HIDDEN ®

New Mexico

HIDDEN®

New Mexico

Including Albuquerque, Santa Fe, Taos and the Enchanted Circle

Richard Harris

FOURTH EDITION

Ulysses Press®
BERKELEY, CALIFORNIA

Published by: ULYSSES PRESS
        P.O. Box 3440
        Berkeley, CA 94703
        www.ulyssespress.com

ISSN 1521-4982
ISBN 1-56975-345-8

Printed in Canada by Transcontinental Printing

10 9 8 7 6

MANAGING EDITOR: Claire Chun
COPY EDITOR: Lily Chou
EDITORIAL ASSOCIATES: Kate Allen, Laura Brancella, Caroline
    Cummins, Marin Van Young
TYPESETTER: Lisa Kester
CARTOGRAPHY: Pease Press
HIDDEN BOOKS DESIGN: Sarah Levin
INDEXER: Sayre Van Young
COVER PHOTOGRAPHY: Larry Ulrich (ristras, strings of
    dried chile peppers, for sale in the Santa Fe area)
ILLUSTRATOR: Glenn Kim

Distributed in the United States by Publishers Group West
and in Canada by Raincoast Books

Write to us!

If in your travels you discover a spot that captures the spirit of New Mexico, or if you live in the region and have a favorite place to share, or if you just feel like expressing your views, write to us and we'll pass your note along to the author.

We can't guarantee that the author will add your personal find to the next edition, but if the writer does use the suggestion, we'll acknowledge you in the credits and send you a free copy of the new edition.

ULYSSES PRESS
P.O. Box 3440
Berkeley, CA 94703-3440
E-mail: readermail@ulyssespress.com

✳

Ulysses Press would like to thank the following readers who took the time to write in with suggestions that were incorporated into this new edition of *Hidden New Mexico*: Kim Asakawa via e-mail; Kent Buckman of Albuquerque, NM; Bonnie Gale via e-mail; Monica Staaf of Foxboro, MA; Donald Tung via e-mail.

What's Hidden?

At different points throughout this book, you'll find special listings marked with a hidden symbol:

◄ HIDDEN

This means that you have come upon a place off the beaten tourist track, a spot that will carry you a step closer to the local people and natural environment of New Mexico.

The goal of this guide is to lead you beyond the realm of everyday tourist facilities. While we include traditional sightseeing listings and popular attractions, we also offer alternative sights and adventure activities. Instead of filling this guide with reviews of standard hotels and chain restaurants, we concentrate on one-of-a-kind places and locally owned establishments.

Our authors seek out locales that are popular with residents but usually overlooked by visitors. Some are more hidden than others (and are marked accordingly), but all the listings in this book are intended to help you discover the true nature of New Mexico and put you on the path of adventure.

Contents

Maps

OUTDOOR ADVENTURE SYMBOLS

The following symbols accompany national, state and regional park listings, as well as beach descriptions throughout the text.

Camping

Hiking

Biking

Horseback Riding

Downhill Skiing

Cross-country Skiing

Swimming

Snorkeling or Scuba Diving

Waterskiing

Windsurfing

Canoeing or Kayaking

Boating

Boat Ramps

Fishing

ONE

The Land of Enchantment

New Mexico is a land unlike any other. It is sheer sandstone cliffs and slickrock mesas, secluded beaches on bright blue lakes, vast deserts alive with giant cacti and unusual animals, high mountain peaks that guard some of the largest wilderness areas in America.

Strange landscapes conceal Indian ruins as old and haunting as Europe's medieval castles. And unlike other parts of the United States, the people who lived in New Mexico when the first white men arrived still live here today. Although it was the first part of the United States where European colonists settled permanently, today it remains, on the whole, one of the least-populated parts of the country.

The state attracts vacationers from around the world at all times of year. It is warm in the winter (some places), cool in the summer (other places) and sunnier than Florida. People come for the climate, the great outdoors, the unique cultural mix and the scenic beauty. Most of all, people come to explore, for the best places are not necessarily marked by big green-and-white signs or entrance gates. In this land of astonishing diversity, you'll find something new and exciting around every curve in the road.

Land of contrasts, proudly provincial, New Mexico lives up to its romantic reputation. Lost cities and hidden treasures await your discovery. If curiosity is in your nature, this is one of the best places on earth to unleash it.

Santa Fe, the most famous New Mexico vacation destination and the starting point for this book, is no larger than Council Bluffs, Iowa, or Troy, New York, or Henderson, North Carolina, or Redding, California. Yet of these small cities, only Santa Fe has a flair—for architecture, art, cuisine and dress—known from Tokyo to Paris. Adobe walls, opera tickets, turquoise-and-silver squash blossom neck-laces, hand-carved wooden saints and coyotes, fiesta dresses, blue-corn tortillas, tongue-blasting green chile stew, the tang of piñon smoke in the crisp fall air, and art and more art everywhere you look all contribute to the now world-famous "Santa Fe Style."

I

As the state capital, Santa Fe has become the epicenter of a cultural kaleidoscope, a marvelous microcosm of New Mexico's varied population. This town has it all, from windburned cowboys, struggling artists and aging hippies to descendants of Spanish colonists and American Indians from more than a dozen tribes, plus generous smatterings of real estate developers, Sikh holy men, gay and lesbian couples, Tibetan refugees, nuclear weapon engineers, movie stars, psychics, and politicians of every conceivable stripe. A few days in Santa Fe will only serve to give you a glimpse at the diversity inherent to the rest of the state.

Few of the 13 million travelers who visit Santa Fe each year realize what riches await in other, less popular parts of the state. The tiny percentage that explore deeper into the backcountry of New Mexico find themselves in a vast and amazingly varied landscape of wide-open roads and small communities as varied and exotic as a traveler might hope to chance upon in any foreign land.

Motorists cruising along any of the three interstates may form an image of New Mexico as a dry and eroded state set against a background of distant, indistinct mountain ranges; even cattle seem scarce in these parts. But first impressions can be deceptive. Just about all the best places in New Mexico are hidden from view. This book is designed to help you find them, whether doing so entails heading up canyons, down dirt roads, on the other sides of mountains or just beyond those trees.

Those game for the adventure of exploring beyond Santa Fe could potentially see the world's largest volcano caldera, with natural hot springs steaming from its slopes. The deserted ruins of what was the biggest city in the Southwest 900 years ago. The remote "sky city" where the descendants of the Mesa Verde cliff dwellers live without electricity or running water. The small Spanish church where pilgrims from all over the state come to pray for miracles. The radio-telescope where scientists scan the heavens for messages from alien beings. The town where Billy the Kid made his reputation as a gunfighter, and the next town north where he was finally gunned down.

Vivid contrasts characterize the New Mexico landscape. The high pine- and fir-covered mountain crests that cover the skyline throughout the state are white with snow eight months out of the year; just a few miles away and 5000 feet lower in altitude lie deserts of crackled clay, lava or gypsum dunes where not only does it never snow, but the rain from summer thunderstorms evaporates before reaching the ground. A short afternoon drive can encompass both primevally lush old-growth forests hidden deep in sheltering canyons and cactus badland mazes of twisting arroyos and dusty riverbeds.

As far as land goes, New Mexico is the fifth-largest state in the country. As you take in the state's vast, often rugged terrain, imagine what it was like when inhabited by nomadic people, or when American Indians built the first large, permanent towns. In what is now the United States, New Mexico was among the first regions with any people at all; it was also one of the earliest areas to be colonized by Europeans. Yet the population today, about 1,800,000, is far less than in any of the other states (Texas, Oklahoma, Colorado, Arizona) that border it.

New Mexico is also among the poorest states (despite the conspicuous wealth of Santa Fe), though it is much more prosperous than its southern neighbor, Old Mexico. In fact, in economy as well as in language and culture, New Mexico stands with one foot firmly planted in Latin America as it hesitantly dips the toes of the other foot into the American mainstream. Like the national economy of Mexico, the economy of New Mexico depends primarily on ranching, drilling for oil, gas and, above all, tourism. As in Mexico, the pride of New Mexico lies in its rich folk art and in the deep and abiding traditions of the cultures that have survived and prospered in this arid, mysteriously alluring and starkly beautiful land.

Hidden New Mexico is designed to help you explore the entire state, starting with the capital, Santa Fe, and venturing out from there in all directions. It covers popular, "must-see" places, offering advice on how best to enjoy them. It also tells you about many off-the-beaten-path spots, the kind you would find by talking with folks at the local café or with someone who has lived in the area all his or her life. It describes the region's history, its natural areas and its residents, both human and animal. It suggests places to eat, to lodge, to play, to camp. Taking into account varying interests, budgets and tastes, it provides the information you need whether your vacation style involves backpacking, golf, museum browsing, shopping or all of the above.

What you choose to see and do is up to you. The old cliché that "there is something for everyone" pretty well rings true in New Mexico. In this book, you'll find free campgrounds with hiking trails and fantastic views as well as a number of

playgrounds for the wealthy and well-known. And you can take some of the most spectacular scenic drives anywhere as well as hikes into wild areas that can't be reached by car. Or check into a bed and breakfast that has galleries and boutiques within walking distance.

There's so much to experience in New Mexico that even most lifelong residents can count on making new discoveries once in a while. First-time vacation visitors are hard pressed just to make brief stops at the region's best-known highlights, while seasoned travelers often prefer to explore a more limited area in depth and then return on later trips to different spots, perhaps in different seasons. Either way, people generally come back, and often to stay. For New Mexico has so many unique ways—food, landscapes, customs, climate, art, architecture, languages—to create lingering memories.

▼▼▼▼▼▼▼▼▼▼▼▼▼▼▼▼▼▼▼▼

The Story of New Mexico

GEOLOGY

The geological features of New Mexico are so varied and spectacular that it is certainly possible to appreciate the landscape for its beauty without knowing how it was formed. But travelers who take a little time to learn about the region's geology in natural history museums or park visitor centers come to see how the many colors and kinds of surface rock connect in a wonderfully complex formation hundreds of miles across. They learn to explore the panorama in three dimensions, not just two.

The delight of New Mexico geology lies not only in its grand overviews but also in its myriad unique details. Dinosaur tracks. Pure white gypsum sand dunes. Ice caves. Fortresslike rock mesas. Solitary mountains that rise like islands from an arid sea. Enormous underground caverns. Parched, overgrazed, alkaline high-desert wasteland that gradually reveals its stark beauty in twisting arroyos and jagged black-lava fields.

Volcanoes created some of the most dramatic scenery in New Mexico. In some places, like Valley of Fires Recreation Area just east of the town of Carrizozo and El Malpais National Monument near Grants, lava has paved the desert floor into tortured surfaces that cannot be crossed, laced with ice caves where water stays frozen even on the hottest summer days. Elsewhere, fields of pumice gravel prevent vegetation from growing but make hiking easy at the foot of picture-perfect volcanic cones.

The Jemez Mountains near Los Alamos formed from the crumbled remnant of what many scientists believe may have been the world's tallest volcano nearly two million years ago. In the canyons of Bandelier National Monument on the slope of the Jemez Mountains stand tent rocks, strange spires left behind when steam vents hardened volcanic ash in the distant past. Farther north, near Taos, the massive lava flow from the Jemez Volcano forms the walls of deep gorges along the Rio Grande. More recent volcanoes produced forbidding black-lava fields such as those at El Malpais and Valley of Fires. There are no active vol-

canoes in New Mexico today, though there's always the possibility of a dormant volcano becoming active again. Volcanoes have
been erupting in the region for millions of years, and the most
recent ones exploded less than a thousand years ago. As geolo-
gists reckon time, a thousand years is just yesterday.

While some mountains in New Mexico originated as volcanos,
others were formed by upheavals in giant earthquakes that shaped
the continent. No two ranges are alike in this region. For instance,
Sandia Crest on the eastern edge of Albuquerque is a piece of the
earth's crust cracked by unimaginable forces and shoved upward
at a sharp angle so that the side facing the city is so steep it looks
almost like a mile-high sheer cliff, while the back side has a gentler slope covered with trees and meadows.

The Sangre de Cristo Mountains above Santa Fe contain a
vast area of peaks and alpine meadows too high for trees to grow
and are only accessible by hiking or horseback.
The Zuni Mountains on and around the Indian
reservation of the same name, broad and gently
rolling, hidden from the view of passing motorists by
ivory and flamingo-colored sandstone cliffs, contain
secluded fishing lakes and many miles of oak, cedar and
pine forests. The Florida Mountains near Deming, sunbaked and barren, attract only rock collectors, while the
cool aspen and fir forests of the Sacramento Mountains
near Ruidoso, with the state's southernmost ski resort, draw visitors from all over West Texas.

> One thousand years ago,
> American Indians of the
> Southwest had exten-
> sive trade contracts,
> including the Toltecs
> of central Mexico.

New Mexico's foremost geographic feature is the Rio Grande,
which is Spanish for "Big River." The Mexican name for the Rio
Grande is "Rio Bravo." The Rio Grande starts in the mountains
of Southern Colorado, slices New Mexico right down the middle
and, upon reaching the western tip of Texas, becomes the Mexican border as it flows 800 more miles, all the way to the Gulf of
Mexico. Ever since about A.D. 1200, at least 90 percent of New
Mexico's people have made their home in the valleys of the upper
Rio Grande—it is one of the few rivers in the state that provides
a reliable water source year-round. Enthusiastic whitewater rafters
and kayakers by the thousands spill down the canyons in the upper
reaches of the river, while farther south a series of dams create reservoirs used by everyone from waterskiers to houseboaters. The
reservoirs are there to capture the precious water from spring
floods and save it for later in the growing season when the chile
farmers of southern New Mexico might otherwise face drought.

NATIVE PEOPLE   Spear points found near Clovis, New Mexico,
prove that human beings lived in the Southwest at least 10,000
years ago. The Clovis points are some of the oldest Indian artifacts
found anywhere, dating back to the last Ice Age. At that time, the

region that is now New Mexico was rich, green countryside where mastodons and giant bison grazed just beyond the reach of glaciers. The hunting and gathering tribes who followed the animals' tracks may have been some of the first people to walk on North American soil. They stayed. Across millenniums, their descendants walked softly through New Mexico leaving few traces—only small bone and obsidian tools.

Less than 2000 years ago, the people of New Mexico learned how to grow corn, beans and watermelons. This new technology allowed them to establish permanent homes. By about A.D. 1000, individual pit houses gave way to cliff dwellings like the ones at Gila in Southwestern New Mexico and large multifamily stone pueblos like the ones at Chaco Canyon in the northwestern part of the state. Besides agriculture and architecture, Pueblo people of the Anasazi, Mimbres and Sinagua civilizations were known for pottery making, cotton weaving and sophisticated astronomical observations and spiritual practices.

The saga of the pre-Columbian New Mexico is one of migration and change. The great Anasazi pueblos of the Four Corners region, then the largest cities in what is now the United States, were occupied for a century or two and suddenly abandoned. Archaeologists disagree about the reasons. The Mesa Verde people may have moved to Acoma, the Mimbres of the Gila canyons to Zuni Pueblo or perhaps Casas Grandes in Old Mexico, the Chacoans to sites along the Rio Grande such as the pueblos at Bandelier National Monument.

During the century just before Columbus' ships reached American shores, a new group of people arrived in the region. They were Athabascans, nomads from the far north who had gradually wandered down the front range of the Rocky Mountains in small groups. They would become the Apache and Navajo nations—but

THE BIRTH OF THE NAVAJO NATION

The Pueblo Revolt created the Navajo nation. To persuade their Athabascan neighbors to help chase away the Spanish, Pueblo leaders agreed that the Athabascans could keep the livestock driven off from ranches they attacked. In that way, the tribe came to own sheep and horses, which would profoundly change their culture. When the Spanish colonists returned, many Pueblo people who had participated in the revolt fled to avoid retaliation and went to live with the nomads, bringing with them such advanced technologies as weaving cloth and growing corn. The Athabascan descendants who herded sheep and farmed became known as the Navajo, while those who held to the old way of life came to be called Apache.

only after another kind of stranger had come to change the character of New Mexico forever.

SPANISH CONQUEST   In the year 1540, a Spanish expedition under the command of *conquistador* Francisco Vasquez de Coronado set out from Mexico City and headed north across the parched, forbidding Chihuahuan Desert in search of the fabled Seven Cities of Cibola. Instead of the gold-paved cities of legend, he found pueblos such as Zuni, occupied by subsistence farmers who drew magical lines of cornmeal in unsuccessful attempts to fend off the Spaniards with their armor, horses and steel swords. Coronado and his followers were the first Europeans to visit the Rio Grande pueblos. For two years they explored the region, but finding no gold they returned to Mexico City with disappointing reports. After that, exploration of the territory Coronado had visited, which came to be called Nuevo Mexico, was left to Franciscan missionaries for the rest of the 16th century.

In 1598, a prosperous mine owner from Zacatecas, Mexico, named Don Juan de Oñate mounted an expedition at his own expense to colonize Nuevo Mexico under a grant from the Spanish government. The group consisted of 400 soldiers and settlers, 83 wagons and 7000 head of livestock. Oñate founded the first permanent Spanish settlement near modern-day Española, New Mexico, but the cost of his expeditions bankrupted him and he resigned his position as governor. The new governor, Don Pedro de Peralta, moved the capital to Santa Fe in 1610.

The Spanish colonists grew in number and established villages, farms and ranches up and down the Rio Grande over several generations, but slavery practices and erratic religious policies toward the Indians inspired the Pueblo Revolt of 1680. The people of the Rio Grande pueblos, aided by fierce Athabascan nomads, attacked the Spanish towns and ranches, killing hundreds of settlers and driving the survivors downriver all the way to the site of present-day El Paso, Texas, where they camped for 11 years before soldiers arrived from Mexico City to help them regain Nuevo Mexico.

After the Pueblo Revolt, Nuevo Mexico endured as an outpost of the Spanish empire for another 130 years. During all of that time, the conquerors and colonists were never able to settle the surrounding areas of the Southwest or even establish roads between Nuevo Mexico and other Spanish colonies in California and central Texas. The lands to the north and east were controlled by warrior horsemen of the Comanche tribe, whose raids forced abandonment of Spanish missions such as those at Pecos and Gran Quivira. To the south and west, the Apache and Navajo people used fear to keep Europeans out of the land that is now Arizona.

Nor did the Spanish settlers have any contact with English-speaking American colonists. Near the end of the colonial era, explorers from the United States, such as early U.S. Army explorer Captain Zebulon Pike, who accidentally strayed into Nuevo Mexico were arrested.

TERRITORIAL PERIOD   Beginning in 1821, distant events changed the lives of the Spanish inhabitants of the region. Mexico won its independence from Spain, and government policies changed. The border was opened, and trade was established along the Santa Fe Trail, which linked Nuevo Mexico to United States territory. At the same time, all Franciscan monks were exiled from Mexican territory, leaving Nuevo Mexico without spiritual leadership. They were replaced by a lay brotherhood of *penitentes* whose spiritual guidance did much to create a uniquely New Mexican culture and tradition that survives to this day in remote mountain villages around Santa Fe and Taos.

When the Texas republic won its independence from Mexico in 1836, many Texans contended that Nuevo Mexico should be part of their new nation—a sentiment that the people of Nuevo Mexico did not share. Texas troops occupied Nuevo Mexico in 1841, but their authority was not acknowledged. Five years later, when Texas had joined the United States and the Mexican War was underway, federal soldiers took possession of Nuevo Mexico. When the war ended in 1848, the peace treaty with Mexico ceded the territories of California and Nuevo Mexico (which included the modern-day states of New Mexico and Arizona) to the United States. To confuse the local people further, 13 years after they had become Americans, the Civil War broke out and Confederate troops from Texas fought numerous battles in New Mexico, briefly capturing Albuquerque, Santa Fe and Mesilla. Before the war ended, New Mexico and its people had been part of five different nations in about 40 years.

The United States government in the late 19th century was far less tolerant of Indians than the Spanish and Mexicans rulers had been. After the Civil War, the Army set out to make the lands ruled by the Comanches, Apaches, Navajos and Utes safe for homesteaders. Some tribes were annihilated. Kit Carson rounded up the entire Navajo tribe and marched them from their homeland to a reservation in eastern New Mexico, but after explorations revealed nothing of value on the Navajo land, and after thousands of Navajo people had died, he marched the survivors back home to the land where they live today.

Law enforcement was unreliable in the territorial era, giving rise to timeless legends of the Wild West. In New Mexico, Billy the Kid and his gang fought against an army of gunmen hired by a ruthless cattle baron in the Lincoln County War. Out of all the turmoil and gunfire emerged a new multicultural society. In 1912 New Mexico became the 47th state in the union.

MODERN TIMES   The traditional Spanish and Indian cultures of
New Mexico remain strong even as waves of visitors and newcomers have swept across the land during the 20th
century. Beginning shortly before World War I,
artists and writers fleeing Paris's West Bank began
to congregate around Taos, New Mexico. Since the
1940s, the Institute of American Indian Arts, the only
federal Indian school dedicated to teaching traditional
and contemporary art, has established Santa Fe, New
Mexico, as the world's leading Indian art market. Exotic
locations and reliable sunshine have drawn myriad film
production companies to New Mexico ever since 1898 and continue to do so. Today, the visual and performing arts form one
of the most important industries in many parts of the region.

The state of New
Mexico is officially
bilingual; one out of
three families speak
Spanish.

In World War II, New Mexico became America's center for
nuclear research. The nation's best physicists were sent to a top
secret base at Los Alamos, deep in a labyrinth of volcanic canyons, to develop the world's first atomic bomb. They tested it in
1945 in the desert near White Sands, New Mexico. After the war
ended, nuclear weapons research continued at Los Alamos, as did
development of peacetime uses for nuclear energy, bringing a
stampede of prospectors and mining companies to the uranium-
rich badlands of the Four Corners area. Today, Los Alamos National Laboratory and other federal laboratories in the region also
study nuclear fusion, geothermal and solar energy research and
genetic studies. The technologies developed at the laboratories
have brought private high-tech companies to the major cities.
Meanwhile, the nuclear industry has reached the top of the list of
environmental controversies that stir heated debate in the region.

Tourism is key among the forces that have shaped the modern New Mexico. With a relatively small population, few manu-
facturing industries and limited agriculture, the economy relies
heavily on travelers, who support hotels, restaurants and other
service businesses. In general, New Mexicans display a friendly,
positive attitude toward tourists. Beauty is one of the region's
most important natural resources, and there is plenty to share.
Besides, as locals like to point out, who would want to live in a
place strangers didn't want to visit?

FLORA

Drivers crossing New Mexico at high speed on interstate highways
can easily form the mistaken impression that this region is mostly
open ranchland so arid that it takes 50 acres to graze a single cow.
This is because main highways follow the flattest, most featureless
routes. All one has to do is take a detour into the mountains and
canyons where the main highways don't go in order to discover

Text continued on page 12.

People of
the Southwest

The population of New Mexico and the entire Southwest is often called "tricultural"—Indian, Spanish and Anglo. Each of the three cultures has been an enemy to the others in centuries past, yet all live in harmony as neighbors today. Through centuries of life in proximity, and despite persistent attempts by both Spanish and Anglos to assimilate the Indian people, each group proudly maintains its cultural identity while respecting the others. The resulting tricultural balance is truly unique to the region.

All three cultural groups share freely in each other's ways. For example, Southwestern cooking blends traditional Anasazi/Pueblo foods—blue corn, beans and squash—with green chile and cooking techniques imported by early Spanish colonists from the Aztecs of central Mexico, and the result is a staple in Anglo kitchens. The distinctive architecture of the desert uses adobe bricks, of Moorish origin and brought to the New World by the Spanish, while the architectural style derives from Anasazi pueblos and incorporates refinements Anglos brought west by railroad.

An Anglo, in local parlance, is anyone who comes from English-speaking America. Anglos first came to the region less than 150 years ago, after the end of the Mexican War, and are still a minority group in many parts today. Newcomers are often surprised to learn that Americans of Jewish, Japanese and African ancestry, among others, are referred to as Anglos. Many Anglos in the more remote parts of the Southwest, from traditional Mormons in rural Utah to residents of old-fashioned hippie communes and artists' colonies in the mountains of New Mexico, hold to ways of life that are a far cry from modern mainstream America.

The Spanish residents of New Mexico trace their ancestry back to the pioneer era around the year 1600—the time of Don Quixote, of the Spanish Inquisition, of the conquest of the New World by the Spanish Armada. Today, the Spanish remain the dominant political and cultural force in many parts of New Mexico, and travelers can still find isolated mountain villages where many aspects of everyday life remain unchanged since the 17th century. Mexican immigration in the 20th century has created a separate Hispanic subculture in southern New Mexico and Arizona.

Visitors today have little opportunity to experience the uniqueness of such tribes as the Apache, Ute, Paiute and other nomadic tribes for whom confinement to reservations has meant adopting conventional ways of rural life. But among groups such as the Pueblo and Navajo people, who still occupy their traditional homelands, the old ways are still very much alive.

The Pueblo people who live along the Rio Grande in Isleta, Santo Domingo, Cochiti, Tesuque, San Ildefonso, Santa Clara, Taos and other Indian communities are descendants of the Anasazi, or "Ancient Ones," who built the impressive castlelike compounds at literally thousands of sites such as those we know as Chaco Canyon, Bandelier, Pecos and Salinas. Although they have lived in close contact with Spanish and Anglo neighbors for centuries, the Rio Grande Pueblo people have carefully guarded their own cultural identity. They often have Spanish names and attend services at mission churches, yet they observe Catholic feast days with sacred dances and kiva ceremonies that reach back to pre-Columbian antiquity. While most Pueblo Indians speak English, they converse among themselves in the dialect of their particular pueblo—Tewa, Tiwa, Towa or Keresan.

The more isolated pueblos of western New Mexico retain their own distinctive cultures. The Acoma people, thought to be descendants of the Mesa Verde Anasazi, practice secret rites that are closed to outsiders. The people of Zuni, who speak a language unrelated to any other Indian group and may be the heirs of the Mimbres who lived in southern New Mexico, follow the ancient kachina religion, becoming embodiments of nature's forces in strange, colorful blessing ceremonies.

Nowhere is the blending of cultures more evident than among the Navajo, the largest Indian tribe in the United States. The roots of their religious traditions stretch far into the past, and their hogan dwellings originated in the frozen northlands from which they came. Since arriving in the Southwest in the 1400s, they have borrowed from their neighbors to create their own unique culture. They learned to grow corn and weave textiles from the Pueblo people, and to herd sheep and ride horses from the Spanish. Early Anglo traders helped them develop their "traditional" art forms, rugs and silver jewelry. Even the more modern aspects of Navajo life—pickup trucks, satellite dishes, blue jeans—are not so much signs of assimilation into the white man's world as of the continuing evolution of a uniquely Navajo way of life.

that the dry climate and extreme elevation changes create a surprising variety of ecosystems, each with its own unique beauty.

At low altitudes where winter temperatures rarely dip to freezing, cacti and other succulents thrive. Ocatillo, century plants, yuccas and prickly pear, barrel and cholla cacti, as well as mesquite and creosote bushes, are found throughout both the Chihuahuan Desert of southern New Mexico. When spring rains come, which may be once in five years or more, the deserts burst forth in a fantastic display of wildflowers.

New Mexico has far more cattle and sheep than people.

Miniature evergreen forests of piñon, juniper and cedar cover the desert hills at higher elevations where winter temperatures fall below freezing. Once every seven years in the fall, piñon trees produce pine nuts, which many consider a delicacy. Cactus and yucca stay small in the high desert; the tallest of them, the cholla cactus, prefer areas that were once stripped of vegetation, such as old Indian ruins.

Mountain forests change with elevation, forming three distinct bands. On the lower slopes of the mountains, ponderosa pine trees stand 50 feet tall and more. At middle elevations, shimmering stands of aspen fill the mountainsides and paint them bright yellow in early October. Douglas fir trees dominate the higher reaches of the mountains. In some parts of the forest, accessible only by hiking trail and out of reach of timber cutters, fir trees 100 feet tall and bigger around than a man's reach stand spirelike in ancient forests dripping with moss and silence.

Of all the various ecosystems that characterize New Mexico, the real gems are the riparian woodlands. Since almost all of the region's landscape is dry and can only support the hardiest of plants, plant life flourishes around even the least trickle of year-round running water. Creek and river banks support thick forests of cottonwood trees and tamarisks, along with isolated stands of hardwood trees such as maple and walnut.

FAUNA

Many animals of Western legend still roam free in the forests and canyons of New Mexico's back country. Mountain lions, rarely seen because they inhabit remote areas and hunt in the dark, sometimes flash past late-night drivers' headlight beams. Many black bears live deep in the mountains, and in drought summers when food is short they may stray into towns to raid trash cans. Coyotes, the most commonly seen Southwestern predators, abound in all rural areas and frequently surround campgrounds with their high-pitched yipping and howling.

Open rangelands support sizable herds of pronghorn antelope alongside grazing cattle. Most visitors to national parks and other protected areas will spot mule deer, and wild horses still roam. The elk population is the largest it has been in this century.

Because elk prefer high mountain meadows, only serious hikers are likely to spot one. Herds of mountain sheep live above timberline on the highest mountains of the Sangre de Cristo ranges, while their solitary relatives, desert bighorn sheep, live in most desert areas.

One of the most distinctive regional birds is the magpie, an exotic-looking, long-tailed, iridescent, black-and-white cousin of Asian myna birds. Another is the roadrunner, which is often seen hunting lizards alongside the highway. Large birds often seen by motorists or hikers include turkey vultures, ravens and a wide variety of hawks. Both golden and bald eagles live throughout New Mexico and are occasionally spotted soaring in the distance. Eagles and vultures are about the same size, and the easiest way to tell them apart is to remember that eagles glide with their wings horizontal, while vultures' wings sweep upward in a V-shape.

A thought that preoccupies many visitors to New Mexico is of living hazards like rattlesnakes, gila monsters, scorpions and tarantulas. Poisonous animals live in most parts of the region except for the high mountains. Yet even local residents who spend most weekends hiking say that they rarely encounter one. When outdoors in desert country, walk loudly and never put your hand or foot where you can't see it.

Where to Go

The "Land of Enchantment" is no more one entity than is Europe. Don't try to "see it all" in a single trip or you may find yourself focused so much on covering large distances that you sacrifice quiet opportunities to appreciate the natural beauty you came to see. Deciding what to see and where to go is a tough choice. The good news is, you'll just have to keep coming back and exploring at different times of the year to get to know the "real" New Mexico.

To help you with your decisions, we'll entice you with a brief description of each area covered in this book. To get the whole story, read the introduction to each chapter, then the more detailed material on the regions that appeal to you.

Visitors to the **Santa Fe Area** find themselves in a magical place where art openings and operas complement rodeos, horse races and wilderness adventures. The sky-high state capital, situated at 7000 feet elevation and backdropped by the spectacular Sangre de Cristo Mountains, is also the oldest colonial city in the United States. Strict guidelines mandate the now familiar Santa Fe–style look of territorial and Spanish Colonial architecture. Thanks to city codes, no high-rises block the mountain views or the ever-changing colors at dawn and dusk.

Northwest of Santa Fe is the city of Los Alamos, birthplace to the atomic bomb. Modern in its technology and scientific findings, Los Alamos' laboratories coexist within a stone's throw of ancient ruins and Indian pueblos—in other words, caveman meets the Jetsons. Those who head southeast of Santa Fe will come across the country's original Las Vegas, a charismatic town that may look familiar at first—and second—glance. That's probably because Las Vegas, New Mexico, has been featured in countless silent movies. Perhaps what's most intriguing about the region, however, is the unique population mix, which includes the world's foremost nuclear scientists and major communities of visual artists, performers and writers, plus a colorful and varied cultural melting pot of Anglo, American Indian and Spanish peoples.

Driving north from New Mexico's capital city, you'll pass vast forests and mountain villages centuries old on your way to **Taos and the Enchanted Circle Area**. Taos is a legendary artists' community, a step down in the frenetic category from the hustle-bustle of Santa Fe. It is a casually sophisticated town where galleries and working artists flourish. Surrounding the city are the raging Rio Grande, the Sangre de Cristo Mountains and the Carson National Forest, making recreational pursuits easily accessible for the many sports-minded people who are drawn to Taos' world-class ski slopes. Visitors can venture into the maze of volcanic canyons in the Jemez Mountains at Bandelier National Monument to see some of the best examples of the ancient pueblos and cliff dwellings found throughout the area. Even more impressive Indian ruins await to the west in the lonely San Juan Basin, once dominated by the Anasazi pueblo city at Chaco Canyon.

Northwestern New Mexico is also known for its rich tapestry of experiences. The areas around Grants and Gallup are close enough that they could be glimpsed as day trips out of Albuquerque, but you might consider them as a vacation destination on their own. Here visitors can explore the Indian pueblos of Acoma and Zuni, where American Indians have lived continuously since long before Christopher Columbus sighted land. Grants is situated at the center of an intriguing array of places—the most ancient continuously inhabited pueblos in New Mexico, a vast and forbidding lava bed with ice caves, a landmark where centuries of explorers left their marks and solitary, massive Mt. Taylor, a sacred mountain in Navajo tradition. Gallup, which bills itself as the "Gateway to Indian Country," presents a cultural contrast as striking as any to be found along the Mexican border, as the interstate brings the outside world to the doorstep of the largest Indian nation in the country. The annual Inter-Tribal Ceremonial and large concentration of American Indians make it a prime place to view native crafts. In the Four Corners area, you can step out of New Mexico into one of three other states or use every limb to simultaneously be in each of the four—New Mexico, Arizona, Colorado and Utah. It's the only spot in the United States where four states come together. Three rivers also meet at this unique junction, feeding a carpet of desert flora in an area that is often perceived as barren.

Billy the Kid once roamed the area that now encompasses **Albuquerque and Central New Mexico**. Now you can, too. The vast ranchland plains east of the Rocky Mountains haven't changed much since the Kid rode into legend more than a century ago. But Albuquerque is another story. Just another small town perched on the banks of the Rio Grande downriver from Santa Fe in the heyday of the Wild West, it has been transformed into a bustling metropolis boasting a unique mosaic of life-styles and cultures. Places, such as the Indian Pueblo Cultural Center, showcase the city's mul-ticultural heritage. But perhaps the best way to gain an understanding of Albuquerque is to walk around the Old Town Plaza, a historic district that preserves the architectural grace of Albuquerque's Spanish Colonial era. Sandia Crest, the enormous moun-tain that flanks the city's Northeast Heights, offers skiing, wil-derness hiking, a thrilling tramway ride and cool forests. With a gnarled old forest of cottonwoods along its banks, the Rio Grande has great secluded trails for urban hiking, jogging, bicycling and horseback riding. Traveling east from Albuquerque takes you into the high plains, where the major tourist spots are all lakes. Driving south takes you to Bosque del Apache, where huge flocks of cranes spend the winter months, or to Salinas Missions, a group of national monument units preserving the ruins of Indian pueb-los and old Spanish missions. This is the Central New Mexico that beckons the traveler: a mixture of the wild and sublime, the small town and the big city, the past and the present.

> Remember that small changes in elevation can mean big variations in climate; as a rule, climbing 1000 feet in elevation alters the temperature as much as going 300 miles north.

Travelers who continue into **Southern New Mexico** face a choice among three different areas, each with its own character. In the east, the premier attraction is Carlsbad Caverns National Park, which draws millions of visitors annually to this remote corner of the state. A visit to Carlsbad Caverns combines easily with a side trip to Ruidoso, a bustling mountain resort town that caters primarily to Texans with its Indian-owned ski slopes and some of the richest horse racing in the country. Nearby, the his-toric town of Lincoln still remembers the days of Billy the Kid, when it was one of the most lawless places in the Wild West. In south central New Mexico, a series of unique sightseeing high-lights—lava fields, wilderness hiking trails, Indian petroglyphs and the vast dunes of White Sands National Monument—invites vacation travelers to leave the interstate and loop through the Tularosa Valley. The dominant feature in the southwestern sector of New Mexico is the Gila Wilderness, the largest roadless area in the 48 contiguous United States. Gila Cliff Dwellings National

Monument is the starting point for hikers entering the wilderness, whether for just an afternoon or a month. Visitors with plenty of time to explore the area can drive around the wilderness boundary to see the well-preserved ghost town of Mogollon or walk up a sheer-sided canyon on a series of narrow footbridges known as The Catwalk.

When to Go

SEASONS

If you're one of the many people who imagine New Mexico to be a scorching hot desert, take heart in the state's benevolent nickname: "Land of Enchantment" hardly describes a hellishly hot destination. Before adopting the appealing moniker, however, New Mexico was known as the Sunshine State; the sun shines here 70 percent of the year.

Around Santa Fe and in Northwestern New Mexico, the high-altitude sun beaming on earth tones helps to create shadows and vibrancies not to be believed. These high, dry mountain towns are pleasingly warm during spring and fall. But winters do get cold enough to make Santa Fe a viable ski area (though even on the coldest days the sun keeps temperatures from being unbearable).

Central New Mexico provides a neat combination of high, cool forests of the Rocky Mountains to the north and the rocky, sunbaked Chihuahuan Desert stretching a thousand miles to the south. In June, when air conditioning becomes essential in Albuquerque, a short drive into the mountains offers shade, refreshing streams and occasional patches of unmelted snow. In January, skiers enjoy nearby slopes and then return to lower elevations where snowfalls are infrequent and light.

Cool islands of high mountain forest offer relief from the scorching summers of the Chihuahuan Desert in the southern portion of the state; on top of this, they're great for winter skiing. The lowlands enjoy a much longer warm season for spring and fall outdoor activities than Albuquerque, Santa Fe or Taos, making the entire region an attractive year-round destination.

Springtime in New Mexico is a mixed blessing. Flooding rivers, chilly winds and sandstorms sometimes await visitors in March and early April, but those who take a chance are more likely to experience mild weather and spectacular displays of desert wildflowers. Leaves do not appear on the trees until late April at moderate elevations, late May in the higher mountains.

Throughout the region, June is the hottest month. Even in cool areas such as northern New Mexico, the thermometer frequently hits the 100-degree mark. In July and August the thunderstorms of what locals refer to as the "monsoon season" usually cool things down quickly on hot afternoons. The majority of the moisture for the entire year falls during these two months, so try to plan outdoor activities in the morning hours. Although New Mexico is pretty much safe from natural disasters like earthquakes, tornadoes and hurricanes, meteorologists have discovered from satellite data that the region has more lightning strikes than anywhere else in the United States.

Autumn is the best time of year throughout the state. Locals used to keep this fact to themselves. Now the secret is out, and record numbers of people are visiting during the fall "shoulder season" to experience fall colors and bright Indian summer days.

CALENDAR OF EVENTS

In addition to all-American-style annual community celebrations with parades, arts-and-crafts shows, concerts and rodeos—most towns in New Mexico trace their heritage back to Spanish colonialism by observing annual fiestas, normally on the feast day of the town's patron saint. Fiestas tend to mix sacred and secular, with solemn religious processions and dancing in the streets.

Albuquerque and Central New Mexico New Year's Day is observed at Cochiti Pueblo with a corn dance.

JANUARY

Taos and the Enchanted Circle Area Participants "ski" the snow slopes with shovels at the annual **Shovel Races** in Angel Fire.

FEBRUARY

Southern New Mexico Each March 9, Columbus holds a military-style **Columbus Raid Commemoration** to remember the victims of Mexican revolutionist Pancho Villa's 1916 raid.

MARCH

Taos and the Enchanted Circle Area The Taos Talking Picture Festival features new films and documentaries from new and up-and-coming artists.
Northwestern New Mexico Swing your partner at the **Square Dance Festival** at the Red Rock State Park near Gallup.
Southern New Mexico Alamogordo's twice-a-year **Trinity Site Tour** (in April and October) is your only chance to see where the first atomic bomb was tested.

APRIL

Santa Fe Area The **Arts & Crafts Fair** in Los Alamos displays work by over 100 artisans.
Taos and the Enchanted Circle Area The Taos **Spring Arts Celebration**, continuing over several weekends, features artists' studio tours, performing arts and live entertainment.
Southern New Mexico **Mayfair**, held on Memorial Day weekend, is the big community festival in Cloudcroft.

MAY

Santa Fe Area The **Spring Festival** at El Rancho de las Golondrinas near Santa Fe presents Spanish Colonial craft demonstra-

JUNE

tions and re-creates 17th-century hacienda life. The **Rodeo de Santa Fe** comes to the state capital with a parade.

Taos and the Enchanted Circle Area The **Taos School of Music Summer Chamber Music Festival**, which runs through August, combines concerts by top classical musicians with educational seminars.

Albuquerque and Central New Mexico **Old Fort Days** in Fort Sumner feature a rodeo, staged bank robbery, melodrama and barbecue. The **New Mexico Arts & Crafts Fair**, held at Albuquerque's State Fairgrounds, is among the state's largest.

JULY

Santa Fe Area The **Santa Fe Opera** season opens and the city's accommodations fill to capacity through August. In Española, **Las Fiestas del Valle de Española**, commemorating the founding of the first Spanish settlement in New Mexico, includes a costumed procession and climaxes in a rowdy all-night street dance.

Taos and the Enchanted Circle Area The **Taos Fiesta** fills the streets with a parade and music.

Southern New Mexico The **Ruidoso Arts Festival** is a major juried arts-and-crafts fair with continuous live entertainment.

AUGUST

Taos and the Enchanted Circle Area **Music from Angel Fire**, held at the Village House, hosts national classical and jazz artists.

Albuquerque and Central New Mexico **Old Lincoln Days** features costumed re-enactments of scenes from the Lincoln County War, including one portraying Billy the Kid's last jailbreak.

Southern New Mexico Deming hosts the **Great American Duck Race of Deming**, where waterfowl race for money and compete in the Duck Queen pageant. Other events include the Tortilla Toss, the Outhouse Race and hot-air balloons.

SEPTEMBER

Santa Fe Area The **Santa Fe Fiesta** starts with the ritual burning in effigy of a 35-foot-tall "Old Man Gloom" and continues through a weekend of parades, processions and wild celebration.

Taos and the Enchanted Circle Area The **Taos Arts Festival** which runs September to mid-October, presents art exhibits, lectures and a crafts fair.

Albuquerque and Central New Mexico In Albuquerque, the **New Mexico State Fair** has horse racing, top country performers, a rodeo and livestock.

Southern New Mexico The **16th of September Fiesta** in Mesilla celebrates Mexico's independence with two days of folk dancing, mariachi music and food.

OCTOBER

Santa Fe Area Costumed volunteers re-create the Spanish Colonial era at **Harvest Festival** at the Rancho de las Golondrinas, a historic hacienda located near Santa Fe.

Albuquerque and Central New Mexico The **Albuquerque Balloon Fiesta** lasts for a week and a half with races, mass ascensions and other events featuring over 800 hot-air balloons—the world's largest such event.

Southern New Mexico Ruidoso celebrates fall foliage with a boisterous **Oktoberfest**, coinciding with Cloudcroft's **Aspencade**. In Las Cruces, the **Whole Enchilada Festival** features a parade, live entertainment, races (including a grocery cart race) and the "World's Largest Enchilada." Columbus observes **Columbus Day** with a street parade, all-day live music and a street dance.

Santa Fe Area The artists of secluded Dixon open their homes and workplaces to the public in the **Dixon Studio Tour**. **NOVEMBER**

Albuquerque and Central New Mexico The **Weems Artfest** focuses on visual arts, presenting the works of over 250 artists at the State Fairgrounds in Albuquerque.

Southern New Mexico Nearly 100 exhibitors participate in the **Renaissance Craftfaire**, a juried art show in Las Cruces.

Santa Fe Area The Christmas holidays hold particular charm in Santa Fe and Taos, where instead of colored lights, building exteriors glow with thousands of small candles called *farolitos*. **DECEMBER**

Albuquerque and Central New Mexico **Luminarias** (altar candles) light up the skyline of Albuquerque's Old Town. For several weekends in December, the town of Madrid lights up for **Christmas in Madrid**. The whole town is decorated and there are **studio tours** and other festivities.

Southern New Mexico Outside Las Cruces, the small community of Tortugas celebrates the **Fiesta of Our Lady of Guadalupe** with a torchlight ascent of a nearby mountain.

CALENDAR OF AMERICAN INDIAN EVENTS

Indian pueblos mark their patron saints' feast days with elaborately costumed ceremonial dances that include a pueblo's entire population, from toddlers to elders. Animal dances are normally held in the winter months and corn dances in the summer. Led by the pueblos' kiva clans, these observances almost certainly evolved from the religious rites of the ancient Anasazi people.

Besides Puebloans, a few other tribes welcome outsiders to ceremonial events. In recent years, however, some Indian groups have opted to minimize the presence of non-Indians. The Zuni and Acoma, for instance, have closed major ceremonies to outsiders. To avoid making yourself and future visitors unwelcome, do not carry a camera during any Indian ceremony; videocameras and sketch pads are also banned. Do not use alcoholic beverages; possession of alcohol is a crime on Indian lands, and obnoxious drunks are not tolerated. Do accord ancient spiritual traditions the respect they deserve.

In addition to ceremonials, all Indian nations host annual powwows—gatherings of people from many tribes around the country who compete for money in colorful contest dances. There are also a growing number of fairs and markets where Indian artisans display and sell their work—often at a fraction of what you'd pay in Santa Fe or Sedona.

JANUARY   **Throughout New Mexico**   New Year's Day is celebrated with dances at Taos, Santa Clara, Jemez, Santa Ana, Cochiti and Santo Domingo pueblos. **King's Day** (January 6) is celebrated with animal dances at most pueblos.

Santa Fe Area   San Ildefonso Pueblo's **Fiesta de San Ildefonso** features all-day animal dances, including an awe-inspiring dawn procession descending from Black Mesa.

Albuquerque and Central New Mexico   New Year's Day is observed at Cochiti Pueblo with a corn dance.

FEBRUARY   **Throughout New Mexico**   Candelaria Day (Candlemas) is observed with ceremonial dances at Picuris and San Felipe pueblos. Later in the month, **deer dances** are held at San Juan Pueblo.

MARCH   **Throughout New Mexico**   Most pueblos celebrate Easter—and the start of the planting season—with basket dances and corn dances. Laguna Pueblo also has dances on the **Fiesta de San José**.

APRIL   **Albuquerque and Central New Mexico**   At the **Gathering of Nations Powwow** in Albuquerque, more than 3000 costumed dancers from all over the country compete for prize money in one of the biggest Indian events staged anywhere. The **Jemez Pueblo Open-Air Market** features food, arts and crafts.

MAY   **Taos and the Enchanted Circle**   Taos Pueblo holds its traditional Blessing of the Fields and Corn Dance.

Albuquerque and Central New Mexico   The Fiesta de San Felipe is observed at the San Felipe Pueblo with a large, spectacular corn dance involving more than 500 dancers. Cochiti Pueblo celebrates the **Fiesta de Santa Cruz** with a corn dance.

JUNE   **Santa Fe Area**   San Juan Pueblo observes the **Fiesta de San Juan** with buffalo and Comanche dances.

Albuquerque and Central New Mexico   On Memorial Day weekend, Jemez Pueblo is the site of the **Jemez Red Rocks Arts & Crafts Show**.

JULY   **Santa Fe Area**   Nambe Pueblo holds its **Waterfall Ceremonial** on the 4th of July. The **Eight Northern Pueblos Arts and Crafts**

Fair, held each year at a different Indian pueblo north of Santa Fe, hosts hundreds of American Indian exhibitors. Picuris Pueblo also hosts its own **Arts & Crafts Fair**. The Jicarilla Apache tribe sponsors the **Little Beaver Roundup and Rodeo**, a weekend-long celebration in Dulce with dances, an Indian rodeo and an arts-and-crafts show.

Taos and the Enchanted Circle   Taos Pueblo holds corn dances on the **Fiesta de Santiago** and the **Fiesta de Santa Ana**.

Albuquerque and Central New Mexico   Corn dances are held at Cochiti Pueblo on the **Fiesta de San Buenaventura** as well as at Santa Ana and Laguna pueblos on the **Fiesta de Santa Ana**.

Southern New Mexico   Visitors have the rare opportunity to witness a ceremony of the secretive Apache people at the **Maidens' Puberty Rites and Mountain Spirits Dance** on the Mescalero Apache Indian Reservation.

Santa Fe Area   Santa Clara Pueblo has corn, buffalo and Co-manche dances during the **Fiesta de Santa Clara**. The **Santa Fe Indian Market**, the largest American Indian arts show and sale anywhere, draws collectors from around the world.   **AUGUST**

Taos and the Enchanted Circle   A corn dance is held at Picuris Pueblo on **San Lorenzo Feast Day**.

Northwestern New Mexico   At the **Inter-Tribal Indian Cere-monial** held in Red Rock State Park near Gallup, American In-dians from more than 50 tribes participate in ritual and contest dances, an arts-and-crafts show, a rodeo and other events. The **Zuni Tribal Fair** includes an arts-and-crafts show, food booths and competition dancing.

Albuquerque and Central New Mexico   As the growing season reaches its peak, the Santo Domingo Pueblo observes the **Fiesta de Santo Domingo** with one of the most spectacular Indian cer-emonials in the Southwest—a huge corn dance in the streets and narrow plazas of this ancient village. Corn dances are also held at Jemez Pueblo on the **Fiesta de Nuestra Señora de Los Angeles**, at Acoma Pueblo on the **Fiesta de San Lorenzo**, at Zia and La-guna pueblos on the **Fiesta de San Antonio** and at Isleta Pueblo on the **Fiesta de San Augustín**. The **Zuni Tribal Fair** includes a rodeo, food booths and competition dancing.

Santa Fe Area   San Ildefonso Pueblo has a corn dance on the **SEPTEMBER** **Fiesta de Navidad de Santa María**. The Jicarilla Apache nation joins in social dances, a rodeo and a powwow at the **Stone Lake Fiesta (Go-jii-ya)** in Dulce.

Taos and the Enchanted Circle   Taos Pueblo celebrates the **Fiesta de San Geronimo** with buffalo, Comanche and corn dances, a trade fair, foot races and a pole climb.

Albuquerque and Central New Mexico   Harvest dances are held at Acoma Pueblo on the **Fiesta de San Estevan**, at Isleta Pueblo on the **Fiesta de San Agustín**, and at Laguna Pueblo on the **Fiesta de Navidad de la Santa María** and the **Fiesta de San José**.

OCTOBER   **Santa Fe Area**   A corn or elk dance marks the **Fiesta de San Francisco** at Nambe Pueblo.

Northwestern New Mexico   The **Shiprock Navajo Nation Fair**, the oldest of Navajo traditional fairs, features a parade, traditional dances, social song and dance contests, arts and crafts, a carnival, a rodeo and beauty pageants.

Albuquerque and Central New Mexico   Laguna Pueblo observes the **Fiesta de Santa Margarita y Santa María** with harvest and social dances.

NOVEMBER   **Santa Fe Area**   Tesuque Pueblo celebrates the **Fiesta de San Diego** with various dances. Jemez Pueblo observes the day with dances and a trade fair.

Northwestern New Mexico   Torchlit processions of masked gods preside over Zuni's traditional **Shalako** house-blessing ceremony. (Tribal leaders sometimes declare this event off-limits to outsiders; check ahead with the New Mexico Department of Tourism.)

DECEMBER   **Throughout New Mexico**   The **Fiesta de Nuestra Señora de Guadalupe** is celebrated at Tesuque, Pojoaque, Santa Clara and Jemez Pueblos with dances. All New Mexico pueblos hold tribal **Christmas dances** on the 24th and 25th, often with masked Matachines dances that depict the Puebloans' first contact with Europeans.

▼▼▼▼▼▼▼▼▼▼▼▼
Before You Go

VISITORS CENTERS

For free visitor information packets including maps and current details on special events, lodging and camping, contact a visitors center or tourism board. As well as large cities, most small towns have chambers of commerce or visitor information centers. Many of them are listed in *Hidden New Mexico* under the appropriate regions. Tourist information centers are usually not open on weekends.

For the state in general, contact the **New Mexico Department of Tourism**. ~ 491 Old Santa Fe Trail, Santa Fe, NM 87503; 800-545-2070, 800-733-6396; www.newmexico.org.

PACKING   The old adage that you should take along twice as much money and half as much stuff as you think you'll need is sound advice as far as it goes, but bear in mind that in many parts of New Mexico you are unlikely to find a store selling anything more substantial than curios and beef jerky.

New Mexicans are casual in their dress and expect the same of visitors. Restaurants with dress codes are few and far between. Even if you attend a fancy $100-a-plate fundraiser or go out for a night at the opera, you'll find that a coat and tie or evening gown and heels instantly brand you as a tourist. Chic apparel in these parts is more likely to mean a western-cut suit, ostrich hide boots and a bolo tie with a flashy turquoise-and-silver slide, or for women, a fiesta dress with a concho belt, long-fringed moccasins and a squash blossom necklace—all fairly expensive items that you may never have an occasion to wear back home. Relax. Sporty, comfortable clothing will pass practically anywhere in New Mexico.

When packing clothes, plan to dress in layers. Temperatures can turn hot or cold in a flash at any time of year. During the course of a single vacation day, you can expect to start wearing a heavy jacket, a sweater or flannel shirt and a pair of slacks or jeans, peeling down to a T-shirt and shorts as the day warms up, then putting the extra layers back on soon after the sun goes down.

Other essentials to pack or buy along the way include a good sunscreen and high-quality sunglasses. If you are planning to camp in the mountains during the summer months, you'll be glad you brought mosquito repellent. Umbrellas are considered an oddity in the Southwest. When it rains, as it sometimes does though rarely for long, the approved means of keeping cold water from running down the back of your neck is a cowboy hat.

For outdoor activities, tough-soled hiking boots are more comfortable than running shoes on rocky terrain. Even RV travelers and those who prefer to spend most nights in motels may want to take along a backpacking tent and sleeping bag for irresistible urges to stay out under star-spangled New Mexico skies. A canteen, first-aid kit, flashlight and other routine camping gear are also likely to come in handy. Cycling enthusiasts should bring their own bikes. Especially when it comes to mountain biking, there are a lot more great places to ride than there are towns where you can find bicycles for rent. The same goes for boating, golf and other activities that call for special equipment.

If you're the kind of person who likes to pick up free souvenirs—in the form of unusual stones, pine cones and the like—be sure to take along some plastic bags for hauling treasures. A camera, of course, is essential for capturing your travel experience; of equal importance is a good pair of binoculars, which let you explore distant landscapes from scenic overlooks. And don't, for heaven's sake, forget your copy of *Hidden New Mexico*.

Lodgings in New Mexico run the gamut from tiny one-room mountain cabins to luxurious hotels that blend Indian pueblo architecture with contemporary elegance. Bed and breakfasts can be found not only in chic destinations like Santa Fe but also in such unlikely locales as former ghost towns and the outskirts of Indian reservations. They come in all types, sizes and price ranges. Typical of the genre are lovingly restored old mansions comfortably fur-

LODGING

nished with period decor, usually with under a dozen rooms. Some bed and breakfasts, however, are guest cottages or rooms in nice suburban homes, while others are larger establishments, approaching hotel size, of the type sometimes referred to as country inns.

The abundance of motels in towns along all major highway routes presents a range of choices, from name-brand motor inns to traditional mom-and-pop establishments that have endured for half a century since motels were invented. Older motels along main truck routes, especially interstate Route 40, offer some of the lowest room rates to be found anywhere in the United States today.

Travelers planning to visit a place in peak season should make advance reservations or arrive early in the day, before the "No Vacancy" signs start lighting up. Those who plan to stay in Santa Fe at any time of year are wise to make reservations well ahead of time.

At the other end of the price spectrum, the height of self-indulgent vacationing is to be found at upscale resorts in some destinations such as Ruidoso and Santa Fe. These resorts offer riding stables, golf courses, tennis courts, fine dining, live entertainment and exclusive shops on the premises so that guests can spend their entire holidays without leaving the grounds—a boon for celebrities seeking a few days' rest and relaxation away from the public eye, but a very expensive way to miss out on experiencing the real New Mexico.

Other lodgings throughout the region offer a different kind of personality. Many towns—preserved historic districts like Lincoln as well as larger communities like Taos—have historic hotels dating back before the turn of the century. Some of them have been lavishly restored to far surpass their original Victorian elegance. Others may lack the polished antique decor and sophisticated ambience but make up for it in their authentic feel. These places give visitors a chance to spice up their vacation experience by spending the night where lawman Wyatt Earp or novelist Zane Grey once slept and awakening to look out their window onto a Main Street that has changed surprisingly little since the days of the Old West.

Whatever your preference and budget, you can probably find something to suit your taste with the help of the regional chapters in this book. Remember, rooms can be scarce and prices may rise during the peak season, which is summer throughout most of the region and winter in low-lying desert communities.

Accommodations in this book are organized by region and classified according to price. Rates referred to are high-season rates, so if you are looking for off-season bargains, it's good to inquire. *Budget* lodgings generally run less than $70 per night for two people and are satisfactory and clean but modest. *Moderate* hotels range from $70 to $110; what they have to offer in the way of luxury will depend on where they are located, but they generally offer larger guest rooms and more attractive surroundings. At *deluxe*-priced accommodations, you can expect to spend between

$110 and $180 for a homey bed and breakfast or a double in a hotel or resort. In hotels of this price you'll generally find spacious rooms, a fashionable lobby, a restaurant and often a group of shops. *Ultra-deluxe* facilities, priced above $180, are a region's finest, offering all the amenities of a deluxe hotel plus plenty of extras.

Room rates vary as much with locale as with quality. Some of the trendier destinations have no rooms at all in the budget price range. In other communities—especially those along interstate highways where rates are set with truck drivers in mind—every motel falls into the budget category, even though accommodations may range from $19.95 at run-down, spartan places to $45 or so at the classiest motor inn in town. The price categories listed in this book are relative, designed to show you where to get the most out of your travel budget, however large or small it may be.

DINING

Restaurants seem to be one of the main industries in some parts of New Mexico. Santa Fe, for example, has approximately 200 restaurants in a city of just 63,000 people. While the specialty cuisine throughout most of New Mexico consists of variations on Mexican and Indian food, you'll find many restaurants catering to customers whose tastes don't include hot chile peppers. You'll also find a growing number of restaurants offering "New Southwestern" menus that feature offbeat dishes using local ingredients. Green-chile tempura? Snow-crab enchiladas? If a newly invented dish sounds tempting, by all means give it a try!

Within a particular chapter, restaurants are categorized by region, with each entry describing the establishment according to price. All serve lunch and dinner unless otherwise noted. Dinner entrées at *budget* restaurants usually cost $8 or less. The ambience is informal, service usually speedy and the crowd often a local one. *Moderately* priced restaurants range between $8 and $16 at dinner; surroundings are casual but pleasant, the menu offers more variety and the pace is usually slower. *Deluxe* establishments tab their entrées from $16 to $24; cuisines may be simple or sophisticated, depending on the location, but the decor is plusher and the service more personalized. *Ultra-deluxe* dining rooms, where entrées begin at $24, are often the gourmet places; here cooking has become a fine art and the service should be impeccable.

Some restaurants change hands often and are occasionally closed in low seasons. Efforts have been made in this book to include places with established reputations for good eating. Breakfast and lunch menus vary less in price from restaurant to restaurant than evening dinners. All restaurants in this book serve lunch and dinner unless otherwise noted.

DRIVING NOTES

The mountains and deserts of New Mexico are clearly the major sightseeing attractions for many visitors. This is a rugged area and there are some important things to remember when driving on the side roads throughout the region. First and foremost, believe it if you see a sign indicating four-wheel drive only. These roads can be very dangerous in a car without high ground clearance and the extra traction afforded by four-wheel drive—and there may be no safe place to turn around if you get stuck. During rainy periods dirt roads may become impassable muck. And in winter, heavy snows necessitate the use of snow tires or chains on main roads, while side roads may or may not be maintained at all.

If you substituted grapes for chiles, New Mexico would be the champagne capital of the world; experts estimate more than 35,000 tons are exported within a single year.

Some side roads will take you far from civilization so be sure to have a full radiator and tank of gas. Carry spare fuel, water and food. In winter, it is always wise to travel with a shovel and blankets in your car. Should you become stuck, local people are usually quite helpful about offering assistance to stranded vehicles, but in case no one else is around, for extended backcountry driving, a cell phone would not be a bad idea.

TRAVELING WITH CHILDREN

Any place that has cowboys and Indians, rocks to climb and limitless room to run is bound to be a hit with youngsters. Plenty of family adventures are available in New Mexico, from manmade attractions to experiences in the wild. A few guidelines will help make travel with children a pleasure.

Book reservations in advance, making sure that the places you stay accept children. Many bed and breakfasts do not. If you need a crib or extra cot, arrange for it ahead of time. A travel agent can be of help here, as well as with most other travel plans.

If you are traveling by air, try to reserve bulkhead seats where there is plenty of room. Take along extras you may need, such as diapers, changes of clothing, snacks and toys or small games. When traveling by car, be sure to take along the extras, too. Make sure you have plenty of water and juices to drink; dehydration can be a subtle but serious problem. Most towns, as well as some national parks, have stores that carry diapers, baby food, snacks and other essentials, though they usually close early. Larger towns often have all-night grocery or convenience stores.

A first-aid kit is a must for any trip. Along with adhesive bandages, antiseptic cream and something to stop itching, be sure to include any medicines your pediatrician might recommend to treat allergies, colds, diarrhea or any chronic health problems your child may have.

New Mexico sunshine is intense. Take extra care for the first few days. Children's skin is usually more tender than adult skin and severe sunburn can happen before you realize it. A hat is a good idea, along with a reliable sunblock.

Many national parks and monuments offer special activities designed just for children. Visitors center film presentations and rangers' campfire slide shows can help inform children about the natural history of the Southwest and head off some questions. However, kids tend to find a lot more things to wonder about than adults have answers for. To be as prepared as possible, seize every opportunity to learn more.

The unique beauty of New Mexico is appealing to many: the wide open spaces stretching for miles and miles invite people who are looking to get away from it all. It's a region that gives people a lot of space, literally, and encourages you to do your own thing, which allows gay or lesbian travelers to feel comfortable here. Whether you're interested in exploring the area's magnificent scenery, sightseeing in the cosmopolitan cities, or just relaxing by the pool, the Southwest has much to offer.

GAY & LESBIAN TRAVELERS

You'll find gay and lesbian communities in a few of the bigger cities such as Santa Fe and Albuquerque. Gay and lesbian publications providing entertainment listings are also available in some of the larger gay enclaves. You can pick up the free monthly *Out Magazine* (not to be confused with the national magazine called *Out*) at bookstores statewide. ~ 505-243-2540; www.outmaga zine.com, e-mail mail@outmagazine.com. *Weekly Alibi*, a free, alternative newspaper, offers entertainment listings specifically for the Albuquerque area. ~ 505-346-0660; www.alibi.com.

Traveling solo grants an independence and freedom different from that of traveling with a partner, but single travelers are more vulnerable to crime and should take additional precautions.

WOMEN TRAVELING ALONE

It's unwise to hitchhike and probably best to avoid inexpensive accommodations on the outskirts of town; the money saved does not outweigh the risk. Bed and breakfasts, youth hostels and YWCAs are generally your safest bet for lodging, and they also foster an environment ideal for bonding with fellow travelers.

Keep all valuables well-hidden and hold onto cameras and purses. Avoid late-night treks or strolls through undesirable parts of town, but if you find yourself in this situation, continue walking with a confident air until you reach a safe haven. A fierce scowl never hurts.

These hints should by no means deter you from seeking out adventure. Wherever you go, stay alert, use your common sense and trust your instincts. If you are hassled or threatened in some way, never be afraid to yell for assistance. It's a good idea to carry change for a phone call and to know the number to call in case of

Text continued on page 30.

Desert Survival

ar travel can be risky in some desert areas described in this guidebook simply because they are so remote. Once you venture beyond paved, well-used roads, if your vehicle breaks down it may be days before another human being comes along. In such a situation, a little survival know-how can save your life.

• Most important, carry more drinking water in your vehicle than you can imagine needing. In hot desert conditions, a human being may require two gallons of water per day to stay alive. Dehydration is the major threat to survival.

• When stranded in the desert, do not drink beer or other alcoholic beverages. Alcohol actually makes your body dehydrate more quickly. Taking small amounts of salt with your water will help prevent dehydration.

• Water is often more plentiful in the desert than it appears. Birds, especially doves, visit small waterholes frequently, and you can follow them there. Green vegetation indicates that water lies just below the surface, where you can collect it by digging a hole and straining it. Water from natural sources must be distilled or purified by boiling or by water purification tablets. Not all tablets protect against giardia, the most common organic contaminant in desert areas.

If water does not support green plants or algae, it may contain poisonous alkali and can only be made safe by distillation. You can distill water with a simple solar still made from a sheet of plastic such as the rain fly for a backpacking tent. Dig a hole. Place a can, jar or other empty container in the center of it, and lay the plastic over the top. Put rocks on the plastic around the hole to hold it in place, then place a stone in the center of the plastic, over the container. As the sun heats the air beneath the plastic, water will evaporate from the bottom of the hole.

It will condense on the underside of the plastic and run down to the lowest point, where it will drip into the container.

• Juice from the red fruit of the prickly pear cactus can provide lifesaving moisture—and it tastes good. (Be careful of the clusters of tiny spines on the outside of the fruit when cutting it open.) Another storehouse of water is the soft flesh inside a barrel cactus. Damaging cacti on federal land is illegal, however, so resort to chopping open a barrel cactus only in desperate circumstances.

• Stay with your vehicle unless someone in your party needs immediate medical attention and you know that help is nearby. If you must walk out in search of help, leave a note on the windshield telling your travel route and direction and the time you left.

• Stay in the shade during midday heat: inside your vehicle with the windows rolled down, under the vehicle or under a lean-to made with a tarp or blanket. If you hide from the hot sun in the shade of a rock formation, bear in mind that rattlesnakes often have the same idea.

• Use any means possible to attract attention. Lay out bright-colored towels, clothing or camping gear in a giant "X"—the international emergency signal for "stranded"—where it can be seen from aircraft. Use oily rags or green leafy brush to build a smokey signal fire. Watch for the dust plumes of distant vehicles and flash sunlight from a mirror in their direction. Keep the hood of your vehicle up at all times so that anyone who sees you can tell immediately that you're in trouble.

• More and more backroad travelers carry cellular phones in case of emergency. Although these phones don't work in the most remote areas or near the huge power lines that run from dams on the Colorado River, they do work more places than not. A CB radio is rarely helpful.

emergency. For more hints, get a copy of *Safety and Security for Women Who Travel* (Travelers Tales).

Most areas have 24-hour hotlines for victims of rape and violent crime. Santa Fe's **Rape Crisis Center** is staffed around the clock. ~ P.O. Box 6484, Santa Fe, NM 87502; 505-986-9111. The **Women's Resource Center** on the University of New Mexico campus offers referrals and counseling. Closed Saturday and Sunday. ~ 1160 Mesa Vista Hall, UNM, Albuquerque, NM 87131; 505-277-3716. Or call the **Albuquerque Rape Crisis Center**. ~ 1025 Hermosa Street Southeast, Albuquerque, NM 87108; 505-266-7711.

SENIOR TRAVELERS   New Mexico is a hospitable place for older vacationers, many of whom turn into part-time or full-time residents thanks to the dry, pleasant climate and the friendly senior citizen communities that have developed in southern Arizona and, on a smaller scale, in other parts of the region. Keep in mind, however, that in the changeable climate of New Mexico, seniors are more at risk of suffering hypothermia. The large number of national parks and monuments in New Mexico means that persons age 62 and older can save considerable money with a Golden Age Passport, which allows free admission. Apply for one in person at any national park unit that charges an entrance fee. Many private sightseeing attractions also offer significant discounts for seniors.

The **American Association of Retired Persons** (AARP) offers membership to anyone over 50. AARP's benefits include travel discounts with a number of firms. ~ 601 E Street NW, Washington, DC 20049; 800-424-3410; www.aarp.org.

Elderhostel offers educational courses that are all-inclusive packages at colleges and universities. In New Mexico, Elderhostel courses are available in numerous locations including Albuquerque, Las Cruces, Santa Fe, Silver City and Taos. ~ 11 Avenue de Lafayette, Boston, MA 02111; 877-426-8056, fax 617-426-0701; www.elderhostel.org.

Be extra careful about health matters. High altitudes may present a risk to persons with heart or respiratory conditions; ask your physician for advice when planning your trip. Many tourist destinations in the region are a long way from any hospital or other health care facility.

In addition to the medications you ordinarily use, it's a good idea to bring along the prescriptions for obtaining more. Consider carrying a medical record with you, including your history and current medical status as well as your doctor's name, phone number and address. Make sure that your insurance covers you while you are away from home.

DISABLED TRAVELERS   New Mexico is striving to make public areas fully accessible to persons with disabilities. Parking spaces and restroom facilities for the handicapped are provided according to both state law and national park regulations. National parks and monuments also post signs that tell which trails are wheel-chair-accessible. You can order *Access New Mexico*, a handbook from the Governor's Committee on the Concerns of the Handicapped. ~ 491 Old Santa Fe Trail, Santa Fe, NM 87501; 505-827-6465.

> The state of New Mexico is roughly the size of Great Britain and Ireland combined.

Organizations offering information for travelers with disabilities include the **Society for Accessible Travel & Hospitality** at 347 5th Avenue, Suite 610, New York, NY 10016, 212-447-7284, fax 212-725-8253, www.sath.org; and the **MossRehab ResourceNet** at MossRehab Hospital, 1200 West Tabor Road, Philadelphia, PA 19141, 215-456-9600, www.mossresourcenet.org.

For general traveling advice, contact **Travelin' Talk**, a networking organization. ~ P.O. Box 1796, Wheatridge, CO 80034; 303-232-2979; www.travelintalk.net. The **Access-Able Travel Service** provides traveling information on the web: www.access-able.com.

Passports and Visas   Most foreign visitors need a passport and tourist visa to enter the United States. Contact your nearest U.S. Embassy or Consulate well in advance to obtain a visa and to check on any other entry requirements.

FOREIGN TRAVELERS

Customs Requirements   Foreign travelers are allowed to carry in the following: 200 cigarettes (1 carton), 50 cigars, or 2 kilograms (4.4 pounds) of smoking tobacco; one liter of alcohol for personal use only (you must be 21 years of age to bring in alcohol); and US$100 worth of duty-free gifts that can include an additional quantity of 100 cigars. You may bring in any amount of currency, but must fill out a form if you bring in over US$10,000. Carry any prescription drugs in clearly marked containers. (You may have to produce a written prescription or doctor's statement for the custom's officer.) Meat or meat products, seeds, plants, fruits and narcotics are not allowed to be brought into the United States. Contact the **United States Customs Service** for further information. ~ 1300 Pennsylvania Avenue NW, Washington, DC 20229; 202-927-1700; www.customs.treas.gov.

Driving   If you plan to rent a car, an international driver's license should be obtained before arriving in the United States. Some car rental agencies require both a foreign license and an international driver's license. Many also require a lessee to be at least 25 years of age; all require a major credit card. Seat belts are mandatory for the driver and all passengers. Children under the age of five or under 40 pounds should be in the back seat in approved child-safety restraints.

Currency   United States money is based on the dollar. Bills generally come in denominations of $1, $2, $5, $10, $20, $50 and

$100. Every dollar is divided into 100 cents. Coins are the penny (1 cent), nickel (5 cents), dime (10 cents) and quarter (25 cents). Half-dollar and dollar coins are rarely used. You may not use foreign currency to purchase goods and services in the United States. Consider buying traveler's checks in dollar amounts. You may also use credit cards affiliated with an American company such as Interbank, Barclay Card, VISA and American Express.

Electricity and Electronics   Electric outlets use currents of 110 volts, 60 cycles. To operate appliances made for other electrical systems, you need a transformer or other adapter. Travelers who use laptop computers for telecommunication should be aware that modem configurations for U.S. telephone systems may be different from their European counterparts. Similarly, the U.S. format for videotapes is different from that in Europe; National Park Service visitors centers and other stores that sell souvenir videos often have them available in European format on request.

Weights and Measures   The United States uses the English system of weights and measures. American units and their metric equivalents are: 1 inch = 2.5 centimeters; 1 foot (12 inches) = 0.3 meter; 1 yard (3 feet) = 0.9 meter; 1 mile (5280 feet) = 1.6 kilometers; 1 ounce = 28 grams; 1 pound (16 ounces) = 0.45 kilogram; 1 quart (liquid) = 0.9 liter.

▼▼▼▼▼▼▼▼▼▼▼▼▼▼
Outdoor Adventures

CAMPING

RV or tent camping is a great way to tour New Mexico. Besides saving a substantial amount of money, campers enjoy the freedom to watch sunsets from beautiful places, spend nights under spectacularly starry skies and wake up to find themselves in lovely surroundings that few hotels can match.

Most towns have commercial RV parks of some sort, and long-term mobile-home parks often rent spaces to RVers by the night. But unless you absolutely must have cable television, none of these places can compete with the wide array of public campgrounds available in national and state parks, monuments and forests. Federal campground sites are typically less developed; only the biggest ones have electrical hookups. National forest campgrounds don't have hookups, while state park campgrounds just about always do. The largest public campgrounds offer tent camping loops separate from RV loops and backcountry camping areas offer the option of spending the night in primeval New Mexico.

For listings of state parks with camping facilities and reservation information, contact the **New Mexico State Park and Recreation Division**, which has information on state park campgrounds. ~ 1220 South St. Francis Drive, Santa Fe, NM 87505; www.nmparks.com.

Information on camping in the national forests is available from the **National Forest Service–Southwestern Region**. ~ 333

Broadway Southeast, Albuquerque, NM 87102; 505-842-3292;
www.fs.fed.us/r3. Camping and reservation information for parks
and monuments is also available from the parks and monuments
listed in this book or from **National Park Service–Intermountain
Support Office**. ~ 1100 Old Santa Fe Trail, Santa Fe, NM 87501;
505-988-6100; www.nps.gov.

Many Indian lands have public campgrounds, which usually
don't appear in campground directories. For information, contact the **Mescalero Apache Tribe**. ~ P.O. Box 227, Mescalero,
NM 88340; 505-671-4494. Also contact **Zuni Pueblo**. ~ P.O.
Box 339, Zuni, NM 87327; 505-5851.

Also see the "Parks" sections in each chapter to discover where
camping is available.

Tent camping is allowed in the backcountry of all national forests   **PERMITS**
here except in a few areas where signs are posted prohibiting it.
You may need a permit to hike or camp in national forest wilderness areas, so contact specific forests for more information. Ranger
stations provide trail maps and advice on current conditions and
fire regulations. In dry seasons, emergency rules may prohibit
campfires and sometimes ban cigarette smoking, with stiff enforcement penalties.

For backcountry hiking in national parks and monuments,
you must first obtain a permit from the ranger at the front desk
in the visitors center. The permit procedure is simple and free. It
helps park administrators measure the impact on sensitive ecosystems and distribute use evenly among major trails to prevent
overcrowding.

Most of the large desert lakes along the Rio Grande and other ma-   **BOATING**
jor rivers are administered by State Parks. Federal boating safety
regulations that apply to these lakes may vary slightly from state
regulations. Indian reservations have separate rules for boating on
tribal lakes. More significant than any differences between federal,
state and tribal regulations are the local rules in force for any par-

CAMPING TIPS

You won't find much in the way of sophisticated reservation systems in New
Mexico. The general rule in public campgrounds is still first-come, first-
served, even though they fill up practically every night in peak season. For
campers, this means traveling in the morning and reaching your intended
campground by early afternoon. In many areas, campers may find it
more convenient to keep a single location for as much as a week and
explore surrounding areas on day trips.

ticular lake. Inquire about applicable boating regulations at a local marina or fishing supply store or use the addresses and phone numbers listed in "Parks" or other sections of each chapter in this book to contact the headquarters for lakes you plan to visit.

Boats, from small power boats to houseboats, can be rented for 24 hours or longer at marinas on several of the larger lakes. At most marinas, you can get a boat on short notice if you come on a weekday, since much of their business comes from local weekend recreation.

River rafting is a very popular sport in several parts of New Mexico, notably on the Chama River and Rio Grande. Independent rafters are welcome, but because of the bulky equipment and specialized knowledge of river hazards involved, most adventurous souls stick with group trips offered by any of the many rafting companies located in Taos and Santa Fe. Rafters, as well as people using canoes, kayaks, windsurfers or inner tubes, are required by state and federal regulations to wear life jackets.

FISHING

In a land as arid as New Mexico, many residents have an irresistible fascination with water. During the warmer months, lake shores and readily accessible portions of streams are often packed with anglers, especially on weekends. Vacationers can beat the crowds to some extent by planning to fish during the week.

Fish hatcheries in all four states keep busy stocking streams with trout, particularly rainbows, the most popular game fish throughout the West. Catch-and-release fly fishing is the rule in some popular areas such as the upper Pecos River near Santa Fe, allowing more anglers a chance at bigger fish. Be sure to inquire locally about eating the fish you catch, since some seemingly remote streams and rivers have contamination problems from old mines and mills.

The larger reservoirs offer an assortment of sport fish, including crappie, carp, white bass, smallmouth bass, largemouth bass and walleye pike. Striped bass, an ocean import, can run as large as 40 pounds, while catfish in the depths of dammed desert canyons sometimes attain mammoth proportions.

For copies of state fishing regulations, inquire at a local fishing supply store or marina. The **New Mexico Department of Game and Fish** can also provide complete information. ~ 1 Wildlife Way, Santa Fe, NM 87507; 505-476-8000, 800-862-9310; www.gmfsh.state.nm.us.

State fishing licenses are required for fishing in national parks and national recreation areas, but not on Indian reservations, where daily permits are sold by the tribal governments. For more information about fishing on Indian lands, contact the tribal agencies listed in "Camping" above.

TWO

Santa Fe Area

Native cultures scoff at the notion that Christopher Columbus discovered this continent. Even as the Europeans trod through the Dark Ages, the Anasazi Indians were well into their building of intricate Chaco Canyon in northwestern New Mexico. In fact, the Pueblo Indians are thought to have come to Santa Fe around A.D. 1200 or 1300, although they were preceded for centuries by the Anasazi, well before Europeans ever dreamed of a New World.

The first Spanish settlers claimed this aptly named "Kingdom of New Mexico" in 1540 and the Spanish made Santa Fe a provincial capital in 1610. Over the next seven decades, Spanish soldiers and Franciscan missionaries sought to convert the Pueblo Indians of the region. Tribespeople numbered nearly 100,000, calling an estimated 70 burnt-orange adobe pueblos (or towns) home.

In 1680 the Pueblo Indians revolted, killing 400 of the 2500 Spanish colonists and driving the rest back to Mexico. The Pueblos sacked Santa Fe and burned most of the structures (save the Palace of the Governors), remaining in Santa Fe until Don Diego de Vargas reconquered the region 12 years later.

When Mexico gained independence from Spain in 1821, so too did New Mexico. But it wasn't until the Mexican-American War that an American flag flew over the territory. In 1848 Mexico ceded New Mexico to the United States and by 1912 New Mexico was a full-fledged state.

Why have people always flocked to this land of rugged beauty? The absolute isolation provided by the fortresslike hills in Los Alamos appealed first to the American Indians, later to scientists. The natural barriers surrounding sky-high Santa Fe, coupled with its obvious beauty, have always made it a desirable city and deserving capital, located at the crossroads of north and south.

Some maintain the lands around Santa Fe are sacred. Each year there's a pilgrimage to the modest Santuario de Chimayo church, said to be constructed on sacred and healing ground. The American Indians, who successfully rejected the white man's attempts to force-feed them organized religion, have blessed grounds and rituals that remain secret to all outsiders. The spirituality takes many forms. For example, semifrequent supernatural occurrences are reported as straight news.

There's also the magic light and intense colors that artist Georgia O'Keeffe captured so accurately on canvas. The high-altitude sun beaming on the earth tones helps to create shadows and vibrancies not to be believed, from subtle morning hues to bold and majestic evenings. Watching a sunset unfold over the Sangre de Cristo and Jemez mountains can be a spiritual experience as oranges, pinks and violets, chalk-colored pastels and lightning-bolt streaks of yellow weave together a picture story with no plot. (Sangre de Cristo is Spanish for "Blood of Christ," a reference to the red hue that can color the mountains at sunset, especially when they are covered with snow.) Color even emerges in everyday life, as blood-red chile *ristras* line highway stands against a big blue sky.

In fact, many of Santa Fe's earliest Anglo residents were painters, sculptors, musicians, novelists and poets. They came to Santa Fe for the same reason Gauguin went to Tahiti and Hemingway to Paris: to immerse themselves in exotic surroundings in hopes of finding new artistic dimensions. Today Santa Fe continues to grow as a regional arts center of international repute, boasting some 200 art galleries, 30 publishers, 17 performance stages and 13 major museums.

Many newcomers, like the region's tourists, are here because of the climate. These high, dry mountain towns are pleasingly warm during spring and fall. Summer can bring intense heat and the winters are cold enough to make Santa Fe and nearby Taos viable ski areas. Summer and fall are particularly popular among vacationers. Santa Fe averages 14 inches of rainfall a year, and 30 to 34 inches of snow.

Others come for the Santa Fe area's cultural mix, which is as colorful and varied as the weather. Anglo, Indian and Spanish peoples coexist, each group more accepting of the others' beliefs yet holding on strong to their own time-honored traditions. New generations living on the pueblos seem less apt to follow the old ways and more interested in the outside world. Whether this is prompted by materialism, survival of the race or both remains to be seen. Still, where other regions have been homogenized by prosperity, in no way are the pueblo peoples tossing aside their proud heritage.

The same goes for the physical remains in the centuries-old cities. Rigorous zoning laws maintain Santa Fe's image by restricting architecture to either the adobe brick or Territorial styles. Fortunately, ordinances make it difficult for developers to raid and tear down. Las Vegas (New Mexico, not the glittering gambling mecca in Nevada) has nine historic districts, with architecture ranging from adobe to Italianate.

The city of Los Alamos, birthplace of the atomic bomb, remains an interesting contrast to the old and new. Modern in its technology and scientific findings, Los Alamos' laboratories coexist within a stone's throw of ancient ruins and Indian pueblos.

Tradition also blends well with modern culinary influences as evidenced in Santa Fe's original cuisine. New styles of cooking in many of the exciting restaurants of the region rely upon old recipes, with a twist. Piquant food is distinctive and uses home-grown chiles and family recipes, blue-corn tortillas and Navajo bread. Rejection of Anglo-izing has made the area unique. Whether it's in the

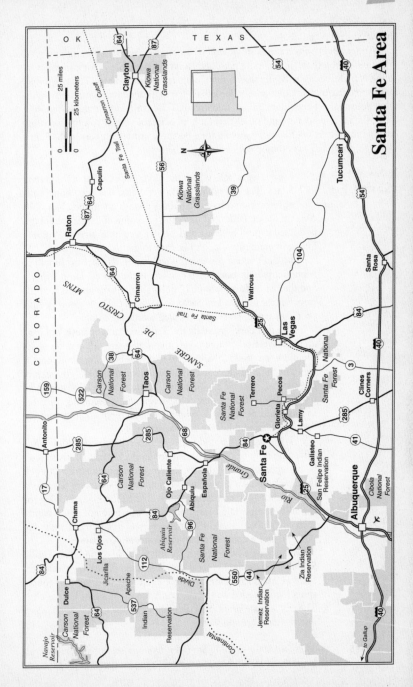

Santa Fe Area

names, lifestyles or biting scents of sage and piñon, in the Santa Fe area, everything has an accent to it.

Above all, however, this is still a land of "mañana," where a majority lives by the philosophy that "if it doesn't get done today, there's always tomorrow." On Sundays, life moves markedly slower than in the rest of the country. This can translate into a frustrating experience as the laissez-faire attitude carries over onto roads that seemingly change numerals in midstream. (The truth is that roads here follow ditches and arroyos and other natural land features.) But if you find yourself lost or learn that your laundry wasn't done on time, just remember: In the Santa Fe area, there's always tomorrow . . . and tomorrow.

▼▼▼▼▼▼▼▼▼
Santa Fe

A trivia game asks what's the oldest state capital in the United States. The answer of Santa Fe, which has been home to a government seat since 1610, is always a stumper. Not only does the "City Different" defy the government center stereotype (a domed capitol building and proper tree-lined streets), but unlike most state capitals, it's not easy to get to.

You can't take a commercial jet or even a train into Santa Fe. Albuquerque, an hour's drive south, is the closest large airport, and the city of Lamy, about 17 miles south, is the nearest Amtrak stop. But the independent Santa Feans seem to like it this way. And once you arrive, you'll find it's well worth the trouble.

Strict guidelines mandate the Territorial and Spanish Colonial architecture that characterizes the well-known Santa Fe style. Thanks to city codes, there are no highrises blocking the mountain views or the ever-changing colors at dawn and dusk. This attractive capital, situated at 7000 feet elevation and backdropped by the spectacular Sangre de Cristo Mountains, is becoming desirable to more and more people who are fleeing their urban homes for Santa Fe's natural beauty and culture.

Those rushing to relocate here either part or full time have driven housing prices to outer-space levels. Fledgling artists aren't being represented in galleries, as owners can only afford to stock their high-rent shops with proven names. Chain stores have been sneaking into the commercial core around the Plaza looking for the all-too-important tourist dollar. The invasion of brand names such as Starbuck's and Banana Republic has sparked local opposition and a clamor to ban chain stores downtown.

By digging a little deeper, it's still possible to find a soul amid Santa Fe's slickening veneer. Avoiding summer holiday weekends, such as Memorial Day or Labor Day, will find favorite tourist spots less crowded and Santa Feans more willing to have a chat. The city is quite beautiful in the fall, when the leaves are changing and the days are still balmy.

SIGHTS   There is plenty to see in Santa Fe, from palaces of worship to galleries to the Indian Market, but save time for the **State Capitol**, one of the only round capitol buildings in the United States. Built in the shape of the Pueblo Indian Zia, the three-story structure, with a red-brick roofline and whitewashed trim, symbolizes the circle of life: four winds, four seasons, four directions and four sacred obligations. It also resembles a much larger version of a Pueblo Indian ceremonial kiva. The roundhouse was built in 1966 to replace an older capitol building (now known as the Bataan Building) down the block. Display cases around the capital rotunda tell the Indian and Spanish history of the state, and you'll find locally made art and furniture scattered throughout. Guided tours of the capitol are available mid-May to mid-October. Open weekdays year-round; open Saturday from Memorial Day through Labor Day. ~ Paseo de Peralta and Old Santa Fe Trail; 505-986-4600; www.legis.state.nm.us, e-mail house@state.nm.us.

The Tlaxcala people from Mexico built the **San Miguel Mission** around 1610, making it the oldest continuously used church in the U.S. But this was probably considered sacred ground before that, as there is evidence of human occupation dating back to A.D. 1300. San Miguel is an amazing archive of everything from pyrographic paintings on buffalo hides and deer skin to a bell from Spain that dates back to 1356! Admission. ~ 401 Old Santa Fe Trail; 505-983-3974.

Constructed by the Spanish in 1609–1610, the Palace of the Governors served as capital of Nuevo Mexico, Spain's northernmost colony in the New World, before the Pilgrims landed at Plymouth Rock.

Not surprisingly, the oldest church is located near the **Oldest House in U.S.**, an earthen structure believed to have been built in 1250. Admission. ~ 215 East De Vargas Street.

Meander up the **Old Santa Fe Trail** through the parklike setting and over the mountain runoff–fed Santa Fe River. Pass by traditional irrigation ditches called *acequias*, which carry moisture from the hills found throughout the city.

Those who believe in miracles must make a point of stopping by the tiny **Loretto Chapel**, patterned after France's Saint Chappelle, which holds the beautiful "miraculous staircase." When the chapel was built, craftsmen failed to install any way to reach the choir loft. Short on funds, the nuns prayed to Saint Joseph, patron of carpenters, for a solution to the problem. The story goes that a man came armed with only a saw, hammer and hot water to shape the wooden staircase. He worked for months and built a staircase that makes two 360-degree turns but has no visible means of support. When it came time for payment, the man mysteriously disappeared. Admission. ~ 207 Old Santa Fe Trail; 505-982-0092, fax 505-984-7921; www.lorettochapel.com, e-mail information@lorettochapel.com.

Continue up the Santa Fe Trail to the **Plaza**, built in 1610 by Don Pedro de Peralta as an end to the Santa Fe Trail. (A marker in the Plaza commemorates its completion.) There's always plenty of excitement revolving around this town square. American Indians roll out their blankets and hawk their wares to tourists on the sidewalks surrounding the Plaza. Their prices have been adjusted to meet Santa Fe's ever-increasing popularity. Groups of young Latino men crowd into big cars and slowly cruise the square's perimeter. If you're lucky, there will be live music and dancing.

America's oldest public building, the **Palace of the Governors** may be more historically significant than the artifacts it houses. Once held by Pueblo Indians, the 1610 adobe fortress has been used as governmental headquarters for Mexico, the Confederacy and the territorial United States. Today the Palace houses exhibits of fascinating regional history. There's also a working exhibit of antique printing presses, as well as a photograph archive, history library and gift shop. Closed Monday. Admission. ~ 105 West Palace Avenue, on the Plaza; 505-476-5100, fax 505-476-5104; www.palaceofthegovernors.org.

Situated west of the Palace of Governors, the **Museum of Fine Arts** is a prototype of the architectural revival style called Spanish-Pueblo. The building is a reproduction of New Mexico's "Cathedral of the Desert" exhibit at the 1915 Panama-California Exposition in San Diego. Completed in 1917, it embodies aspects of the Spanish mission in the region. Notice the ceilings of split cedar *latillas* and hand-hewn vigas. Housing more than 7000 pieces of art, the museum is a repository for works of early Santa Fe and Taos masters as well as contemporary artists. Closed Monday. Admission. ~ 107 West Palace Avenue, on the Plaza; 505-827-4455, fax 505-476-5076; www.museumofnewmexico.org, e-mail ezieselman@mnm.state.nm.us.

The **Georgia O'Keeffe Museum** occupies three moderately historic buildings connected by hallways in a formerly nondescript part of downtown now known as "the O'K District." You'll find it behind the Eldorado Hotel, three blocks west of the Museum of Fine Arts. Grouped in stark exhibit spaces with otherwise bare white walls and sandstone floors are more than 100 paintings and small sculptures by New Mexico's most celebrated artist, who lived in Santa Fe for the last decade before her death at the age of 90. Closed Monday. Admission. ~ 217 Johnson Street; 505-995-0785, fax 505-995-0786; www.okeeffemuseum.org, e-mail main@okeeffemuseum.org.

Before leaving the Plaza area, you'll want to pop into **La Fonda Hotel**, which calls itself the "inn at the end of the trail," for a drink in the popular bar or a meal in its impressive dining room. You can glean as much information here about what's going on in town as you can at the chamber of commerce. ~ 100 East San Francisco Street; 505-982-5511, 800-523-5002; www.lafondasantafe.com, e-mail manager@lafondasantafe.com.

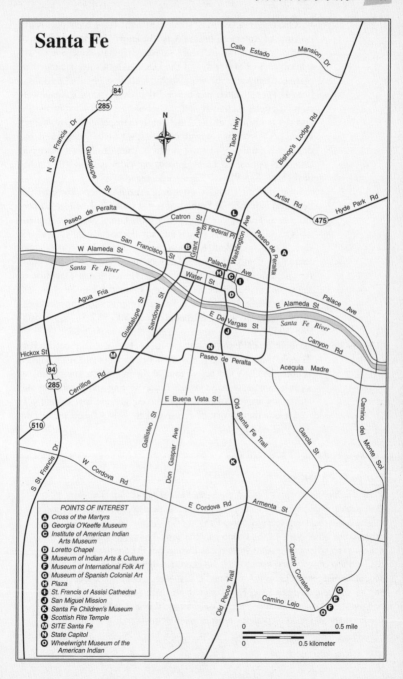

Santa Fe

Calle Estado
Mansion Dr
84
285
N St Francis Dr
Guadalupe St
Old Taos Hwy
Bishop's Lodge Rd
Artist Rd
Hyde Park Rd
475
Paseo de Peralta
Catron St
L
S Federal Pl
Washington Ave
Paseo de Peralta
San Francisco St
Grant Ave
B
A
W Alameda St
Palace Ave
Santa Fe River
H
Water St
C
I
Agua Fria
D
Guadalupe St
Sandoval St
E De Vargas St
E Alameda St
Palace Ave
Santa Fe River
J
Hickox St
Canyon Rd
M
N
Paseo de Peralta
84
285
Cerrillos Rd
Acequia Madre
510
E Buena Vista St
Gallisteo St
Don Gaspar Ave
Old Santa Fe Trail
Garcia St
Camino del Monte Sol
S St Francis Dr
W Cordova Rd
K
E Cordova Rd
Armenta St
Camino Corrales
G
E
Old Pecos Trail
Camino Lejo
F

POINTS OF INTEREST

- Ⓐ Cross of the Martyrs
- Ⓑ Georgia O'Keeffe Museum
- Ⓒ Institute of American Indian Arts Museum
- Ⓓ Loretto Chapel
- Ⓔ Museum of Indian Arts & Culture
- Ⓕ Museum of International Folk Art
- Ⓖ Museum of Spanish Colonial Art
- Ⓗ Plaza
- Ⓘ St. Francis of Assisi Cathedral
- Ⓙ San Miguel Mission
- Ⓚ Santa Fe Children's Museum
- Ⓛ Scottish Rite Temple
- Ⓜ SITE Santa Fe
- Ⓝ State Capitol
- Ⓞ Wheelwright Museum of the American Indian

0   0.5 mile

0   0.5 kilometer

One of Santa Fe's most significant sightseeing highlights is the **Institute of American Indian Arts Museum**. This downtown museum is part of the federally chartered Indian college-level art school (one of only three in the U.S.). Exhibits are arranged to place contemporary artwork within a context of tribal tradition. For instance, located just beyond the main entrance is the welcoming circle, a circular space symbolic of the cycles of nature and the continuity of the American Indian people. Here, before viewing the exhibits, visitors can gather their thoughts in the quiet, contemplative manner in which American Indians have traditionally approached art appreciation. Admission. ~ 108 Cathedral Place; 505-983-1777; www.iaiancad.org.

If you're interested in attending church services, consider the beautiful Santa Fe **St. Francis of Assisi Cathedral**, whose cornerstone was laid in 1869 by Archbishop Lamy. With its stained-glass windows, bronze panels and smaller Sacrament Chapel, it's certainly the grandest church in the Southwest. In a corner is the sacred La Conquistadora ("Lady of the Conquest"), the oldest representation of the Madonna in the United States. Devotion to the woodcarved statue has been maintained for more than 300 years. In the early morning light, La Conquistadora appears positively heavenly. ~ 131 Cathedral Place; 505-982-5619, fax 505-989-1952.

HIDDEN ► Built in 1911 and situated north of the plaza, the **Scottish Rite Temple** may be familiar to Santa Fe residents but it's a hidden gem to the city's visitors. A tour of the building allows a look at a professional stage, a vintage theater seating area, costumes and a dressing area for the Masons who congregate here once a year to act out the history of Freemasonry. ~ 463 Paseo de Peralta; 505-982-4414.

PUEBLO PRIDE

While Pueblo Indians have lived in the Santa Fe area for at least 800 years, the pueblos within Santa Fe County nowadays are quite small, totaling only a few hundred residents. Many of Santa Fe's American Indian residents are drawn from other parts of the country by the Santa Fe Indian School, a college prep school for youths from tribes throughout the Southwest, and the Institute of American Indian Arts, the nation's only college-level art school for indigenous people. Artists and craftspeople from many tribes rely on the abundance of Santa Fe galleries that exhibit contemporary and traditional American Indian art, as well as special events such as the huge annual Indian Market, for most of their income.

If you're traveling with kids consider a stop at the **Santa Fe Children's Museum**. Budding architects can design and build a room from PVC pipes; young musicians can compose original tunes on an assortment of xylophones; and future physicists can marvel at the echoing sound dishes. Earthworks, an educational, one-acre garden, harbors a greenhouse, wetlands and humming-bird and butterfly gardens. Closed Monday and Tuesday. Admission. ~ 1050 Old Pecos Trail; 505-989-8359, fax 505-989-7506; www.santafechildrensmuseum.org, e-mail children@santafechildrensmuseum.org.

A recent addition to the city's roster of museums, SITE **Santa Fe** is a private nonprofit "artspace" designed to accommodate traveling art exhibits. Free from the strictures of government-run museums, SITE Santa Fe often presents more daring and progressive shows than can be found elsewhere in town. The vast free-form space—it used to be a warehouse—is flexible enough to fit all kinds of visual-arts exhibits and also hosts nationally known poets and performance artists. Admission. ~ 1606 Paseo de Peralta; 505-989-1199, fax 505-989-1188; www.sitesantafe.org, e-mail sitesantafe@sitesantafe.org.

Impressive is a good way to describe the privately owned **Wheelwright Museum of the American Indian**. Though the permanent collection (not available to the public) has a lot of Navajo weavings, changing exhibits feature historic and contemporary American Indian art. ~ 704 Camino Lejo; 505-982-4636, 800-607-4636, fax 505-989-7386; www.wheelwright.org, e-mail info@wheelwright.org.

The nearby **Museum of International Folk Art** houses the world's largest collection of folk art—130,000 artifacts from all around the globe. Toys, miniatures, textiles and religious art are colorfully displayed in the Girard Wing. The Hispanic Heritage Wing highlights four centuries of New Mexico's Latino folk culture. Costumes, textiles and quilts number among the exhibits in the Neutrogena Wing and Lloyd's Treasure Chest. The museum plaza, café and parking lot also afford a spectacular view of the Jemez Mountains, southwest of Santa Fe, and the Sangre de Cristos to the north. Closed Monday. Admission. ~ 706 Camino Lejo; 505-476-1200, fax 505-476-1300; www.moifa.org.

Southwestern American Indians are the focus of the **Museum of Indian Arts & Culture**, with exhibits drawn from extensive collections of the museum's Laboratory of Anthropology. Ancient and contemporary pottery is displayed in the Buchsbaum Gallery; the library and archives contain countless records, photographs and manuscripts. Docent tours are available. Closed Monday. Admission. ~ 710 Camino Lejo; 505-476-1250, fax 505-476-1330; www.miaclab.org, e-mail info@miaclab.org.

Inaugurated in 2002, the **Museum of Spanish Colonial Art** boasts a varied collection of more than 3500 pieces that spans five continents and four centuries. Specializing in Spanish colonial pieces, its rotating and permanent exhibition consists of furniture, paintings, metal work, weaving and pottery, displayed in a historic 1930 adobe designed by John Gaw Meem. There's also creations by 20th-century Hispanic artists on view. Closed Monday. Admission. ~ 750 Camino Lejo; 505-982-2226; www.span ishcolonial.org, e-mail info@spanishcolonial.org.

Wandering up to **Canyon Road** (see "Art Everywhere You Look" and "Shopping" below), you'll pass by historic haciendas and witness firsthand the center of Santa Fe's burgeoning arts community. This shopping district is where the founders of Santa Fe's artist community resided, and in 1935 the first gallery was established (it's no longer there). Early in the 20th century the narrow old river road ran through a low-rent district with secluded compounds of small residences and studios. Now it's home to literally hundreds of galleries, and an important landmark for artists everywhere. Yet Canyon Road does not flaunt its history, focusing instead on the business at hand: buying and selling art.

If you continue up Canyon Road beyond the galleries and shops and the broad, green neighborhood park, you'll come to **Cristo Rey Church**. Don't be deceived by the historic look of this adobe church. It was actually built in 1940 in the style of Spanish Colonial mission churches (such as those in Chimayo, Las Trampas and Truchas on the High Road to Taos) to house a stone altarpiece dating back to 1760. This treasure, one of the finest works of early New Mexican religious sculpture, depicts God and a number of saints. ~ At the corner of Cristo Rey Street and Canyon Road; 505-983-8528, fax 505-992-6836; www.cristorey catholicchurch.org, e-mail cristorey@qwest.net.

Randall Davey Audubon Center is named for a painter known for his horse-racing themes. When he died in the early 1980s, Davey left his 135-acre estate to the National Audubon Society. As you stroll the easy walking trails that circle the oak and piñon terrain, you may encounter a wide variety of animal life, including rabbits, skunks, raccoons and deer. Birdwatchers are likely to spot magpies, piñon jays, ravens and dozens of songbird species. A visitors center includes a bookstore with an excellent selection on the natural history of New Mexico. The home, including Davey's studio and an exhibition of his works, opens for tours on an irregular basis. Closed Sunday during winter. Admission. ~ 1800 Upper Canyon Road; 505-983-4609, fax 505-983-2355.

To take in the whole picture of Santa Fe, hoof it up to the **Cross of the Martyrs,** located in the city's Marcy Park section.

There are stairs by Paseo de Peralta and Washington Avenue that you have to climb to earn the bird's-eye view of the city.

Settle into a private hot tub overlooking the mountains under the starlit sky at **Ten Thousand Waves**, located just a few minutes from downtown Santa Fe. This authentic Japanese health spa also offers a variety of full-body massages, facials and herbal wraps. Fee. ~ 3451 Hyde Park Road; 505-982-9304, fax 505-989-5077; www.tenthousandwaves.com, e-mail info@tenthousandwaves.com.

Adjacent to the Loretto Chapel, the striking Pueblo-style **Inn at Loretto** features interior wall murals and Southwest decor that reflect the heritage of New Mexico. Some of the 141 rooms and suites have kiva fireplaces and private balconies. Those looking for mind/body rejuvenation will enjoy the services of the on-site spa. Other amenities include a restaurant with an outdoor terrace. ~ 211 Old Santa Fe Trail; 505-988-5531, 800-727-5531, fax 505-984-7988; www.hotelloretto.com, e-mail lorettorooms@compuserve.com. ULTRA-DELUXE.

LODGING

Red-brick coping and windows trimmed in white signal the traditional Territorial-style architecture of the **Hotel Plaza Real**. Situated around a central courtyard, the hotel's 55 rooms feature massive wood beams and Southwest-style furniture. Nearly all units have a fireplace and most have a patio or balcony. But a word to the wise: Some rooms are small and second-floor units feature steep, narrow staircases. The restaurant serves breakfast and lunch. Underground hotel parking is $10. ~ 125 Washington Avenue; 505-988-4900, 800-279-7325, fax 505-983-9322; e-mail agarcia@buynm.com. DELUXE TO ULTRA-DELUXE.

AUTHOR FAVORITE

I love the **Inn of the Anasazi**'s personal touch, from the homemade juice and introduction letter at check-in to the escorted tour of the hotel by a bellman, and thoughtful turn-down service and dimming of bedroom lights. Its understated elegance has made the Anasazi a favorite among well-heeled visitors. Decor throughout the small inn is decidedly low key—neutral tones prevail. The 59 guest rooms are charmingly bedecked with four-poster beds, viga ceilings, kiva fireplaces, cast-iron furniture, angelic figurines and handknitted cotton blankets. Instead of "do not disturb" signs, hotel attendants place leather-tied blocks over doorknobs. ~ 113 Washington Avenue; 505-988-3030, 800-688-8100, fax 505-988-3277; www.innoftheanasazi.com. ULTRA-DELUXE.

Considering the amount of noise on the street it fronts, guest rooms at the **Inn on the Alameda** are surprisingly quiet. Everything emphasizes sunny and clean—from the pristine adobe walls to the beautiful slate tiles and the modern artwork. Many guest rooms are pleasantly decorated in Southwest style, with wicker and wood-cane furniture; all come with fluffy robes for guest use. Breakfast is included. There's also complimentary wine and cheese in the afternoon. ~ 303 East Alameda Street; 505-984-2121, 800-289-2122, fax 505-986-8325; www.innonthealameda.com, e-mail info@inn-alameda.com. ULTRA-DELUXE.

Literally the "inn at the end of the Santa Fe Trail," **La Fonda Hotel** is a Santa Fe institution. Though the original 1610 adobe hotel is gone, the latest incarnation still caters to weary travelers in search of pleasant lodging and fine food. Each room is unique, with hand-painted wooden furniture and room accents; many feature balconies and fireplaces. A central meeting spot for area sightseeing tours and recreational activities, La Fonda hums with excitement. A newsstand, an art gallery, shops, a restaurant and a cantina all add to the bustle. ~ 100 East San Francisco Street; 505-982-5511, 800-523-5002, fax 505-988-2952; www.lafonda santafe.com, e-mail reservations@lafondasantafe.com. ULTRA-DELUXE.

Guests and staff alike often report sightings of Santa Fe's most notorious phantom, the ghost of Julia Staab, on the grand staircase that ascends from the lobby of **La Posada de Santa Fe**. The sprawling downtown resort has been expanded over the years to completely surround the mansion of a 19th-century local banker, and while the old house remains Victorian in character, the rest of the hotel blends classic and contemporary Southwestern styles. Luxurious rooms and suites, many with kiva fireplaces, fill not only the main inn but also casitas clustered throughout six acres of beautifully landscaped grounds. There's a large spa facility that includes steam rooms, whirlpools, exercise facilities, a heated outdoor pool and a juice bar terrace. ~ 330 East Palace Avenue; 505-986-0000, 800-727-5276, fax 505-982-6850; www.laposadadesantafe.com. ULTRA-DELUXE.

Reputed to have been built in 1910 by a Spaniard for his bride, the **Hacienda Nicholas** exudes old-time Southwest charm. Light and airy, all seven guest bedrooms are outfitted with *viga* ceilings, rustic Mexican furniture and four-poster beds; some have kiva fireplaces and open onto the courtyard. Breakfast and afternoon tea are served in the inn's flower-strewn garden, and an outdoor kiva fireplace provides warmth on chilly days. ~ 320 East Marcy Street; 505-986-1431, 888-321-5123, fax 505-982-8572;

Typically, the farther you move away from Santa Fe's Plaza, the more hotel prices drop. But beware of a few of the 1950s-style hotels lining Cerrillos Road—some are dives!

www.haciendanicholas.com, e-mail haciendanicholas@aol.com.
DELUXE.

If you find bigger is always better, then be sure to book a room
at the looming, yet lovely, 219-room **Eldorado Hotel**. Lovers of
classic Santa Fe architecture just about choked when this monolith was constructed. Yet few who venture inside find fault with
the brass-and-chrome-fixtured lobby bar, heated rooftop pool,
two cocktail lounges and adjacent shops. Double rooms are done
in a very Southwestern style. ~ 309 West San Francisco Street;
505-988-4455, 800-955-4455, fax 505-995-4544; www.eldorado
hotel.com, e-mail rez@eldoradohotel.com. ULTRA-DELUXE.

How many different ways can you say sweet? The **Grant
Corner Inn** is a turn-of-the-20th-century restored Colonial manor
transformed into a wonderful bed and breakfast famous for its
morning repasts. Located next door to the Georgia O'Keeffe Museum, the Grant Corner Inn is filled with gorgeous white wrought-
iron furnishings, shiny brass beds, handsome quilts, Ralph Lauren
bedding and an amusing collection of bunny art. ~ 122 Grant
Avenue; 505-983-6678, 800-964-9003, fax 505-983-1526; www.
grantcornerinn.com, e-mail info@grantcornerinn.com. DELUXE TO
ULTRA-DELUXE.

Afternoon tea attracts a high-tone crowd to the **Hotel St.
Francis**, one of the prettiest properties in town. Each of the 83
rooms and suites is unique with high ceilings, casement windows,
brass and iron beds and antique furniture. Original hexagonal
tile and porcelain pedestal sinks give the bathrooms a lush yet
historic feel. A spacious lobby hosts the famous afternoon tea,
complete with finger sandwiches and scones. ~ 210 Don Gaspar
Avenue; 505-983-5700, 800-529-5700, fax 505-989-7690; www.
hotelstfrancis.com, e-mail reservations@hotelstfrancis.net. MOD-
ERATE TO ULTRA-DELUXE.

Small and intimate, **Dos Casas Viejas** is an eight-room bed and
breakfast housed in three adobe buildings that date back to the
1860s. Each room features a kiva fireplace and private patio along
with the ubiquitous Southwestern furnishings. The inn, walled in
on all sides, also has a private brick pool where twig lounge chairs
with overstuffed cushions provide a sublime place for sunbathing.
Afternoon wine breaks occur in the lobby while in-room massages can also be booked. Peruse the on-site CD library and take
a disc or two back to your room. Owners Susan and Michael
Strijek offer an expansive continental breakfast. ~ 610 Agua Fria
Street; 505-983-1636, fax 505-983-1749; www.doscasasviejas.
com, e-mail doscasas@earthlink.net. ULTRA-DELUXE.

The scent of piñon wood pervades the polished and contem-
porary **Hotel Santa Fe**, located on the edge of Santa Fe's historic   ◄ HIDDEN
Guadalupe district. Large rooms, many of which have a separate

sitting area, are handsomely decorated in those oh-so-familiar Southwestern colors and hand-carved furniture. The first off-site Indian project in the state, the hotel is more than half-owned by the Picuris Indian Pueblo. The Picuris run its gift shop, while other American Indians work in the rest of the hotel. ~ 1501 Paseo de Peralta; 505-982-1200, 800-825-9876, fax 505-984-2211; www.hotelsantafe.com, e-mail hotelsantafe@newmexico.com. DELUXE TO ULTRA-DELUXE.

Providing some of the most luxurious lodging in town, **Las Brisas de Santa Fe** offers *viga* ceilings and kiva fireplaces (stocked with plenty of wood) in its Santa Fe–style adobe units. Choose between one and two bedrooms, both of which have queen- or king-size beds and fully equipped kitchens. If it's a warm night, you can enjoy dinner on your private patio. Located eight blocks from the downtown plaza in a compound on a quiet residential side street, these time-share condominiums rent by the night, so the number of units available varies seasonally. ~ 624 Galisteo Street; 505-982-5795, fax 505-982-7900; www.lasbrisasdesanta fe.com, e-mail lasbrisas@cybermesa.com. ULTRA-DELUXE.

Not to be confused with the neighboring Hotel Santa Fe, the **Santa Fe Motel and Inn** has bungalow-style dwellings and standard lodge rooms, some with kitchenettes. Given its prime location, within walking distance of the Plaza, the Santa Fe Motel is probably the best value for the money. A continental-style breakfast is included. ~ 510 Cerrillos Road; 505-982-1039, 800-745-9910, fax 505-986-1275; www.santafemotelinn.com. MODERATE TO DELUXE.

The **El Rey Inn**, with its lush garden property filled with fountains and patios, stands tall against neighboring hotels. Decor varies between Indian pueblo, Victorian and Spanish. Some rooms have oriental rugs; others feature brick floors. Omnipresent in all the units is a keen attention to detail and cleanliness. ~ 1862 Cerrillos Road; 505-982-1931, 800-521-1349, fax 505-989-9249; www.elreyinnsantafe.com. MODERATE TO DELUXE.

HIDDEN ►   The **Inn of the Turquoise Bear** is located in a secluded southside adobe mansion that originally belonged to poet/philanthropist Witter Bynner, a leader of Santa Fe's literary community for four decades beginning in the Roaring Twenties. Among the many luminaries who stayed here as Bynner's houseguests were composer Igor Stravinsky, poet Robert Frost, actors Errol Flynn and Rita Hayworth, and playwright Thornton Wilder. Each of the ten guest rooms has traditional Santa Fe–style decor and modern amenities from VCRs to terry-cloth robes and fresh, fragrant flowers. The inn is pleasantly shaded by lofty ponderosa pines on an acre of grounds with terraced gardens, old stone benches and flagstone footpaths. Gay-friendly. ~ 342 East Buena Vista

Street; 505-983-0798, 800-396-4104, fax 505-988-4225; www. turquoisebear.com, e-mail bluebear@newmexico.com. MODERATE TO ULTRA-DELUXE.

DINING

Homemade granola and goat's milk yogurt start the day at the **Inn of the Anasazi**. The innovative kitchen creates indescribable cuisine that blends many elements, flavors, exotic grains and organic ingredients. Homemade breads, seafoods and wild game feature prominently in the menu. The inn's beautiful 92-seat dining room alone is worth a visit. ~ 113 Washington Avenue; 505-988-3236, 800-688-8100; www.innoftheanasazi.com, e-mail reserva tions@innoftheanasazi.com. DELUXE TO ULTRA-DELUXE.

Named simply **Paul's**, this restaurant offers "modern and international" cuisine that is far from simple. Open seven days a week (no lunch Sunday), Paul's and its namesake chef Paul Hunsicker serve such delights as grilled sesame chicken with asparagus and oriental vegetables over fettuccini and baked salmon in pecan-herb crust with sorrel cream sauce. There are many fine vegetarian dishes on the menu as well. The restaurant is small, decorated with walls of lively colored folk art. ~ 72 West Marcy Street; 505-982-8738 or 505-982-2090; www.paulsofsanta fe.com. MODERATE TO DELUXE.

> In the 1700s, some people used red chile as a meat preservative, while others rubbed it on their gums for toothaches.

Though the wait for a table can be long, don't pass up the opportunity to breakfast or brunch at **The Grant**, an intimate restaurant (it only seats about 30 inside; the 30-seat patio is available when the weather's nice) located within the Grant Corner Inn. While the regular menu has first-rate fare (waffles, egg dishes, soufflés), your best bet is the full brunch special, which includes a fruit frappe, a choice between three entrées, pastries and fresh-ground Colombian coffee or high-end tea. They'll occasionally have a buffet brunch. Fresh flowers adorn every table and service is extremely attentive. Open Monday through Saturday for breakfast, Sunday for brunch. Reservations are a must! ~ 122 Grant Avenue; 505-983-6678, fax 505-983-1526; www.grantcornerinn.com, e-mail info@grantcornerinn.com. MODERATE.

Caffe latte never tasted so good as in the Bohemian atmosphere of the **Aztec Café**, where you'll find lively conversation, tasty bagels and sandwiches, and art worthy of discussion but, alas, too much cigarette smoke. ~ 317 Aztec Street; 505-983-9464; www.azteccafe.com. BUDGET.

Modern American cuisine in a hip setting with good people-watching makes **Zia Diner** a fun place to come on your own. Sit at the counter or come with pals and the kids and grab a big table. There's food here for everyone, like meatloaf, burgers, pizza and a

Text continued on page 52.

Colorful Cuisine

Chances are the one question you'll be asked after a New Mexico vacation is, "How was the food?" Like Cajun cooking in Louisiana or spicy Szechuan dishes in China, authentic New Mexican cooking can delight the senses as much as any scenic panorama. Odds are, long after you've left the state, your palate will still savor the flavorful (sometimes fiery) tastes of New Mexico.

Bottom line ... New Mexican cooking is not Mexican or Tex-Mex. It is distinctive cuisine with strong roots in the state's Indian culture as adapted by Spanish and Anglo settlers. From flavors to cooking techniques, all are delicately balanced, with the result a literal feast of tastes, textures, smells and colors: green chiles, yellow cheese, blue corn.

This mélange dates back hundreds (maybe even thousands) of years. New Mexico's early inhabitants dined on rabbit and venison. But these meats were quickly replaced by beef, *chorizo* (a spicy pork sausage) and mutton after the Spanish arrived. Corn, beans, squash and nuts originated with American Indians. Europeans brought wheat, rice, fruit, onions, garlic and grapes. From Mexico came tomatoes, avocados and chocolate.

Today's New Mexican cooking uses such unusual fruits and vegetables as jicama, chayote (or vegetable pear), *nopales* (the flat green pads of the prickly pear cactus), tomatillos (with their tart lemon flavor) and plantains. Cumin is the predominant spice, though oregano, cilantro, *epazote*, mint, cinnamon and coriander are also utilized.

Traditionalists will tell you there are four basic elements to a true New Mexican meal—chile, corn, cheese and beans. If all four aren't served, you aren't getting an authentic dinner.

Ah, yes, the chile: heart and soul of New Mexican cooking. Politics, religion, who'll win the Super Bowl, no topic generates more dispute than red versus green and hot versus mild. New Mexicans consume more chiles per capita than any other state and it's the state's second-largest cash crop. If you were to compare chiles to grapes, New Mexico would be the champagne capital of the world. Local experts estimate more than 35,000 tons are exported within a single year.

The chile (not to be confused with chili powder or chili in a bowl) may have existed as early as 700 B.C. Columbus found "chile" (the Aztec name for the wrinkled, fiery pods) in the West Indies in 1493 and brought them to the New World. Pueblo Indians were growing a mild version along the banks of the Rio Grande when the Spanish arrived in the 1500s.

Nowadays, some still believe a hot dose of chiles will clear the sinuses. True or not, chiles are high in vitamins A and C. Most of us recognize at least a few of the many varieties—green bell pepper, *poblano* (a large, dark green chile), jalapeño, serrano and *chipotle* to name a few. Almost everyone quickly recognizes the New Mexico red chile strung in wreaths and chains called *ristras*.

Members of the nightshade family (which includes tomatoes and potatoes), chiles used before they are ripe are green in color. Once ripe, they turn red. They can be picked and eaten in both stages. Not all chiles are naturally "hot." The amount and variety of chile and whether it is fresh, dried or ground determines the hotness.

One of the best ways to learn all there is about New Mexican cooking is at the **Santa Fe School of Cooking**. Here, expert chefs demonstrate the history and techniques of New Mexico cuisine. Best of all, students get to sample the finished product. ~ 116 West San Francisco Street, Upper Level, Plaza Mercado, Santa Fe; 505-983-4511; www.santafeschoolofcooking.com, e-mail cookin@nets.com.

If enrolling in a two-and-a-half hour class isn't your idea of a vacation, it's at least a good idea to master a few Spanish terms for the basic dishes. For example, *carne asada* means roasted meat (though it now sometimes includes grilled meat). *Carne adovada* refers to meat marinated in red chile. Chicken in chile sauce is known as *mole*.

A traditional tamale is a combination of minced meat and red pepper rolled in corn meal, wrapped in corn husks and baked or steamed. The ever-popular *chile relleno* refers to a large, battered, fried green chile, stuffed with cheese, avocado, shrimp, pork, etc. *Chile con queso* is a chile and cheese pie. A side order of *frijoles* will get you a plate of pinto beans. *Sopapilla* translates to "pillow," an apt description for the light, puffy fried dough typically served drizzled with honey.

Tortillas are the "bread" of New Mexico. Usually made of white cornmeal, they come hot and fresh with almost every dish. Some cooks favor flour or blue cornmeal for preparing tortillas. And yes, blue corn is really "blue." Finally, you should never be embarrassed to ask questions or request your chile on the side. New Mexicans take great pride in their colorful cuisine and want you to enjoy all the magnificent flavors it holds.

Mount Everest–size pile of fries. Zia moves a good crowd through. The Zia bar in the rear hops, too. ~ 326 South Guadalupe Street; 505-988-7008, fax 505-820-7677. BUDGET TO MODERATE.

In the old railroad station is **Tomasita's,** which on the surface looks like a tourist trap. But the food—Tomasita's wins raves for its green chile and *chiles rellenos*—and the margaritas wipe away any disparaging thoughts. Closed Sunday. ~ 500 South Guadalupe Street; 505-983-5721, fax 505-983-0780. BUDGET.

Southwestern cuisine and Continental-style entrées with a tangy Creole snap dominate the menu at **Pink Adobe,** where the favorite entrée is steak served with green chiles and mushrooms. No lunch on Saturday and Sunday. ~ 406 Old Santa Fe Trail; 505-983-7712, fax 505-984-0691; www.thepinkadobe.com, e-mail enchantjoe@earthlink.net. MODERATE TO DELUXE.

If you're hankering for prime beef, the **Bull Ring** is an upscale steak house with white linen tablecloths and an extensive wine list. No lunch on Saturday and Sunday. ~ 150 Washington Avenue; 505-983-3328, fax 505-982-8254; e-mail bullrest@aol.com. DELUXE TO ULTRA-DELUXE.

Of the four Japanese restaurants in Santa Fe, **Shohko Café** has the freshest food and best sushi bar. Sake and tempura ice cream are very viable accompaniments. No lunch on Sunday. ~ 321 Johnson Street; 505-983-7288, fax 505-984-1853. MODERATE TO DELUXE.

The Coyote Café made a big splash when it first opened and was soon ranked among the top 100 restaurants in the country. The ever-evolving menu typically includes honey-poached and rotisseried duck with cumin-stewed mango and chile-glazed beef short ribs with corn dumplings. Some locals feel the Coyote is overrated, but it remains a favorite among the visiting crowd. ~ 132 West Water Street; 505-983-1615, fax 505-989-9026; www.coyote-cafe.com, e-mail reservations@coyote-cafe.com. ULTRA-DELUXE.

AUTHOR FAVORITE

My stomach rumbles at the thought of the **Santacafé,** where herbs are exalted and only the freshest of foods find their way to the table. The combination of flavors never disappoints, from the starter (shiitake and cactus spring rolls, for instance) to the grand finale (warm toffee pudding with bourbon–brown sugar sauce, anyone?). What's best about Santacafé is it doesn't try too hard when delivering its New American cuisine. Then again, it doesn't have to. ~ 231 Washington Avenue; 505-984-1788, fax 505-986-0110; www.santacafe.com, e-mail santacafe@aol.com. DELUXE TO ULTRA-DELUXE.

A bright, cheerful second-story restaurant in the downtown Plaza Mercado, **Blue Corn Café** is another favorite. The New Mexican menu covers all the basics (enchiladas, tacos and tamales). Many dishes come with a delicious blue-corn *posole* (hominy). ~ 133 West Water Street; 505-984-1800, fax 505-984-2104. BUDGET TO MODERATE. They also operate a brew pub. ~ 4056 Cerrillos Road; 505-984-1800.

Designed by architect Alexander Girard, who is best known for the amazing collection he donated to the Museum of International Folk Art, **The Compound Restaurant** is where you'll probably want to go for a very special evening. Foie gras, lamb, duck, caviar and fresh fish are attentively served in this restored hacienda. The impressive wine cellar has some rare vintages. No lunch on Saturday and Sunday. ~ 653 Canyon Road; 505-982-4353, fax 505-982-4868; www.compoundrestaurant.com. ULTRA-DELUXE.

Serving "eclectic global gourmet," there is almost no culinary territory that **Geronimo's** won't tread upon. Its menu offers a varied mix of Italian to Thai–inspired entrées made exclusively from local, organic sources. There's Amish pork, New Zealand lamb and beautiful sushi and sashimi-like plates. The decor is as clean and crisp as the cuisine; the art on the wall and the leather banquettes lend a feel of stunning minimalist. No lunch on Monday. ~ 724 Canyon Road; 505-982-1500; www.geronimorestaurant.com. MODERATE TO ULTRA-DELUXE.

El Farol has an ambience as good as its food. Hot and cold Spanish *tapas* and entrées are its forte. Try one of the house specialties—paella, cold curry chicken or shrimp sautéed in garlic, lime and sherry—for an inexpensive and filling meal. ~ 808 Canyon Road; 505-983-9912, fax 505-988-3823. MODERATE TO DELUXE.

Considered one of Santa Fe's finest restaurants, **La Casa Sena** boasts both a main dining room and a smaller cantina. The restaurant, part of a restored 1860 adobe casa, covers its walls with paintings by early Santa Fe masters. Fine, fresh ingredients are used (even the water is from their own well), resulting in fabulous dining adventures. Entrées take regional favorites and give them a creative twist like grilled Colorado lamb chops with a tropical fruit *insalata*, and grilled herb-crusted sea bass served with a legume mushroom sauté. Don't miss the carmelized banana tepee with coconut sauce. Outrageous! ~ 125 East Palace Avenue, Sena Plaza; 505-988-9232, fax 505-820-2909. MODERATE TO ULTRA-DELUXE.

Lines form early at **La Casa Sena Cantina** because no reservations are accepted. But in this bustling crowded space, everything from food to song is artistically presented. In fact, nowhere else in Santa Fe does the blue-corn chicken enchilada come with a rousing rendition of "Phantom of the Opera" (or whatever the server's in the mood for).The limited menu includes such specialties as grilled chicken and jack cheese *quesadillas* with blue cheese, pears, red chile pecans and habañero salsa. Waiters and waitresses perform excerpts from popular musicals, then follow with a sampling of show tunes. Patrons come and go between sets, making their way among the tiny butcher-block tables and baby grand piano. ~ 125 East Palace Avenue, Sena Plaza; 505-988-9232, fax 505-820-2909. MODERATE TO ULTRA-DELUXE.

If a huge old Mexico–style lunch followed by a siesta is what you're after, then seek out **The Shed**, where wise eaters come before noon to avoid the lines. Blue-corn tortillas wrapped around cheese and onion specialties are served on sizzling plates with *posole* on the side. Consider starting your meal with some fresh mushroom soup and ending it with lemon soufflé. Dinner reservations recommended. Closed Sunday. ~ 113½ East Palace Avenue; 505-982-9030, fax 505-982-0902; www.sfshed.com. BUDGET TO MODERATE.

Café Pasqual's is a bustling bistro with some of the most intriguing decorations and inviting dishes in the city. Small and popular, Pasqual's serves breakfast, lunch and dinner in an atmosphere of Mexican tiles, hanging *piccatas* and lavish hand-painted Oaxacan murals. For breakfast there are quesadillas; lunch favorites include the salmon burrito with herbed goat cheese. The ever-changing menu may include grilled squash and red onion enchiladas with jack cheese or *huevos motuleños* with black beans and a roasted jalapeño salsa. Chocoholics won't want to miss the "killer cake" off the dessert card. Reservations required for dinner. ~ 121 Don Gaspar Street; 505-983-9340, fax 505-988-4645; www.pasquals.com. DELUXE TO ULTRA-DELUXE.

An inexpensive downtown favorite is **Tia Sophia's**, a long-established restaurant known for its breakfast burrito. This spicy entrée consists of scrambled eggs and chili rolled in a tortilla, a combination that has gained popularity throughout the West. You can't beat the original version pioneered right here. Choose from daily breakfast and lunch specials as well as a wide variety of traditional New Mexican selections. The Southwestern-style decor is bright and homey. No dinner. Closed Sunday. ~ 210 West San Francisco Street; 505-983-9880. BUDGET.

HIDDEN ▶ Secluded in an enclosed courtyard reached by an inconspicuous walkway from San Francisco Street one block west of the Plaza, **Tribes Coffee House** serves design-it-yourself salads and assorted deli sandwiches as well as bakery goods and gourmet coffee drinks in a hideaway atmosphere that offers refuge from the busy streets of downtown. Paintings by lesser-known artists making their debuts in the Santa Fe scene adorn the walls. ~ 139 West San Francisco Street; 505-982-7948. BUDGET.

With the unlikely name of **Dave's Not Here,** this great little neighborhood spot serves typical Mexican food and a yummy Greek salad. But the burgers are what keep folks coming back. You can have them with guacamole, green chile, onions or just plain naked. By the way, namesake Dave really isn't here—he sold the restaurant a long time ago. Closed Sunday. ~ 1115 Hickox Street; 505-983-7060. BUDGET.

When you gotta have a pizza fix, head for **Il Primo Pizza** for some cheesy, Windy City–style deep dish. ~ 234 North Guadalupe Street; 505-988-2007. BUDGET TO MODERATE.

A saloon and gambling house had this address in the mid-1800s; now the site has gone upscale as the **Palace Restaurant & Saloon,** a popular place that pays tribute to its past with saloon-style doors. The Continental menu with regional Italian specialties includes such specialties as truffled duckling mousse pâté and *pâillard* of free-range chicken breast in a kalamata olive sauce with angel-hair pasta. The current owners hail from Italy's Lake Como district. No lunch on Sunday. ~ 142 West Palace Avenue; 505-982-9891, fax 505-988-7151; www.thepalacerestaurant.com, e-mail palace@aol.com. DELUXE TO ULTRA-DELUXE.

The artist crowd tends to hang out at the **Cloud Cliff Bakery and Café.** The main reason is that it's adjacent to Second Street Studios, a large complex where many artists have their workspaces, but the flaky, sweet pastries and inexpensive lunch choices come in a close second. Drop by for breakfast or a light midday meal. Works by local artists serve as decor, a nice touch since most of the workspaces next door are not open to the public. Open for breakfast and lunch. ~ 1805 2nd Street; 505-983-6254,

ALL ABOARD

Although the Atchison, Topeka and Santa Fe is one of the grand old names of the American rail system, Amtrak trains don't call on the capital city. Now, however, you can take the **Santa Fe Southern** south through scenic foothill country to the village of Lamy, the Amtrak stop closest to Santa Fe. In the summer, the tourist train leaves Tuesday, Thursday, Saturday and Sunday mornings and Friday evenings (there's an abbreviated winter schedule). Passengers can bring their own picnic lunches to dine on board or at Lamy. This excursion runs several hours ahead of the daily eastbound and westbound Amtrak trains. Admission. ~ Santa Fe Southern Railroad Depot, off Guadalupe Street, southwest of downtown; 505-989-8600, fax 505-983-7620; www.sfsr.com.

fax 505-986-0205; www.cloudcliff.com, e-mail inbox@cloudcliff. com. BUDGET.

Breakfast lovers head to the homey little **Tecolote Cafe**, which whips up heart-healthy breakfast burritos in addition to omelettes bursting with gooey filling, and baskets of biscuits and muffins. Singles sit at a community table, ideal for meeting local folks. For lunch, the burgers, enchiladas and burritos are popular. No dinner. Closed Monday. ~ 1203 Cerrillos Road; 505-988-1362. BUDGET.

SHOPPING   In a city known for its history and architecture, what everyone remembers about Santa Fe is . . . the shopping. Myriad arts-and-crafts shops plus oodles of galleries crowd the Plaza and nearby Canyon Road, a two-mile street lined with fine art stores.

For silver jewelry, pottery and handwoven blankets of exquisite detail, look no further than beneath the portal of the Palace of Governors on the Plaza where Indian artisans gather to market their wares.

HIDDEN ▶   Always-exciting images by well-known 19th- and 20th-century shooters can be viewed at **Andrew Smith Gallery**. ~ 203 West San Francisco Street; 505-984-1234; www.andrewsmith gallery.com.

Nedra Matteucci Galleries features folk art, early and contemporary Taos and Santa Fe painters as well as American Indian jewelry. The sculpture garden and fountains add to the atmosphere. ~ 1075 Paseo de Peralta; 505-982-4631; www.matteucci.com.

The **LewAllen Contemporary** is modern, hooked into "the scene" and always worth your time. Closed Sunday except in July and August. ~ 129 West Palace Avenue; 505-988-8997; www.lewallenart.com.

Well-priced casual clothing makes **Chico's** a good place to purchase wearable souvenirs. ~ 328 South Guadalupe Street, 505-984-1132; and 135 West Palace Avenue, 505-984-3134.

GLOBAL SHOPPING

The past decade has seen Santa Fe emerge as a collectors market for ethnic art from all over the world. Following is a sampling of Santa Fe's international diversity. **Project Tibet** works with Santa Fe's Tibetan community to aid refugees internationally. The gallery here carries *thankas* (sacred paintings), Buddhist religious objects, clothing and books. ~ 403 Canyon Road; 505-982-3002. **Fourth World Cottage Industries** carries imported handicrafts, textiles and the like from around the world. ~ 102 West San Francisco Street, upstairs; 505-982-4388. **Origins** is a chic boutique with traditional and designer clothing for women from many lands. ~ 135 West San Francisco Street; 505-988-2323.

Operated by Joseph Sisneros, great-grandson of the Jaramillo pioneer family, **Rancho de Chimayo Collection** features works of Spanish-Colonial and American Indian masters. The collection includes 19th- and 20th-century santero art, Pueblo pottery and contemporary gold and silver, American Indian jewelry, painting and sculpture. ~ In the Sena Plaza, 127 East Palace Avenue; 505-988-4526; www.ranchochimayo.com, e-mail gallery@ranchochimayo.com.

Bodhi Bazaar, in the Sambusco Center, has women's contemporary casual and dressy clothing. ~ 500 Montezuma Street; 505-982-3880.

An unusual bookstore, **The Ark** is found well off the beaten track in a hideaway hacienda. Books on healing and UFOs, crystals and incense fill this New Age haven. ~ 133 Romero Street; 505-988-3709.

Find gold jewelry and brilliant earth stones like sugilite at **Spirit of the Earth**. ~ 108 Don Gaspar Street; 505-988-9558. **LewAllen and LewAllen Jewelry** has branched out from designer Ross LewAllen's original ear cuffs into pendants, safari bracelets, beading and wildlife-theme wearables. ~ 105 East Palace Avenue; 505-983-2657.

Silver and gold buckles shake hands with serpent and leather belts as well as custom-made Western boots at **Tom Taylor Co.** ◄ HIDDEN
~ La Fonda Hotel, 100 East San Francisco Street; 505-984-2231.

Cotton garments and accessories for women and children fill the shelves at **Pinkoyote**. ~ 220 Shelby Street; 505-984-9911.

For outrageous greeting and postcards, try the **Marcy Street Card Shop**. Closed occasionally on Sunday. ~ 75 West Marcy Street; 505-982-5160. **The Chile Shop** has pottery, *ristras*, chile powders and cookbooks. Closed Tuesday in January and February. ~ 109 East Water Street; 505-983-6080.

For tribal arts there are numerous choices, including **La Fonda Indian Shop**. ~ La Fonda Hotel, 100 East San Francisco Street; 505-988-2488. You can also try **Tin-Nee-Ann** for Southwestern arts and crafts. Closed Sunday. ~ 923 Cerrillos Road; 505-988-1630.

CANYON ROAD While art abounds everyday in the City Different, from public sculpture to stylishly dressed Santa Feans, one of the greatest concentrations of galleries can be found on Canyon Road. High rents have made the old artist-working-in-the-back-room an anomaly and turned Canyon Road into a rather exclusive enclave. There are plenty of beautiful things to be viewed here—from clothing and jewelry to furniture and paintings—satisfying most palates if not every pocketbook.

Karen Melfi Collection displays a plethora of contemporary gold and silver inlaid jewelry. ~ 225 Canyon Road; 505-982-3032.

Text continued on page 60.

Art Everywhere
You Look

During the early days of Santa Fe's art colony, painters shipped their works by rail to be sold back East. Today, though, some 200 art galleries are within walking distance of the Plaza, and the world comes to Santa Fe for art.

The place to start a gallery tour is midway between the Plaza and Canyon Road, at the **Gerald Peters Gallery**, the largest private art gallery in the U.S. Its rooms are full of museum-quality 19th- and 20th-century American works by such notables as Frederic Remington and Georgia O'Keeffe. There's also a magical gallery of wildlife art. Closed Sunday. ~ 1011 Paseo de Peralta; 505-954-5700, fax 505-954-5754. Next door, **Nedra Matteucci Galleries** also ranks among the finest in town. Here you'll find works by artists such as early Western landscapists Albert Bierstadt and Thomas Moran as well as paintings by legendary Santa Fe and Taos painters of the 1920s and a secluded one-acre sculpture garden. Closed Sunday. ~ 1075 Paseo de Peralta; 505-982-4631. Farther north along Paseo de Peralta, the **Laurel Seth Gallery** is run by a second-generation Santa Fe art dealer and carries works by early New Mexico painters, including Santa Fe's famed Cinco Pintores and members of the original Taos art colony, along with contemporary works. Closed Sunday and Monday. ~ 1121 Paseo de Peralta; 505-988-7349; www.sethgallery.com. Nearby, the **Wyeth Hurd Gallery** represents N. C. Wyeth, Peter Hurd, Andrew Wyeth, and a dozen other members of this four-generation dynasty of American artists. Closed Sunday. ~ 839 Paseo de Peralta; 505-989-8380.

Among the myriad galleries on the streets surrounding the Plaza, a fascinating place that often goes unnoticed is **Andrew Smith Gallery**. This shop is stacked with limited-edition prints by Ansel Adams, Elliott Porter and many others, including photo portraits of Ernest Hemingway and Albert Einstein. ~ 203 West San Francisco Street; 505-984-1234. **Owings-Dewey Fine Art** carries works by classic Santa Fe artists and serves as estate representative for two of the city's leading early painters, William Penhallow Henderson and Will Shuster. Closed Sunday. ~ 76 East San Francisco Street; 505-982-6244; www.owings dewey.com.

There is a cluster of galleries along West Palace Avenue between the Plaza and the Georgia O'Keeffe Museum. The **LewAllen Contemporary** is modern, hooked into "the scene" and always worth your time. Closed Sunday. ~ 129 West Palace Avenue; 505-988-8997. Directly across the street, the **Wadle Galleries** exhibit the finest in representational art. Closed Sunday. ~ 128 West Palace Avenue; 505-983-9219.

The greatest concentration of galleries can be found along Canyon Road, which runs east (uphill) from Paseo de Peralta. The center of Santa Fe's original art colony, Canyon Road is now a rather exclusive enclave given over to retail galleries instead of back-room studios. Lovers of bronze sculpture should check out **Meyer Gallery** and its huge selection of impressionist paintings by well-known artists. ~ 225 Canyon Road; 505-983-1434. In the same compound is one of the country's oldest galleries (in business since 1860), **Munson Gallery**, featuring paintings and sculpture. ~ 225 Canyon Road; 505-983-1657; www.munsongallery.com. Important American Modernists, Regionalists and contemporary painters are shown at **Cline Fine Art Gallery**. Closed Sunday. ~ 526 Canyon Road; 505-982-5328; www.clinefineart.com. **Allene Lapidus Gallery** is another purveyor of contemporary art. Closed Sunday, and Monday from October through March. ~ 558 Canyon Road; 505-984-0191. Situated in an 1850s historic adobe home, the **Waxlander Gallery** displays the works of 18 artists in individual spaces and exhibits large sculptures in an outdoor garden amid colorful flowers and fruit trees. ~ 622 Canyon Road; 505-984-2202; e-mail art@waxlander.com. Sharing one space, **Anthony Sobin Fine Art** features pre-1940s American art while **Moondance Gallery** has contemporary sculpture and art. ~ 707 Canyon Road; 505-982-3421.

Galleries open new exhibits by hosting receptions, with snacks, wine and an opportunity to meet the artist, on Friday evenings between 5 and 7 p.m. year-round. Listings of the week's receptions are found in the weekly *Santa Fe Reporter* and in the Friday *Pasatiempo* supplement to the *Santa Fe New Mexican*. During the summer months, Canyon Road gallery owners band together to sponsor **Canyon Road Art Walks** with refreshments and music during the Friday 5-to-7 time slot.

Stunning Southwestern scenes of adobes and more are found at **Ventana Fine Art**. ~ 400 Canyon Road; 505-983-8815; www.ventanafineart.com.

The **Hahn Ross Gallery** showcases the whimsical contemporary art—paintings, sculpture, monoprints—of over 20 artists. ~ 409 Canyon Road; 505-984-8434; www.hahnross.com.

With much of the selection dating to the 18th century, **Morning Star Gallery** is the most successful gallery in the United States dealing exclusively in antique American Indian artwork and artifacts. Museum-quality pueblo pottery is displayed here, along with Plains Indian beadwork, Navajo silverwork and Northwest Coast woodcarvings. ~ 513 Canyon Road; 505-982-8187, fax 505-984-2368; www.morningstargallery.com.

For functional art for everyday use, check out **Off the Wall**. This is not your typical upscale housewares store—designs tend to be way out on the wild side. Add a decorative touch of excitement to your dining table or kitchen. ~ 616 Canyon Road; 505-983-8337; www.offthewallnm.com.

Bellas Artes is an intriguing gallery featuring significant works in painting, clay, sculpture, photography and fibers as well as some African and pre-Columbian art. Closed Sunday and Monday. ~ 653 Canyon Road; 505-983-2745; www.bellasartes gallery.com

In business since 1974, **Tresa Vorenberg Goldsmiths** enjoys a reputation as one of the finest jewelry stores in a city awash with jewelry. Hand-wrought one-of-a-kind pieces are the specialty. Call for winter hours. ~ 656 Canyon Road; 505-988-7215.

Antique American Indian jewelry, basketry and textiles are among the artifacts found at **Kania-Ferrin Gallery**. ~ 662 Canyon Road; 505-982-8767.

Carol LaRoche Gallery has monotypes, abstract and representational art that was created by LaRoche herself as well as sculptures by Ron Allen. ~ 701 Canyon Road; 505-982-1186; www.laroche-gallery.com.

Houshang's Gallery represents many of the top artists in the Southwest today, including J. D. Challenger, Brad Smith and Nancy Cawdrey, though it tends toward contemporary impressionist paintings. ~ 713 Canyon Road; 505-988-3322, www.houshangart.com. (This elegant gallery has a second Santa Fe location at 235 Don Gaspar Avenue; 505-982-4442.)

Natural-fiber clothing designs and handmade garments have made **Judy's Unique Apparel** popular. ~ 714 Canyon Road; 505-988-5746.

And let's not forget about **Artisan/Santa Fe**, the one-stop shop for Santa Fe artists in the market for paints and canvases. ~ 717 Canyon Road; 505-988-2179; www.artisan-santafe.com. (If you want to make another stop, try their other location at 2601 Cerrillos Road; 505-954-4179.)

Folk art, 19th-century American Indian art, Western art and vintage photos are found at **Alan Kessler**. ~ 836 Canyon Road; 505-986-0123.

Just about every Santa Fe home contains an item of decor from **Jackalope**, one of the most unusual shopping spots in town. Far from the chic shops of the Plaza and Canyon Road, the huge store sprawls across a six-square-block tract of the city's westside motel strip. Living up to its slogan of "Folk Art by the Truck-load," the complex shows off the heaps of pottery, Spanish colonial furniture, handmade clothing, tropical cactuses and other wares that have made it the largest Mexican import retailer in the United States. You'll also find buildings full of antiques and exotica from India and Bali, as well as an outdoor cantina with live music, a prairie dog enclosure and maybe even a chainsaw sculptor at work. It's the closest thing to a theme park in Santa Fe, and admission is free. ~ 2820 Cerrillos Road; 505-471-8539, fax 505-471-6710; www.jackalope.com.

When light shines through colored glass, wonderful things happen, and the **Dunbar Stained Glass Studio and Gallery** sparkles with glasswork. Closed Saturday and Sunday. ~ In the Design Center, 418 Cerrillos Road, Suite F1; 505-984-8515.

La Casa Sena has singing waiters and waitresses and one heck of a wine list. ~ 125 East Palace Avenue, Sena Plaza; 505-988-9232.

NIGHTLIFE

For a nightcap, try the gracious Victorian bar in **La Posada de Santa Fe** with its chandeliers and leather chairs and cushy couch by the fireplace. If the weather's nice, take a sip on the outdoor patio. ~ 330 East Palace Avenue; 505-986-0000.

A mix of politicians, tourists and plain old working folks can be found at the **Pink Adobe**, a handsome watering hole located around the corner from the State Capitol. ~ 406 Old Santa Fe Trail; 505-983-7712.

SANTA FE LAKE

Whether you get there by hiking, biking, or riding the chairlift at Santa Fe Ski Basin, the summit of Lake Peak offers a spectacular view of the high peaks of the Pecos Wilderness. It is also the only vantage point from which you can see **Santa Fe Lake**, the headwaters of the Santa Fe River. This secluded natural lake, surrounded by cliffs thousands of feet high, is also the source of Santa Fe's drinking water. There is no public access to the lake shore.

Get ready to kick up your heels at **Rodeo Nites,** a rowdy nightclub for lovers of country-and-western music. Live bands play nightly: country bands entertain Tuesday, Wednesday, Friday and Saturday, *Nuevo Mexicano* groups perform on Thursday, and big-name Mexican outfits take the stage on Sunday. Cover Thursday through Sunday. Closed Monday. ~ 2911 Cerrillos Road; 505-473-4138.

El Farol is a cantina where locals love to hang out and drink. With a spirit all of its own, El Farol attracts real people (including loads of tourists who have discovered its just-like-real-Santa-Fe ambience). You can hear live music here every night, including flamenco, R&B and jazz. Cover on Wednesday, Friday and Saturday. ~ 808 Canyon Road; 505-983-9912, fax 505-988-3823.

Even more down home is the mucho macho **Evangelo's,** where the beer is cheap, cheap, cheap. Live music, mostly rock-and-roll, jazz and blues every night. Occasional cover. ~ 200 West San Francisco Street; 505-982-9014.

The lounge in the **La Fonda Hotel** during happy hour gurgles with the energy of locals and visitors. Hot hors d'oeuvres and music are fine accompaniments to the loaded margaritas. ~ 100 East San Francisco Street; 505-982-5511, fax 505-988-2952; www.lafondasantafe.com.

The Palace Restaurant offers piano music, jazz and other genres every night of the week except Sunday, along with well-poured drinks and reliable service. ~ 142 West Palace Avenue; 505-982-9891; www.palacerestaurant.com.

For a relaxed atmosphere right on the Plaza, go to the **Ore House.** Live music, including blues, folk and country, Thursday through Sunday. ~ 50 Lincoln Avenue; 505-983-8687.

Vanessie of Santa Fe is where the drinks may be the most expensive in town, but you're in *the* place to see and be seen. Pianist Doug Montgomery, who performs at this upscale piano bar Sunday through Tuesday, is a local celebrity. The rest of the week other entertainers step in and keep the Steinway concert. Gay-friendly. ~ 434 West San Francisco Street; 505-982-9966, fax 505-982-1507.

HIDDEN ▶   For live Norteño (traditional northern New Mexican) dance music and a local crowd, drop into **Tiny's Lounge** any weekend night. It's hidden toward the back of a small shopping center near the intersection of St. Francis Drive and Cerrillos Road southwest of downtown. ~ 1015 Pen Road; 505-983-9817. Or dance the

HIDDEN ▶   night away to salsa music at **Club Alegria,** about three miles east of downtown, where a local band led by a Catholic priest has for years been serving up hot, spicy sounds for enthusiastic crowds. ~ Agua Fria Road; 505-471-2324.

OPERA, THEATER, SYMPHONY AND DANCE Music and moonlight fill the **Santa Fe Opera,** one of the country's most famous

(and finest) summer opera companies. Blending seasoned clas
with exciting premieres, the Opera runs from late June thro
August in the open-air auditorium. Though all of ●●●●●●●●
the seats are sheltered, the sides are open and warm
clothing and raingear are suggested, since evenings
can be cold and/or wet. ~ Route 84/285; 505-986-
5900, fax 505-995-3030; www.santafeopera.org.

The n
mesa top of the Santa Fe
National Forest's Caja
del Rio area provides a
sanctuary for wild
horses and bighorn
sheep.

Community theater of the highest order is found
at **Santa Fe Playhouse**, the oldest continuously running
theater company west of the Mississippi. It offers year-
round theatrical entertainment with musicals, comedies,
dramas and dance. ~ 142 East De Vargas Street; 505-988-
4262.

The beautiful Paolo Soleri Outdoor Theater of the Santa Fe
Indian School campus serves as home to the **Santa Fe Summer
Concert Series**, which brings big-name acts to town May through
September. ~ On the campus of the Santa Fe Indian School, 1501
Cerrillos Road; 505-989-6320.

The **Santa Fe Symphony** performs both traditional and contemporary classical works at Lensic Performing Arts Center from
October through April. ~ 211 West San Francisco Street; box office: 505-983-1414, 800-480-1319.

Santa Fe Stages mixes national and international theater,
dance and music productions with some of its own at both the
Lensic Performing Arts Center and The Armory for the Arts. The
season runs from late May to mid-September. ~ 422 West San
Francisco Street; 505-982-6683; www.santafestages.org.

Founded in 1980, the **Santa Fe Pro Musica** performs from
September through May at Lensic Performing Arts Center (211
West San Francisco Street) and the Loretto Chapel (211 Old Santa
Fe Trail). ~ 505-988-4640, fax 505-984-2501; www.santafepro
musica.com.

Saint Francis Auditorium (inside the Museum of Fine Arts)
and Lensic Performing Arts Center both play host to the **Santa Fe
Concert Association** (505-984-8759) and **Santa Fe Chamber
Music Festival** (505-983-2075).

The sizzling **Teatro Flamenco** returns to Santa Fe each summer (late June through August) for a series of flamenco dance
concerts under the direction of Maria Benitez. Performances are
held at the Radisson Santa Fe (750 North St. Francis Drive). ~
505-955-8562, 888-435-2636; www.mariabenitez.com.

GAY SCENE Santa Fe has long been known as a safe haven for
gay individuals and has a large and highly visible lesbian community. There is not much of a gay cruising scene, however, and gay-
oriented clubs come and go at whim. The most popular dance
club in town, **The Paramount** used to be primarily a gay and les-

bian club, but now draws an eclectic mix of gay and straight clientele. It hosts live entertainers as well. Cover. ~ 331 Sandoval Street; 505-982-8999.

PARKS

HYDE MEMORIAL STATE PARK 🏃🏊 A small park (350 acres) in the mountains high above Santa Fe, Hyde Park's woodsy and sheltered feeling gives visitors the impression they're light years away from the city. This park is a good base for cross-country skiing or hiking in the Santa Fe National Forest. There are picnic areas, restrooms and a sledding hill. Day-use fee, $4 per vehicle. ~ Route 475, about seven miles northeast of Santa Fe; 505-983-7175, fax 505-983-2783.

▲ There are 43 tent sites, $10 per night; and 7 RV sites with electric hookups, $14 per night. Reservations (mid-May to Memorial Day only): 877-664-7787.

SANTA FE NATIONAL FOREST 🏃🚴🐎🛶🏊🚣 The Sangre de Cristo unit of this 1,589,000-acre national forest encompasses the southernmost part of the Rocky Mountains, including half of the Pecos Wilderness, a vast area of alpine meadows and lakes among 12,000-foot peaks. The main forest access from Santa Fe is the paved Hyde Park/Ski Basin Road, which climbs through the world's largest contiguous aspen forest to an elevation of 10,500 feet at the Santa Fe Ski Basin. The Pecos Wilderness trailhead is on the north edge of the ski area parking lot. The Caja del Rio area is an isolated mesa on the east bank of the Rio Grande across from Bandelier National Monument and the town of White Rock. ~ Route 475, 17 miles northeast of Santa Fe; 505-438-7840, fax 505-438-7582.

▲ Black Canyon Campground has 42 campsites (no hookups); $9 per night; 505-982-8674.

The other major roadless area in this part of the forest is the **San Pedro Parks Wilderness**, a rarely explored expanse of springs, marshes and meadows set among 10,000-foot peaks, reached from a trailhead at San Gregorio Reservoir, on a mesatop east of Cuba. ~ Off Route 96 between Abiquiu and Cuba.

▲ There are 12 sites (no hookups) at Clear Creek Campground, and 15 sites at Rio de Las Vacas (no hookups), 12 miles east of Cuba on the road past San Gregorio Reservoir; $5 per night. ~ 505-289-3264.

▼▼▼▼▼▼▼▼▼▼▼

Road to Taos

Route 68, the main highway from Santa Fe to Taos, parallels the Rio Grande, where early summer motorists can see whitewater rafters and kayakers by the hundreds—and plenty of traffic. Taos makes for an inviting day trip from Santa Fe (or vice-versa), traveling one way by the slower High Road to Taos and returning via the main highway. If this is your plan, avoid Española, midway between Santa Fe and Taos, on weekend evenings, when slow-cruising lowriders can paralyze highway traffic.

As you leave the Santa Fe area en route to Taos, take a detour through Tesuque, home to a number of film and TV celebrities and perhaps Santa Fe's most beautiful suburb.

En route, if you can keep from being intrusive, visit Archbishop Lamy's private chapel at the **Bishop's Lodge**. Small, private and very holy are words that characterize this sanctuary along the Little Tesuque Stream. Vigas have replaced the former rafters in this intimate chapel, but the archbishop's cloak, hat and crucifix

SIGHTS

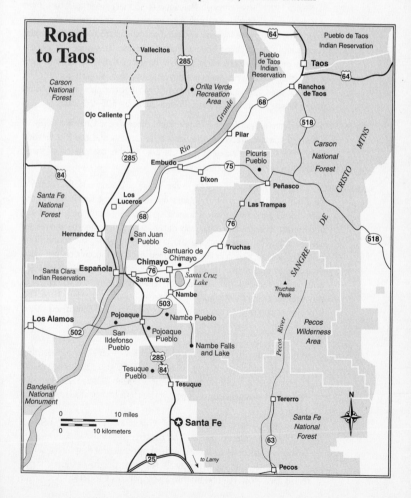

Road to Taos

The High Road to Taos

This paved backroad route takes you through a series of traditional villages along the foothills of the Sangre de Cristo Range, where ways of life have not changed much since territorial times. Although it is only slightly longer than the main highway route—52 miles versus 45 miles—it takes about twice as long thanks to winding roads, village speed zones and irresistible photo opportunities.

NAMBE PUEBLO   Drive through Pojoaque to County Road 503; turn right and drive three miles to a turnoff marked by a sign to Nambe Lake. Make a right onto the paved highway and wind past the cottonwoods to Nambe Pueblo and the sparkling Nambe Falls picnic site. This area was once a Spanish province where early settlers developed their communal land grants. Many Nambe residents are descendants of those early settlers. The falls are closed late September to mid-March. Photography fee; admission to the falls. ~ Route 1, Nambe; 505-455-2036, fax 505-455-2038.

CHIMAYO   Turn left on Route 520 and head through the Chimayo Valley to Chimayo. Located between the Sangre de Cristos and the Rio Grande Valley, the Chimayo Valley is a fertile area at the confluence of three streams.

SANTUARIO DE CHIMAYO   Within the village of Chimayo is the Santuario de Chimayo, the place of countless miracles. Legend has it that in the early 1800s a man who saw a shining light coming from the ground dug and found a crucifix. The cross was moved to a church nearby and placed on the altar. The next morning the crucifix was gone, and found in its original location. The crucifix was moved back to the church, but again disappeared and ended up in its original location. This kept happening until people realized that someone or something wanted it to remain at this site. So, a church was built in Chimayo between 1814 and 1816. This is probably one of the reasons why people believe the Santuario's dirt is

remain. Enter by way of an old church key! It's quite possible a visit here will inspire you to read Willa Cather's classic, *Death Comes for the Archbishop*. ~ Bishop's Lodge Road, Santa Fe; 505-983-6377; www.bishopslodge.com, e-mail bishopslodge@bishopslodge.com.

Across Route 285 from the village of Tesuque is **Tesuque Pueblo**. Considered one of the most traditional of the pueblos, Tesuque continues to have a strong agricultural emphasis, which results in organic food products for sale. Bright designs characterize their pottery. The pueblo also operates Camel Rock Casino, blessed. El Santuario, "The Shrine," remains a magic place where people with ailments come to feel God's healing touch. There's an annual pilgrimage to the church beginning on Good Friday. Testaments to its healing powers are everywhere, as discarded crutches, braces and *retablos* (paintings of saints done on wood) fill the church's side rooms. ~ County Road 98; 505-351-4889.

TRUCHAS   After visiting Chimayo, head north on Route 76 to the town of Truchas with its little weaving and woodcutting shops. It is a burgeoning arts center whose people are undoubtedly inspired by the splendid scenery of the Sangre de Cristos and New Mexico's second-highest mountain, 13,102-foot Truchas Peak.

LAS TRAMPAS   Continue north on Route 76 to Las Trampas. Once a walled adobe village—to protect it from "wild" Indians—Las Trampas is home to the 18th-century **Church of San Jose**, an oft-photographed mission church with mud plastering and early paintings. ~ Route 76, Las Trampas.

PICURIS PUEBLO   After passing through Las Trampas you'll come to Peñasco. Turn on Route 75 through the Picuris Pueblo to see the native pottery, weaving, silversmithing, beadwork and remains of a pueblo from the 13th century. Picuris, with its standing roundhouse, remains one of New Mexico's smallest pueblos. Admission. ~ Route 75, Peñasco; 505-587-2519, fax 505-587-1071; www.picurispueblo.com.

SAN FRANCISCO DE ASIS   From Picuris, rejoin Route 75 for a few miles until you connect with Route 518 and pass over the landmark U.S. Hill Vista, an early, tortuous trading route. After driving over hill and dale, when Route 518 meets with Route 68, head straight to the Ranchos de Taos. There you'll find San Francisco de Asis, a Spanish Colonial adobe church that was the favorite of photographers like Eliot Porter and Ansel Adams. It's home to Henri Ault's amazing *The Shadow of the Cross*, which some say is miraculous. Ault's painting depicts Christ carrying a cross when observed from one angle. In different light, however, the cross cannot be seen. Admission to *The Shadow of the Cross*. ~ Route 68, Ranchos de Taos; 505-758-2754, fax 505-751-3923.

where the main highway crosses tribal land. No cameras. Call for hours. ~ Route 84/285, Tesuque; 505-983-2667, fax 505-982-2331.

   Pojoaque Pueblo, one of the smallest of the northern Rio Grande Indian pueblos, hosts special fiesta days and has a visitors center where handcrafted items are sold. The pueblo's **Poeh Cultural Center** (505-455-3334) includes a museum and a reconstruction of part of the original pueblo, which was abandoned in the 1920s. The tribe has converted its old elementary school building into the glitzy neon Cities of Gold Casino. ~ Route 84/285; 505-455-3460, fax 505-455-7151 (visitors center).

Go left on Route 502 to **San Ildefonso Pueblo**, where you'll see beautiful burnished black matte pottery in the tradition of the late Maria Martinez. Current potters here continue to create artistic wonders. There's also a museum on site displaying jewelry, costumes and religious artifacts. Visitors must register at the visitors center. Photography is allowed with a permit. Admission. ~ Route 502; 505-455-3549, fax 505-455-7351.

If you opt not to take the High Road to Taos and continue north out of Santa Fe on Route 285, you'll come across the jolly sandstone **Camel Rock Monolith**.

Continuing north past Española, where the highway divides, drive a little farther on Route 68 to the San Juan Pueblo sign. **San Juan Pueblo** was the site of the first capital of New Mexico in 1598. Geometric designs and luster define the red-incised pottery. Woodcarvings and weavings are also for sale on site. ~ 505-852-4400, fax 505-852-4820.

Near San Juan Pueblo, on the east side of the highway, stands the controversial **Don Juan Oñate Monument**. This controversial $4 million bronze statue, a larger-than-life mounted figure of the first conquistador to attempt to colonize New Mexico, is considered by some to be a political boondoggle and an affront to the Indians of the Española Valley. Latinos, however, view it as a tribute to their proud cultural heritage. Notice where one of Oñate's boots has been welded back on; parties unknown once sawed it off in protest because Oñate cut the left legs off Acoma Pueblo warriors following an uprising in 1608.

HIDDEN ►   Continuing north on Route 68, the unpaved **River Road** parallels the highway and Río Grande. The oldest road in the valley, it serves several old haciendas that date back to colonial times. To explore it, follow any of the marked roads that turn west off the highway and intersect it. Of particular interest is Los Luceros, a hacienda that grew into a village and served as the county seat from 1821 to 1860.

sights   AUTHOR FAVORITE

As far as art galleries go, none is quite like the **Shidoni Foundry**, where bronze pourings take place on Saturdays. The art foundry, gardens and contemporary gallery are world-renowned among purveyors of fine art. You can experience Shidoni's charm with a stroll through the foundry's two large, peaceful parks, where dozens of metal sculptures—many of them monumental in size and price—await corporate buyers. Closed Sunday. ~ Bishop's Lodge Road, Tesuque; 505-988-8001, fax 505-984-8115; www.shidoni.com, e-mail shidoni@shidoni.com.

Another 15 miles or so north on Route 68 takes you to the turnoff to the verdant town of **Dixon**, where artists hold studio visits the first weekend in November. ~ Route 75; information on studio visits: 505-579-4363.

In this fragrant valley is the **La Chiripada Winery**, which has a tour (by appointment only) and tasting room (tasting fee). ~ Route 75, Dixon; 505-579-4437, 800-528-7801; www.lachiripa da.com, e-mail chiripa@cybermesa.com.

From there it's just a couple more miles on the "river road" to Pilar and the **Orilla Verde Recreation Area**, a nice rest stop on the river's edge. (See Chapter Ten for more information.)

If you return to Route 68 to travel north toward Taos, you'll discover that the highway was built by the U.S. Army and first called Camino Militar. Completion of this road helped end centuries' worth of isolation in Taos.

On the northern edge of town are two rather rural alternatives to the city lodging experience. The **Bishop's Lodge** is the better of the two primarily because of its rich history. The property along the Little Tesuque Stream was once the private retreat of Archbishop Jean Baptiste Lamy. The bishop's sacred, private chapel still stands behind the main lodge and can be entered by borrowing a special key from the front desk. Since 1917, the 440-acre ranch has hosted guests who choose from horseback riding, swimming, meditative hikes and tennis. Well-kept guest rooms are decorated in ranch motif. ~ Bishop's Lodge Road, off Route 84/285, Santa Fe; 505-983-6377, 800-732-2240, fax 505-989-8739; www.bish opslodge.com, e-mail bishopslodge@bishopslodge.com. ULTRA-DELUXE.

LODGING

A similar resort experience is offered at **Rancho Encantado**, which has fancier accommodations but less overall ambience and attention to service than the Bishop's Lodge. Handsome tree-lined grounds are criss-crossed with cobblestone paths linking the main building to the *casitas*, corral, tennis courts and cantina. Spanish Colonial and ranch styles prevail in the spacious and thoughtfully furnished rooms and cottages, the latter featuring fireplaces. The resort is currently closed for renovations; call for status. ~ State Road 592, Tesuque; 505-982-3537, 800-722-9339, fax 505-983-8269; www.ranchoencantadosantafe.com. ULTRA-DELUXE.

Located on the famed high road to Taos, **Hacienda Rancho de Chimayo** is a splendid seven-room retreat. Antique beds made of mahogany and iron, as well as traditional Chimayo handwoven draperies and rugs, give the rooms a homey feel. All rooms adjoin a beautiful courtyard and have fireplaces crafted from adobe as well as pine floors and *vigas*. The inn itself is adjacent

◀ HIDDEN

to a popular New Mexican restaurant. This place is a real gem. ~ County Road 98, Chimayo; phone/fax 505-351-2222; e-mail rdc@espanola-nm.com. MODERATE.

DINING

HIDDEN ►

Before it gets any trendier, check out the **Tesuque Village Market** and its casually chic atmosphere. The Tesuque chile-cheeseburger, stir-fry veggie plate and salads are highly recommended. There's a full wine cellar and good choices by the glass. ~ Route 591 and Bishop's Lodge Road, Tesuque; 505-988-8848, fax 505-986-0921. BUDGET TO MODERATE.

Tucked into the mountains about 40 minutes north of Santa Fe, **Restaurante Rancho de Chimayo** serves authentic New Mexican meals in an adobe house. Bill of fare includes tamales, enchiladas, tacos and flautas plus specialties like steak, trout, marinated pork cutlets served in a red-chile sauce and chicken breasts topped with chile sauce and melted cheese. Leave room for the homemade *sopapillas* and honey. During summer months, ask for the outdoor patio seating. Closed Monday from November through April. ~ Country Road 98, Chimayo; 505-351-4444. MODERATE.

The tough little town of Truchas was home to John Nichol's 1988 film *The Milagro Beanfield War.*

Dine alfresco on the banks of the Rio Grande at **Embudo Station**, a glass-walled adobe restaurant located a couple miles west of Dixon and half an hour south of Taos. Red-chile beer is the novelty item on a menu of traditional favorites such as smoked trout, beef brisket and black-bean burritos. Closed Monday and from November to mid-April. ~ Route 68, Embudo; 505-852-4707, fax 505-852-2479; www.embudostation.com. MODERATE.

SHOPPING

HIDDEN ►

When you're writing a guidebook about New Mexico, it's hard to decide whether the **Tesuque Pueblo Flea Market** belongs in the shopping or sightseeing section. Just as every flea market reflects its surrounding community, this northern New Mexico gathering place contains Spanish, Anglo and American Indian traders alike. Pull over to the side of the road, shuffle through the dust and you'll find everything from pinto beans to auto parts to fine turquoise jewelry. The flea market is open every Friday, Saturday and Sunday. ~ To get there head seven miles north from Santa Fe on Route 84/285, turn left after the opera house; 505-995-8626.

From moccasins to colorful masks and hand-coiled pottery, **Pojoaque Visitors Center** covers the gamut of American Indian folk art. It's a large gift shop, worth a good hour of browsing, and you'll no doubt walk away with a souvenir. Perhaps a storyteller doll or a kachina. ~ 96 City of Gold Road, Pojoaque; 505-455-3460, fax 505-455-7151.

For eight generations the Ortega family has been weaving brilliant sashes, vests, purses and jackets as well as world-famous rugs at their wonderful little shop, **Ortega's Weaving**. Closed Sunday from November through March. ~ County Road 98, Chimayo; 505-351-4215.

Next door, the **Galeria Ortega** is a good place to check for Southwestern gifts (pottery, kachinas, paintings, candles) and books on regional topics. Closed Sunday from November through March. ~ County Road 98 and Route 76, Chimayo; 505-351-2288.

For a sampling of local talent in Truchas, stop by the **Hand Artes Gallery,** featuring folk and fine art. Closed Sunday. ~ Route 76, Truchas; 505-689-2443, 800-689-2441, fax 505-689-2443; www.collectorsguide.com/handartes.

Also in Truchas is the **Cardona-Hine Gallery**, featuring the contemporary paintings of Alvaro Cardona-Hine and his wife, Barbara McCauley. ~ Off Route 76, on County Road 75, Truchas; 505-689-2253, 866-692-5070, fax 505-689-2903; www.cardona hinegallery.com.

NAMBE FALLS AND LAKE 🏃 ⛵ A double-drop waterfall tumbles down from Nambe Lake to a small picnic and camping area among the cottonwoods that line the Río Nambe. The lake is generously stocked with trout, and since it is on tribal land a New Mexico fishing license is not required. Instead, anglers pay a daily fee to the pueblo; these fees are the primary source of income for this small tribe. The falls are closed October to mid-March. Day-use fee, $10. ~ To get there, turn east at Pojoaque onto Route 503 and continue for six miles, past the pueblo turnoff, to the lake entrance; 505-455-2304, fax 505-455-2038.

▲ The Nambe Falls campground has six tent/RV sites with water and hookups; $20 to $30 per night.

PARKS

When early pleasure travelers from the east stepped down from the Santa Fe train, they must have felt much as modern-day Amtrak passengers do when they arrive at the depot in Lamy, a one-street town right out of the Old West. Although Santa Fe is just over the hill, the open countryside south of the city remains mostly empty grazing land. Each of the few scattered towns has a unique character of its own.

South of Santa Fe

Located 18 miles south of Santa Fe, **Lamy** is populated almost exclusively by artists. It's as quiet as small towns come—except for the daily arrivals of Amtrak trains. (The station here serves Santa Fe, since the tracks there were too steep for early-day locomotives pulling full-length trains. As a result, Santa Fe–bound cars were disconnected in Lamy and pulled into the city by a shuttle.)

SIGHTS

Galisteo, a tiny village about five miles south of Lamy on Route 41, dates back to the early 17th century, when a cluster of Spanish colonial haciendas appeared along the banks of the Galisteo River. In earlier centuries, the surrounding Galisteo Basin was one of the most densely populated areas in the region, with some 3000 people in 11 pueblos (one of which is currently under excavation). Perhaps it was this rich historic tradition that inspired radio personality Arthur Godfrey to build his hacienda-style home just outside of town in the 1960s.

More recently, a number of New Age institutes have made their headquarters in Galisteo's larger houses. The rest of the population seems to be divided between old Spanish families and Anglo artists, many of whom keep studios here.

About 15 miles southwest of Santa Fe is **Rancho de Las Golondrinas,** a restored Spanish hacienda dating back to 1710. It was once the last *paraje* (inn) before Santa Fe on the grueling journey along El Camino Real, the "Royal Highway," which brought traders and settlers from Mexico City to Northern New Mexico. The 200-acre grounds still operate as a working ranch, growing Indian corn and raising sheep. Coming here is like stepping back in time. Call for theme weekends and seasonal closures. Admission. ~ Route 25, Exit 276, go to 334 Los Piños Road; 505-471-2261, fax 505-471-5623; www.golondrinas.org, e-mail mail@golondrinas.org.

LODGING

For many weary travelers, the highlight of Galisteo is the **Galisteo Inn,** an authentic hacienda set on eight acres of landscaped grounds in the middle of the village. Many of the original features have been preserved, including hand-hewn *vigas*, plank floors, and antique Mexican tilework. The 12 rooms range from tiny twin-bedded units to accommodations with private fireplace. Room rates include full breakfast. ~ 9 La Vega, Galisteo; 505-466-8200, fax 505-466-4008; www.galisteoinn.com, e-mail galisteoin@aol.com. MODERATE TO ULTRA-DELUXE.

DINING

The **Galisteo Inn** has a good reputation as a restaurant specializing in Continental cuisine—creative, gourmet meals using traditional New Mexico ingredients. The prix-fixe menu changes weekly. No dinner on Monday and Tuesday. ~ 9 La Vega, Galisteo; 505-466-8200, fax 505-466-4008; www.galisteoinn.com, e-mail galisteoin@aol.com. ULTRA-DELUXE.

Las Vegas Area

The slow-paced town of Las Vegas, with its refreshingly real central plaza, is the county seat of three-million-acre San Miguel County. A practically undiscovered gem, it reflects the heritage of northern New Mexico. The surrounding region takes in the Pecos River, rushing from the high peaks of the

Pecos Wilderness down a deep canyon and past ancient Indian
ruins, as well as the magnificent mountain country around Hermit's Peak. To the north lies the strangely silent land around
Mora, one of a small cluster of traditional villages that are slowly
turning into ghost towns. Few travelers take the time to explore
the Las Vegas area, just an hour's drive from Santa Fe; for those
who do, a wealth of history and natural beauty awaits.

By driving the back road (Routes 84 and 25), that follows the   **SIGHTS**
Santa Fe Trail between the capital city and Las Vegas, you'll first
pass the **Glorieta Battlefield**, the site of the westernmost skirmish
of the Civil War, the 1862 Battle of Glorieta Pass. This engage-
ment was triggered by a Texas unit of the Confederate Army that
tried to capture Santa Fe as a base for seizure of the Colorado
and California goldfields. Defeat of the rebels at Glorieta Pass put
an end to this audacious plan.

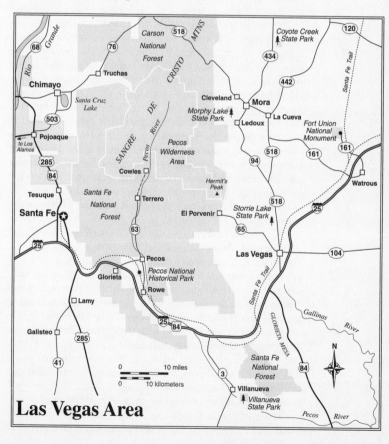

Las Vegas Area

Seven miles from Glorieta (a few miles off of Route 25 midway between the capital and Las Vegas) is **Pecos** (population 1500), a tiny town that consists of a gas station, a general store, a National Forest Service ranger station and two places typical of every New Mexican village: a Catholic mission church and a bar. Much of the predominantly Spanish-speaking population ekes out a living in the surrounding national forest, cutting *vigas*, *latillas* and firewood or grazing small herds of cattle, horses and goats. Unpaved roads (many of them passable by passenger car—check at the ranger station for suggestions) lead into the forest in all directions from the village; it's a beautiful area, full of spotted, rolling hills.

When the late actress Greer Garson and her husband donated 365 acres to preserve a postclassic pueblo civilization, they made possible the creation of **Pecos National Historical Park**. Walk among ruins dating back to A.D. 1200, a pueblo thought to have stood four to five stories back in 1451 when it had a population of 2000 (more than live in the Pecos area today). By the 17th century the Franciscan monks had taken over the pueblo and built a pair of mission churches. You can still see the remains of the huge church, *convento* and garden walls alongside the ancient pueblo ruins. Rampant disease and famine coupled with Comanche Indian raids in the mid-1800s led to the pueblo's abandonment, but survivors moved to Jemez Pueblo, where even today they form a separate clan and speak a dialect distinct from other Indians at the pueblo. When visiting, be careful to respect the privacy of the spirits that may haunt this incredible site. The ancient pueblo people were quite leery of strangers, forbidding them to set foot on pueblo land even when Pecos Pueblo was a center for trade with the Plains people. Trading parties actually had to camp outside the city wall. Admission. ~ Route 63, two miles south of Pecos; 505-757-6414 ext. 240, fax 505-757-8460; www.nps.gov/peco, e-mail peco_visitor_information@nps.gov.

Going west from the park and Pecos village, the road winds along a scenic river canyon painted with scrub oak. Along the way you'll pass a lake where the locals fish for dinner, a trout hatchery, a monastery and clusters of summer cabins. The upper Pecos River is renowned for its catch-and-release fly fishing, and on summer weekends you'll find the riverbanks lined with fishermen.

North of Pecos on Route 63 is the settlement of **Terrero**, the site of a long-abandoned refinery that used to process gold and other ores from the surrounding mountains. The pavement ends about four miles north of Terrero, and the unpaved road, steep and rough in spots, continues to a series of trailheads and large, well-developed campgrounds at the south portal of the Pecos Wilderness.

About 50 miles from Pecos is the country's original **Las Vegas**. The area's modern-day roots go back to the railroad's heyday, when Las Vegas was an important mercantile center. Las Vegas' destiny to become a major port of entry for supply wagons on the Santa Fe Trail began in 1835, when the Mexican government gave land grants to 29 individuals. By 1879, railroad tracks were laid east of the Gallinas River in "New Town"; not surprisingly, Railroad Avenue and the neighborhood boomed. But by 1905, railroad traffic was diverted south and the once-expanding city, whose population in the late 1800s rivaled Denver's, dwindled.

The diverse origins of people who came during Las Vegas' prime left an architectural legacy of everything from Territorial and Italianate styles to Victorian designs. In fact, Las Vegas has nine historic districts and more than 900 historically designated buildings. Movie buffs may recognize the distinctive-looking town as the setting of numerous silent films.

As you enter the city, you'll want to first head to the historic **Plaza**, the center of Old Town. The Plaza dates back to the 1600s with the Spaniards, although archaeological digs in Las Vegas show that the Paleo Indians lived here as early as 8000 B.C.

Afterward, stop by the **Las Vegas–San Miguel Chamber of Commerce** for maps of walking tours, hiking trails and information on Las Vegas' history. Closed weekends. ~ 513 6th Street, Las Vegas; 505-425-8631, 800-832-5947; www.lasvegasnewmex ico.com, e-mail chamber@worldplaces.com.

Next to the municipal courts is **The City of Las Vegas Museum & Rough Rider Memorial Collection**, which has mementos of the Spanish-American War donated by Rough Riders. It also exhibits artifacts and other historical items from northeastern New Mexico, starting with the Santa Fe Trail. Closed Saturday and Sunday from November through April. ~ 727 Grand Avenue, Las Vegas; 505-454-1401, fax 505-425-7335.

> Well-marked natural hot springs baths, located right off the highway in view of the United World College, are offered in varying temperatures.

Pretty buildings line the street of **New Mexico Highlands University**, which was established in 1893, bridging the rivaling Old and New Towns. The school is well known for its fine arts, performing arts and technical programs. ~ 901 University Avenue, Las Vegas; 505-425-7511, fax 505-454-3599; www.nmhu.edu.

Yet the pride of the area is the **United World College**, a beautiful red-slate structure that looks like a castle, complete with turrets. The school's unique setting and approach to learning draw students from around the world. To find the college, drive up pretty **Hot Springs Canyon** past painted barns, a picturesque little church and a couple of colorful wall murals. ~ Near the former spa of Montezuma, Las Vegas; 505-454-4200, fax 505-454-4274; www.ahuwc.k12.nm.us.

For a splendid drive, continue on Route 65 through Gallinas Canyon into the heart of the Sangre de Cristos and on up to the hiker's paradise of 10,263-foot **Hermit's Peak**.

Backtracking to Las Vegas and then north on Route 518 takes you to the boardsailing-haven of **Storrie Lake State Park**. A short drive farther north on scenic Route 518 puts you in **Mora**, known as the breadbasket of the area during the heyday of the Santa Fe Trail when it grew wheat.

In the nearby town of **Cleveland** is the **Cleveland Roller Mill Museum**, a 1900s flour mill that operated until 1947. The building, which is on the National Register of Historic Places, has original mill equipment and also covers local and regional history. The outside of the mill is open year-round; open weekends from Memorial Day through October. Admission. ~ Off Route 518, Cleveland; 505-387-2645; e-mail dancas@nnmt.net.

Northeast of Las Vegas via Route 25 is **Fort Union National Monument**, which beginning in 1851 and throughout most of the 19th century was the largest military post in the region and headquarters for soldiers who protected Santa Fe Trail travelers from Indian raids. A self-guided trail and visitors center explains its rich history. Admission. ~ Route 161, Watrous; 505-425-8025, fax 505-454-1155; www.nps.gov/foun.

LODGING
Victoriana is alive in the center of Las Vegas at the historic **Plaza Hotel**. Originally built in 1882 in the Italianate bracketed style, the Plaza was the first major inn constructed after the railroad's arrival. A century later, original features such as tin ceilings and window bracketing were uncovered. Rooms are decorated in period furniture, antiques and floral accents typical of late-19th-century buildings in the West. There's an on-site restaurant and lounge. ~ 230 Plaza, Las Vegas; 505-425-3591, 800-328-1882,

DAY TRIP TO LA CUEVA

La Cueva National Historic Site, part of the Mora land grant of 1835, is an exceptionally beautiful sight in the springtime. Built around a hacienda completed in 1863, La Cueva was a major agricultural center and the home of an adobe mill that ground flour for generations. Electricity was generated here until 1949. You can visit the old mill and the Mercantile Building, now the **Salman Ranch Store**, a peaked-roof adobe that sells locally produced jams, syrups and the like, along with dried flowers and wildflower seeds. Closed Tuesday and Wednesday from January to mid-May. Northeast of the store is **San Rafael Mission Church**, a building graced with handsome French Gothic windows. ~ Route 442, off of Route 518, 25 miles north of Las Vegas; 505-387-2900.

fax 505-425-9659; www.lasvegasnewmexico.com/plaza, e-mail plazahotel@worldplaces.com. MODERATE.

Or drive just a few miles to the "new" section of town and the hacienda-style **Inn on the Santa Fe Trail** for the best rooms for the price in the area. The property is handsomely decorated in oak and whitewashed pine furniture crafted by a Las Vegas artisan. Southwestern paintings cover pink walls. Fiberglass tubs are found in the bathrooms. ~ 1133 Grand Avenue, Las Vegas; 505-425-6791, 888-448-8438, fax 505-425-0417; www.innon thesantafetrail.com, e-mail information@innonthesantafetrail. com. BUDGET TO MODERATE.

There's no belfry at the **Carriage House Bed and Breakfast,** but if you're outside at sundown, you might spot the bats that live in the attic—that's when the furry creatures tend to emerge. Bats are only one of the attractions at this circa 1893 Victorian inn, the perfect base for exploring historic Las Vegas. The five rooms are furnished with bird's-eye maple chests and chenille bedspreads; elegant public areas complement the accommodations. This charming hostelry is on the National Register of Historic Places. ~ 925 6th Street, Las Vegas; phone/fax 505-454-1784, 888-221-9689; www.newmexicocarriagehouse.com, e-mail carriagebb@zialink.com. BUDGET TO MODERATE.

DINING

The **Landmark Grill**, the most elegant restaurant in Las Vegas, has an English look highlighted by Corinthian columns and floral-patterned tablecloths. Indulge in the chicken piccata, the linguine alfredo with shrimp or the rib-eye steak served with red or green chile. The intimate setting has been known to whet appetites of all kinds. ~ Plaza Hotel, 230 Plaza, Las Vegas; 505-425-3591; www.lasvegasnewmexico.com/plaza, e-mail plazahotel@world places.com. MODERATE TO DELUXE.

◄ HIDDEN

Located between a used-car lot and a hair salon, the **Mexican Kitchen** is the kind of place you'd normally pass right by. But we took a seat at one of the formica tables and noticed signed autographs from "General Hospital" soap opera stars who stopped by this redecorated drive-in while shooting an episode nearby. Perhaps the word-of-mouth reviews had already started. For excellent burritos, tacos and enchiladas at inexpensive prices, we wouldn't hesitate to return. Breakfast, lunch and dinner are served. ~ 717 Grand Avenue, Las Vegas; 505-454-1769. BUDGET TO MODERATE.

Don't be deterred by the shabby exterior of **Estella's Café.** Thoughtfully prepared American and Mexican cuisine dominate the menu. The green chile comes highly recommended. Open Monday through Wednesday for lunch, Thursday through Saturday for lunch and dinner. Closed Sunday. ~ 148 Bridge Street, Las Vegas; 505-454-0048. BUDGET TO MODERATE.

A reader s suggestion brought us to **El Rialto Restaurant & the Rye Lounge,** where you can down a few Mexican beers amid models of old trains and cars before stepping into the dining room. Fare such as fajitas, steak and enchiladas are prepared Southwest/New Mexican style; steaks and lobster have deluxe to ultra-deluxe price tags. ~ 141 Bridge Street, Las Vegas; 505-454-0037. BUDGET TO ULTRA-DELUXE.

SHOPPING   On the historic Plaza in Las Vegas is **La Galeria de los Artesanos Book Store,** where you ll find used and rare books on New Mexico and the Southwest, guidebooks, fiction and nonfiction housed in a former law office. Closed Sunday and Monday. ~ 220 North Plaza, Las Vegas; 505-425-8331.

NIGHTLIFE   In Las Vegas, try a spot that was named after a ghost, **Byron T s Saloon,** for a selection of libations. Live music on Friday. ~ Plaza Hotel, 230 Old Town Plaza, Las Vegas; 505-425-1455, fax 505-425-9659.

PARKS   **VILLANUEVA STATE PARK** 🚣 ⛺ 🛶 ⛵ ♨ This 1600-acre park on the banks of the Pecos River, 14 miles south of Route 25, is a local favorite for picnicking. Fishing is excellent for rainbow and brown trout. A visitors center provides information about the area s history and natural resources. Facilities are limited to showers and restrooms. ~ Route 3; 505-421-2957, fax 505-421-3231.

▲ There are 31 campsites (no hookups), $10 per night; and 12 RV sites with electricity, $14 per night.

SANTA FE NATIONAL FOREST 🚶 🚴 🐎 🎿 ⛷ ♨ Trails head into the 230,000-acre Pecos Wilderness, the heart of this vast national forest, from both Pecos and Las Vegas. From Pecos, the Pecos River Canyon Road runs north for 20 miles the last six of them unpaved and rough to a series of campgrounds and trailheads along the wilderness boundary. From Las Vegas, a paved road leads to El Porvenir, the least-used of the Pecos Wilderness portals, at the foot of Hermit s Peak. Access to the wilderness area is by foot or horseback only; no bicycles or motorized vehicles. In addition to the wilderness area, the forest encompasses 11,661-foot Elk Mountain, the subject of a seemingly endless conservation dispute between environmentalists and timber interests, and Glorieta Mesa, an uninhabited 60-mile-long, piæon-forested island in the sky that can be reached on an unpaved road that climbs to the mesa top from the village of Rowe, just off Route 25. ~ Route 63, 20 miles north of Pecos; and on Route 65, 17 miles northwest of Las Vegas; 505-757-6121, fax 505-757-2737.

▲ Holy Ghost, Iron Gate, Jack s Creek and Cowles campgrounds, all located along the wilderness boundary at the upper end of the Pecos River Canyon, have a total of 86 campsites (no hookups). Cowles has water, but Iron Gate does not (it does have four horse corrals). Cowles has a camping fee of $6 per night; Iron Gate is $4. Holy Ghost has a fee of $8 per night, while Jacks Creek is $10. El Porvenir Campground west of Las Vegas has 13 sites (no hookups); $8 per night.

STORRIE LAKE STATE PARK 🏊 🚣 ⛵ 🚤 🍴 A pretty mountain lake thats favored by gung-ho windsurfers who like the consistent breezes, and families who enjoy the jewel of a setting and the swimming. There is a visitors center, picnic area, toilets and showers. Entrance closes at sunset year-round. Day-use fee, $4 per vehicle. ~ Route 518, four miles north of Las Vegas; 505-425-7278, fax 505-425-0446.

> The first atomic bombs bore the nicknames Fat Man and Little Boy.

▲ There are 46 developed sites (25 with RV hookups); tent sites are $10 per night and hookups are $14 per night. Primitive camping is allowed along the lakes shore; $8 per night.

MORPHY LAKE STATE PARK 🏊 🚤 🍴 A scenic mountain lake and park thats a popular fishing spot for everyone and a swimming hole for only the very hearty. Unspoiled barely does justice to this little jewel. There are pit toilets, tables and grills. No motorboats are allowed. Closed November through March. Day-use fee, $4 per vehicle. ~ Route 94, four miles west of Ledoux; 505-387-2328, fax 505-387-5628.

▲ There are 20 developed sites ($10 per night) and primitive sites ($8 per night).

COYOTE CREEK STATE PARK 🚶 🍴 Fishing and camping are the main attractions in this compact 80-acre park, but there are also hiking trails, picnic sites and a playground as well as a visitors center. Amenities include restrooms and showers. Day-use fee, $4 per vehicle. ~ Route 434, 17 miles north of Mora; 505-387-2328, fax 505-387-5628.

▲ There are 67 sites including 17 with electric hookups and 20 primitive sites. Fees per night are $8 for primitive sites, $10 for standard sites and $14 for hookups. Reservations (mid-May to September): 877-664-7787.

Los Alamos Area

The Pajarito Plateau, a broad, pine-forested shelf of lava and ash, spans the eastern slope of the Jemez Mountains. This unusual mountain range is circular because some 200,000 years ago it was the base of a single volcano larger than any active volcano on earth today. The elements have carved the plateau into canyons with sheer orange-and-white walls where ancient cliff-dwellers made their homes.

This geological labyrinth made the plateau a perfect place for the government to hide its top-secret A-bomb laboratory during

World War II. Throughout the Cold War, as the brains behind the bomb continued to move into the area, Los Alamos boomed to become the wealthiest town in the state. Today, the future of this community surrounded by wilderness is uncertain as it slips into post–Cold War history.

In fact, history is an ever-present reality throughout the land between Santa Fe and Taos. It can be captured in such places as Bandelier National Monument, with its ruins of Indian pueblos and cliff dwellings from the 13th century, as well as still-inhabited Indian pueblos and Spanish mountain villages, where the ways of life from centuries past still endure.

SIGHTS   **Los Alamos** was developed in the early 1940s by the U.S. government for scientists working on the highly secretive Manhattan Project. The isolated town in the high-altitude Jemez Mountains boasted a spectacular setting, with scenery of dense forest and Indian pueblos; an extinct volcano formed a natural barrier on the other side. About the only thing here was the private Los Alamos Ranch School for Boys, but it was easily closed and the Manhattan Project, an experiment that would change the course of history, was underway.

Bright young minds were imported to create the first atomic bombs that eventually helped end World War II. But, alas, the inventors and their families were forced to live behind a wall of secrecy, where mail was subject to a censor's pen and passes were needed for leaves. It was physicist Robert Oppenheimer, architect of the atomic bomb, who once said: "The notion of disappearing into the New Mexico desert for an indefinite period disturbed a good many scientists."

Los Alamos National Laboratory remains the major presence in the city and accounts for the lion's share of local jobs. The Department of Energy still owns the laboratory that employs more than 7000 for national security studies, metallurgy, genetics information and geothermal and solar research. Los Alamos, obviously, still attracts the intelligentsia.

Los Alamos is warming (no pun intended) to visitors after decades as an ultra-insular community. The bomb was invented under a veil of secrecy; people in Santa Fe (only about 35 miles away) didn't even know what was going on "up there."

No matter how you feel about the atomic age, a visit to the **Bradbury Science Museum** is a must. Three dozen exhibits are interspersed with photographs, a timeline, films and letters, including one from Albert Einstein to President Roosevelt; the Robert Oppenheimer story is detailed. The museum is alternately frightening and enlightening. A recent exhibit discussed laboratory research to protect the environment. ~ 15th and Central streets,

Los Alamos; 505-667-4444, fax 505-665-6932; www.lanl.gov/external/museum, e-mail museum@lanl.gov.

To understand a little more about this unique town, be sure to stop at the **Los Alamos Historical Museum**, which covers pre-bomb history dating back to the Pleistocene era, artifacts from the defunct boy's school and items from the World War II era. There is a small pre-Columbian Indian pueblo ruin in the park behind the museum. ~ 1921 Juniper Street, Los Alamos; 505-662-4493, fax 505-662-6312; www.losalamos.com/historicalsociety, e-mail historicalsociety@losalamos.com.

Adjacent to the historical museum is a 1928 log building, home of the **Art Center at Fuller Lodge**. This national landmark, once a recreation hall for ranch school students, hosts exhibits by native and visiting artists. Closed Sunday. ~ 2132 Central Avenue, Los Alamos; 505-662-9331, fax 505-662-9334; www.losalamos. org/flac, e-mail artful@losalamos.com.

Nearby is the gleaming **Larry R. Walkup Aquatic Center**, the highest-altitude Olympic-size indoor pool in the United States, serving athletes and recreational swimmers who enjoy a splash. Closed Sunday from June through August. Admission. ~ 2760 Canyon Road, Los Alamos; 505-662-8170, fax 505-662-8034.

The earth is hot around Los Alamos less because of radioactivity than its volcanic history, and hot springs bubble forth to the delight of those who enjoy a refreshing and relaxing dip. In their natural state are the **Spence Hot Springs** (Route 4, about seven miles north of Jemez Springs) and **Battleship Rock Warm Springs** (Route 4, about five miles north of Jemez Springs). Short, well-trod foot paths take off from the respective parking areas.

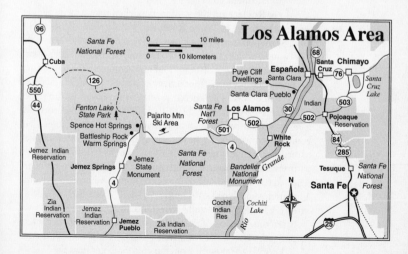

At the more developed **Jemez Springs Bathhouse,** private indoor tubs and a private outdoor hot tub are available, as well as massages, facials, manicures and pedicures. Admission. ~ Route 1 near the town of Jemez Springs; 505-829-3303, fax 505-829-3093; www.jemez.com/baths.

One mile north of the city of Jemez Springs is the **Jemez State Monument.** The monument, officially recognized in 1935, honors pre-Columbian Indian ruins, including the ruins of a pueblo and the remains of a Spanish mission, the Church of San Jose de los Jemez, which was built in 1621–22. A tiny museum offers exhibits that explain some of the Jemez history. Closed Tuesday. Admission. ~ Route 4; phone/fax 505-829-3530; www.nmculture.org.

> Roughly 7000 archaeological sites are said to surround the Los Alamos area.

Valle Grande was created about a million years ago when a volcano's summit seemingly crumbled and spewed ash as far east as Kansas. It left a broad basin called a caldera (thought to be the largest of its kind) that stretches about 15 miles in diameter. The Valle Grande is also home to one of the largest elk herds in the United States. It was nominated for national park status three times between 1926 and 1990, but the move was repeatedly blocked for political reasons. Finally, in 1999, Congress approved the acquisition of the Valle Grande by the Valles Caldera Trust. Now called the **Valles Caldera National Preserve,** this experiment in land management allows you a more solitary experience than you might get in other wilderness areas. Reservations required; check their website for details. ~ Route 4, 14 miles west of Los Alamos; 505-661-3333, fax 505-661-0400; www.vallescaldera.gov.

HIDDEN ▶ Along Route 4 on the way to Bandelier, take a two-mile detour in the town of White Rock and follow signs to the **Overlook.** Sitting on this volcanic peninsula you can gaze down to the Rio Grande, which curves in a broad sweep far below. Sedimentary cliffs and a tableau of distant mountains complete the panorama.

Bandelier National Monument encompasses 32,737 acres of scenic wilderness. The Pueblo people, who settled in the Jemez Mountains between A.D. 1100 to 1550, centuries before white men arrived, farmed this comparatively lush area in Frijoles Canyon. The canyon walls bear their symbols. Most of Bandelier, named for archaeologist Adolph Bandelier, is wild backcountry, with several riparian oases. Strenuous climbs up steep cliffs are required to explore much of the backcountry. Admission. ~ Route 4, ten miles south of Los Alamos; 505-672-0343, 505-672-3861 ext. 517, fax 505-672-9607; www.nps.gov/band.

Start your perusal of the park at the visitors center with a ten-minute slide show of "The Bandelier Story." The short, self-guided Main Loop Trail takes off from the visitors center near the Frijoles

Creek and passes **Tyuonyi** ("Meeting Place"), a circular village believed to have once stood three stories high. Its single entrance has led to speculation that this large and impressive structure was used for defending the village.

Behind Tyuonyi is **Talus House**, which has been completely reconstructed to give visitors an idea of what the homes along the cliff would have looked like. The trail continues to the longest structure at Bandelier, aptly named **Long House Ruin**, nestled under a cliff. It's full of ancient pictographs and petroglyphs.

You can continue on the trail for a half mile and scramble up several somewhat scary ladders to the **Ceremonial Cave**, which affords a great overall view of the canyon. Backtracking to the visitors center, hike down Frijoles Canyon across the creek to the **Upper Falls** and then view yet another waterfall about a half-mile down the path.

If your appetite is whet for ruins, then drive a few dozen miles northwest to the **Puye Cliff Dwellings**, a fascinating little ancient city. Inhabited by up to 1500 people between the years of 1250 to 1577, Puye is currently operated by the neighboring Santa Clara Pueblo, whose occupants are probably descendants of the original settlers. The excavated ruins of the ancient apartmentlike complexes are evident from miles away as you approach the site. Upon arrival, choose either the Cliff Trail or the Mesa Top Trail for exploring. Admission. The dwelling is currently closed due to fire damage. Closed until 2004; call for more information. ~ Located seven miles off Route 30, south of Española; 505-753-7330.

◄ HIDDEN

The **Cliff Trail** takes off from above the parking lot and offers you a chance to walk through cavelike rooms and past petroglyphs and the outlines of buried masonry dwellings for more than a mile along the south face of the Puye mesa. Rock inscriptions of spirals and masks, serpents and humans are carved along the caves and cliffs. You'll also see outlines of buried masonry dwellings known as talus rooms. Stepping places and hand grips lead to kivas and the grand Community House from the cave rooms (or cavate rooms) below. Near the base of the cliffs are two kivas. But there may be more ceremonial chambers and other treasures lying undiscovered, well beneath the earth's surface.

It's possible to drive up to the second trail, appropriately called **Mesa Top Trail**, by following the road past the visitors center. From there, the Puye's 740-room pueblo, with its restored room, can be examined. Historians imagine the structure loomed as high as three stories tall. When perusing the remains, take a look around at the splendid views of the Rio Grande region. Puye villagers of so long ago likely enjoyed a similar panorama.

After exploring the cliff dwellings, drive six miles west to gorgeous **Santa Clara Canyon**, a nice place for a picnic lunch or fishing stop.

LODGING

HIDDEN ►

They'll loan you golf clubs, tennis rackets or bikes, recommend hikes and heap up plenty of free advice at **Renata's Orange Street Inn Bed and Breakfast**, a quiet alternative to the hotel scene. The suburban-looking house—one almost expects to see June Cleaver at the door—offers eight rooms, four of which share two baths. Each room is furnished differently; some have a Southwest style and others have antiques, though all have thick, soft comforters on the beds. The morning meal is included and the fridge is open for frozen yogurt during the day and wine in the afternoon. ~ 3496 Orange Street, Los Alamos; 505-662-2651, 800-662-3180, fax 505-661-1538; www.losalamos.com/orangestreetinn, e-mail renatas@losalamos.com. BUDGET TO MODERATE.

At the **Los Alamos Inn**, the 100 rooms are bright and pleasant with pastel bedspreads and art class–variety paintings. The inn is in a wooded area of town. Sitting by the swimming pool and sauna will make you feel miles away from the city. Full breakfast included. ~ 2201 Trinity Drive, Los Alamos; 505-662-7211, 800-279-9270, fax 505-661-7714; e-mail lainmx@aol.com. MODERATE.

A similar dwelling is the **Best Western Hilltop House Hotel**, which caters to businesspeople with mini-suites and executive suites outfitted with full kitchens. Amenities include a hot tub and sauna, an indoor heated pool and a 24-hour deli. ~ Trinity Drive and Central Street, Los Alamos; 505-662-2441, 800-462-0936, fax 505-662-5913; e-mail hilltop@losalamos.com. MODERATE.

Perched on a high-desert hilltop, **Amrit Nivas** (also known as The Inn of Nectar) is an unusual and peaceful getaway that caters to families. This 1000-square-foot home can sleep up to eight people and is fully equipped with a dishwasher, washer/dryer, satellite TV and VCR. Extras include an outdoor hot tub and meditation pavilion. The kitchen is strictly vegetarian, but an outdoor grill is provided for other food preparation. Catered vegetarian meals and yoga instruction are available upon request. ~ P.O. Box 970, Santa Cruz, NM 87567; 505-753-5086, 888-809-0885, fax 505-753-9259; www.cyberzones.com/amritnivas, e-mail nam@newmexico.com. DELUXE.

DINING

For light fare such as croissants, sandwiches, pastries and espresso, pay a visit to **Café Allegro**. No dinner. Closed Sunday. ~ 800 Trinity Drive, Los Alamos; 505-662-4040. BUDGET.

On your way toward an afternoon picnic, swing by **Allied Foods** for goodies to go. Vegetarians may not be thrilled here, but meat lovers will enjoy the breakfast burritos (with sausage, ham or bacon), daily sandwich specials (which might be cheesesteak, corned beef or pastrami) or custom-made deli sandwiches. Because what's a picnic without pastrami? Closed Sunday. ~ 751 Central Avenue, Los Alamos; 505-662-2777, fax 505-661-6111; www.losalamos.com/allied. BUDGET.

Taking a Chance

Nothing in recent years has changed the look of New Mexico's major highways as much as the rise of Indian gaming. Advertised by glittering billboards and bright computerized displays, the state's Pueblo and Apache tribes operate 11 gambling casinos throughout the state, including four between Santa Fe and Taos. Although gaming is largely unrestricted, most casinos offer blackjack, craps, roulette, poker, Caribbean stud, pai gow poker, video poker, slot machines and bingo. Most also have budget-priced all-you-can-eat buffets.

Indian gaming has been a highly controversial topic in New Mexico since it first appeared in 1997. Opponents assert that it encourages compulsive gambling, ruins lives and drains the local economy. There can be no doubt, though, that casinos have improved the finances of Indian tribes. Visitors to Tesuque Pueblo, for instance, can see how beautifully the once-crumbling center of the pueblo has been restored, and gaming proceeds have financed the development of other businesses such as Tesuque Natural Farms, a tribal enterprise that raises llamas and grows amaranth, a traditional Aztec grain. Casinos provide employment for about 2000 people in northern New Mexico.

The closest casino to Santa Fe, Tesuque Pueblo's **Camel Rock Casino** is known for its Las Vegas–style showroom concerts, which run the gamut from country and Norteño bands to oldies-but-goodies rock groups. ~ nine miles north of Santa Fe Route 84/285; 505-984-8414.

New Mexico's largest casino, **Cities of Gold** at Pojoaque operates over 700 slot machines in a building that used to be the local high school. It is also the first Indian casino in the state to build adjacent lodging accommodations. ~ Route 84/285, 16 miles north of Santa Fe; 505-455-3313.

Santa Clara Pueblo has not yet opened a casino but has entered into a compact for a large planned gaming resort in Española, where much of the town is on Indian land. Meanwhile, Española residents risk their money at San Juan Pueblo's **OhKay Casino**. ~ One mile north of Española; 800-752-9286.

Taos Pueblo has the state's smallest gaming facility, **Taos Mountain Casino**, located near the turnoff from the highway to the pueblo—and some ambitious plans. The tribe has applied for state permission to buy the Kachina Lodge in the center of Taos and convert it into a gambling resort. ~ Two miles north of Taos; 505-737-0777.

Los Alamos pizza aficionados head for **Tony's Pizzeria**, a local dive with good pies. You can get them New York or Sicilian style. They also serve pasta, sandwiches and subs. The only problem with Tony's is that they close early (8:30 p.m.) and on weekends. Otherwise, that's *amore*. ~ 723 Central Avenue, Los Alamos; 505-662-7799; www.losalamos.com/pizza, e-mail pizza@losalamos.com. BUDGET.

Before New Mexico adopted the moniker of Land of Enchantment, it was known as the Sunshine State.

South of Los Alamos, you'll discover **Katherine's Fine Dining**, an anomaly out here in the blissful middle of nowhere. Try the artichoke hearts baked in brie as an appetizer; then move on to the medallions of beef zinfandel. Local art and hanging quilts add to the decor. No lunch on Saturday. Closed Sunday and Monday. ~ 121 Longview, White Rock; 505-672-9661, fax 505-672-1038; www.losalamos.com/katherines. MODERATE TO ULTRA-DELUXE.

NIGHTLIFE They roll up the sidewalks early in Los Alamos; a big night out may consist of a brew at the corner pub (the likes of which are admittedly few and far between). You could, however, give the **Hot Club of Los Alamos** a try. Held in the Allied deli (out front during the summer), live local and international musicians give intimate performances accompanied by coffee and desserts. Call for schedule. Occasional cover. ~ 751 Central Avenue, Los Alamos; 505-662-7279; www.losalamos.com/allied.

PARKS **BANDELIER NATIONAL MONUMENT** 🏃 Nestled in the Jemez Mountains are cave and cliff dwellings and Pueblo sites abandoned about 450 years ago by the farming ancestors of the present Pueblo people. Hiking trails lead the curious visitor around this secret honeycombed world. There's a visitors center to get you started. Food service is available in the park. No pets allowed. A fee of $10 per private vehicle is good for seven days. ~ Route 4, about ten miles south of Los Alamos; 505-672-0343, 505-672-3861 ext. 517, fax 505-672-9607; www.nps.gov/band.

▲ There are 94 sites during the summer, about 30 sites during the off-season; $10 per night for individual sites, $35 per night at group sites (reservations required). Call 505-672-3861 ext. 534 for group campsite reservations.

SANTA FE NATIONAL FOREST 🏃 🚵 🏇 🛶 ⛺ 🎣 The Jemez unit of this national forest encompasses two of New Mexico's most remarkable natural features—the huge ancient volcano caldera of Valle Grande and the rugged canyonlands of the Pajarito Plateau. Cliff dwellings and pueblo ruins built by ancestors of the present-day Pueblo Indians are found all over the plateau, which had a much larger population in the 13th and 14th centuries than it does today. There are also numerous waterfalls and natural hot springs. The Dome Wilderness, adjoining the western boundary of Bandelier National Monument, was engulfed by an explosive forest fire in 1996. There are six picnic areas; Spanish Queen and Battleship are wheelchair-accessible. All have restrooms. ~ Route 4, west of Los Alamos; 505-829-3535, fax 505-829-3223.

▲ There are nine forest service campgrounds in the Jemez unit of Santa Fe National Forest, with approximately 200 total sites. There are no electrical hookups, but there are sites large enough for RVs. There is one wheelchair-accessible campground, Vista Linda. Campsites are also available adjacent to the national forest, Fenton Lake State Park and Jemez National Monument.

FENTON LAKE STATE PARK 🚲 🏕 🚤 🛷 ⛵ Sheltered in a   ◄ HIDDEN
ponderosa pine forest below 1000-foot red cliffs, the park surrounds a 37-acre trout lake that allows no motorboats or swimming. (But rowboats are allowed and there is access.) In winter, cross-country skiers appreciate the two miles of groomed trails and enjoy gliding around the frozen lake through deep snow. Campsites fill early in the summer, in spite of the fact that Fenton Lake's 7800-foot elevation makes for cool, cool nights. There are picnic areas and restrooms throughout the park and accessible fishing areas as well. Day-use fee, $4 per vehicle. ~ Take Route 4 until you reach Route 126, 45 miles west of Los Alamos; 505-829-3630, fax 505-829-3412.

▲ There are 37 developed tent sites, $10 per vehicle; and 5 sites with electricity and water, $14 per vehicle.

Heading north on Route 84 from Santa Fe will eventually lead to Chama, a forgotten town near where a little-used backcountry highway crossed the Colorado state line— until the railroad returned. Now thousands of visitors each summer come to Chama to ride the narrow-gauge steam train into the aspen forests of the Colorado mountains and back. Along the way you'll pass through Georgia O'Keeffe country with its bluebird skies, yucca plants and red-brushed hills in the high desert. The muddy, red-tinged Rio Chama sidles along the highway.

Chama Area

Traveling from the Los Alamos area, driving north on Route 84 you pass through **Española**. Founded in the 1880s as a railroad stop (although it was discovered by the Europeans as early as 1598), you'll notice the community remains true to its Hispanic heritage in everything from culture to churches. Although it has evolved into a bedroom community for Santa Fe, Española's claim to fame has always been as the "Low-rider Capital" of the world. Cruise Main Street on a Saturday night to see spiffed-up vehicles and macho young men.

SIGHTS

Turning west on Route 84 at Española takes the traveler through the ink spot of a town called Hernandez. Stop at **Romero's Fruit Stand** to pick up authentic *ristras* (strings of chiles), local honey and raspberry and cherry cider before continuing your trip north. ~ Route 84, Hernandez; 505-753-4189.

The scenery of sage-filled hills and open vistas will probably start to look more and more familiar as you continue north on Route 84. This is the region that inspired artist Georgia O'Keeffe to create her magic on canvas. The small town of **Abiquiu**, which was settled in the 1700s on an American Indian ruin at the river's bend, was O'Keeffe's home for many years. The **Georgia O'Keeffe House**, the celebrated artist's winter home for 35 years, is where she painted some of her most famous pictures. O'Keeffe's home is open for public tours by reservation only. Plan ahead! The tours, which run Tuesday, Thursday and Friday from April to mid-November, are booked up one to two months in advance; call the **Georgia O'Keeffe Foundation** in Abiquiu. Admission. ~ P.O. Box 40, Abiquiu, NM 87510; 505-685-4539, fax 505-685-4551.

Ghost Ranch, originally a dude ranch frequented by Hollywood celebrities in the 1930s, is now operated by the Presbyterian Church as one of the most popular conference centers in the state, thanks partly to its spectacular setting among bright-colored cliffs and spires of sandstone, limestone, gypsum and shale. The ranch is also a paleontologist's dream. Dinosaur skeletons found on the grounds include the crocodile-like *Phytosaur*, the rare armored *Typothorax*, and lots of examples of the ten-foot-long, flesh-eating *Coelophysis*, New Mexico's official state fossil. You can see them on display in the **Ruth Hall Museum of Paleontology** on the conference center grounds. Museum is closed Monday. ~ Route 84, Abiquiu; 505-685-4333, 877-804-4678, fax 505-685-4519; www.ghostranch.org.

HIDDEN ►

When steep, pastel-colored cliffs, part of the shifting formation called the Gallina Fault Zone, come into view, you'll know you're nearing the **Piedra Lumbre Visitors Center**. Environmental education is a theme at this unique learning center. Operated by the U.S. Forest Service, the center's short walking tours showcase the local ecology. You'll find current and useful facts about the Rio Chama as well as the Gateway to the Past exhibit, which features displays regarding the culture and peoples of the region. Also here is the one-acre **Beaver National Forest**, one of the smallest national forests in the country. Closed Monday. Admission. The visitors center is currently closed for renovations; call ahead. ~ Route 84, Abiquiu; 505-685-4312, fax 505-685-4558.

HIDDEN ►

About a mile north of Ghost Ranch, an unpaved road turns off Route 84 to the west and follows the Chama River for 13 rough miles to the **Monastery of Christ in the Desert**. The modernistic, freeform adobe complex was hand-built by three Benedictine

HIDDEN ►

monks from New York between 1964 and 1974. Today's dozen or so resident monks grow their own food and make a living by selling handcrafts and renting out a dormitory-style guesthouse where visitors can experience the monastic way of life for a few days or weeks. In keeping with the creativity and spirituality that seem to pervade the Abiquiu area, much of the music sung in the daily masses is composed by the brothers themselves. This is also one of the few places in the world where monks still practice calligraphy and illumination, copying sacred texts by hand. There are no phones, though the monks *do* have a site on the World Wide Web. ~ Forest Road 151, Abiquiu; www.christdesert.org, e-mail porter@christdesert.org.

A few miles north again on Route 84 takes you to the trails and natural wonder of **Echo Amphitheater**. Years of erosion have hollowed out this gargantuan sandstone theater. A picnic area and campground are available.

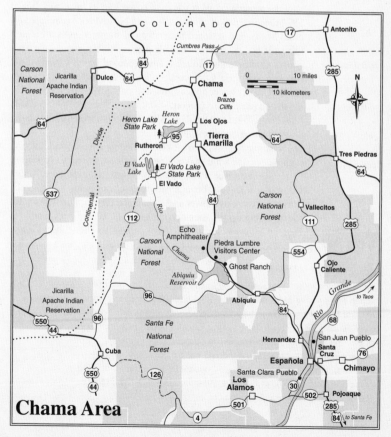

At an altitude of 8000 feet, **Chama,** located in the southern San Juan Mountains just nine miles from the Colorado border, is becoming more and more popular as a recreation area. Although Chama has only about 1000 residents, it is the largest town in this wild mountain area where most of the population lives scattered in tiny, traditional Spanish villages or down narrow dirt roads into the solitary reaches of the Apache lands. Summer is still high time, but with more than 300 miles of trails in the Carson National Forest, snowmobile safaris are common in the little town that bills itself as the "Snowmobile Capital of the Southwest."

Tourism, ranching and lumbering are the lifeblood of Chama, which experienced its first population explosion in the early 1880s with the building of the railroad. The train served mining camps that were digging into this rich region. Records show those were wild times, as bustling saloons and rowdy gambling halls lined the main drag.

Like most Wild West towns, Chama had its bust, too. But in 1974 the governments of Colorado and New Mexico purchased 64 miles of rail and restored the coal-fired steam train as a historic tourist attraction. The "double-header" (twin-engine narrow-gauge) **Cumbres and Toltec Scenic Railroad** leaves Chama daily between Memorial Day weekend and mid-October to chug over hill and dale, through meadows and past groves of piñon, oak, aspen and juniper. Admission. ~ Route 17, Chama; 505-756-2151, 888-286-2737, fax 505-756-2694; www.cumbresandtoltec.com, e-mail rrinfo@cumbrestoltec.com.

HIDDEN ►

Nestling against the river's edge, fording a trestle and hugging high passes, the train makes a 64-mile one-way trip to Antonito, Colorado (you ride a van back), or shorter roundtrips to Osier, Colorado. It travels through the valley of Los Piños River, which bursts with iris, sunflower and Indian paintbrush. The steam train moves along up the four percent grade of 10,015-foot Cumbres Pass and burrows through two tunnels to the Toltec Gorge.

AUTHOR FAVORITE

sights

When I've been sitting in the car all day, my neck tends to stiffen and my shoulders develop knots—I know it's time for a soak in some mineral hot springs and maybe a massage. About a half-hour drive north from Española is the no-frills spa called **Ojo Caliente Mineral Springs**, one of the oldest health resorts in the country. Soak in the springs or perhaps take an herbal wrap or indulge in a massage. Five minerals— iron, soda, lithia, sodium and arsenic—bubble up from the ground. Admission. ~ Route 285, Ojo Caliente; 505-583-2233, 800-222-9162, fax 505-583-2045; www.ojocalientespa.com.

Autumn is a nice time to see the aspen trees alight the forest. No matter what the season, the ride may be chilly and snow always a possibility. It's not a ride for anyone in a hurry. The trip takes six and a half hours.

Ten miles south of Chama on Route 84 is **Los Ojos**, a town that was founded around 1860. Plenty of Los Ojos' original houses remain standing. The architecture mixes traditional adobe construction with turn-of-the-20th-century pitched roofs, Victorian influences and gingerbread trim. Here you can visit the **Tierra Wools Cooperative Showroom**, where artisans keep centuries-old native weaving traditions alive. Closed Sunday from November through May. ~ Route 84, Los Ojos; 505-588-7231, 888-709-0979, fax 505-588-7044; www.handweavers.com.

The **Brazos Cliffs** abut the skyline south of Chama, and for about three weeks each spring a waterfall of snow runoff cascades off 11,289-foot Brazos Peak. ~ Route 512, seven miles east of Route 84.

The tribal members residing on the unspoiled **Jicarilla Apache Indian Reservation** (505-759-3255, fax 505-759-3457; www.jica rillaonline.com) open up their lands for hunting, fishing and camping on the mountain lakes. In the Jicarilla's commercial center of **Dulce**, on Route 64, 25 miles west of Chama, you'll find a tribal arts-and-crafts shop and a small museum.

LODGING

Aside from the Monastery of Christ in the Desert, the only place to spend the night—or dine out—in the Abiquiu area is the **Abiquiu Inn**. Owned and operated by Abiquiu's Islamic mosque, this 14-room motor inn has contemporary guest rooms decorated in earth tones, outfitted with the conventional amenities. In addition, there are five *casitas*, three with private verandas and hammocks. Management of both the motel and the restaurant has been spotty over the years, and staff is often inexperienced. The inn's greatest appeal is location: It is hard to imagine where one might sleep further from city lights or closer to starry skies than in Abiquiu. ~ Route 84, Abiquiu; 505-685-4378, 800-447-5621; www.abiquiuinn.com, e-mail abiquiuinn@computeratwinx.com. BUDGET TO DELUXE.

If the rugged outdoors call you, along with elegance and a hot tub, try **The Lodge at Chama**, an interesting combination of the deluxe and the downhome. The 22 Southwestern-style rooms are clean and spacious and the spa facility is the epitome of luxury. Room packages aren't cheap, but they include various combinations of recreational activities on the 36,000-acre ranch such as hiking, hunting and fishing, as well as upper-end meals in the lodge's fine restaurant. ~ P.O. Box 127, Chama, NM 87520; 505-756-2133, fax 505-756-2519; www.lodgeatchama.com, e-mail reservations@lodgeatchama.com. ULTRA-DELUXE.

Chama has seen the renovation and conversion of several of its early-20th-century homes into B&Bs. One successful transformation is the **Lightheart Inn**, across the street from the railroad depot. This one-and-a-half-story Victorian offers five guest rooms, plenty of hospitality and a complimentary breakfast served early enough to allow plenty of time to catch the train. ~ 631 Terrace Avenue, Chama; 505-756-2908, 800-976-2297; www.lightheartinn.com, e-mail terry@cvn.com. MODERATE.

DINING   **El Parasol** is a legend around these parts. Nothing more than a busy, fast-food taco stand, it turns out surprisingly tasty, authentic Mexican favorites. So authentic in fact, that you'd be hard-pressed to find an English-speaking employee. The *carne adovada* burritos and crispy chicken tacos doused in green or red salsa are crowd pleasers. ~ 602 Santa Cruz Road, Española; 505-753-8852. BUDGET.

The **Abiquiu Inn Café** specializes in Middle Eastern, Southwest and Italian food. Breakfast, lunch and dinner are served; no dinner from November through March. ~ Route 84, Abiquiu; 505-685-4378, 800-447-5261; www.abiquiuinn.com, e-mail abiquiuinn@computeratwinx.com. BUDGET TO MODERATE.

Let your nose lead you: The spicy, peppery smell of native cuisine hails from **Vera's Mexican Kitchen**, where *rellenos*, burritos and enchiladas await. Closed Wednesday. ~ Route 84, Chama; 505-756-2557. BUDGET.

American standards and Mexican favorites are served at the **High Country Restaurant and Lounge**. Choose between such entrées as filet mignon, a seafood platter, steak *asada* or *pico de gallo*. ~ Route 84, Chama; 505-756-2384. MODERATE TO DELUXE.

SHOPPING   The **Narrow Gauge Gift Shop** sells train-related souvenirs such as engineers caps (naturally!) and T-shirts at fair prices. Closed November through April. ~ Route 17, Chama; 505-756-2963.

The timeless art of weaving is revitalized by the wool artisans and growers of **Tierra Wools**, who gladly offer their wares through a cooperative showroom. Closed Sunday from October through April. ~ Off Route 84, Los Ojos; 505-588-7231.

NIGHTLIFE   **Foster's Hotel, Restaurant and Saloon**, a historic hotel where you will want to stop for a drink, has been in business since 1881. ~ 4th and Terrace streets, Chama; 505-756-2296.

PARKS   **ABIQUIU RESERVOIR**   All water sports are permitted in this 4000-acre reservoir, an Army Corps of Engineering project, which was created by damming the Rio Chama. The colors of the day, especially sunsets, are splendid in the wonderfully pastel-colored country that artist Georgia O'Keeffe loved so much. Fishing yields channel catfish, salmon, smallmouth bass and a variety of trout. Facilities include picnic areas, bathrooms and showers. Boat launch fee, $3 per day. ~ Route 84, seven miles northwest of Abiquiu; 505-685-4371, fax 505-685-4647; www. spa.usace.army.mil/abiquiu.

▲ Riana Campground (505-685-4561) has 54 sites. Fees are $5 per night for walk-in sites, $10 for vehicle-accessible sites and $14 for hookups. Free from October to early April, when all water is shut off. Reservations are recommended: 877-444-6777.

EL VADO LAKE STATE PARK This is a beautiful mountain lake for waterskiing and fishing (the latter of which is popular year-round). In the winter, ice anglers head for the frozen waters. There are picnic areas and playgrounds. Day-use fee, $4 per vehicle. ~ Route 112, 14 miles southwest of Tierra Amarilla; information through State Parks Department, phone/fax 505-588-7247.

▲ There are 80 developed sites, $10 per night; unlimited primitive sites, $8 per night; and 19 RV sites, $14 per night. Reservations: 877-664-7787.

Use bait or fly, but don't head home without taking back some tall fish tales from your trip to the Enchanted Circle. Pack your pole and perambulate over to the Pecos River or one of the area's lakes.

Outdoor Adventures

FISHING

SANTA FE In the Santa Fe area, the fish are probably biting at the **Pecos River**. In the upper reaches of the canyon, all fishing is catch-and-release. If you want to eat the trout you catch, head for **Monastery Lake**, on the river just north of Pecos and downstream from the state trout hatchery. Try **High Desert Angler** for tackle rental and flyfishing guide service. ~ 435 South Guadalupe Street; 505-988-7688. Bait is available at **Adelo's Town and Country Store** in Pecos. ~ 505-757-8565.

> Ice skating in New Mexico? Why not? Check out Genoveva Chavez Community Center's chilly arena. ~ 3221 Rodeo Road, Santa Fe; 505-955-4001.

ROAD TO TAOS **Nambe Lake**, on the Nambe Pueblo reservation, is well stocked with rainbow trout; a state fishing license is not required, but a day-use fee is charged.

LAS VEGAS AREA Serious anglers head for the **Upper Pecos River**, a designated catch-and-release area that boasts trout of formidable size, midway between Santa Fe and Las Vegas. If you want to keep your catch and cook it, the place to go is **Monastery Lake** on the north edge of the village of Pecos. A large state trout hatchery just upriver keeps the lake jumping, and many Pecos residents depend on it as a year-round food source. **Adelo's Town and Country Store** (505-757-8565) at the main road intersection in Pecos (on Route 63) carries fishing supplies and sells licenses. Near Las Vegas, **Morphy Lake State Park** and **Storrie Lake** are stocked with trout.

HIDDEN ▶ **LOS ALAMOS AREA** A truly hidden local fishing hole is **Los Alamos Lake**. The former town reservoir is now used exclusively by the few anglers who find their way to it along the rough two-mile forest road that starts from *under* the big bridge near the Los Alamos National Laboratories administration building at the west end of town.

BOATING & WIND-SURFING Some prefer playing on the water when it's not rushing over large rocks. If you don't have your own windsurfing or boating equipment, you can hunt down one of the Storrie Lake sailboard-rental outfits, or go with a boat rental on scenic Heron Lake, a "no-wake" lake.

In the Chama area, hire an 18-foot pontoon boat or 17-foot V-hull and boat from Stone House Lodge. ~ 95 Heron Lake Road, Los Ojos; 505-588-7274.

RIVER RUNNING Shooting the rapids is an increasingly popular activity in the Santa Fe area, so get your feet wet on a tame or tumultuous guided tour of the Rio Grande or the Rio Chama. Many outfitters are ready and willing to help immerse you in the fun of wave riding.

SANTA FE Although the Santa Fe River rarely flows, several Santa Fe–based rafting companies shuttle the adventurous northward to get their feet wet on tumultuous guided tours of the Rio Grande near Taos or tamer ones on the Rio Chama near Abiquiu. Many outfitters are ready and willing to help immerse you in the fun of wave riding. Rafting season is late spring through early summer, when the rivers are swollen by runoff from the melting mountain snow pack. Weekend releases of water from El Vado Lake near Chama keep the river flowing all summer. **New Wave Rafting Co.** runs daily tours from Santa Fe in rafting season, including overnight trips on the Rio Grande and three-day runs on Rio Chama. Food and gear are provided. ~ Route 5, Box 302-A; 505-984-1444, 800-984-1444; www.newwaverafting.com. Another outfitter for the region is **Santa Fe Rafting**, which offers half-day, full-day, evening and overnight trips on the Rio Grande and the Chama. ~ 1000 Cerrillos Road; 505-988-4914, 800-467-7238; www.santaferafting.com. **Kokopelli Rafting Adventures** embarks on half- and full-day whitewater excursions on the Rio Grande and the Rio Chama (class II to class IV rapids). They also have inflatable kayak trips on the river and sea kayaks on some of the local lakes. Food is provided. ~ 541 West Cordova Road; 505-983-3734, 800-879-9035; www.kokopelliraft.com.

SWIMMING Swim with the bigshots at the most elevated Olympic-size pool in the country (altitude-wise, that is). Or just splash around in one of the several public pools in the area.

SANTA FE Take a Santa Fe splash at the **Salvador Perez Pool.** ~ 601 Alta Vista Street; 505-955-2604. Also in the area is the the **Tino Griego Pool.** ~ 1730 Llano Street; 505-955-2661. The **Alto/ Bicentennial Pool** opens in late May for summer swims. ~ 1121 Alto Street; 505-955-2650. **Genoveva Chavez Community Center** has an Olympic-size pool and another outfitted with a waterslide. ~ 3221 Rodeo Road; 505-955-4001.

LAS VEGAS AREA The junior Olympic-size pool at **New Mexico Highlands University** is open to the public Monday through Friday. ~ 2118 8th Street, Las Vegas; 505-454-3073.

LOS ALAMOS AREA The **Larry Walkup Aquatic Center** has the highest altitude Olympic-size indoor pool in the nation (athletes use it for endurance training). It's open to the public for lap swimming. ~ 2760 Canyon Road, Los Alamos; 505-662-8170.

Don't be fooled by the seemingly dry New Mexico landscape: The mountains are situated in a moisture belt that in an average year receives more snow than the Colorado Rockies. When storm clouds part, be prepared for warm, sunny days in the high desert. The ski season runs from Thanksgiving through April, weather permitting, but may vary from resort to resort.

SKIING

SANTA FE How many capital cities have a full-service ski area within a 30-minute drive? **Ski Santa Fe**, located up the winding, twisting Hyde Park/Ski Basin Road, 17 miles northeast of the Plaza, has six lifts and 43 trails— 20 percent beginner, 40 percent intermediate and 40 percent advanced—covering 550 skiable acres with a vertical drop of 1650 feet. There are no limits on snowboarding. Ski and snowboard rentals and lessons for children and adults are available. ~ Route 475; 505-982-4429, fax 505-986-0645; www.skisantafe.com.

> The Santa Fe Ski Basin is the most heavily traveled trailhead for access to the vast, rugged expanse of the Pecos Wilderness.

The **Santa Fe Nordic Ski Area**, located just west of Ski Basin Road about two miles from the downhill ski slopes, is groomed by a local ski club to offer an array of cross-country ski challenges designed for racing practice but suitable for all skill levels. ~ Santa Fe National Forest, Vegas District; 505-425-3534.

LOS ALAMOS AREA **Pajarito Mountain Ski Area**, located eight miles west of Los Alamos up a startlingly steep paved road, is one of the state's least-known large ski areas, with 37 trails and a 1200-foot vertical drop. Across the road a free, groomed ten-kilometer course takes cross-country skiers into the high meadows of the Jemez Mountains. It operates Friday through Sunday from mid-December to mid-March. ~ Camp May Road; 505-662-5725; www.skipajarito.com, e-mail ski@skipajarito.com. Park Service rangers work with Los Alamos' local ski club to groom a cross-country ski area on the west edge of **Bandelier National Monument**. Though less than three miles long, the trail offers deep snow and dramatic scenery, climaxing in a thrill-a-second run along the canyon rim. ~ Route 4; 505-672-3861, fax 505-672-9607; www. nps.gov/band.

CHAMA AREA   In Chama, the community-trail system maintains nearly four miles of groomed cross-country tracks in the **Rio Grande National Forest**.

There's cross-country skiing along the six-mile service road running from Aspen Vista picnic area on the Ski Basin Road to the broadcast towers on the 12,000-foot summit of Lake Peak. (In the summer months a chairlift takes sightseers up to the top of the mountain.)

Between Taos and Santa Fe is the **Sipapu Ski Area**, with 31 trails and four lifts with a vertical drop of 1065 feet. Ski and snowboard rentals are available. ~ Route 518, Vadito; 505-587-2240.

Ski Rentals   For Nordic and alpine skis, snowboards and snowshoes, try **Alpine Sports**. Closed Sunday from April to November. ~ 121 Sandoval Street, Santa Fe; 505-983-5155. Telemark, cross-country ski and snowshoe rentals, backcountry supplies and repairs, and maps of the Cumbres Pass are available through **Chama Ski Service**. Closed mid-April through November. ~ 1551 Alamo Drive, Chama; 505-756-2492.

GOLF

Believe it or not, the New Mexico desert harbors great golfing. Lush courses provide a cool respite from summer heat and primo playing conditions even in the dead of winter. (And there's no charge for the fabulous scenery.) Most courses have club and cart rentals as well as a resident pro.

SANTA FE   Practice your swing on the 18-hole semiprivate course or driving range at the **Santa Fe Country Club**. ~ 1000 Country Club Drive; 505-471-0601. The public **Marty Sanchez Links de Santa Fe** has both an 18-hole championship course and a par-3, 9-hole course offering mountain views. A driving range, putting green and pro shop are additional features. ~ 205 Caja del Rio; 505-955-4400.

LAS VEGAS AREA   In Las Vegas, tee off at **New Mexico Highlands University Golf Course**, a nine-hole course that is open to the public. They also have a driving range. ~ East Mills Avenue and Country Club Drive; 505-425-7711.

LOS ALAMOS AREA   Duffers in Los Alamos play at the **Los Alamos Golf Club**, one of the first 18-hole golf courses in New Mexico. ~ 4250 Diamond Drive; 505-662-8139.

TENNIS

There's plenty of space to serve and volley in the Enchanted Circle. Hit one of the area sports stores and head for the parks.

SANTA FE Santa Fe vacationers can take a swing at any of several municipal courts—**Atalaya Park** (717 Camino Cabra; two courts), the **Fort Marcy Complex** (Old Taos Highway and Morales Road; two courts) and **Larragoite Park** (Agua Fria Street and Avenida Cristobal Colon; two courts). All have hard-surface public courts for daylight use only, first-come, first-served. **Alto Park** (1121 Alto Street), **Herb Martínez/La Resolana Park** (2240 Camino Carlos Rey) and **Salvador Pérez Park** (610 Alta Vista Street) have four lighted courts each. Court information is available at 505-955-2100.

Cyclists often outnumber cars on Route 4, the Los Alamos area's breathtaking (in more ways than one) paved two-lane highway.

LOS ALAMOS AREA In Los Alamos, there are four hard-surface lighted courts at **Urban Park** (48th and Urban streets) and two unlit courts at **Canyon Road Tennis Courts** (Canyon Road and 15th Street) and three unlit courts at **Barranca Park** (Barranca Road and Loma de Escolar). ~ 505-662-8170.

Wondering how to acquire that true Western swagger? Hop in the saddle and ride the range—or just take a lesson—with one of the several outfitters in the area.

RIDING STABLES

SANTA FE For a unique riding experience, the **Broken Saddle Riding Company** offers one- to three-hour small group tours of the Cerrillos Hills, site of historic turquoise and silver mines, on well-trained Tennessee Walkers and Missouri Fox Trotters. ~ Cerrillos; 505-424-7774; www.brokensaddle.com.

ROAD TO TAOS You can saddle up at **Bishop's Lodge**, where daily guided trail rides follow Tesuque Creek into the Sangre de Cristo foothills. ~ Bishop's Lodge Road, Santa Fe; 505-983-6377, fax 505-989-8739; www.bishopslodge.com. **Vallecitos Stables** offers two- to five-hour guided trail rides through mountain meadows and forests. ~ P.O. Box 1214, Vallecitos, NM 87581; 505-582-4221, 800-797-7261; www.vallecitosstables.com.

LAS VEGAS AREA Tererro Riding Stables offers one-hour to all-day guided trips (lunch not provided) into the Pecos Wilderness from mid-May to early September. ~ Box N, Tererro; 505-757-6193.

If you haven't noticed the high altitude yet, why not get in touch with your environment by going for a two-wheeled spin? You'll be amply rewarded for your huffing and puffing with breathtaking views.

BIKING

SANTA FE From the Santa Fe Plaza, pedal to **Ski Basin Road**, which takes cyclists up a windy and at times steep 17-mile two-lane road through heavily wooded national forest land to the Ski Santa Fe area. To enjoy a shorter trip at a more forgiving altitude (the ski area is at 10,400 feet), just ride the eight miles to Hyde State Park.

A killer ten-mile ride for mountain bikers starts north of the Picacho Hotel on St. Francis Drive, crosses Dead Man's Gulch and Camino La Tierra before heading into the foothills of **La Tierra**. Circle back to the hotel via Buckman Road.

The most spectacular mountain-bike trip in the Santa Fe area starts at **Aspen Vista**, on Ski Basin Road midway between Hyde Park and the ski area. A six-mile access road for the broadcast towers on top of 12,010-foot Tesuque Peak is off-limits to motor vehicles but open to cyclists. It offers a long climb through a shimmering aspen forest, ending with a panoramic view of the Pecos Wilderness from a perch at the edge of a sheer cliff that drops 2000 feet to inaccessible Santa Fe Lake. Coasting back down is a mountain bikers' thrill of a lifetime.

LAS VEGAS AREA   The jeep road that starts at the village of La Cueva, off Route 50 midway between Glorieta and Pecos, makes for a wonderful mountain bike trip climbing eight miles to the 10,199-foot summit of **Glorieta Baldy**. Also near Pecos, **Glorieta Mesa** is an "island in the sky" where nearly level national forest roads wander among stands of piñon and along thousand-foot cliffs above the Pecos River Valley; the only access road to the mesa top starts from the village of Rowe just off Route 25.

LOS ALAMOS AREA   Sweeping curves and roller-coaster hills make **Route 4** through White Rock to Bandelier National Monument the most popular paved-road cycle tour in the state. For a break from automobile traffic, detour onto the wide, paved bike trail that loops through the town of White Rock. Among the many unpaved Santa Fe National Forest roads suitable for mountain biking is the **St. Peter's Dome Road**, which starts from Route 4 at Valle Grande and follows the rim of the ancient volcano caldera south for nine miles to a mountaintop fire lookout at the edge of the Dome Wilderness. About five miles south of Jemez Springs, take Route 485, which cuts northwest for about ten miles through the hills and two narrow-gauge railroad tunnels. Join the Crimson Rock dirt road that follows the river up to **Fenton Lake State Park** and its headwaters. Once you get to Fenton Lake, there are miles of dirt roads within these environs.

Bike Rentals   In Santa Fe, **Sun Mountain Bike Rental**, located in El Centro, offers mountain-bike rentals, plus beginning to expert mountain-bike tours. Grab a latte from their espresso bar while suiting up. ~ 102 East Water Street; 505-982-8986; www. sunmountainbikeco.com.

HIKING   When it comes time to travel without wheels, rest assured that the hiking trails in this region offer plenty of incentive for lacing up your boots. Just outside the city limits of Santa Fe, national forest land beckons and the hiker can disappear almost immediately into the dozens of trails that dip around peaks and to mountain lakes. All distances listed are one way unless otherwise noted.

SANTA FE **Atalaya Trail** starts at a trailhead parking lot near St. John's College on Santa Fe's eastern edge and climbs 2000 feet in less than three miles to the summit of Atalaya Mountain. The higher you climb, the better the view of the city and the desert and mountains that surround it.

The **Winsor Trail** (9 to 14 miles) meanders from 7000 to 11,000 feet, sidling along Big Tesuque Creek. Start at the top of Ski Basin Road and traipse through stands of aspen and evergreen and, finally, above timberline to 12,000-foot-plus Santa Fe Baldy. If you prefer a longer hike, begin in Tesuque along the creek. The gentle Borrego Trail branches off of Winsor.

LAS VEGAS AREA A trail to **Hermit's Peak** (4 miles) gains nearly 3000 vertical feet after starting at 7500 feet. A narrow and rocky path, the view is spectacular. Find it by following Route 65 to the parking lot at El Porvenir, 15 miles northwest of Las Vegas.

LOS ALAMOS AREA The majority of Bandelier National Monument is considered undisturbed backcountry. Several forest fires have scorched areas of the plateau within the monument boundary. A large forest fire in 1996 burned a vast expanse of forest west of **Painted Cave** near the south boundary, a 12-mile backpacking expedition that takes all day one way. The tough six-mile trail to the ancient **Yapashi pueblo site** passes near a 1997 forest fire area in Lummis Canyon, then scales down one side and up the other of 600-foot-deep Alamo Canyon.

Plenty of gratification without a whole lot of effort is found on the **Main Loop Trail** (1 mile roundtrip) in Frijoles Canyon at Bandelier National Monument. Start from the visitors center and walk past the big kiva and the condominium-style dwelling (known as Long House) built into the canyon wall.

AUTHOR FAVORITE

Bandelier National Monument has miles of maintained hiking trails in a wilderness area known as **Tsankawi**, which is located in a separate section of the monument. Tsankawi is accessible by a 1.5-mile loop trail that winds through lush piñon-juniper woodland, past petroglyphs to a high mesa and the unexcavated Tsankawi Ruins, a condo-style site and nearby cliff dwellings. The trail provides spectacular views of the Española Valley.
~ The trailhead is near the intersection of Routes 4 and 502.

Trail to the Falls (1.5 miles) crosses Rio de los Frijoles, follows the creek and passes some impressive cliffs and tent rocks before arriving at the falls.

CHAMA AREA   Concealed among the stark badlands and sheer cliffs that surround Abiquiu are surrealistic landscapes of Georgia O'Keeffe's paintings. One of the most dramatic is Plaza Blanca, often called The White Place, a maze of deep arroyos with a trail that winds between weird gypsum spires and hoodoos for about three miles.

▼▼▼▼▼▼▼▼▼▼▼
Transportation

CAR

Route 25 is the favored north–south road through New Mexico, accessing Las Vegas and Santa Fe. Route 68 heads south from Taos to Santa Fe, while Route 285/84 heads north from Santa Fe through Española all the way to Chama and the New Mexico/Colorado border.

Route 64 skirts across the northern edge of New Mexico passing through the Four Corners Area and across to Chama. For New Mexico road conditions, call 800-432-4269.

AIR

Most visitors to the Santa Fe area fly into Albuquerque (see "Transportation" in Chapter Five). Santa Fe Municipal Airport (505-955-2900) has daily flights via United Express (800-241-6522) from Denver, Colorado. Sandia Shuttle Express (888-775-5696), and Herrera Santa Fe Shuttle (888-833-2300) offer service between the Albuquerque Airport and Santa Fe.

BUS

TNM&O Coaches services Santa Fe and Las Vegas. ~ 858 St. Michaels Drive, Santa Fe; 505-471-0008.

TRAIN

Amtrak serves Santa Fe via the village of Lamy, 17 miles from town. ~ 800-872-7245; www.amtrak.com. The Lamy Shuttle can take you into Santa Fe. Reservations required. ~ 505-982-8829.

CAR RENTALS

Avis Rent A Car (800-831-2847) has offices both at the Santa Fe airport and in town. Hertz Rent A Car (800-654-3131) has an office at the airport. Enterprise Rent A Car (800-325-8007) offers free shuttle service from the airport. Budget Rent A Car (800-527-0700) has an office in town.

PUBLIC TRANSIT

With their chic tan and turquoise paint jobs designed by local artist Sally Blakemore, the natural gas–propelled Santa Fe Trails buses are an excellent way to navigate Santa Fe. Bus #10 takes you from the downtown area to the Indian Arts, Folk Art and Wheelwright museums as well as to St. John's College. Route #2 serves the crop of motels along Cerrillos Road and continues to the Villa Linda Mall, located on the far west side of town. This bus also makes it possible to avoid nasty downtown parking problems by leaving your vehicle at the De Vargas Mall (Guadalupe Street at Paseo de Peralta) and taking a five-minute bus ride downtown. Buses run every half hour from 6:30 a.m. to 10 p.m. weekdays, 8 a.m. to 7:30 p.m. on Saturday on all routes; no service on Sunday. ~ 505-955-2003, 505-955-2001.

In Los Alamos, the **Los Alamos Bus System** provides regularly scheduled bus service on a variety of routes. No weekend service. ~ 505-662-2080.

TAXIS

Santa Fe's only taxi service is **Capital City Cab Co.** ~ 505-438-0000.

WALKING TOURS

Perhaps the most down-to-earth method of touring cities like Santa Fe and Taos is via a walking tour. Local guides provide rich historical and personal insight to their communities as you stroll ancient streets and narrow lanes. Most tours last about two to three hours and may include visits inside area museums. For information on tours, contact **Santa Fe Walks**. Reservations required. ~ Hotel St. Francis lobby, 210 Don Gaspar Avenue; 505-988-2774.

Afoot in Santa Fe conducts two-hour morning jaunts. Fee includes admission to the Loretto Chapel. ~ Inn at Loretto, 211 Old Santa Fe Trail; 505-983-3701.

THREE

Taos and the Enchanted Circle

Painters Ernest Blumenschein and Bert Phillips were on their way to Mexico in 1898 when their wagon broke an axle and they found themselves stranded in Taos. In the end, however, it mattered very little. For in the people, the landscape and the crisp mountain light they found subject matter so compelling that their paintings inspired a generation of artists from the East and Europe to follow in their talented footsteps.

The Sangre de Cristo Mountains ("Blood of Christ") abut the town of Taos, which sits at an altitude of nearly 8000 feet above sea level on the east, and the Rio Grande River forms the city's western boundary. The Enchanted Circle is the name commonly given to an 80-mile loop route from Taos that crosses the crest of the Sangre de Cristos and circles all four sides of Wheeler Peak (elevation 13,161 feet), the highest mountain in New Mexico. The drive along the Enchanted Circle affords incomparable vistas of the heart of the high country, perspectives that could hardly help but inspire great works of art.

By the 1920s, Taos enjoyed a reputation as one of the greatest artists' colonies in America, thanks in large part to the sponsorship of local grand dame Mabel Dodge Luhan, a flamboyant New York heiress who married a man from Taos Pueblo and invited guests such as D. H. Lawrence, Georgia O'Keeffe, Ansel Adams, Willa Cather and Aldous Huxley to visit. (Her house is now a bed-and-breakfast inn.)

In the late 1960s, Taos gained brief notoriety for its hippie communes, where young people from the city joined in attempts to return to the Pueblo Indian way of life. Clearing the land and building communal homes of adobe, they sought to create a simple lifestyle in tune with nature. Simple it wasn't. Besides the hard physical labor they experienced, these freewheeling pioneers had to cultivate their own food, debate communal politics and wrestle with the problems and possibilities of their newfound sexual freedom. Life became a grand experiment. The old-time communes were revealed to the outside world in former Taos filmmaker Dennis Hopper's '60s epic *Easy Rider*. Soon over 3000 hippies set up house in the Taos area. Although the days of drugs and free love have long since vanished, the pursuit of spiritual enlightenment remains a strong force here.

But the fact that artists and idealists have taken to this part of New Mexico has hardly disrupted the deep cultural traditions that have characterized this area for thousands of years. Powwows, for instance, began in the days when Taos was one of the most distant outposts of the Rio Grande Pueblo Indians. These intertribal gatherings provided opportunities for trade, dancing and politics between the Pueblo Indians and the nomadic Arapahoe and Ute people who roamed the plains and mountains to the north. Today, powwows at Taos Pueblo attract participants from as far away as Canada. The pueblo itself draws throngs of non-Indian travelers from around the world each year to see this tiny, five-story town where the residents continue to live without electricity or running water in accordance with ancient custom.

After the first Spanish settlers came, Taos served as a marketplace for trade between the colonists and the Indians. In the 1820s, it became the outpost where mountain men emerged from the southern Colorado Rockies to trade for supplies. (At least one legendary frontiersman, Kit Carson, settled down in Taos, where he lived out his later years as one of the few Anglos in the Spanish and Indian community.) Today, tourism is the town's main industry. It seems that Taos residents (native Pueblo people, descendants of Spanish settlers and contemporary artists and sculptors alike) still support themselves in the same time-honored traditions— trading with visitors from the outside world.

Taos Area

Just as Santa Fe is a unique city, with all the social and economic complexity that term implies, Taos (population 6200) is a unique small town, not exactly easy to understand but certainly direct in its unconventionality. Painters and writers form the backbone of this peaceful yet eccentric frontier outpost, where American Indians, graying hippies and Spanish villagers alike walk in extraordinary beauty. The hodgepodge of architectural styles—Victorian-era frame houses, now stuccoed over in hues of tan, clustered with adobe haciendas from the Spanish Colonial period and Indian houses stacked like honeycombs—only serves to enhance the town's compelling landscape.

SIGHTS

Surrounded by mesas, canyons and mountain peaks, Taos has plenty of outdoor recreation year-round. The Taos Box, a wilderness canyon through which the Rio Grande tumbles and roars, offers plenty of whitewater rafting in early summer. Visitors who rent horses from the stables at Taos Pueblo can ride into the reservation's forested mountain highlands, which are otherwise off-limits to non-Indians. Hikers and backpackers find an alpine wonderland among the 13,000-foot summits of the Wheeler Peak area. For those who prefer more conventional sports, the biggest challenge to playing any of the area's golf courses and tennis courts is focusing on the ball instead of the stunning mountain scenery.

Given the superb natural setting, it's ironic that stifling grid-lock and auto pollution plague Taos' main artery, Paseo del Pueblo, in all but the slowest seasons. But there's really no other way to get to Taos, and given the large local opposition to airport expansion, it could remain this way for a while. So be ecologically minded, leave your car at your residence and walk around the compact commercial core.

The **Historic Taos Plaza**, as is true in so many Southwestern towns, is its lifeblood. The Plaza has for centuries remained the commercial center for tourism and throughout the centuries, three flags—Spanish, American and Mexican—have flown over the stucco buildings. Plaza galleries and shops merit at least a day's visit. You can pick up sightseeing information at the **Taos Chamber of Commerce**. ~ 1139 Paseo del Pueblo Sur; 505-758-3873, 800-732-8267, fax 505-758-3872; www.taoschamber.com, e-mail info@taoschamber.com.

Kit Carson Park is a 25-acre verdant park in the center of town that houses the grave of frontiersman Kit Carson. There are picnic areas, a playground and restrooms. ~ 211 Paseo del Pueblo Norte, Taos; 505-758-8234, fax 505-758-2493.

The following six museums can be visited with one discounted ticket (available at all locations) that's both transferable and good for one year:

Mountain man and scout Kit Carson purchased half of a 12-room adobe home in 1843 as a wedding gift for his bride, Josefa Jaramillo. Today the **Kit Carson Home and Museum** showcases the Old West, with a living room, bedroom and kitchen that re-create the period when Carson's family lived there. There is also a gun exhibit. Admission. ~ Kit Carson Road, Taos; 505-758-4741, fax 505-758-0330; www.taosmuseums.org.

Blending the sophistication of European charm with a classic Taos adobe, the **E. L. Blumenschein Home and Museum** showcases the paintings of Blumenschein (a co-founder of the Taos Society of Artists); his wife, Mary Greene Blumenschein; their daughter, Helen; and many other Taos artists. The fully restored home, built in the late 1700s, is filled with furnishings from the early 20th century, as well as European antiques. Admission. ~ 222 Ledoux Street, Taos; 505-758-0505, fax 505-758-0330; www.taosmuseums.org.

Two blocks southwest of the Plaza, at the west end of historic Ledoux Street, is the **Harwood Museum**, New Mexico's second-oldest museum. A Pueblo Revival–style adobe compound, the Harwood showcases the brilliant work of the Taos Society of Artists, core of the local artists' colony. It also includes the octagonal Agnes Martin Gallery, featuring work by the internationally acclaimed artist and Taos resident. The museum's collection of 19th-century *retablos* (religious paintings on wood) will also fas-

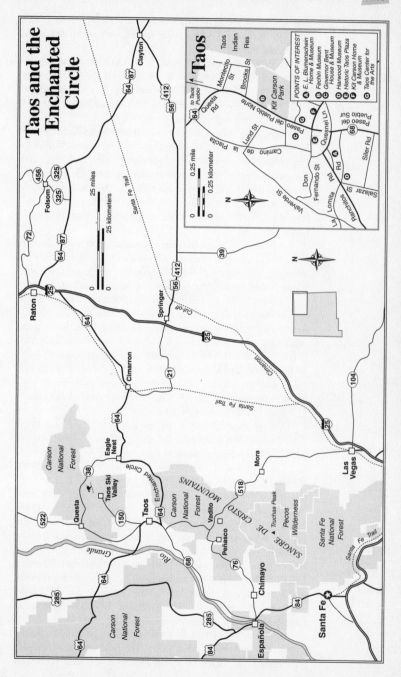

Taos and the Enchanted Circle

Taos

POINTS OF INTEREST

Ⓐ E. L. Blumenschein Home & Museum
Ⓑ Fechin Museum
Ⓒ Governor Bent House & Museum
Ⓓ Harwood Museum
Ⓔ Historic Taos Plaza
Ⓕ Kit Carson Home & Museum
Ⓖ Taos Center for the Arts

cinate. Closed Monday. Admission. ~ 238 Ledoux Street, Taos; 505-758-9826, fax 505-758-1475; www.taosmuseums.org, e-mail harwood@unm.edu.

The **Fechin Museum/Institute** is full of handcarved woodwork in the former adobe of Russian artist Nicolai Fechin, who also designed the building. Closed Monday and Tuesday. Admission. ~ 227 Paseo del Pueblo Norte, Taos; 505-758-1710, fax 505-758-9826; www.taosmuseums.org.

American Indian and Hispanic art fill the **Millicent Rogers Museum**, a memorial to the late Standard Oil heiress. Within the 15 galleries are rare examples of jewelry, textiles, basketry, paintings and pottery, as well as some exhibits by contemporary artists. Closed Monday from November through March. Admission. ~ Off Route 522, four miles north of Taos Plaza; 505-758-2462, fax 505-758-5751; www.millicentrogers.org, e-mail mrm@milli centrogers.org.

South of Taos at the **Martinez Hacienda**, you might discover craftsmen chinking the dark wooden walls of a sheep barn to ward off winter's cold. One of the only fully restored Spanish Colonial adobe haciendas in New Mexico, the fortresslike home is constantly being replastered to maintain its structural integrity. Inside, area artisans who perpetuate century-old skills through a living-history program demonstrate weaving, quilting, wood carving and other folk arts. Admission. ~ Ranchitos Road, Route 240; 505-758-1000, fax 505-758-0330; www.taosmuseums.org.

Governor Bent House and Museum has American Indian artifacts and war-era memorabilia from the first governor of New Mexico. It's worth about 15 minutes of your time. Admission. ~ 117 Bent Street, Taos; 505-758-2376.

Three miles north of the city, the distant past endures at the **Taos Pueblo**, the northernmost of all pueblos. These original adobe buildings appear much as they did when Spanish explorers first viewed them in 1540. This village is a First Living World Heritage Site and follows traditional ways, with no electricity or running water for the remaining families living in the pueblo buildings. Food is sometimes cooked in an outdoor *horno* (oven) and water is drawn from the river that breeches the heart of the pueblo. Local artisans sell mica-flecked pottery, silver jewelry, moccasins, boots and drums here. Authentic Indian fry bread, hot and drizzled with honey, is a firsthand way to sample American Indian cooking. Since the pueblo closes occasionally for ceremonial purposes, call ahead. Admission; camera and artist sketching fees. ~ Route 64; 505-758-1028, fax 505-758-4604; www.taospueblo.com, e-mail tourism@taospueblo.com.

Just north of the turnoff to the pueblo turn right on Route 150 for a trip to the **Taos Ski Valley**. The road rises and rolls past churches and tiny hotels through the sleepy towns of Arroyo Seco

and Valdez. Making the 12-mile trip at dusk, when the lig
flects from the aspen trees in ever-changing hues, can be a
ical experience.

Located south of the historic district, the **Sagebrush Inn**
just like any other Pueblo-style hotel from the outside. But open
the hefty front door and it's a totally different world. Rooms are
dark and romantic, usually decorated with Navajo rugs and pottery and equipped with fireplaces. A pool and hot tubs are nice
amenities. Breakfast is included. ~ 1508 Paseo del Pueblo Sur, Taos;
505-758-2254, 800-428-3626, fax 505-758-5077; www.sagebrush
inn.com, e-mail sagebrush@newmex.com. MODERATE TO DELUXE.

Distinctive Pueblo-style architecture marks the **Holiday Inn
Don Fernando de Taos**. Rooms are designed around central courtyards and connected by walkways that meander through landscaped grounds. Standard rooms are oversized, while suites have
living rooms, fireplaces and hospitality bars. All feature Southwestern styles, including hand-carved New Mexican furniture. A

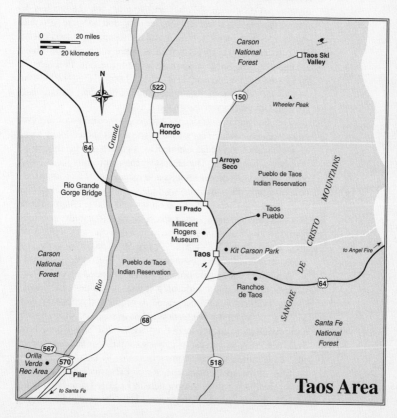

Taos Area

large heated pool, a hot tub, a tennis court and an on-site restaurant and lounge add to the friendly ambience. Complimentary shuttle service within a five-mile radius is offered. ~ 1005 Paseo del Pueblo Sur, Taos; 505-758-4444, 800-759-2736, fax 505-758-0055; www.holiday-taos.com, e-mail holiday@newmex.com. DELUXE.

From the friendly "welcome home" greeting by the front-desk clerk to the hearty skillet breakfasts, the **Ramada Inn of Taos** is big on comfort and warmth. Refurbished in nouvelle-adobe style and pastel colors, the Ramada capably handles groups—even in the hot tub, where après ski is often shoulder to shoulder—without neglecting individuals. There's an indoor swimming pool. ~ 615 Paseo del Pueblo Sur, Taos; 505-758-2900, 800-659-8267, fax 505-758-1662. MODERATE TO DELUXE.

The most economical closed-in lodging in Taos is the **Best Value Indian Hills Inn–Taos Plaza**, a vintage pueblo-style hotel that dates back to the early 1900s with an annex of rooms added in 1997. Located just two blocks from the plaza, within walking distance of dozens of galleries and restaurants, the inn has 55 rooms, most facing a peaceful interior patio and one-acre yard with shade trees and picnic tables. Standard rooms have two queen-size beds and typical motel amenities, while upgrade rooms have a king-size bed, Southwestern-style furniture and fireplaces. ~ 233 Paseo del Pueblo Sur, Taos; phone/fax 505-758-4293, 800-444-2346; www.taosnet.com/indianhillsinn, e-mail indianhills@taosnet.com. BUDGET TO MODERATE.

Taos bed and breakfasts are extraordinary and becoming ever more popular. Hidden on a lovely lane about three blocks south of the Plaza is **Casa de las Chimeneas**, a guesthouse for those who love being pampered. The largest of the eight units has a living room with a collection of books and magazines. The rooms have oak furniture, tiled bathrooms and views of the formal garden and fountains. There's a hot tub on site and a large common area, as well as an exercise room, a spa, a sauna and laundry facilities. Breakfast and a buffet dinner are included in the rates. ~ 405 Cordoba Road, Taos; 505-758-4777, fax 505-758-3976; www.visit taos.com, e-mail casa@newmex.com. DELUXE TO ULTRA-DELUXE.

A hermit could easily hole up for an extended period of time in the **Sonterra Condominiums**, a special little side-street retreat. Quiet, comfortable and decorated in bright contemporary New Mexican style, all the Sonterra units have separate sitting spaces and private patios; three have fireplaces. ~ 206 Siler Road, Taos; 505-758-7989, 888-482-2042; www.sonterracondos.com, e-mail sonterra@sonterracondos.com. MODERATE TO DELUXE.

One of the area's original bed and breakfasts, **La Posada de Taos** provides a homey atmosphere in its huge book-filled living room and open, sunny dining room. The 100-year-old house has been lovingly remodeled with six guest units, each with tiled baths and antique furnishings. Five of the units are inside the inn itself, the sixth is a honeymoon cottage across the adobe-walled courtyard. All but the Taos Room sport private patios and kiva fireplaces; some have jacuzzi tubs. ~ 309 Juanita Lane, Taos; 505-758-8164, 800-645-4803, fax 505-751-3294; www.lapo sadadetaos.com, e-mail laposada@laposadadetaos.com. MODERATE TO DELUXE.

At least one legendary frontiersman, Kit Carson, settled down in Taos, where he lived out his later years as one of the few Anglos in the Spanish and Indian community.

La Doña Luz Inn is a remarkable inn with 14 units, each a treat in itself. Built around a patio overflowing with flowers, each room features a spiral staircase, *vigas*, an American Indian fireplace and cowboy motifs. The whimsical Sonrisa Room has a canopied bed with a wedding-ring quilt, while the Kit Carson Room has a log bed, a sitting room with a cast-iron wood-burning stove and a clawfoot tub in the bathroom. This inn includes a wheelchair-accessible unit. ~ 114 Kit Carson Road, Taos; 505-758-4874, 800-758-9187, fax 505-758-4541; www.ladonaluz.com, e-mail info@ladonaluz.com. BUDGET TO ULTRA-DELUXE.

Every room at **Casa Benavides Bed & Breakfast Inn** is unique, but they share a common quality—luxury. Several meticulously restored buildings, including an old trading post and an artist's studio, make up the 35-room complex. This crème de la crème property is elegantly furnished with tile floors, handmade furniture, kiva fireplaces, down comforters and a bevy of unusual antiques. The cost of a room includes a sumptuous breakfast served in a bright, airy dining room, and afternoon tea. The inn also has lavish gardens and two hot tubs, as well as a lovely art collection. ~ 137 Kit Carson Road, Taos; 505-758-1772, 800-552-1772, fax 505-758-5738; www.taos-casabenavides.com, e-mail casabena@ newmex.com. MODERATE TO ULTRA-DELUXE.

◄ HIDDEN

Mabel Dodge, Georgia O'Keeffe, Ansel Adams, D. H. Lawrence and Dennis Hopper were but a few of the inventive minds that spent quality time at the historic, Pueblo-style **Mabel Dodge Luhan House**. Located on a secluded street off Kit Carson Road, its nine rooms, a two-bedroom cottage and an adjacent eight-room guesthouse are charmingly decorated and offer ample opportunity to relax amid cottonwood and willow trees after a hard day of sightseeing. Reserve the glass-enclosed solarium for views of the Sacred Mountains; light up the kiva fireplace before curling up with a book on the hand-carved bed in Mabel's room. Full breakfast included. ~ 240 Morada Lane, Taos; 505-751-9686, 800-846-2235, fax 505-737-0365; www.mabeldodgeluhan.com, e-mail mabel@mabeldodgeluhan.com. MODERATE TO DELUXE.

Epicenter of Taos activity is the enormously popular **Historic Taos Inn**. A National Historic Landmark, the inn comprises several separate houses from the 1800s. Thirty-six rooms are decorated in a Southwestern motif with Mexican tile, locally designed furniture and hand-loomed Indian bedspreads; most have fireplaces. If the inn is booked, which it may very well be, set aside an evening to enjoy a drink in the lobby, which is as comfortable as any living room. A favorite hangout for locals, also known as "Taoseños," the inn's lobby is showplace to the recurring "Meet the Artist Series." ~ 125 Paseo del Pueblo Norte, Taos; 505-758-2233, 800-826-7466, fax 505-758-5776; www.taosinn.com, e-mail taosinn@newmex.com. MODERATE TO DELUXE.

Sharing six wooded acres with the Fechin Museum/Institute, the two-story **Fechin Inn** is a visual wonderland that pays tribute to the Russian-born artist and long-time Taos resident, Nicolai Fechin. The eye-catching hand-carved doors, woodwork and furniture reflect his unique style within a Southwestern framework of *viga* ceilings and stucco walls. Each guest suite displays prints of his paintings; most boast fireplaces, patios or balconies. Also on the grounds are a bar, an open-air hot tub and an exercise room. ~ 227 Paseo del Pueblo Norte, Taos; 505-751-1000, 800-811-2933, fax 505-751-7338; www.fechin-inn.com, e-mail info@fechin-inn.com. MODERATE TO ULTRA-DELUXE.

Certainly one of the finest bed and breakfasts in the state, **Hacienda del Sol** is a glorious adobe that epitomizes the Southwestern experience. The 11 guest rooms and *casitas* feature Spanish Colonial and American Indian decor, with twig screens and kiva fireplaces. Architectural touches include *viga* and *latilla* ceilings, stained glass and skylights. A shady stand of cottonwoods, pines, spruce and willow trees nicely blocks out nearby traffic noise. The hacienda is difficult to find, so call ahead for directions. ~ 109 Mabel Dodge Lane, Taos; 505-758-0287, fax

AUTHOR FAVORITE

The **Laughing Horse Inn** is a century-old hacienda transformed into a European-style pension. As the name implies, it helps to have a sense of humor when staying here: one guest room has chile pepper–motif lights and the inn's floor varies between old wood and varnished dirt. What it may lack in luxury, it more than makes up for in personality with its low *viga* ceilings, dirt floors polished with ox blood, and memorabilia from the early New Mexico literary-magazine publisher who had his printing press here. The communal kitchen offers light snacks for next-to-nothing prices. ~ 729 Paseo del Pueblo Norte, Taos; 505-758-8350, 800-776-0161, fax 505-751-1123; www.laughinghorseinn.com, e-mail laughing horse@laughinghorseinn.com. BUDGET TO DELUXE.

505-758-5895; www.taoshaciendadelsol.com, e-mail sunhouse@
newmex.com. MODERATE TO ULTRA-DELUXE.

Visit the **Dreamcatcher Bed and Breakfast**. Choose from a
room with a sunken bedroom or one with traditional *viga* furniture. Saltillo tile floors, kiva fireplaces, and private entrances also
characterize some of the seven quiet rooms. A hot tub is available and a full breakfast is included with a night's stay. ~ 416 La
Lomita Road, Taos; 505-758-0613, 888-758-0613, fax 505-751-
0115; www.dreambb.com, e-mail dream@taosnm.com. MODERATE
TO DELUXE.

It's hard not to get lost while walking around the compound
known as the **Quail Ridge Inn**. Low-slung buildings containing
fully equipped apartment-size rooms dot the landscape. A casual,
country-club variety of clientele clogs the pool, tennis and squash
courts and fitness center. The self-contained resort offers so many
on-site amenities and diversions that you need not ever leave the
complex, which would be a crying shame considering all there is to
see in Taos. Rates sometimes include breakfast. ~ Taos Ski Valley
Road, Taos; 505-776-2211, 800-624-4448, fax 505-776-2949;
www.quailridgeinn.com, e-mail quail@quailridgeinn.com. DELUXE.

Skiers, hikers and other adventuresome spirits looking for an
ultra-cheap experience should seek out the **Hostelling International
—Taos**, also known as the **Abominable Snowmansion**. The hostel
has seven dorm rooms (four can be converted into private family
rooms) with large closets, dressing areas, bathrooms and showers.
A piano, pool table, fireplace and conversation area are also available to guests. There are Indian tepees or a bunkhouse for additional sleeping arrangements. Camping is also allowed. Showers
and use of the kitchen are included in the price. ~ Taos Ski Valley
Road, Arroyo Seco; 505-776-8298, fax 505-776-2107; www.taos
webb.com/hotel/snowmansion, e-mail snowman@newmex.com.
BUDGET.

Close to the Taos Ski Area, with outrageous views of the Sangre de Cristo Mountains, is luxurious **Salsa del Salto**. Goose-down
comforters warm the king-size beds. Leather couches in the common area are placed in front of the two-story stone fireplace—a
good place for getting horizontal after a long day on Taos' tough
slopes. The pool, tennis courts and hot tub help take the edge off
as well. Guests rave about the omelettes served here. ~ Route 150,
one mile north of Arroyo Seco; 505-776-2422, 800-530-3097,
fax 505-776-5734; www.bandbtaos.com, e-mail salsa@taosnm.
com. DELUXE TO ULTRA-DELUXE.

If long days of skiing and multicourse meals are enough to sat-
isfy you, consider a stay in the Taos Ski Valley at one of several
European-flavored lodges like the simple but comfortable **Hotel
St. Bernard**. Location, location, location and a family atmosphere

prevail at this 28-room chalet-style dwelling. Reservations are usually made by the week only; all meals are included in the price. Closed early April through Thanksgiving. ~ Taos Ski Valley Road, Taos; 505-776-2251, fax 505-776-5790; www.stbernardtaos.com, e-mail stbtaos@newmex.com. DELUXE.

Located about one and a half miles from the ski area is the **Austing Haus B&B**, the largest timber-frame building in North America. As the name implies, this charming 24-unit bed and breakfast has an Austrian ambience. The glass dining room (open in winter only) is truly elegant. Closed mid-April to mid-May. ~ Taos Ski Valley Road, Taos; 505-776-2649, 800-748-2932, fax 505-776-8751; www.taoswebb.com/hotel/austinghaus, e-mail austing@newmex.com. DELUXE.

DINING

Lamb entrées top the list of house specialties at **Lambert's of Taos**. Established in 1989 by the former chef at Doc Martin's, Lambert's serves imaginative presentations of mahimahi, salmon, swordfish and other fresh seafood in the parlor rooms of a refurbished Territorial-era house that exudes an atmosphere of gracious frontier living. The menu also includes beef, veal and poultry selections. Dinner only. ~ 309 Paseo del Pueblo Sur, Taos; 505-758-1009. MODERATE TO DELUXE.

Pizza Emergency has great New York–style pizza and a name you won't quickly forget. Also on the menu are baked pastas, hot submarine sandwiches and salads. They have free delivery in the Taos area, but only until 9:30 p.m.—well before the pizza bug typically strikes. ~ 316 Paseo del Pueblo Sur, Taos; 505-751-0911. BUDGET TO MODERATE.

For basic, traditional Mexican fare that's wildly popular with the locals, stop by **Guadalajara Grill**. Burritos, tacos and seafood plates number among many other dishes from the to-go counter at this fast food–style restaurant. ~ 1384 Paseo de Pueblo Sur, Taos; 505-751-1450. BUDGET.

HIDDEN ▶

Delicious whole-grain breads and fresh-squeezed juices (plus tarts to undo all the good you've put in your body) are common at the **Main Street Bakery**, specializing in vegetarian and vegan fare. If you're shy about garlic, don't order the home-style potatoes. This is a great place to catch up on local gossip. Breakfast and lunch weekdays, breakfast until 12:30 p.m. on weekends. ~ 112 Doña Luz Road, Taos; 505-758-9610. BUDGET.

Housed in an old adobe building, **Roberto's** offers Northern New Mexican cuisine. The menu features tacos, enchiladas, homemade tamales and *chiles rellenos*. Dinner only. Closed Tuesday in summer; closed every day but weekends and holidays November and December. ~ 122-B Kit Carson Road, Taos; 505-758-2434. MODERATE.

Taos Counterculture Lives On

Back in the 1960s, young people from all over the country abandoned city life and migrated to the mountains of New Mexico. Soon, over 3000 hippies set up house in the Taos area.

Clearing the land and building communal homes of adobe, they sought to create a simple lifestyle in tune with nature. Simple it wasn't. Besides the hard physical labor they experienced, these freewheeling pioneers had to cultivate their own food, debate communal politics and wrestle with the problems and possibilities of their newfound sexual freedom. Life became a grand experiment.

In the forefront of this back-to-the-land movement, the New Buffalo Commune in Arroyo Hondo north of Taos was featured in *Look* and *Life* magazines, as well as *Playboy*, *Newsweek* and *Esquire*. Actor-filmmaker Dennis Hopper chose it as the location for an idyllic segment of the movie *Easy Rider*. Craft industries and spiritual connections thrived here—but it was the nudity, rock-and-roll and drugs that made the headlines. By the 1980s, the commune had collapsed, and in 1989 it was converted into the New Buffalo Bed & Breakfast.

Not far away, the commune of Lama was founded by a utopian sect under the leadership of psychologist-turned-guru Baba Ram Dass. Formerly known as Dr. Richard Alpert, he had taught at—and been fired from—Harvard alongside Timothy Leary. But while Leary became an outspoken LSD advocate, Ram Dass took a different path, retreating to the New Mexico mountains to practice Buddhist meditation with a select group of followers. Lama grew into a villagelike, family-oriented spiritual community that endured a 1996 forest fire, which destroyed everything except the central dome housing the library, a meditation kiva and a ceremonial area.

After the fire, New Buffalo threw open its guest rooms to the homeless residents of Lama. In doing so, the owners forfeited their summer tourist trade, and the bed and breakfast went out of business. **New Buffalo Bed & Breakfast** reopened in 2002 with fine guest accommodations (shared bath) in a traditional-style adobe compound, two greenhouses and loads of charm and culture. ~ P.O. Box 257, Arroyo Hondo, NM 87513; 505-776-2015; www. newbuffalotaos.com, e-mail info@newbuffalotaos.com. BUDGET TO MODERATE.

Although the days of drugs and free love have long since vanished, the pursuit of spiritual enlightenment remains a strong force in the Taos area. Baba Ram Dass worked tirelessly raising funds to rebuild Lama until he suffered a disabling stroke in 1997. ~ 505-758-8622, fax 505-556-1964; www.lama foundation.org, e-mail info@lamafoundation.org.

Caffe Tazza, a newsstand café, makes for a wonderful stop in the middle of the day. ~ 122 Kit Carson Road, Taos; 505-758-8706. BUDGET.

You could eat three meals a day in the award-winning **Doc Martin's** and never get bored. Blue-corn and blueberry hotcakes at breakfast make the mouth water, as does potato gnocchi with sun-dried tomatoes for lunch. But it's at dinnertime when the kitchen really shines. Savor the grilled pork tenderloin with tomato jam and specials like the piñon-crusted salmon with pesto and try to save room for dessert. ~ 125 Paseo del Pueblo Norte, Taos; 505-758-1977, fax 505-758-5776; www.taosinn. com. MODERATE TO ULTRA-DELUXE.

The funky sign on local institution **Michael's Kitchen** might grab you, but the sweets' cabinet could lock you into a stranglehold. Spill-off-your-plate-size breakfasts pack 'em in on ski mornings; diner-type meals are served the rest of the day. Closed November. ~ 304 Paseo del Pueblo Norte, Taos; 505-758-4178; www.michaelskitchen.com, e-mail ninneman@michaelskitchen. com. MODERATE.

The emphasis is on fresh at the **Apple Tree**, a charming house converted into a restaurant. The Apple Tree offers innovative interpretations of standard poultry, fish and meat dishes. Killer desserts top off the menu. ~ 123 Bent Street, Taos; 505-758-1900; e-mail appletree@newmex.com. MODERATE.

With the best view in town of the central plaza from its second-story balcony, **Ogelvie's** serves such Southwest Nouveau cuisine as trout piñon and garlic and pepper ribeye steaks. Traditional New Mexican dishes such as *quesadillas* and chicken or beef fajitas are also served in this dimly lit restaurant and lounge. ~ 103-I East Plaza, Taos; 505-758-8866, fax 505-758-0728. MODERATE TO DELUXE.

Just north of Taos, **Orlando's New Mexican Café** is a tiny, family-owned eatery that manages to stand out in a sea of restaurants also offering New Mexican cuisine. Its simple, home-cooked

AUTHOR FAVORITE

Fine dining is one of my passions, and in my subjective opinion the finest in Taos is at **Joseph's Table**. Candlelight and frescoed walls set the stage for outstanding cuisine at this chef-owned restaurant. The menu, which changes daily, emphasizes organic ingredients. A typical dinner might be an appetizer of New Mexico squash blossoms stuffed with crab and buffalo mozzarella, followed by an entrée of apricot rosemary–glazed salmon. Dinner only. ~ 4167 Paseo del Pueblo Sur, Ranchos de Taos; 505-751-4512. DELUXE TO ULTRA-DELUXE.

meals, prepared with local ingredients, are just like grandma's. Classic offerings include chilis, enchiladas and burritos. No lunch on Sunday. ~ 1114 Don Juan Valdez Lane, El Prado; 505-751-1450. MODERATE.

Momentitos de la Vida Restaurant is simply delicious. The New American cuisine is prepared with fresh, organic ingredients whenever possible. Menu recommendations (and it's all recommended) include the blue crabcakes appetizer, goat cheese and warm pear salad, and the Madras prawns (shrimp on basmati rice with apple curry butter and almonds). The kitchen will gladly whip up unlisted delights to satisfy any type of dietary restrictions. And you'll be sure to find the perfect accompaniment from their extensive wine list. ~ 474 Route 150, Arroyo Seco; 505-776-3333; e-mail vida@newmex.com. MODERATE TO ULTRA-DELUXE.

For outstanding margaritas, *chiles rellenos*, blue-corn tortillas and other regional food plus Caribbean seafood specialties and fish tacos, try the **Old Blinking Light Restaurant**. And did I mention the margaritas? Dinner only. ~ Mile Marker 1, Taos Ski Valley Road, four miles north of Taos; 505-776-8787; e-mail mike@theoldblinkinglight.com. MODERATE.

Sate après-ski hunger by moseying on down the hill to **Tim's Stray Dog Cantina**. Quaff multiple varieties of margaritas served in pitchers while chowing down on the rich tequila shrimp, homemade green-chile stew and mud pie that will push your cholesterol count right off the Richter scale. ~ Cottam's Alpine Village, Taos Ski Area; 505-776-2894, fax 505-776-1350. BUDGET TO MODERATE.

The Taos "mystique" has always lured artists and craftsmen, so expect to find lots of shops and galleries around the Plaza and surrounding streets.

SHOPPING

For a deal on moccasins, stop by the **Taos Moccasin Company**. ~ 216 Paseo del Pueblo Sur; 505-751-0032. **Old Taos Traders** is a traditional favorite for Mexican imports. ~ 127 North Plaza, Taos; 505-758-1133.

Antiques and beautiful oriental rugs fill the front and back yards of **Patrick Dunbar Colonial Antiques**, which is interesting to visit even if you can't afford a single thing. Closed Sunday in winter. ~ 222 Paseo del Pueblo Norte, Taos; 505-758-2511.

Touristy, yes, but wonderful too, is R. C. Gorman's **Navajo Gallery**, which specializes in Gorman's paintings and sculpture of Navajo women. ~ 210 Ledoux Street, Taos; 505-758-3250; www.rcgormangallery.com.

Taos has a plethora of art galleries. Here's a sampling of what you'll find. **The Clay and Fiber Gallery** has beautiful bowls, jewelry and textiles. Closed Sunday in winter. ~ 201 Paseo del Pueblo Sur; 505-758-8093. The **New Directions Gallery** specializes in contemporary Taos painting and sculpture. Closed Sunday in winter. ~ 107-B North Plaza, Taos; 505-758-2771. Another gallery that merits a visit is **Wade Gallery of Taos**. Closed Monday and Tuesday. ~ 208 Paseo del Pueblo Norte; 505-758-7500.

There are many great bookstores in Taos. A favorite is **Moby Dickens Bookshop**, which has plenty of places to sit and read. A cat guards the door. ~ 124-A Bent Street; 505-758-3050. **Brodsky Bookshop** has lots of new and used American Indian and Southwestern titles as well as poetry and literature. Closed Sunday. ~ 226-A Paseo del Pueblo Norte; 505-758-9468. The **Taos Book Shop** purports to be the oldest book shop in the state. ~ 122-D Kit Carson Road; 505-758-3733.

Taos Artisans Gallery is an impressive cooperative of iron sculpture, jewelry, pottery and woven clothing. ~ 107-A Bent Street; 505-758-1558. Another gem of an art cooperative is **Open Space Gallery**, where more than a dozen local artists show their work. ~ 103-B East Plaza, Taos; 505-758-1217.

La Lana Wools uses fine natural fibers to make sweaters, coats, yarns and jackets. Native plants are used to dye the fiber. ~ 136 Paseo del Pueblo Norte, Taos; 505-758-9631. **Taos Mountain Outfitters** sells outdoor garb and equipment for trekking into the high country. ~ 114 South Plaza, Taos; 505-758-9292.

NIGHTLIFE To taste the local flavor or take a gander at the recurring local artists' series, swing by the **Taos Inn's Adobe Bar**. Jazz, flamenco and American Indian flute can be enjoyed several nights a week. ~ 125 Paseo del Pueblo Norte, Taos; 505-758-2233; www.taos inn.com, e-mail taosinn@newmex.com.

The **Taos Center for the Arts** hosts a wide variety of events ranging from films and music and dance performances to art shows that suit all tastes and ages. ~ 133 Paseo del Pueblo Norte, Taos; 505-758-2052, fax 505-751-3305; www.taoscenterforthe arts.org.

Hot times are had at the **Sagebrush Inn Bar**, with nightly live music and country-and-western dancing. No music Sunday and Monday. ~ 1508 Paseo del Pueblo Sur, Taos; 505-758-2254.

Taos' best sports bar, complete with brewpub and a boisterous crowd, is the **Old Blinking Light**, which occasionally features live music. Don't leave without trying a margarita. ~ Mile Marker 1, Ski Valley Road, Taos; 505-776-8787.

For a drink in the Taos Ski Valley, check out the margaritas at **Tim's Stray Dog Cantina**. ~ Cottam's Alpine Village, Taos Ski Area; 505-776-2894. Located just 150 yards from the main lift at the Taos Ski Area, the Thunderbird Lodge's **Twining Tavern** is another good bet. Closed mid-April to mid-December. ~ 3 Thunderbird Road; 505-776-2280.

CARSON NATIONAL FOREST 🚶 🚴 🏇 🎿 ⛵ The challenge of scaling Wheeler Peak, whose 13,161-foot summit is the highest point in New Mexico, brings mountaineers from all over the country. The lower, gentler mountains southeast of Taos, which local villagers have been using communally as a source of firewood and summer pasturage for centuries, contain hundreds of miles of rough forest roads, many of which are ideal for mountain-bike and four-wheel-drive adventures in the summer months and cross-country skiing in the winter season. Farther south, the 13,102-foot Truchas Peak crowns the roadless immensity of the Pecos Wilderness. Roads and amenities are closed January through April. ~ Accessed by Route 150 (Taos Ski Valley Road) and by Routes 518, 75 and 76 (collectively called the High Road to Taos); 505-758-6200, fax 505-758-6213; www.fs.fed.us/r3/carson.

PARK

The Taos economy in the late 16th century included slavery—Navajo warriors traded Hopi and Zuni captives for livestock.

▲ **Capulin** and **La Sombra Campgrounds**, located one half mile apart on Route 64 about seven miles east of Taos, have a total of 24 tent and RV sites (no hookups); $8 to $15 per night. Farther west, off of Route 518 near Tres Rito, **Agua Piedra** and **Duran Canyon Campgrounds** have a total of 56 campsites (no hookups); $8 to $15 per night. These campgrounds are closed October through April.

ORILLA VERDE RECREATION AREA 🚶 🚴 🛶 ⛵ Situated on the banks of an ultrascenic stretch of the Rio Grande, the park is renowned for its trout fishing but equally popular for day outings and weekend camping. The only facilities are picnic areas and restrooms. Day-use fee, $3. ~ Route 570, two miles north of Pilar; 505-758-8851, fax 505-758-1620.

▲ There are 32 campsites (no hookups); $7 per night. No water in winter.

The Enchanted Circle is the name given to the 84-mile loop formed by Routes 522, 38 and 64. From Taos, the paved route winds through subalpine evergreen forests around the base of Wheeler Peak, the highest mountain in New Mexico (elevation 13,161 feet). Along the way you'll find ski resorts, a recreational lake in a basin surrounded by mountain peaks, and a moving tribute to the men and women who served in the Vietnam War.

Enchanted Circle Area

On a hillside overlooking Eagle Nest Reservoir, midway through the Enchanted Circle tour (see "Driving Tour" in this chapter), the **Vietnam Veterans National Memorial** pays tribute to soldiers who fought in Vietnam. Set against the backdrop of the Sangre de Cristo Mountains, this 24-acre monument is one of the largest in

SIGHTS

the country. It includes a visitors center with extensive exhibits dedicated to the memory of those who lost their lives as well as access to computerized archives of KIA (killed in action) and MIA (missing in action) soldiers. There's also an interdenominational chapel on the premises. ~ Route 64, Angel Fire; 505-377-6900, fax 505-377-3223; www.vietnamveteransnationalmemorial.org, e-mail info@vietnamveteransnationalmemorial.org.

Just 11 miles southwest of Questa, where the Enchanted Circle tour rejoins the main highway, is the **Wild Rivers Recreation Area**, the ideal place to see the Rio Grande and Red River in their natural state. The Art Zimmerman Visitors Center features geologic exhibits, interpretive displays and rangers who will help you make the most of this scenic area. Most visitors flock to La Junta Point overlooking the junction of these free-flowing rivers. Self-guiding nature trails show you how the Rio Grande Gorge was etched out over the centuries by wind and water. The numerous hiking trails in this area include several steep climbs leading down to the water. Proceed with caution. Admission. ~ Route 378; 505-770-1600, 505-758-8851, fax 505-751-1620.

Thirteen miles south of Questa is the **D. H. Lawrence Ranch**, a memorial to the British writer built by his widow, Frieda. When Mabel Dodge Luhan gave the land that is now the D. H. Lawrence Ranch to the writer's wife, Frieda returned the favor with a gift: the original manuscript to *Sons and Lovers*. Now a field center for the University of New Mexico, it can be readily visited during the daytime hours. ~ Off Route 522, 15 miles north of Taos; 505-776-2245, fax 505-776-2408.

Another 13 miles south is the junction of Routes 522 and 64. Go west on Route 64 until you reach the **Rio Grande Gorge Bridge**. You may want to hold your breath while crossing this suspension bridge, 650 feet over the Rio Grande.

LODGING   Bring the family to the full-service **Angel Fire Resort Hotel**, where ultraspacious guest rooms, bedecked in pastel colors and Southwestern styles, offer plenty of closet space and can easily accommodate rollaway beds. ~ North Angel Fire Road, Angel Fire; 505-377-6401, 800-633-7463, fax 505-377-4200; www.angel fireresort.com, e-mail reserve@angelfireresort.com. MODERATE TO ULTRA-DELUXE.

Also in Angel Fire, the **Wildflower Bed & Breakfast** is a traditionally designed contemporary home with a wide front porch and sunny back deck area, both looking out on meadows that are full of colorful native flowers in the warm months. Second-floor dormers contain the five guest bedrooms, three with private baths. Perhaps the best part of a stay at this B&B is the gourmet breakfast, featuring such items as banana french toast, Swedish oatmeal pancakes and sourdough biscuits with eggs. There's a two-night minimum stay in winter. ~ P.O. Box 575 (40 Halo Pines Terrace), Angel Fire, NM 87710; 505-377-6869; www.angelfirenm.com/wildflower, e-mail wildflower@angelfirenm.com. MODERATE TO DELUXE.

The guest accommodations at **Cottonwood Lodge** are situated above the Enchanted Circle area's most unique gift store (items featured are chainsaw-carved). Each of the three units opens onto a conversation area, and each has a TV with VCR and a full kitchen with microwave and dishwasher; the rooms are furnished with antiques. The shore of Eagle Nest Reservoir is just a short walk away. ~ 124 East Therma Street, Eagle Nest; 505-377-3382, fax 505-377-2446; www.angelfirenm.com/cottonwood, e-mail cotton wood@angelfirenm.com. MODERATE.

Prices drop at the **Laguna Vista Lodge**, just 12 miles north of Angel Fire on the pretty road to Eagle Nest. Motel rooms and suites are available. ~ Route 64, Eagle Nest; 505-377-6522, 800-821-2093, fax 505-377-6626; www.lagunavistalodge.com, e-mail laguna@newmex.com. BUDGET TO MODERATE.

For a laidback vacation complete with rustic cabins, a small private fishing lake and easy access to the Red River, head for **Rio Colorado Lodge**. Paneled with tongue-and-groove knotty pine,

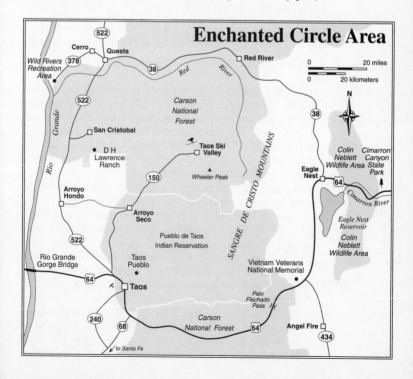

Enchanted Circle Area

The Enchanted Circle

The Enchanted Circle is the name given to the 84-mile loop formed by Routes 522, 38 and 64.

PALO FLECHADO PASS   Drive south of downtown Taos to Route 64 and cruise over scenic Palo Flechado Pass, which was used by American Indians and Spaniards who came from the plains via the Cimarron River. Along the way are several places to pull over for a picnic or snapshot.

ANGEL FIRE   Upon reaching the intersection of Route 434, turn south for a quick visit to the resort town of Angel Fire. In winter it's a favorite destination for intermediate skiers, while in summer, golfers, hikers and lovers of chamber music flock to Angel Fire.

WHEELER PEAK   Back on Route 64 you'll soon come to **Eagle Nest Reservoir**, a fine sailing, windsurfing and fishing lake that affords a spectacular lookout. Be sure to get a good look at Wheeler Peak, the state's highest peak at 13,161 feet above sea level.

EAGLE NEST   At the lake's north shore is the village of Eagle Nest, with a handful of restaurants and shops. From there it's 24 windy miles to

the 21 one- to three-bedroom units come with full kitchens and chenille bedspreads. Many offer fireplaces, and most are fully carpeted. Families especially appreciate the large picnic areas (with barbecue pits) and playground for the kids. ~ 515 East Main Street, Red River; 505-754-2212, 800-654-6516, fax 505-754-3063; www.redrivernm.com/riocolorado, e-mail riocolorado@redrivernm.com. BUDGET TO MODERATE.

A short walk to the ski slopes, **Lifts West Condominium Resort Hotel** features contemporary, two-story units, all with fireplaces and wall-to-wall carpeting. Many have complete kitchens and balconies or decks. A heated pool, restaurant and shopping mall are on the premises. Summer rates are budget while winter rates skyrocket to the ultra-deluxe category. ~ 201 West Main Street, Red River; 505-754-2778, 800-221-1859, fax 505-754-6617; www.taoswebb.com/hotel/liftswest, e-mail lifts@redriver.org. MODERATE TO ULTRA-DELUXE.

On the banks of the Red River by the ski lifts is the **Alpine Lodge**. Rooms and apartments are well-maintained, all with porch or balcony. An on-site restaurant and nearby ski rental make the Alpine a convenient spot for skiers. ~ 417 West Main

Cimarron through the Cimarron Range (one of the easternmost ranges of the Sangre de Cristo Mountains), the Colin Neblett Wildlife Area and Cimarron Canyon.

CIMARRON CANYON STATE PARK   Three miles east of Eagle Nest are the towering walls of Cimarron Canyon State Park. Be sure to watch your speed, and after dark be on the lookout for deer as you travel through the narrow canyon. ~ Route 64; 505-377-6271.

RED RIVER   Return to Eagle Nest; just north of the town (where Route 64 becomes Route 38) is an open and pretty valley ringed with high mountains. Drop down Bobcat Pass into Red River, yet another Wild West village. Though touristy, this early-20th-century goldmining town retains a certain charm from its rip-roaring gambling, brawling and red-light district days. A ski area rises out of its center and national forest land surrounds it completely.

QUESTA   Continuing east on the Enchanted Circle, which hugs Red River, you'll drive past plenty of forest and camping spots until you reach the honey-producing town of Questa. From Questa, 22 miles south on Route 522 will bring you back to Taos. Along the way, you may wish to stop and visit the D. H. Lawrence Ranch, the Rio Grande Gorge Bridge or the Millicent Rogers Museum.

Street, Red River; 505-754-2952, 800-252-2333, fax 505-754-6421; www.thealpinelodge.com, e-mail reservations@thealpine lodge.com. BUDGET TO MODERATE.

The 26 rooms at **The Lodge at Red River** are rustic, but the central location is appealing. Closed April to mid-May and October to mid-November ~ 400 East Main Street, Red River; 505-754-6280, 800-915-6343, fax 505-754-6304; www.redrivernm. com/lodgeatrr, e-mail lodge@newmex.org. MODERATE.

DINING

Eager to trade fast-food drive-ins for a table set with real silverware? Then take a seat in the beam-ceilinged dining room at **The Lodge at Red River**. Specialties like rainbow trout, charbroiled pork chops and fish tacos will make up for all the cheeseburgers you've suffered. Entrées come with salad or soup and vegetables, and extra helpings on these items are available at no extra charge. The bar is a pleasant après-ski stop. Breakfast, lunch and dinner are served. Closed April to mid-May. ~ 400 East Main Street, Red River; 505-754-6280, 800-915-6343; www.redriver nm.com/lodgeatrr, e-mail lodge@redrivernm.com. MODERATE TO DELUXE.

You can't top **Angelina's** for chicken-fried steak, enchilada plates and a generous soup and salad bar. The Southwest-style pastel decor includes ceiling fans and booth seating. Reduced hours during the off-season; call ahead. ~ 112 West Main Street, Red River; 505-754-6177. BUDGET TO MODERATE.

For stuffed *sopapillas*, fajitas or other New Mexican specialties try **Sundance**. The beautiful wood-paneled dining room is appointed with *vigas* and Southwestern paintings. Dinner only. ~ Copper King Trail and High Street, Red River; 505-754-6271. BUDGET TO MODERATE.

Corny as it may sound, you won't waddle away hungry from **Texas Red's Steakhouse**, which specializes in slabs of beef, big hamburgers and other hearty Western-style meals. Dinner only. Limited hours in April and November. ~ 111 Main Street, Red River; 505-754-2964, fax 505-754-2309. MODERATE TO DELUXE.

NIGHTLIFE **Music from Angel Fire** is a great place to rub elbows with New Mexico's patrons of the arts. Celebrating its 20th season in 2003, the organization hosts a variety of rotating artists whose music will soothe the most savage of beasts. There are also regular chamber music recitals and festivals. ~ P.O. Box 502, Angel Fire; 505-377-3233, fax 505-989-4773; www.musicfromangelfire.org.

Over the mountain in Red River, stop in at **Bull o' the Woods Saloon**, where a deejay plays country music and classic rock on weekends. Closed in April. ~ 401 Main Street; 505-754-2593. A bar with live country-and-western on weekend nights is the **Motherlode** at The Lodge at Red River. Closed April and May. Cover. ~ 400 East Main Street, Red River; 505-754-6280.

Melodramas are staged several nights a week from mid-June to mid-August at the **Red River Inn**. Call ahead for performance days and times. ~ 300 West Main Street, Red River; 505-754-2930.

PARKS **CARSON NATIONAL FOREST** 🚶 🚴 🐎 🏕 ⛵ Like the Santa Fe National Forest, which adjoins it on the south, Carson National Forest is split by the Rio Grande Valley into two separate units. The western part extends from the spectacular red, white and yellow cliffs around Abiquiu northward to the Colorado state line, encompassing the gently rolling pine forests of the San Pedro and Canjilon Mountains. The portion of the Rio Chama above Abiquiu Lake has been designated a National Wild and Scenic River by the U.S. Congress and is a popular rafting area. The Canjilon Lakes and a number of other remote lakes reached by forest roads in the north are favorites with local anglers. ~ Accessed by numerous forest roads off Route 84 between Española and Chama; 505-684-2486, fax 505-684-2486; www.fs.fed.us/r3/carson.

▲ The lakeside campground at Canjilon Lakes has 40 sites (no hookups); $5 per night. Closed September through May.

In the Land of Three Cultures

No other place reflects the tricultural heritage of northern New Mexico as much as Taos does. Here, at the northern gateway to the Pueblo lands, the native people met and traded with nomadic outlanders such as the Utes, Apaches and Comanches for many centuries before the first Spanish conquistadores set foot in New Mexico. Here, too, as in few other places around the region, Spanish settlers built a town within easy walking distance of a large Indian pueblo. And here, at the dawn of the 20th century, artists and writers came from such faraway places as New York, Great Britain, France and Russia to establish a colony dedicated to capturing the traditions of the local people.

Multiculturalism has not always translated into tolerance or brotherly love, though. In the early days of Spanish colonialism, Puebloans from Taos south to the Albuquerque area revolted and killed the majority of the settlers, driving the survivors out of New Mexico. Taos Plaza is also reputed to have been the site of a market where Navajo raiders brought people kidnapped from Zuni and other western pueblos and sold them to the Spanish as slaves. And when New Mexico became United States territory in the 1840s, newly appointed governor Charles Bent, whose house is now a museum (page 397), was assassinated by the locals after serving less than a year in office. Cultural conflicts have plagued Taos as recently as the late 1960s and early '70s, when the town became a mecca for hippies, whose philosophy of psychedelics and free love offended the conservative, mostly Catholic populace.

On the whole, however, the three cultures have maintained a surprisingly peaceful balance over the centuries. Indian fighter Kit Carson retired to Taos with his Hispanic wife and became an ally of the local Puebloans. New York heiress Mabel Dodge married Tony Luhan, an Indian from Taos Pueblo, and became the artist colony's leading patron. Some hippie communes from the 1960s grew into spiritual centers, while others became bed and breakfasts. When the nearby Buddhist spiritual community of Lama was destroyed by a forest fire in 1996, the entire town and Pueblo of Taos rallied together to provide food and shelter for the homeless Lama residents.

Today, more than any other community in northern New Mexico, Taos is dedicated almost entirely to tourism. This town with a population of only about 5000 plays host to approximately three million visitors a year. Viewed in historical perspective, the tourist trade is a continuation of Taos' centuries-old role as the place where New Mexico meets the rest of the world.

CIMARRON CANYON STATE PARK 🏃 🚲 🐎 ⚓ ⏬ Granite formations tower above a sparkling stream where brown and rainbow trout crowd the waters and wildlife congregates. There are some hiking trails, but fishing is the most popular park activity. Facilities are limited to picnic areas and restrooms. ~ Route 64, 14 miles west of Cimarron; 505-377-6271, fax 505-377-2259.

▲ There are 88 developed sites (no hookups); $10 per vehicle per night. No water from mid-September to early May.

East of Cimarron

Known as *Los Llanos*, "the plains," the wide-open country spills from the edge of the mountains across the empty northeastern corner of New Mexico and on into Oklahoma and the Texas Panhandle. Those who take the time to visit Capulin Volcano can stand at the top of this extinct, solitary cone that rises out of the prairie and appreciate the vastness of this land. Most travelers, however, hurry through the area on the interstate without realizing that the two-lane highway from Raton through Cimarron and through the Sangre de Cristo Mountains is a beautiful shortcut to both Taos and Santa Fe. Both Cimarron and Raton preserve their frontier heritage in historic buildings and small museums full of Old Western artifacts.

SIGHTS

The settlement of **Cimarron**, where plain and pasture meet rugged mountains, was founded in 1848 with entrepreneur Lucien Maxwell's land grant. Life was cheap at this outpost on the mountain branch of the Santa Fe Trail; death from a gunfight was not uncommon. Cimarron the town and Cimarron the river lived up to the Spanish translation of their name—wild and untamed. While that may have described Cimarron a century ago, these days it's just a mellow small town. The rambling river waters too have been calmed by the establishment of Eagle Nest Reservoir.

A trip to Cimarron wouldn't be complete without a peek inside the historic **St. James Hotel**, with its partly renovated interior and completely authentic funkiness. Built in 1873 by one of Abraham Lincoln's chefs, some say the St. James is haunted by outlaw ghosts of the past. ~ Route 21, Cimarron; 505-376-2664.

Originally built as a grist mill, the **Old Mill Museum** now offers a panoramic view of local history from chuckwagons to regional paintings. And while the collection does include sleighs and American Indian pottery shards, it focuses on ranching, mining and homesteading in the Cimarron area. You'll be surrounded by treasures of the past. This exhibit is not to be missed. Closed Thursday and October through April, weekends only in May and September. Admission. For information about the museum call the Cimarron Chamber of Commerce. ~ Off Route 21, Cimarron; phone/fax 505-376-2417; www.cimarronnm.com, e-mail chamber@cimarron.springercoop.com.

More down to earth is the **Philmont Scout Ranch**, the nation's largest scouting camp. In 1922, the Tulsa oil baron Waite Phillips bought a 300,000-acre ranch south of Cimarron. In 1941, he donated a total of 137,000 acres to the Boy Scouts of America. Today, a small museum features local artifacts and works of Ernest Thompson-Seton, one of the founders of the Boy Scouts. Also here is **Villa Philmonte** (admission), the former home of Waite Phillips. There are guided tours of the mansion every half hour in summer and once or twice daily off-season. ~ Route 21, about four miles south of Cimarron, Philmont; 505-376-2281, fax 505-376-2636; www.scouting.org/philmont, e-mail philstaff@cimarron. springercoop.com.

Seven miles south of the Philmont Scout headquarters is the **Kit Carson Museum**, an intriguing living-history exhibit illustrating the life of 1850s-era settlers like Kit Carson (who lived here). Operated by the Boy Scouts of America, this old adobe compound is a terrific place to learn pioneer arts and crafts; the place even boasts a hardworking blacksmith and candlemakers. Closed late August through May, except by appointment. ~ Route 21, Rayado; 505-376-4621 (summer), 505-376-2281 ext. 256 (winter), fax 505-376-2602.

Continuing another 38 miles northeast of Cimarron on Routes 64 and 25, you'll come to **Raton** (elevation 6666 feet), a small New Mexican city located on the original Santa Fe Trail. Raton,

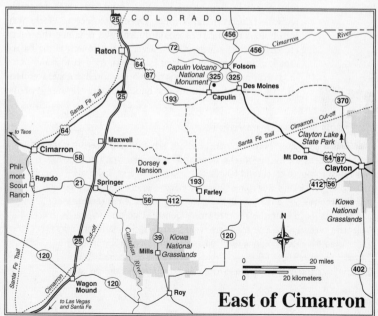

East of Cimarron

with its scenic mesas, sits at the foot of Raton Pass and was first founded as a railroad outpost.

Visits to Raton should begin with a walking tour of the **Raton Downtown Historic District**, one of New Mexico's most distinguished Main Street districts. Some of the buildings have been completely restored, others are in the midst of rehabilitation and a few cry out for love and care. This is an opportunity to see an array of styles and period pieces from the late 19th to the early 20th centuries—truly an architectural timeline. This area is on the National Register of Historic Places. Pick up the walking-tour brochure at the **Raton Chamber and Economic Development Council**. ~ 100 Clayton Road, Raton; 505-445-3689, 800-638-6161, fax 505-335-3680; www.raton.com, e-mail chamber@raton.com.

The walking tour begins at the **Santa Fe Depot** on 1st Street, a Mission Revival structure adorned with colorful portals. Other highlights on this block include **Cooks Hall**, the Corinthian-pilastered **Roth Building** and the red-brick **Investment Block**. Continue over to 2nd Street and the **Shuler Theater**, clearly Raton's architectural masterpiece. If you can't get inside to view the rococo interior, be sure to at least see the fine WPA murals. Continue on for a look at the **Foote Hotel** and the **A. H. Carey Hardware Store**, a handsome stone building featuring a brick facade.

On Cook Street you'll see the neoclassical **Raton Public Library** and the **International State Bank** building. The latter structure, originally named the Swastika Hotel, was once decorated with the famous Indian symbol. During the Second World War, for obvious reasons, this establishment was renamed the Yucca Hotel. Another worthy Cook Street establishment is the **Palace Hotel**, a fine structure built of locally quarried sandstone.

Next door on 1st Street is the ivory-colored brick **Haven Hotel**. It's adjacent to the Coors Building, now the home of the

AUTHOR FAVORITE

Dorsey Mansion may be a long way from anywhere, but it's definitely worth the excursion. The stone and log mansion was once the heart of a ranch rumored to extend 60 miles in length. Now it's a landmark—listed on the National Register of Historic Places—adorned with an Italian marble fireplace and a number of intriguing gargoyles. Carved rattlesnakes and bobcats lunge from the intricate stone fountain. Don't try to visit in inclement weather; the clay roads are exceptionally slick when wet. Tours are offered daily. Reservations required. Admission. ~ From Springer, drive 24 miles east on Route 56, then 12 miles north on a dirt road; 505-375-2222; www.dorseymansion.com, e-mail shenning@dorseymansion.com.

Raton Museum. This storefront collection features Santa Fe Trail memorabilia, including historic photos and crockery. Old West buffs will especially like the rail and mining exhibits. Closed Sunday and Monday from May through November, and Sunday through Wednesday from December through April. ~ 216 South 1st Street, Raton; 505-445-8979.

The most worthwhile area attraction is the **Capulin Volcano National Monument.** Now dormant, the mile-wide cone of the volcano rises more than 1200 feet above the flat plains. The volcano is believed to be 56,000 to 62,000 years old. A visitors center and small museum provide information on the natural wonder. ~ Route 64/87, Capulin, 30 miles east of Raton; 505-278-2201, fax 505-278-2211; www.nps.gov/cavo, e-mail cavo_administration@nps.gov.

Route 325 leads north from here to the town of **Folsom.** This short (seven miles) and beautiful trip is backcountry New Mexico driving at its best. Winding through picturesque valleys you'll descend to this little hamlet, worth visiting if only to see the impressive turn-of-the-20th-century native stone Catholic church and the 1888 Folsom Hotel. There are also a number of intriguing old adobe houses.

Housed in what used to be a general store, the **Folsom Museum** features the original display cases from the store. There's also a vault and rolling ladders that served the higher shelves. The exhibits include old telephone switchboards, x-ray machines and spittoons. You'll also see a replica of a pioneer law office, saddles and gems. And the collection of regional history books should answer any questions you have about these objects. Closed October through April. Admission. ~ Main Street, Folsom; 505-278-2122.

Hop on Route 325 until you reach the junction with Route 64 at Des Moines. Forty-five miles east on Route 64 will bring you to the town of Clayton. Rich in dinosaur history, this area of northeastern New Mexico has plenty of giant tracks to prove it. If you yearn to play amateur paleontologist, visit the **Clayton–Union County Chamber of Commerce,** where they make dinosaurs their business. Closed Saturday and Sunday from Labor Day through Memorial Day. ~ 1103 South 1st Street, Clayton; phone/fax 505-374-9253, 800-390-7858; www.claytonnewmexico.org, e-mail cuchamber@plateautel.net.

The kind folks at the COC will no doubt direct you to **Clayton Lake State Park,** where you can see 500 dinosaur tracks from over 100 million years ago. First found in 1982 after a flood removed a layer of silt, the tracks here are etched in Dakota mudstone. ~ Route 370, 12 miles north of Clayton; 505-374-8808, fax 505-374-2461.

Dinosaur relics from the area are displayed alongside railroading and farming equipment at the **Herzstein Memorial Museum**. Rounding out the collection is memorabilia of the museum's benefactors, the Herzstein family, and a replica of a Depression-era doctor's office. Stained-glass windows add a lovely touch to this space, which occupies a former Methodist Church. Open Tuesday through Sunday, afternoons only. ~ 2nd and Walnut streets, Clayton; 505-374-2977; www.herzsteinmuseum.org.

LODGING

Best bet by far in Cimarron is the spooky **St. James Hotel,** where famous residents such as Buffalo Bill Cody and Annie Oakley hung their Wild West duds. Built in 1880 and then lovingly restored and reopened a century later, this landmark has rooms with original cast-iron period furniture. Each unit is unique and ghosts haunt the hallways, so you may ask to inspect your room before renting. Phones and TVs are available in an adjoining motel annex but not in the rooms of the historic hotel. ~ Route 21, Cimarron; 505-376-2664, 800-748-2694, fax 505-376-2623; e-mail stjhotel@ cimarron.springercoop.com. MODERATE TO DELUXE.

Casa del Gavilan is a charming white adobe bed and breakfast. Period antiques are omnipresent; all five guest rooms have private baths. ~ Route 21, Cimarron; 505-376-2246, 800-428-4526, fax 505-376-2247; www.casadelgavilan.com, e-mail info@ casadelgavilan.com. MODERATE TO DELUXE.

Quiet and well-priced, **Budget Host Raton** is convenient to Raton's historic downtown district. Each of these 27 units offers king-size or double beds with floral print spreads. ~ 136 Canyon Drive, Raton; 505-445-3655, 800-421-5210. BUDGET.

Among the least expensive lodging in town, the circa-1902 **El Portal** offers spacious older units with hardwood floors and double beds. Antique and painted Southwestern furniture creates a cheery setting, and the upper stories have nice views. ~ 101 North 3rd Street, Raton; phone/fax 505-445-3631. BUDGET.

The family-owned **Clayton Motel** is a 26-unit motor court that's clean and quiet. In the process of gradual renovation, the rooms are large with contemporary oak furniture. Morning coffee and doughnuts are complimentary. This low-priced establishment is an excellent choice for a good night's sleep. ~ 422 Monroe Street, Clayton; 505-374-2544, fax 505-374-6102. BUDGET.

DINING

The knotty pine–paneled **Kit Carson Restaurant** offers frontiersman-size breakfasts, as well as chile burgers, taco salads, steaks and enchilada plates for lunch and dinner. If you're watching your waistline, there's a generous salad bar. The paneling in the adjacent lounge is stamped with local cattle brands. ~ Route 64, Cimarron; 505-376-2288, fax 505-376-9214. BUDGET TO MODERATE.

Green Chile,
Blue Corn & Piñon Nuts

New Mexico's distinctive cuisine has strong roots in the Pueblo Indian culture as adapted by Spanish settlers. It is set apart from Tex-Mex and Mexican food by three ingredients that are unique to the state.

Green chile, which is ubiquitous in New Mexican restaurants and kitchens, is the same hot pepper that is crushed into chili powder—in fact, New Mexico produces virtually all of the chili powder in the United States—but locals prefer to harvest it before it turns red and eat it as an ultra-spicy vegetable. Grown mainly in the small communities of Hatch and Chimayo, it is sold by the bushel during the late August to mid-September harvest season. The seller roasts the chiles, making the inedible outer skin easy to remove, and the buyer divides them into bags and freezes them to last the rest of the year. Green chile is almost never served outside New Mexico. If the plant is grown elsewhere, the green chile pods lose their flavor, as they do when dried or canned. Enjoy it while you can. If you want to take the taste of New Mexico home as a souvenir, your best bet is green chile preserves, sold in many Santa Fe and Taos curio shops.

Blue corn, a variety of Indian maize, has been cultivated by the Pueblo people for at least 1200 years. They hold it sacred because it is the color of the sky and of turquoise, the most precious of stones among Southwestern Indians. Spanish settlers grew blue corn obtained from the Indians, and it accounts for much of the corn grown in New Mexico today. The corn kernels have tough outer shells and so cannot be eaten directly off the cob. Instead, they are traditionally crushed into meal, mixed with water and made into tortillas or ground into a fine powder and boiled in water to make a souplike beverage called *atole*, which Indian shamans and Spanish *curanderos* claim has healing powers.

Piñon nuts form inside the cones of the piñon trees that dot the hills and mesas of northern New Mexico. All the trees in a particular area produce nuts at the same time, but only once every seven years. Local villagers harvest them by placing a sheet around the bottom of a tree, then lassoing the treetop with a rope and shaking it vigorously until the nuts fall out. The nuts are then sold by the roadside or wholesaled to local supermarkets. It is a common practice in northern New Mexico to mix piñon nuts, shell and all, with whole-bean coffee and grind them together, giving the coffee a rich, chocolatelike flavor. Coffee with piñon is sold in many supermarkets and makes an unusual souvenir or gift.

Heck's Hungry Traveler is an unpretentious coffee shop where you'll enjoy tripledecker club sandwiches, half-pound hamburgers and cheese enchiladas. Booth and table seating are available. Be sure to try the homemade soups and pies. No breakfast during the week. ~ Route 64, Cimarron; 505-376-2574. BUDGET TO MODERATE.

The bullet holes in the ceiling are the last reminders of **Lambert's** days as a saloon and gambling hall. Today, the chandeliers, upholstered chairs and candles set the mood for elegant dining. Raspberry shrimp; filet mignon stuffed with roasted red peppers, mushrooms and olives; and vegetarian fettuccine Alfredo might be a few of the selections from the diverse menu. Breakfast, lunch and dinner are served. Call ahead for days of operation. ~ St. James Hotel, Route 21, Cimarron; 505-376-2664, fax 505-376-2623. MODERATE TO DELUXE.

A pine counter taken from a circa-1920 coffee shop is the architectural highlight at the **Brown Hotel Restaurant,** a small café decorated with antique tableware and glass lamps. *Huevos rancheros* and french toast round out the breakfast menu, while dinner and lunch include green-chile enchiladas, pork chops and chicken-fried steak. No dinner on Sunday. ~ 302 Maxwell Street, Springer; 505-483-2269, fax 505-483-0053. BUDGET.

For morning coffee and hot-out-of-the-oven cinnamon rolls, go to **Eva's Bakery**. They also serve omelettes and breakfast burritos; sandwiches on homemade bread are available at lunch. Breakfast and lunch only. Closed Sunday and Monday. ~ 134 North 2nd Street, Raton; 505-445-3781. BUDGET.

Founded by Jim Pappas and Gus Petritsis in 1923, **Pappas' Sweet Shop Restaurant** was such a popular candy store and soda fountain that the owners added a full-fledged restaurant. Run today by Jim's son, Mike, the Territorial-style establishment overflows with memorabilia: historic photos, train sets, classic car models and gilt-framed mirrors. The eclectic menu ranges from lobster tail and prime rib to stuffed jalapeños; several vegetarian entrées are also available. Toasted coconut pie and fried ice cream are just a few of the choices for dessert. Closed Sunday. ~ 1201 South 2nd Street, Raton; 505-445-9811, fax 505-445-3080; e-mail papcfy@aol.com. MODERATE TO ULTRA-DELUXE.

Restaurant options are few and far between in eastern New Mexico, but there's one thing you can count on. Out here, where cattle ranching is the only industry, the food at steak houses is a big, juicy cut above what you'll find at freeway-exit fast-food eateries.

If it's atmosphere you are looking for, it's hard to beat the velvet-cushioned banquettes at the **Eklund Dining Room and Saloon**. Built in 1892, this two-story rock-walled landmark is a real find. Mounted game oversee the hand-carved bar, one of the most beautiful in the state. Appointed with gold floral wallpaper, a marble fireplace and historic photographs, the dining room may tempt you to take out your camera. The menu emphasizes New Mexican specialties, though it also offers surf and turf and prime rib. ~ 15 Main Street, Clayton; 505-374-2551, fax 505-374-2500. MODERATE TO DELUXE.

Knotty pine paneling, *vigas* and handcrafted furniture make **Hi Ho Café** an inviting place to try American and Mexican specialties. Steaks and burgers are always popular here, but you can opt for the soup and salad bar. Sandwiches and child's plates are also available. Breakfast, lunch and dinner are served. ~ 1201 South 1st Street, Clayton; 505-374-9515. BUDGET.

SHOPPING

Looking for squash blossom jewelry, kachinas or scouting memorabilia? Or perhaps you'd like to pick up a regional history book? If so, be sure to visit the **Villa Philmonte Gift Shop**, a one-stop souvenir shop. ~ Route 21, Philmont; 505-376-2281 ext. 256.

Cowboys and cowgirls (and Western wanna-bes) will find all the proper accessories at **Solano's Boot & Western Wear**, one of the largest shops of its kind in northern New Mexico. Saunter on in and "git" yourself a custom-made hat or an embroidered shirt. A wide selection of jackets and belt buckles completes the inventory. ~ 101 South 2nd Street, Raton; 505-445-2632; www.solanos westernwear.com, e-mail epicdigital@bacavalley.com.

As you could no doubt guess from the name, the **Heirloom Shop** carries antiques and collectibles, including advertising signs. This shop also boasts an excellent array of quilts, Depression glass and china. ~ 132 South 1st Street, Raton; 505-445-8876.

One way to beat Santa Fe's high prices for American Indian artifacts and collectibles is to head for **Santa Fe Trail Traders**. The

AUTHOR FAVORITE

For a special treat and a wide selection of pottery (including turquoise fetish pots), I pay a visit to the **Cimarron Art Gallery**. Sculpture, paintings, jewelry and earrings are found here, as well as books on the Southwest. And it is probably the only gallery in the Southwest with a working 1937 soda fountain—yes, they do serve ice cream in the gallery, and no, I generally can't resist indulging myself. ~ 337 9th Street, Cimarron; 505-376-2614; www.cimarronartgallery.com, e-mail wdbd gers@springercoop.com.

Navajo, Hopi and Zuni artwork, from jewelry, fetishes and sand-paintings to kachinas and blankets, is well priced for such high-quality merchandise. Closed Sunday in winter. ~ 100 South 2nd Street, Raton; 505-445-2888.

If you're planning to fish, camp, hike or golf in beautiful north-eastern New Mexico, head over to **Knott's Sportsman Supply**. Just about everything you could possibly need for life in the outback is on sale here, including maps, regional guides and athletic equipment. Anglers are certain to appreciate the complete selection of fishing rods, lures and flies. Closed Sunday. ~ 1015 South 1st Street, Clayton; 505-374-8361.

NIGHTLIFE   The **Raton Arts and Humanities Council** presents an impressive year-round calendar of adult and children's drama, musical soloists, symphony orchestras and touring dance companies. Most of the events are staged in the rococo Shuler Theater (131 North 2nd Street), opened to the public in 1915 and restored in the early 1970s. Original show curtains are in use today and the lobby murals are a must-see. ~ 145 South 1st Street, Raton; phone/fax 505-445-2052; www.ratonarts.com, e-mail artinfo@ratonarts.com.

PARKS   **CLAYTON LAKE STATE PARK** 🏃 🚤 🛶 🎣 This prairie lake is a good spot for birding. Not only do Canada geese and several species of ducks winter here, bald eagles are also a common sight. Anglers also find that the lake offers excellent trout, catfish and bass fishing, and four state-record walleyed pikes have been caught here. Perhaps the most unusual feature of the park is its dinosaur trackway. Along the lake's spillway, more than 500 dinosaur footprints have been preserved and identified. Interpretive markers identify the prints of several different types of herbivorous and carnivorous dinosaurs and ancient crocodiles. Day-use fee, $4. ~ Off Route 370, 12 miles northwest of Clayton; 505-374-8808, fax 505-374-2461.

▲ There are 30 developed sites ($10 per night), and an additional 7 with electric and water hookups ($14 per night). The campground has restrooms with showers.

BLACK JACK KETCHUM'S FINAL DAYS

The notorious bandit Black Jack Ketchum committed his last crime near Twin Mountain, just four miles away from Folsom. He was apprehended and brought to Folsom after wounding himself during a train robbery. Following his conviction a year later, Ketchum was convicted and hung in Clayton on April 25, 1901. His last words were: "Let her rip."

Anglers find the fishing grand in these parts. ▼▼▼▼▼▼▼▼▼▼▼▼▼▼
Near Taos, head for the Rio Grande. Roads run **Outdoor Adventures**
to the river at Orilla Verde and Wild Rivers
Recreation Areas. More adventuresome anglers can hike down the   **FISHING**
steep volcanic cliffs of the Rio Grande Gorge to remote stretches
of the river in search of trophy-size rainbow and brown trout.

TAOS AREA   Los Rios Anglers sells and rents flyfishing tackle
and guides half- and full-day fishing trips along the Rio Grande
and its tributaries. ~ 126 West Plaza Drive, Taos; 505-758-2798.
In the summer, tackle is available at **Cottam's Skiing and Outdoor
Shop.** ~ 207-A Paseo del Pueblo Sur; 505-758-2822.

ENCHANTED CIRCLE AREA   Dos Amigos Anglers Co. provides
bait and tackle in Eagle Nest. They also offer instruction, half-
day lake fishing trips and full-day flyfishing trips. ~ Route 64;
505-377-6226.

West of Taos, the Rio Grande flows through a spectacular 400-   **RIVER
foot-deep gorge nicknamed the Taos Box. Both the Rio Grande   RUNNING**
and the Chama River, which flows into the Rio Grande midway
between Taos and Santa Fe, have been designated by the United
States government as Wild and Scenic Rivers, with environmental protection similar to federal wilderness areas. Both are full of
river rafts and kayaks during the late spring and early summer
when the rivers are swollen with runoff from snow melting in the
nearby mountains.

TAOS AREA   There are several rafting guide services in the Taos
area. **Los Rios River Runners** takes half-day, full-day and overnight trips on the Class III and V rapids of the Rio Grande and
the smooth current of the Rio Chama. Overnight trips on the
Class V Dolores River in southern Colorado are also available.
If you really want to go all out, they'll arrange for an astronomer,
a Celtic musician, a yoga teacher or a wine expert to accompany
you. All meals, tents and camping gear are provided. ~ 23 Route
150 (Taos Ski Valley Road); 505-776-8854, 800-544-1181; www.
losriosriverrunners.com, e-mail whitewater@newmex.com.

Native Sons Adventures also guides whitewater raft trips
through the Class II to IV Taos Box and the Class II and III
Lower Gorge (a good starting trip for beginners). ~ 1033 Paseo
del Pueblo Sur; 505-758-9342, 800-753-7559; www.nativesons
dventures.com.

Far Flung Adventures operates out of El Prado and runs the
Taos Box and the Rio Chama. They offer half-day, full-day and
overnight trips. Meals and tents are provided. ~ P.O. Box 707,
El Prado, NM 87529; 505-758-2628, 800-359-2627; www.far
flung.com.

SKIING   This area boasts New Mexico's best alpine skiing. The ski season runs roughly from Thanksgiving through March, but may begin earlier or end later depending on weather conditions. Ski rentals and instruction are available at all the resorts listed here.

TAOS AREA   Granddaddy of New Mexico's alpine ski resorts is **Taos Ski Valley**, with a summit elevation of nearly 12,000 feet above sea level and a vertical drop of 2612 feet. Taos boasts more than 1000 acres of bowls and chutes served by ten chairs and two surface lifts. Taos has a reputation as one of the most challenging ski areas in the Rocky Mountains, with about half of the trails designated as expert. Snow conditions at Taos Ski Valley are available 24 hours a day by calling 505-776-2916. ~ Route 150/Taos Ski Valley Road; 505-776-2291; www.skitaos.org, e-mail tsv@skitaos.org.

Taos Ski Area is so popular that Taos has become the only town in New Mexico where winter, not summer, is the peak tourist season.

ENCHANTED CIRCLE AREA   Forty-five minutes away from Taos, **Red River Ski Area** is an increasingly popular family ski area with a 1600-foot vertical drop. Seven lifts serve 290 acres of trails, rated 32 percent beginner, 38 percent intermediate and 30 percent expert. Snowboarding is allowed. Snow conditions at Red River are available 24 hours a day by calling 505-754-2220. ~ Route 38, Red River; 505-754-2223; www.redriverskiarea.com, e-mail redriver@newmex.com.

An even gentler ski area is **Angel Fire**, where five lifts carry skiers up to 10,677 feet elevation for a vertical descent of 2077 feet on 31 percent beginner, 48 percent intermediate and 21 percent expert trails. Snowboarding is allowed on all runs as well as in the terrain park. ~ Route 434; 505-377-6401, 800-633-7463.

HIDDEN ▶   **Sipapu Ski Area**—the oldest ski slope in northern New Mexico, built in 1952—is especially popular with snowboarders. The small ski area covers only 37 acres, with a peak elevation of just over 9000 feet and an 865-foot vertical drop. Three lifts serve 19 trails: 20 percent beginner, 50 percent intermediate and 30 percent expert. ~ Route 518, Vadito; 505-587-2240, 800-587-2240; www.sipapunm.com; e-mail resort@sipapunm.com.

Cross-country skiers who prefer the peaceful sounds of nature will enjoy gliding through the **Enchanted Forest**, which has no services save for a warming hut. ~ Route 38, Red River.

Ski Rentals   To rent your sticks in Taos, visit **Cottam's Skiing and Outdoor Shop**, where they will set you up with downhill and cross-country skis, snowboards and snowshoes. ~ 207-A Paseo del Pueblo Sur; 505-758-2822. You'll find cross-country equipment and snowshoes at **Taos Mountain Outfitters**. ~ 114 Taos Plaza South; 505-758-9292.

Angel Fire Resort Rental Shop at the mountain base rents downhill and Nordic equipment. They also offer repairs and tunings. ~ Angel Fire; 505-377-4290, 800-633-7463. **SkiTech Dis-**

count **Ski Rentals**, convenient to Angel Fire, rents downhill and cross-country skis, snowboards and snowblades. ~ North Angel Fire Road, Village Center; 505-377-3213, 800-531-7547. Get your snowboards and skis in Red River at **River City Sports/Calamity Jane's** near the mountain base. ~ 325-B Main Street, Red River; 505-754-2428. For cross-country ski or snowshoe rentals, lessons or a moonlight ski tour, check in at **Millers Crossing**, a shop that runs the ski area at Enchanted Forest. ~ 417 West Main Street, Red River; 505-754-2374, 800-966-9381; www.enchanted forestxc.com.

Beautiful terrain and varied trails make this a great area to see on horseback. Several ranches in the region outfit trips, including one run by a local tribe that leads trips on reservation land.

RIDING STABLES

TAOS AREA   Ride with the American Indians on the Great Spirit's property at the **Taos Indian Horse Ranch**, where tribal guides lead groups of one to twenty riders on two-hour and longer tours through parts of Taos Pueblo's mountainous 100,000-acre reservation. Children's rides are also available. ~ 1 Miller Road, Taos Pueblo; phone/fax 505-758-3212.

ENCHANTED CIRCLE AREA   East of Taos, one-hour to half-day trail rides are offered by **Roadrunner Tours, Ltd.** You can also take an overnight camping trip on horseback or join a cattle drive on the mountainous 10,000-acre CS Ranch. ~ Route 434, Angel Fire; 505-377-6416, 800-377-6416.

The scenic mountain roads lend themselves to bicycle rides of all lengths and levels.

BIKING

TAOS AREA   A relatively difficult five-mile loop trail called **Devisadero** allows for a good view of the town of Taos. Start across from the El Nogal picnic area on Route 64 and get ready to climb 1300 vertical feet of elevation.

ENCHANTED CIRCLE AREA   La Jara Canyon (Route 64, on the horseshoe between Taos and Angel Fire) is a meandering two-mile climb to an alpine meadow that appeals especially to those new in the (bike) saddle.

Wait until late afternoon to take the three-mile **Cebolla Mesa Trail** (Route 522, about 18 miles north of Taos) for the splendid sunsets. Pedal near the rim of the 800-foot Rio Grande Gorge at Cebolla Mesa. Start the trip at the intersection of Cebolla Mesa Road and Route 522 and ride to the campground.

EAST OF CIMARRON   Although travelers on most major highways get the impression that eastern New Mexico is flat and featureless, the prairie conceals an occasional natural wonder such as Mills Canyon on the Canadian River. The rough unpaved road that descends into the 700-foot-deep canyon and climbs out the far side was originally the Butterfield Overland stagecoach route, a major "highway" in the 1870s. Today, it's an ideal biking-and-hiking expedition. The old road leaves Route 39 heading west from the tiny town of Mills (36 miles southeast of the Springer exit from Route 25) and stretches across the sparse, uninhabited Kiowa National Grasslands for about seven miles to the canyon, where the descent is marked with a sign that reads "Primitive Road—Not Maintained." On the far side, it continues for eight miles to join Route 120 in empty rangeland about 13 miles east of Wagon Mound and Route 25. The ruins of an old stone stagecoach station and ranch house stand by the river that meanders through the broad canyon rippling with knee-deep buffalo grass. The canyon extends for six miles upriver and 13 miles downriver; you can bike for about two miles and walk for the entire length of the canyon.

Bike Rentals & Tours   **Gearing Up Bicycle Shop** rents mountain bikes, sells new bicycles and accessories and has a repair shop on the premises. ~ 129 Paseo de Pueblo Sur, Taos; 505-751-0365. Along with mountain-bike rentals, **Native Sons Adventures** offers half- and full-day bike tours. The Pedal to Paddle excursion combines biking and river rafting in the Rio Grande Gorge. ~ 1033-A Paseo de Pueblo Sur; 505-758-9342, 800-753-7559; www.nativesonsadventures.com.

HIKING   From a gentle trail following a creek to a challenging ascent of New Mexico's highest mountain, 13,161-foot Wheeler Peak, the Enchanted Circle is filled with enchanting hiking possibilities. All distances listed are one way unless otherwise noted.

TAOS AREA   Most hiking trails in the Taos area start from the Ski Valley. The ultimate hike is the seven-mile trail to the summit of **Wheeler Peak**. Though not particularly steep, the rocky trail is for conditioned hikers only because of the high altitude.

The **Carson National Forest** near Taos has more than 20 marked trails of varying difficulty that wind in and around some of the state's more magnificent scenic spots.

Yerba Canyon Trail (4 miles) begins in the aspens and willows, but snakes through fir and spruce trees as you approach the ridge. As its name would suggest, the trail follows Yerba Canyon for most of its length and makes a difficult 3600-foot climb before reaching Lobo Peak. The trailhead is on Taos Ski Valley Road, a mile up the hill from Upper Cuchilla Campground.

From roughly the same access point as the Yerba Canyon Trail is the **Gavilan Trail** (2.4 miles), a colorful though difficult hike that primarily follows alongside Gavilan Creek. Steep in its early section, the trip flattens out as it opens into meadows near the ridge.

In the Red River area you'll find the trail to **Middlefork Lake** (2 miles), which climbs 1200 vertical feet to a glacier lake.

Another way to the summit of Wheeler Peak, longer and more difficult than the route from the Taos Ski Valley, the **East Fork Trail** (10 miles) starts from a trailhead near the end of Route 578, the road that serves the vacation cabin area south of Red River.

ENCHANTED CIRCLE AREA   Perhaps the most spectacular high-mountain hike in the Sangre de Cristos is the **Truchas Peak Trail** (11 miles), which starts at the Pecos Wilderness portal at Santa Barbara Campground off the High Road to Taos. The long, gradual ascent leads to the long ridgeline connecting the triple peaks of this 13,102-foot mountain where mountain sheep are often seen grazing on the alpine slopes.

Transportation

CAR

From Santa Fe, head north on **Route 285/84**. Near Española, **Route 68** leads north to Taos. **Route 64** weaves across the northern area of the state, passing through Taos and Cimarron. Note: Parts of the highway that cross high through Carson National Forest are closed during the winter. For New Mexico road conditions, call 800-432-4269.

AIR

Most visitors to the Taos area usually fly into **Albuquerque International Sunport** (see "Transportation" in Chapter Five). Both **Faust's Transportation** (505-758-3410, 888-830-3410) and **Twin Hearts Express** (505-751-1201, 800-654-9456) provide shuttle service to Taos from the Albuquerque airport.

Air charters to Taos are available; contact the **Taos Airport**. ~ 505-758-4995. **Rio Grande Air** provides scheduled service from Taos to Albuquerque and Ruidoso as well as Durango, Colorado. Charter service is provided to other areas of New Mexico and southern Colorado. ~ 505-737-9790, 877-435-9742.

BUS

TNM&O Coaches provides service to Taos from Albuquerque via Santa Fe. The line continues northeast to Eagle Nest, Cimarron and Raton. ~ 505-758-1144.

CAR RENTALS

If you'd like to rent a car in Taos, try **Dollar Rent A Car**. ~ Taos Airport; 505-758-3500, 800-800-4000. **Enterprise Rent A Car** also rents in Taos. ~ 1137 Paseo del Pueblo Sur; 505-737-0514, 800-325-8007. **United Chevrolet and Toyota** rents cars in Raton. ~ 505-445-3644.

PUBLIC TRANSIT

You need a car in this region because public transportation is nearly nonexistent. Most visitors flying into Albuquerque will rent a vehicle there. There is a bus system, **The Chili Line**, which provides limited service in Taos only. ~ 505-751-4459.

WALKING TOURS

Call **Taos Historical Walking Tours** if you'd like to stroll about the ancient streets of Taos with a local guide. Tours leave at 10:30 a.m. from the Mable Dodge Luhan House at 240 Morada Lane. Available Monday to Saturday from June through September. They also offer guide services for bus tours. ~ Phone/fax 505-758-4020.

FOUR

Northwestern New Mexico

Half-wild horses gallop across the sagebrush desert around Chaco Canyon in northwestern New Mexico, a land of timeless mystery and profound loneliness. These beautiful creatures are owned, in a loose way, by Navajo herders, none of whom are seen. Traditional Navajo people choose to live in isolation, building their homes out of sight of main roads and other houses. The only signs of human habitation are the strange, scarecrowlike effigies marking the turnoffs to hidden dwellings.

Although deserted now, the San Juan Basin was the site of one of the great capital cities of the Americas nearly a thousand years ago. An Anasazi city stood at the center of this trade empire that spanned the Southwest, linked by an impressive network of ancient "highways." Travelers who venture on dusty washboard roads across the Indian lands to Chaco Canyon will discover mysterious ruins, all that is left of this enigmatic ancient site. Chaco Canyon's fame has spread in recent years, enough to draw hundreds of visitors in a single day, but why the Anasazi chose to build in this desolate place remains a mystery (and why they abandoned it likewise a puzzle). A visit still provides an experience best described as mystical.

The Navajo nation, the largest and fastest-growing Indian tribe in the United States, controls most of the northwestern quadrant of New Mexico. Royalties from coal mining on the reservation provided the means of purchasing vast sprawls of arid rangeland east and south of the official reservation boundary. And while overpopulation, air pollution and economic depression characterize this part of the state, it also boasts colorful people, an incomprehensible language and fascinating folk ways. In short, Navajoland is a true Third World country within the borders of the wealthiest nation on earth.

Other tribes inhabit the region, as well. The Jicarilla Apache Indian Reservation lies to the east of the Navajo lands, and farther south are a string of pueblos that have been occupied since the very first Spaniard, a shipwrecked accountant named Cabeza de Vaca ("Cow's Head"), stumbled upon them after trekking clear across Texas in 1527. Among the pueblos are Acoma, with its fairytale setting overlooking an enchanted landscape of strange rock formations from the top of a steep, isolated mesa, and ancient Zuni, where the people speak a language utterly unlike any other on earth. The American Indians have been here so long that their legends, passed on by spoken word from each generation to the next, contain eyewitness accounts of the volcanic eruptions that created the huge malpais, or lava badlands, on the outskirts of the town of Grants.

Nowhere is the memory of the Spanish soldiers who explored this region in the mid-1500s as vivid as in the mesas south of Route 40 between Grants and Gallup. Here, in the poor and remote villages of the Zuni Indian Reservation, lies the reality behind the "golden cities of Cibola" legend that lured the first explorers northward from Mexico City. Here, too, stand the cliffs of El Morro, where Indians, Spanish explorers and Anglo settlers alike carved messages in stone to create a "guest register" spanning 800 years.

The town of Grants, formerly the center of the uranium boom that swept northwestern New Mexico in the 1950s and died in the 1970s, is now little more than an inexpensive place for interstate truckers to spend the night. Yet its location, sandwiched between the lava badlands and the forested slopes of Mt. Taylor, is ideal for taking advantage of the wonders of the surrounding lands.

Near the western boundary of New Mexico, Gallup is the largest border town adjoining the Navajo Indian Reservation. It presents a cultural contrast as striking as any to be found along the Mexican border, as the interstate highway brings the outside world to the doorstep of the largest Indian nation in the United States.

▼ ▼ ▼ ▼ ▼ ▼ ▼ ▼
Grants Area

Just over an hour's drive west of Albuquerque on Route 40, Grants is situated at the center of an intriguing array of places—the most ancient continuously inhabited pueblos in New Mexico, a vast and forbidding lava bed with ice caves that bear the marks of centuries of explorers, and a mountain held sacred in Navajo tradition.

SIGHTS

More than 7000 native people reside in **Laguna Pueblo**, a pueblo that dates back to the turn of the 17th century. Old Laguna is situated on a hillside overlooking the interstate midway between Albuquerque and Grants; the centerpiece is **San Jose de Laguna Church**, a mission church in use since the pueblo's founding. Most Laguna residents live in modern villages scattered across the reservation. ~ 505-552-6654, fax 505-552-6941.

Travelers in no particular hurry and tired of dodging trucks on the interstate can catch a remnant of **Old Route 66** at Laguna. The road parallels Route 40 and plays peekaboo with it all the way to the Acoma reservation.

Acoma Pueblo (Sky City) has been inhabited continuously since it was built on a solitary mesa top above a valley of stone pillars in the 12th century—earlier than the pueblos at Salinas, Bandelier or Pecos. New houses are still being built on the roofs of houses centuries old. There is no school bus service, electricity or running water on the mesa, so today only 15 families live in Sky City year-round. Most work as potters or pottery painters. More than 400 well-maintained homes in the old pueblo are used as spiritual retreats and summer houses by their owners, who live in modern reservation towns near the interstate. Shuttle buses carry visitors up the steep road, built by a motion-picture crew in 1969, for an hour-long guided tour of the pueblo. Those who choose to can hike back down on the short, steep trail used by Acoma residents for at least 800 years before the road was built. For schedule information, call the **Acoma Visitors Center.** Fee for photographing. Admission. ~ Located 15 miles east of Grants on Route 40, take Exit 89 and drive another 15 miles south on Indian Road 38; 505-469-1052, 800-747-0181, fax 505-552-7204.

Grants got its start as a railroad stop back when the region's major industry was carrot farming. In 1950 a Navajo sheepherder discovered a strange yellow rock that turned out to be radioactive, and Grants suddenly became the center of a uranium mining boom.

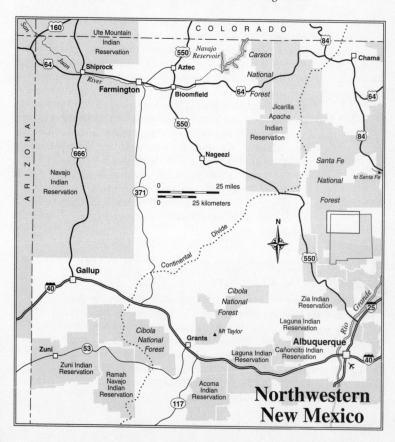

Northwestern New Mexico

Today, despite its prime location amid many of western New Mexico's best sightseeing highlights, Grants is a low-key highwayside town with few of the trappings of a tourist mecca.

Those who wish to learn more about the uranium era can do so at the **New Mexico Mining Museum**, where visitors ride an elevator down from the museum's main floor to explore an underground mine replica. The Grants Chamber of Commerce shares the same building. Closed Sunday from September through April. Admission. ~ 100 North Iron Street, Grants; 505-287-4802, 800-748-2142, fax 505-287-8224; www.grants.org, e-mail discover@grants.org.

Route 53, a quiet secondary highway, leads south and west of Grants to two national monuments—the first ever established in the United States and one of the newest. The highway continues across the Ramah Navajo and Zuni Indian reservations. Near the pueblo of Zuni, Route 602 goes north and returns to Route 40 at Gallup.

Malpais is Spanish for "badland," and the 114,277-acre **El Malpais National Monument** protects one of the largest lava beds in New Mexico. The highways that border the lava flow—Route 53 on the west and Route 117 on the east—are connected by County Road 42, a rugged dirt road that runs along the west and south perimeters; these roads should only be attempted in a high-clearance vehicle. Though there are no developed campgrounds, primitive camping is allowed (free backcountry permits are available at the monument's Information Center). Hiking opportunities in the national monument are discussed in the "Hiking" section at the end of the chapter.

For a spectacular panoramic view of El Malpais, stop at **Sandstone Bluffs**, an overlook 200 feet above the monument. From here you'll spy Mt. Taylor to the north, the chain of craters to the west and the lava bed–filled valley. ~ Route 117, ten miles south of Route 40.

AUTHOR FAVORITE

A rewarding stop on a quick visit to El Malpais is **Bandera Crater and Ice Cave**, a privately owned tourist concession that eventually will be acquired as part of the monument. Separate easy trails take visitors to the crater of one of the volcanoes that made the lava field and to a subterranean ice cave, a lava tube where the temperature stays below freezing even on the hottest summer days. Admission. ~ Route 53, 25 miles south of Route 40; 505-783-4303, 888-423-2283, fax 505-783-4304; www.icecaves.com, e-mail icecaves@cia-g.com.

Stock up on maps and information at **El Malpais Information Center**, located on Route 53, 23 miles south of the Route 40 turnoff. A hiking trail, part of the Continental Divide National Scenic Trail, and geological exhibits are the center's highlights. Backcountry tent camping is allowed with a permit. ~ On Route 53 between mile markers 63 and 64; phone/fax 505-783-4774; www.nps.gov/elma.

At **El Morro National Monument,** a 15-minute drive west on Route 53 from Bandera Crater, a white-sandstone bluff marks the location of a 200,000-gallon waterhole. Atop the high bluff are the ruins of Atsina, a 13th-century pueblo where about 1500 people lived. The Indians carved petroglyphs along the trail between the pueblo and the waterhole, starting a tradition that would last 800 years. When conquistador Don Juan de Oñate camped by the pool in 1605, returning after his discovery of the Gulf of California, he scratched an inscription in the sandstone to memorialize his passing. Spanish explorers added their often-lengthy messages to the rock face until 1774. The absence of inscriptions for 75 years bears mute witness to the social turmoil surrounding the Mexican Revolution and the Mexican War. The first English inscription appeared in 1849, and soldiers, surveyors and pioneers continued to carve their names in the cliff until 1904. Two years later, President Theodore Roosevelt declared El Morro the nation's second national monument, and defacing the rock with its historical graffiti has been prohibited ever since. Admission. ~ Route 53, Ramah; 505-783-4226, fax 505-783-4689; www.nps.gov/elmo.

LODGING

There are about 15 motels in town. The more modern franchise motels, located near the easternmost Grants exit from Route 40, include the **Best Western Inn and Suites,** with large rooms as well as amenities like an indoor swimming pool and a sauna. Breakfast is included in the rates. ~ 1501 East Santa Fe Avenue, Grants; 505-287-7901, 800-528-1234, fax 505-285-5751. BUDGET.

Farther west along Santa Fe Avenue are a number of independent motels, all budget. Several of them formerly belonged to national chains, still recognizable under fresh coats of paint. The 24-room **Sands Motel** is a block off the main route and offers a little more peace and quiet. There are refrigerators in every room and a complimentary continental breakfast is served. ~ 112 McArthur Street, Grants; 505-287-2996, 800-424-7679, fax 505-287-2107; www.sandsmotelonroute66.com, e-mail management@ sandsmotelonroute66.com. BUDGET.

◄ HIDDEN

A genuinely different bed-and-breakfast inn near Grants is the **Cimarron Rose Bed & Breakfast,** a ranchlike compound among the ponderosa pines at 7700 feet elevation on the Continental Divide. The location is secluded and ideal for hiking, mountain biking, cross-country skiing, birdwatching and honeymooning.

Zuni Country

You can drive form Grants to Gallup—a distance of 65 miles—in less than an hour on Route 25 and see very little of interest. But if you're willing to turn this leg of your journey into an all-day trip, the paved two-lane route outlined here will show you some of New Mexico's best "hidden" sights.

EL MALPAIS   Taking Route 40 Exit 82 at Grants, head south on Route 53, which skirts the edge of the jagged, black lava flow known as El Malpais ("the badland"). Continue for 26 miles until you enter the ponderosa forest. Stop a minute at Sandstone Bluff for a panoramic view of the lava flow.

BANDERA CRATER AND ICE CAVE   Visit Bandera Crater and Ice Cave (page 142), a private concession within El Malpais National Monument. Take a hot hike up a gentle lava slope to the interior of the volcanic crater, then cool off in the ice cave. Allow one and a half hours.

Accommodations are in modern, comfortable suites with full kitchens, and breakfast—featuring hosts' specialties such as blue corn pancakes and crepes along with juice and fruit—is delivered to your room in a basket. ~ 689 Oso Ridge Route, 30 miles southwest of Grants; 505-783-4770, 800-856-5776; www.cimarron rose.com. MODERATE TO DELUXE.

DINING   Grants has several low-priced restaurants that serve good New Mexican food. The family-style **Monte Carlo Restaurant** is known for its sheepherder sandwich—a steak on a tortilla with chili and cheese. Breakfast, lunch and dinner are served. ~ 721 West Santa Fe Avenue, Grants; 505-287-9250. BUDGET TO MODERATE.

Jaramillos Mexi-Catessen, a local favorite, offers a choice of eating on the premises or ordering take-out for a spicy picnic lunch. Closed Saturday and Sunday. ~ 213 North 3rd Street, Grants; 505-287-9308. BUDGET.

Fancier, but still inexpensive, is **El Jardin**, featuring more sophisticated Southwestern cuisine such as chimichangas, flautas, fajitas and *machaca* burritos. Closed Sunday. ~ 319 West Santa Fe Avenue, Grants; 505-285-5231. BUDGET.

A bustling local haunt, **El Cafecito** serves up hearty fare all day long. The menu offers both Mexican and American food, and on any given day, families can be seen here enjoying stuffed *sopapillas* and burgers. The breakfasts are large and inexpensive.

EL MORRO NATIONAL MONUMENT   Continue for 16 more miles on Route 53 to the turnoff for El Morro. Visit El Morro National Monument (page 143). Many tourists are content with a look at the inscriptions around the spring at the base of the cliff left by early Spanish and Anglo exploration parties, but take time to climb the petroglyph-lined trail up the back side of the rock and be surprised by the spectacular setting of the ancient Indian ruins on top. Allow one and a half hours.

ZUNI PUEBLO   Continue on Route 53 for 32 more miles to Zuni Pueblo, where it's best to park near the highway and see the pueblo on foot. Take a walk through the back streets of Zuni Pueblo (page 148), where modern construction materials blend seamlessly with stone walls that were ancient when conquistador Coronado saw them 460 years ago and mistook the pueblo for a legendary city of gold. Allow one hour.

HAWIKUH   If you have extra time, take the 12-mile unpaved road from Zuni south to the ruins of Hawikuh, an ancestral pueblo of the Zuni people. From Zuni, backtrack six miles on Route 53 and turn north on Route 602. A 25-mile drive through beautiful pink and white hills will bring you back to Route 40 at Gallup.

Closed Sunday. ~ 820 East Santa Fe Avenue, Grants; 505-285-6229. BUDGET.

For a fancier, more upscale night out in Grants, **La Ventana** is it. Dark and intimate, the one-room restaurant is decorated in a typical Southwestern motif, with kachinas on the walls and Indian rugs underfoot; there's a sunken bar upon entering. The food varies from steak and seafood to prime rib. Sandwiches at lunch might include turkey and guacamole on seven-grain bread. Closed Sunday. ~ 110½ Geis Street, Grants; 505-287-9393, fax 505-287-7490. BUDGET TO DELUXE.

For simple good food and plenty of it, consider the **Iron Skillet** at the Petro Truck Stop west of Grants. This is one of the largest truck stops along the length of Route 40, and the restaurant confirms the adage that the best food is the place with the most semi-trailers parked out front. Open 24 hours daily, the Iron Skillet offers both full family menus and an impressive all-you-can-eat buffet and salad bar as well as daily specials. Each booth has a telephone. ~ Route 40 at Horizon Boulevard, Milan; 505-285-6621, fax 505-287-7078. BUDGET TO MODERATE.

BLUEWATER LAKE STATE PARK   Secluded in a valley halfway between Grants and Gallup, this picturesque reservoir dates back to the 1920s. The lake, stocked with trout and catfish, is said to have one of the highest fish-catch rates of all

PARKS

New Mexican lakes. A variety of watersports is allowed; swim at your own risk. One of the several hiking trails here begins near the campground and leads down to a lush side canyon. Facilities include picnic tables, restrooms and showers. Day-use fee, $4. ~ Route 412, seven miles south of Exit 63 from Route 40, which is 19 miles west of Grants; 505-876-2391, fax 505-876-2307.

▲   There are 135 sites (14 with RV hookups); primitive camping is allowed near the lake. Fees per night are $8 for primitive sites, $10 for developed sites and $14 for hookups.

RAMAH LAKE   Mormon settlers created this small lake (pronounced "ray-mah") in the 1880s for irrigation. It operated for generations as a private fishing lake and has been open to the public since 1987. Fishing is good for trout; there are also a few bass and bluegill. Facilities are limited to restrooms and a small boat dock. ~ Route 53, just north of Ramah. Ramah is near the eastern boundary of the Zuni Indian Reservation, 55 miles southwest of Grants. Information about the lake can be found at the Lewis Trade Center, which also issues fishing licenses; 505-783-4368, fax 505-783-4372.

▼ ▼ ▼ ▼ ▼ ▼ ▼ ▼ ▼ ▼

Gallup Area

Gallup is the largest town on the boundary of the Navajo Indian Reservation, which sprawls across vast tracts of New Mexico, Arizona and Utah. Most of the 200,000 Navajo people live scattered across the land, no home within view of another, on a reservation larger than the states of Connecticut, Vermont and Massachusetts put together. The Navajo people come to Gallup to shop and sell their jewelry, rugs and other handicrafts to traders. Today, as savvy collectors are visiting Gallup in search of good bargains on high-quality work by Navajo and Zuni artisans, the previously decrepit downtown area is being gentrified and occupied by fine art galleries and shops.

SIGHTS   The main feature at **Red Rock State Park** is its rodeo grounds nestled in a sheer-walled canyon. A small museum exhibits ancient, historic and contemporary American Indian arts and crafts, including pottery, kachinas, baskets, masks and oil paintings, by artists from various tribes in the region. The park also contains archaeological sites dating back over a thousand years. Closed Saturday and Sunday from October through May. ~ Off Route 40, just east of Gallup; 505-722-3839, fax 505-863-1297; e-mail rrsp@ci.gallup.nm.us.

Gallup rests astride old Route 66 (called Historic 66 in Gallup) just 22 miles from the Arizona border. Located near both the Navajo and Zuni Indian reservations, this historic town of 20,000 bills itself as the "Gateway to Indian Country." Pawn shops, bars and a row of neon motels lend a hard edge to the local ambience,

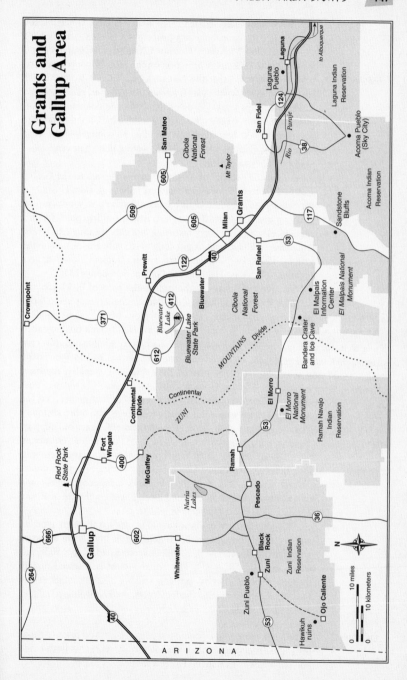

Grants and Gallup Area

ARIZONA

to Albuquerque

Laguna
Laguna Pueblo
124
Laguna Indian Reservation
San Fidel
Rio Paraje
38
Acoma Pueblo (Sky City)
Acoma Indian Reservation

San Mateo
Cibola National Forest
Mt Taylor
605
509
605
Grants
Milan
117
Sandstone Bluffs
122
40
53
San Rafael
El Malpais Information Center
El Malpais National Monument
Prewitt
Bluewater
412
Bluewater Lake
Bluewater Lake State Park
612
Cibola National Forest
Bandera Crater and Ice Cave
Crownpoint
371
MOUNTAINS
Divide
El Morro
Continental Divide
Continental Divide
ZUNI
53
El Morro National Monument
Ramah Navajo Indian Reservation
Fort Wingate
400
Red Rock State Park
McGaffey
Ramah
53
Nutria Lakes
Pescado
36
666
Gallup
602
Black Rock
Whitewater
Zuni
Zuni Indian Reservation
264
Zuni Pueblo
Ojo Caliente
53
Hawikuh ruins

N

0   10 miles
0   10 kilometers

but the annual Inter-Tribal Ceremonial and large concentration of American Indians make it a prime place to view native crafts.

The **Gallup-McKinley County Chamber of Commerce** is a good place to pick up information on the area. While you're here, take a moment to visit the **Navajo Code Talkers Room**, which showcases these World War II heroes. Awards and photos chronicle the wartime experiences of the 200 code talkers, with particular attention paid to the first 29 inductees. Closed Sunday in summer; closed Saturday and Sunday in winter. ~ 103 West Historic 66, Gallup; 505-722-2228; www.gallupchamber.com, e-mail hwy66@cia-g.com.

HIDDEN ►

A limestone statue of a Navajo greets visitors to the **Gallup Cultural Center**, housed in a restored railway station. Upstairs is the Storyteller Museum with narrated displays on sandpainting, weaving and Gallup's days as a bustling trading post. On the same level is an art gallery featuring monthly rotating exhibits of American Indian artists. A gift shop and a café are located on the ground floor. In summer, there are traditional Indian dances nightly. ~ 201 East Historic 66, Gallup; 505-863-4131.

Situated on Route 53 about 30 miles west of El Morro and 40 miles south of Gallup is **Zuni Pueblo**, the largest pueblo (population approximately 10,000) in New Mexico. The modern town of Zuni has evolved from a pueblo called Halona, which had been established for centuries when Coronado arrived in 1540, believing it to be one of the fabulously wealthy, mythical "Seven Golden Cities of Cibola." The town does not look like anything special at first glance, but the more you wander the back streets, the more antiquity reveals itself. Stone foundations 800 years old support many modern buildings in Zuni Pueblo, and crumbling stone storage sheds in people's yards may have been built long before Christopher Columbus first set sail. Keep your ears perked here, for the Zuni people speak a language unlike any other known American Indian dialect. Photography fee. ~ Route 53; 505-782-4481, fax 505-782-7202.

Some of the illustrious guests at El Rancho Hotel included John Wayne, Humphrey Bogart, Spencer Tracy, Katharine Hepburn, Alan Ladd and Kirk Douglas.

The long history of Zuni Pueblo is recalled through artifacts and historical photographs in the fledgling **A:shiwi Awan Museum and Heritage Center**. ~ 02E Ojo Caliente Road, Zuni; 505-782-4403, fax 505-782-4503. This tribal project is financed mainly through sales of jewelry, pottery, fetishes and paintings at the **Pueblo of Zuni Arts and Crafts Center**. ~ 1222 Route 53, Zuni; 505-782-5531, fax 505-782-2136.

LODGING

Gallup has more motels comparable in quality and price to those in Grants. It also has one unique historic hotel that is both rustic and elegant. The **El Rancho Hotel** was built in 1937 by the brother of film producer D. W. Griffith. This is where movie stars stayed while shooting Westerns in the surrounding red-rock canyon country. Ronald Reagan (surely you remember him before he was president) checked in here in the 1940s. Rich, dark wood polished to a gleam predominates in the larger-than-life two-story lobby. There are accommodations in both the old hotel and the modern annex next door. There's also an outdoor pool. ~ 1000 East Historic 66, Gallup; 505-863-9311, 800-543-6351, fax 505-722-5917; www.elranchohotel.com, e-mail elrancho@cnetco.com. BUDGET.

The only lodging on the Zuni Reservation is the **Inn At Halona,** situated close enough to the pre-Columbian pueblo that guests feel like a part of the timeless village life. The eight-room inn looks like a family home, with a shared kitchen, laundry room and baths and local Indian art on the walls. The owners enjoy sharing their knowledge of Zuni traditions, and each guest is given a small handcrafted fetish bear as a memento of their stay. ~ 23-B Pia Mesa Road, Zuni; 505-782-4118, fax 505-782-2155; www.halona.com, e-mail halona@nm.net. MODERATE.

◄ HIDDEN

In Gallup, an unusual eatery is the restaurant in the historic **El Rancho Hotel**. The food is fairly conventional American fare, but movie stars like John Wayne, Humphrey Bogart and Ronald Reagan once ate here and now have menu items named after them as well as publicity photos on the walls—a little bit of old Hollywood in Indian country! Breakfast, lunch and dinner are served. ~ 1000 East Historic 66, Gallup; 505-863-9311, fax 505-722-5917; www.elranchohotel.com. BUDGET TO MODERATE.

DINING

New Mexican food is served up at **Genaro's,** a well-hidden café specializing in stuffed *sopapillas*. Closed Sunday and Monday, as well as two weeks at the end of June and two weeks at the end of December. ~ 600 West Hill Avenue, Gallup; 505-863-6761. BUDGET.

New Mexican beef dishes such as *carne adovada* and greenchile steak appear on the menu at **Panz Alegra**. They also serve Italian fare and seafood. Closed Sunday. ~ 1201 East Historic 66, Gallup; 505-722-7229. MODERATE TO DELUXE.

Another quite popular mid-range restaurant is the **Ranch Kitchen**, where waiters serve American and Mexican fare in a casual atmosphere. Breakfast, lunch and dinner are served. ~ 3001 West Historic 66, Gallup; 505-722-2537, fax 505-722-2328. MODERATE TO DELUXE.

Prices for American Indian wares are normally lower in Gallup than in Santa Fe or Albuquerque, but quality varies. State law protects American Indians and collectors alike from fraud in the sale of American Indian–made goods, but it can still require a

SHOPPING

discerning eye to distinguish handmade crafts from those made in factories that employ American Indians or determine which items are genuinely old as opposed to "antiqued." Still, the region has been a major American Indian arts-and-crafts trading center for more than a century, and it is possible to find valuable turn-of-the-20th-century Germantown blankets and forgotten pieces of "old pawn" turquoise and silver jewelry.

The largest concentration of American Indian traders is found along Historic 66 between 2nd and 3rd streets. The oldest shop on the block is **Richardson's**, where the modest facade gives little hint of the treasures in several large rooms inside. This is one of several downtown pawn shops that serve as "banks" for the Navajo people, continuing the tradition whereby the American Indians store their individual wealth in the form of handmade jewelry, using it as needed for collateral and redeeming it for ceremonials. Closed Sunday. ~ 222 West Historic 66, Gallup; 505-722-4762, fax 505-772-9424.

Those interested in the materials and techniques of making American Indian jewelry can learn about them on a visit to **Thunderbird Jewelry Supply**. Closed Sunday. ~ 1907 West Historic 66, Gallup; 505-722-4323.

Recently, galleries have been appearing along Coal Street, Gallup's main drag situated a block south of Historic 66. Several of them emphasize contemporary American Indian and Southwestern arts.

Zuni Pueblo has several well-stocked American Indian galleries, particularly **Turquoise Village**. Closed Sunday. ~ Route 53; 505-782-5522, 800-748-2405.

For just about everything including maybe the kitchen sink, visit **Ellis Tanner Trading Company**. There's a plethora of American Indian crafts and jewelry, as well as cookware and even rug-making materials in case you feel inspired to make your own souvenir. Closed Sunday. ~ 1908 Route 602, Gallup; 505-863-4434; www.etanner.com.

JEWELRY CENTRAL

American Indian jewelry is said to be the leading industry in Gallup. The number of wholesalers, galleries and pawn shops specializing in jewelry (and rugs) supports this claim, as does the presence of buyers and collectors from all over the world. As the biggest town on the edge of the Navajo Indian Reservation and the nearest town to Zuni (the largest of New Mexico's Indian pueblos), Gallup is the natural location for trading companies dealing directly with American Indian artists and craftsworkers.

As its name suggests, **Tobe Turpen's Indian Trading Company** specializes exclusively in American Indian arts and crafts: pottery, baskets, rugs, kachinas and dreamcatchers. Closed Sunday. ~ 1710 South 2nd Street, Gallup; 505-722-3806; www.pn trader.com.

There's not much in terms of nightlife in Gallup, but there are a few bars and sports clubs mostly within local chain hotels around town. The **City Lights Lounge and Sports Bar** is located in the Holiday Inn. ~ 2915 West Historic 66; 505-722-2201. Another is **Rookies Sports Bar** at the Best Western Inn & Suites. ~ 3009 West Historic 66; 505-722-2221.

NIGHTLIFE

ZUNI LAKES ⛵ 🚣 The Zuni tribe operates several fishing lakes in the hills of the reservation. (A permit must be obtained from tribal headquarters on Route 53 in Zuni, Major Market in Zuni or Lewis Trading Post in Ramah.) Boating is allowed, though gasoline motors are prohibited. Blackrock Lake has picnic facilities and a playground. Boating fee, $1. ~ Blackrock Lake is three miles east of Zuni off Route 53. Eustace Lake is within Zuni village limits. Nutria Lakes are seven to eleven miles north of Route 53 on an unpaved road. Ojo Caliente is 17 miles south of Zuni on Tribal Route 2. Pescado Lake is 17 miles east of Zuni off Route 53; 505-782-5851, fax 505-782-2726.

PARKS

▲ There are primitive sites at Blackrock Lake, Ojo Caliente, Nutria Lakes, No. 4 and Eustace Lake. Campgrounds at six of the lakes are open all year; $5 per night and $3 each additional night.

RED ROCK STATE PARK 🏃 Named for the red sandstone cliffs that lend an austere beauty to the surrounding area, the 640-acre park's main feature is its rodeo grounds, which can be found clinging to the side of the canyon. There are also picnic tables, restrooms, showers, a museum and trails. The park is the site of several important Indian events, concerts and community activities, including the annual Inter-Tribal Ceremonial, the largest powwow in the United States. Closed Saturday and Sunday from October through May. ~ Located just off Route 40 east of Gallup; 505-722-3839, fax 505-863-1297; e-mail rrsp@ci.gallup.nm.us.

▲ There are 134 sites with hookups; $18 per night.

Four Corners Area

Farmington is the natural base camp for sightseeing in the Four Corners area, the sole hub in the continental United States where four states— New Mexico, Arizona, Colorado and Utah—meet. Three rivers, the San Juan, Animas and LaPlata also converge here, dispelling the notion that this is dry, dusty desert country. In fact, Farmington was founded on farming, hence its name, although the easy-going town now has industry and mining at its financial base.

The true highlight of the region, however, is its rich American Indian history. The area abounds in Pueblo ruins and offers numerous museums that provide a glimpse into the religious and cultural lives of the ancient Navajo, Chaco and Anasazi tribes.

SIGHTS   Start your sightseeing tour of the region on Route 666, about 30 miles southwest of Farmington at **Shiprock Peak**. Solidified lava and igneous rock comprise this neck of a volcano, which can be seen by air from more than 100 miles away. The towering Shiprock rises from a great stretch of nothing but sand and rock. (American Indians called it a "rock with wings.") The site has no services. ~ Off Route 666.

When you're done admiring the natural beauty at Shiprock pinnacle, head north on Route 666 until you reach the town of Shiprock. From here, it's another 30 miles east on Route 64 to the laidback town of Farmington.

Take your brochures and maps to **Orchard Park**, in the center of downtown, where you can peruse your options. ~ Main and Orchard streets, Farmington.

For an overview of the area's cultural and outdoor offerings, check in at the **Gateway Park Museum and Visitors Center** (505-599-1174, fax 505-326-7572), where there's a photograph of New Mexico's fifth-largest city during frontier days, a children's gallery, a reconstruction of a 1930s trading post and an exhibit of the geologic history of the San Juan Basin. Also here is the **Farmington Convention and Visitors Bureau**, where you can get your fill of town literature. Closed Sunday. ~ 3041 East Main Street, Farmington; 505-326-7602, 800-448-1240, fax 505-327-0577; www.farmingtonnm.org.

Next you'll find **Salmon Ruin**, which has remains from an 11th-century pueblo, including a large kiva, built by the Chaco people. Ongoing stabilization of the site's exposed structures continues to this day. Admission. ~ 6131 Route 64, Bloomfield; 505-632-2013, fax 505-632-1707.

At Salmon Ruin is **Heritage Park**, a re-creation of habitation units, from sand dune campgrounds to tepees and hogans, representing man's occupation in the San Juan Valley. The on-site museum houses regional artifacts, too.

Driving from Farmington northeast on Route 550 brings you to the charming town of **Aztec**, which boasts ancient Indian ruins and turn-of-the-20th-century buildings. Aztec's modern-day renaissance, which took place in the 1890s, still shows its Victorian influence in the downtown area. For more information, call the **Aztec Chamber of Commerce & Visitors Center**. Closed Sunday; closed Saturday from December through April. ~ 110 North Ash

Street, Aztec; 505-334-9551, fax 505-334-7648; www.aztecnm. com, e-mail aztec@cyberport.com.

Your first stop on a whirlwind tour of Aztec should begin at the old City Hall, where the **Aztec Museum** displays all kinds of bric-a-brac, like minerals and rocks, Victorian fashions, sleighs and buggies, tools used by the early settlers, an oilfield exhibit and a pioneer village with an authentically furnished post office, general store, bank and log cabin. Closed Sunday. Admission. ~ 125 North Main Street, Aztec; 505-334-9829, fax 505-334-7648; e-mail aztecmuseum@cyberport.com.

Strolling along Aztec's Main Street, you'll see many turn-of-the-20th-century buildings, including the **Odd Fellows Hall** (107 South Main Street) and **Miss Gail's Inn** (300 South Main Street). On a side street is the **Presbyterian Church** (201 North Church Street), which was built of adobe brick in 1889.

Another building worth a look-see is the **Denver & Rio Grande Western Railway Depot.** No tracks remain on the site of this commercial building turned residence, but the 1915 structure is a classic reminder of the railway's heyday. ~ 408 North Rio Grande, Aztec.

Aztec's buildings seem perfectly modern in comparison to the ancient **Aztec Ruins National Monument,** a major prehistoric settlement chock full of 12th-century pueblo ruins, including a restored kiva. (Despite its misleading name, no Aztec Indians ever inhabited this area.) Both the Chaco civilization to the south and the Mesa Verde settlement to the north probably influenced

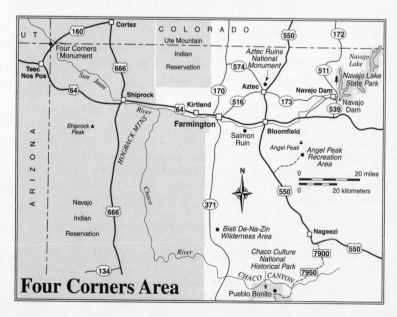

Four Corners Area

Aztec's development. Admission. ~ Ruins Road, Aztec; 505-334-6174, fax 505-334-6372; www.nps.gov/azru, e-mail tracy_bod nar@nps.gov.

A visit to the ruins is a must, for its sheer accessibility as much as for its wonders. First take the self-guided trail that begins just outside the visitors center. You'll come upon the **West Ruin** and the magnificently restored **Great Kiva**. West Ruin could be compared to a present-day apartment building because as many as 300 people may have lived there at a single time; most unusual is a line of green sandstone on one outer wall. The kiva, an underground chamber that's traditionally used for religious ceremonies, was carefully constructed of sandstone blocks from materials that were hand-carried from quarries miles away. The kiva was excavated in 1921 and reconstructed about 12 years later.

The open plaza area was the center of daily life in Aztec. Wandering north out of the main ruins takes you to the **Hubbard Site**, a kiva that's unique in that it has three concentric circular walls. Presumably this building was used for religious ceremonies (it's now back-filled for protection). Another tri-walled kiva, largely unexcavated, exists in a nearby mound.

Off the beaten path is the **East Ruin** and its annex, thought to be the second and later civilization at Aztec. Both are largely unexcavated and must be viewed from a distance. Adjacent to the Aztec ruins is a tree-lined picnic area, a nice shady place for a snack or repose after wandering through the ancient cultural center.

To return to ruin sightings like desolate Angel Peak, you must backtrack to Aztec or take Route 550 south through Bloomfield toward Albuquerque.

Angel Peak, a multimillion-year-old geologic formation, is a sacred dwelling place to the Navajos. A five-mile unpaved, dirt road along the rim offers great views of the pastel-hued mesas

FOUR CORNERS MONUMENT

There's something both silly and irresistible about driving to **Four Corners** to stick each foot in a different state (Colorado and Utah) and each hand in still two others (Arizona and New Mexico) while someone takes your picture from a scaffolding. But then, this is the only place in the United States where you can simultaneously "be" in four different states. The inevitable Navajo crafts booths offer up jewelry, T-shirts, paintings, sandpaintings, fry bread and lemonade—a splendid way to make something festive out of two intersecting lines on a map. ~ From Farmington, head west on Route 64 until you cross the Arizona/New Mexico border. At Teec Nos Pos, Arizona, head north on Route 160 for about ten miles.

and buttes. Camping and picnicking are allowed, though no water is available. After Angel Peak, continue on to Chaco Canyon, the epicenter of Anasazi life.

Reflecting the simplicity of lifestyle and slower pace of the region's people, the lodging choices in and around Four Corners are characterized by their cleanliness and efficiency.

LODGING

Cast-iron sculptures honoring the "ancient ones" decorate the walls of the pink-hued rooms at the **Anasazi Inn**. Handsome quilt prints in a Southwestern scheme and spotless bathrooms are reason enough to try this centrally located lodge. ~ 903 West Main Street, Farmington; 505-325-4564, fax 505-326-0732. BUDGET.

If bigger is better, then **Best Western Inn and Suites** has something over its chain competitors on the same street. Extra-large rooms are great for families and help give the inn a leg up. A sizable indoor pool in a tropical setting may make you forget you're in desert country. A fitness center and a game room for children are also available. ~ 700 Scott Avenue, Farmington; 505-327-5221, 800-528-1234, fax 505-327-1565; www.newmexico-innandsuites.com. MODERATE.

With just 33 rooms, the **Farmington Lodge** falls into the small, no-frills category. Most of the well-maintained rooms have refrigerators. ~ 1510 West Main Street, Farmington; 505-325-0233, fax 505-325-6574. BUDGET.

Kokopelli's Inn may be the most "hidden" accommodation in this guidebook. The owner, a consulting geologist, originally built the manmade-cave-cum-B&B as his office—but clients couldn't find it. In fact, the single-unit bed and breakfast is in a manmade cave beneath 70 feet of rock, with its entrance at the base of a sheer sandstone cliff outside of town. The luxury guest apartment is complete with handmade furniture, Indian rugs, VCR, CD stereo system, microwave, dishwasher and laundry room, as well as a stone jacuzzi under a waterfall shower. Make reservations well in advance. Closed end of November through February. ~ 206 West 38th Street, Farmington; 505-325-7855, fax 505-325-9671; www.bbonline.com/nm/kokopelli, e-mail kokoscave@hotmail.com. ULTRA-DELUXE.

◄ HIDDEN

Its location on a busy highway is definitely a drawback, but you can shut out most of the world's noise in the 20 tidy rooms of the **Enchantment Lodge**. ~ 1800 West Aztec Boulevard, Aztec; 505-334-6143, 800-847-2194, fax 505-334-9234. BUDGET.

Most people come to Aztec for the mysterious ruins. But a visit to its historic Main Street is well worth your time. Smack in the middle of the main drag is **Miss Gail's Inn**, a 1905 palace of antiques. The Country Victorian rooms—some with partial kitchens—are large enough for multiday living. Weekly rates avail-

Text continued on page 158.

In the Land
of Ancient Ones

An intricate highway system, irrigation ditches and 13 great house ruins have led archaeologists to speculate that Chaco was once a center for the Anasazi civilization. The canyon has remained in a comparatively pristine state largely because access is difficult on rutted dirt roads. A debate continues on whether the road should be upgraded, but those who believe Chaco remains in better shape because of its inaccessibility have prevailed so far. Unless you're driving an expensive sports car or the road is slippery from rain, it's worth the bumpy ride to view 13 major ruins and the remains of a culture suspected to have begun in Chaco around A.D 900. Note: Services are virtually nonexistent, so come fully prepared with food, water and gas.

The fascinating civilization of 1000 years ago has left in its wake traces of advanced art forms like pottery and weaving. The Chaco Anasazi were farmers who probably fled the drought-stricken area in the 13th century. Chaco is considered to be the center of Anasazi culture (the developed road network tells us that) and religious ceremony (as all the kivas left behind indicate). Site excavation began in the late 1890s and continues today through the University of New Mexico's Chaco Research Institute.

Park rangers conduct informational walks through Chaco Canyon, or you can grab a map from the visitors center and chart your own path through this eerily silent land. Self-guided trails are found at Pueblo Bonito, Chetro Ketl and Casa Rinconada. Admission. ~ Located 54 miles south of Bloomfield via Route 550 and County Roads 7900 and 7950; 505-786-7014, fax 505-786-7061; www.nps.gov/chcu.

Closest to the visitors center is the partially excavated **Una Vida** ruin, with its five kivas and 150 rooms. Because it was built on a mound, Una Vida appears higher than it actually is. Petroglyphs and remains from hogans huddle in the surrounding rock. From the paved park road is the **Hungo Pavi** ruin, an easy trek from the car. Down the road is **Chetro Ketl**, with its estimated 500 rooms and 16 kivas one of the largest Chacoan villages. Chetro Ketl's expansive plaza section is thought to be typical of great houses of that time.

A short jaunt in the other direction from the same trailhead brings you to the amazing **Pueblo Bonito**, which was probably the heart and soul of Chaco. In fact, it could be considered to have been the New York City of its day with multiple rooms and kivas crammed into a relatively tight space. The four-story stone masonry complex is obviously the product of painstaking craftsmanship.

Pueblo del Arroyo, a high-standing D-shaped house, with its 280 rooms and 20 kivas, is found nearby along the paved road. **Kin Kletso**, which was built in two stages, had 100 rooms and five kivas. It may have risen as high as three stories. Take the trail that begins here to the prehistoric **Jackson Stairs**, one of the more impressive stairways in the Anasazi world, and try to figure out the farming terraces of the Anasazi.

Past Kin Kletso is Casa Chiquita, where the hike from the central canyon to the unexcavated great house of **Peñasco Blanco** is well worth the effort. On the south side of the paved park road is **Casa Rinconada**, one of the largest kivas in the Southwest. A trail that begins here winds to the South Mesa and the great house of **Tsin Kletsin**, a structure seven rooms strong.

The more adventurous and archaeology-minded can wander in search of "outlier" sites of Chaco Canyon, like Pueblo Pintado and Kin Ya-ah. Free backcountry permits (required before setting out) and directions are available from the visitors center. Camping is also permitted here, but you should be well prepared: Campers in Chaco Canyon must come equipped with plenty of provisions, although water is available. The closest groceries and gas are 21 miles away, most of them on dirt roads, near the County Road 7900 turnoff on Route 550. Gallo Campground is located about one mile east of the visitors center. There are 48 sites, including 5 RV sites (no hookups); $10 per night.

able fall and winter are a bargain. It's a good place to hang your hat if you plan on thoroughly exploring the Four Corners area. Breakfast included. ~ 300 South Main Street, Aztec; 505-334-3452, 888-534-3452, fax 505-334-9664. BUDGET TO MODERATE.

HIDDEN ►

Two miles north of the turnoff to Chaco Canyon ruins is a welcome respite from the dust and heat. The **Chaco Inn at the Post** is a bed and breakfast that promotes a family-style atmosphere—the innkeepers live on the premises and pride themselves on keeping the guests comfortable. The three rooms are quaint, with clean lines and wooden floors. Closed late November to early March. ~ Route 44, Nageezi; 505-632-3646; e-mail chaco@ fifi.net. MODERATE.

DINING

Spinach-and-feta-cheese croissants served piping hot out of the oven, raspberry granola bars and multigrain breads are only a few of the healthy, homemade delectables at **Something Special Bakery & Tea Room**. It's open for breakfast and lunch. Vegetarian entrées available. Closed occasional weekends; call ahead. ~ 116 North Auburn Avenue, Farmington; 505-325-8183, fax 505-327-2859. BUDGET.

Among the many restaurants offering wholesome "American cuisine" that dot downtown Farmington, **TJ's Downtown Diner** is just a tad better. Along with homemade soups and pies, TJ's also features daily Mexican specials. Breakfast and lunch only. Closed Sunday. ~ 119 East Main Street, Farmington; 505-327-5027. BUDGET.

How hot do you like your green chile? For authentic Mexican cuisine, try the **El Charro Cafe**. ~ 737 West Main Street, Farmington; 505-327-2464. BUDGET. Its primary competition is the **Los Rios Café**, which serves New Mexican cuisine as well as burgers and fries. Closed Sunday. ~ 915 Farmington Avenue, Farmington; 505-325-5699. BUDGET.

While the name suggests a trip back to merry old England, the menu is closer to south-of-the-border. Still, **Chelsea's London Pub & Grill** is a good choice for an ale and sandwich, steak or enchilada. Sorry, no kidney pie. ~ Animas Valley Mall, 4601 East Main Street, Farmington; 505-327-9644, fax 505-327-0866. BUDGET TO MODERATE.

SHOPPING

Try the **Foutz Trading Co.** for splendid Navajo crafts such as silver jewelry and intricately beaded barrettes. Closed Sunday. ~ Route 64, Shiprock; 505-368-5790.

If you've been on the road for awhile and could use some "herbal fitness," stop in at **Herbal Alternatives** and pick up natural remedies for all that ails you. Closed Sunday. ~ 6510 East Main Street, Farmington; 505-327-3205.

Victorian gifts and decor, candles, teddy bears and antique laces and linens can be found at **Echoes**. Closed Sunday. ~ 103 South Main Street, Aztec; 505-334-9302.

NIGHTLIFE

Farmington is not exactly a late-night town, but it does boast a few nightclubs with live music. Check out the **Top Deck Bar** for live country Wednesday through Saturday and karaoke on Sunday and Monday. Cover charge Wednesday through Saturday. ~ 515 East Main Street, Farmington; 505-327-7385.

Lively and colorful dramas, including *Black River Traders*, are performed mid-June to mid-August at the **Lions Wilderness Park Amphitheater**. ~ College Boulevard, Farmington; 505-326-7602, 877-599-3331 (tickets).

PARKS

NAVAJO LAKE STATE PARK   New Mexico's second-largest lake offers boating, fishing, swimming and even scuba diving at three recreation areas—Pine River, Sims Mesa and the San Juan River. Navajo Lake's sparkling waters and nearly 200 miles of shoreline is chock full of cold and warm water species of game fish, including trophy trout, catfish, pike and bass. The park features a visitors center, marinas, picnic sites and restrooms. Day-use fee, $4. ~ Take Route 173 to Route 511, 23 miles east of Aztec; 505-632-2278, fax 505-632-8159; e-mail navajolake@cyberport.com.

> Scuba diving isn't usually associated with New Mexico's waters. But diving opportunities abound at Navajo Lake State Park.

▲ There are 157 sites at Pine (54 with electricity and 9 with full hookups), 46 at Sims Mesa (24 with hookups) and 47 (23 with hookups) at Cottonwood Campground on the San Juan River. Fees are $10 per night for standard sites, $14 for electricity and $18 per night for full hookups. Reservations: 800-667-2757.

ANGEL PEAK RECREATION AREA   A heavenly looking 40-million-year-old geologic formation appears to be suspended within a lovely colored canyon. The five-mile-long road around the canyon rim offers fine vistas of the buttes and badlands in this land of the "sacred ones." The only facilities are picnic tables and restrooms. ~ Take Route 550 to the Angel Peak turnoff, about 17 miles southeast of Bloomfield; 505-599-8900, fax 505-599-8998.

▲ There are eight primitive sites, no water; no fee.

BISTI DE-NA-ZIN WILDERNESS AREA   Nearly 45,000 acres of eroded shale, clay and sandstone spires, mesas and sculpted rock that defy description were naturally sculpted in this former inland sea. Large reptiles and mammals were thought to walk these lands about 70 million years ago; fossils and petrified wood are all that remain in this desolate area of badlands. No developed trails, facilities or signs mar this protected wilderness, pronounced "bis-tye." No bicycles allowed. ~ Route 371, 36 miles south of Farmington; 505-599-8900, fax 505-599-8998.

▲ Primitive camping allowed, no water; no fee.

Outdoor Adventures

FISHING

A variety of catches are found in the lakes of the Four Corners area, so try your luck with the plentiful trout or one of the other fish often caught here. Equipment is available at some sites; others are more remote.

FOUR CORNERS AREA The San Juan River at the base of the Navajo Dam in **Navajo Lake State Park** is the site of quality waters teeming with trout. One of the largest lakes in New Mexico, Navajo provides angling opportunities for bluegill, bass, trout, pike and catfish. Try **Born-n-Raised on the San Juan River** for flyfishing equipment and guide services. ~ 1791 Route 173, Navajo Dam; 505-632-2194. **Rizuto's Fly Shop** rents flyfishing gear and also offers half- and full-day fishing float trips on the San Juan River. ~ 1796 Route 173, Navajo Dam; 505-632-3893.

Morgan Lake produces trophy largemouth bass, and is also great for catfish. ~ Four miles south of Kirtland, next to Four Corners Power Plant.

SKIING

Who needs a resort? Excellent cross-country skiing can be found on county and national forest roads—minus the crowds and lift lines.

GRANTS AREA Primitive roads on **Mt. Taylor** are used for cross-country skiing in winter. For information on routes and conditions, contact the Cibola National Forest–Mt. Taylor District Ranger Station in Grants. ~ 1800 Lobo Canyon Road; 505-287-8833, fax 505-287-4924.

AUTHOR FAVORITE

In the spring and fall months, El Malpais National Monument south of Grants presents some unusual hiking possibilities. One of my memorable adventures in the lava lands was hiking the **Acoma-Zuni Trail** (7.5 miles), which crosses the lava fields between routes 53 and 117. Said to be part of a trade route that linked the Zuni and Acoma pueblos in ancient times, the trail is level, but the lava is so rough and uneven that even a short walk from either trailhead will prove quite strenuous. If you decide to do the entire seven and a half miles, plan for a full day of hiking or arrange a two-vehicle shuttle.

Opportunities for mountain biking abound in a region with beautiful scenery and many unpaved roads.

BIKING

GRANTS AREA Mountain biking is allowed on trails and roads throughout the **Cibola National Forest**. Many bikers recently have been testing their skills on the **Mt. Taylor summit trail** and the **McGaffey region**. Trails in the BLM **Conservation Area** on Route 117 near El Malpais National Monument are also open to bikers.

FOUR CORNERS AREA There's only one trail in Chaco Canyon where you can ride nonmotorized bikes, and that's the mile-and-a-half **Wijiji Trail**.

Bike Rentals Mountain-bike rentals, repairs, sales and ride recommendations can be found at **Scoreboard Sporting Goods**. Closed Sunday. ~ 107 West Coal Avenue, Gallup; 505-722-6077.

Northwestern New Mexico boasts several national forests and monuments with trails for hiking. From 11,000-foot peaks to fascinating archaeological sites to rugged, trailless wilderness areas, there's something for everyone to explore. All distances are one way unless otherwise noted.

HIKING

GRANTS AREA Unpaved roads lead through **Cibola National Forest** to within a mile of the summit of **Mt. Taylor**, the 11,301-foot mountain that dominates the skyline north of Grants. A trail that starts near the junction of Forest Roads 193 and 501 climbs more than 2000 feet up the southwest side of the peak to the mountaintop in three miles. Another, the Gooseberry Trail, begins near La Mosca Peak Overlook and ascends the north ridge to reach the summit of Mt. Taylor in a mile.

Though there are no defined trails at **Sandstone Bluffs** you can descend to the bluffs' base for a trek alongside the lava beds.

Other trails into El Malpais start along unpaved County Road 42, which skirts the western and southern edges of the monument. The road requires a high-clearance vehicle. The **Big Tubes Area Route** (2-mile loop) leads to Big Skylight Cave, which then branches off to Caterpillar Collapse, Seven Bridges and Four Window Cave; Big Skylight and Four Window are both entrances to the same immense lava tube, part of a system that is 17 miles long. For more information, call 505-783-4774.

To the west of Albuquerque on **Route 40**, it is a two-hour drive to Grants and another hour to Gallup. From Gallup, head north on **Route 666**, which meets with Route 64 near Shiprock. **Route 64** skirts across the northern edge of New Mexico, passing through the Four Corners area and across to Chama. For New Mexico road conditions, call 800-432-4269.

▼▼▼▼▼▼▼▼▼▼
Transportation

CAR

AIR

Most visitors will fly into **Albuquerque International Sunport**; see Chapter Twelve for more information.

Charter service to **Four Corners Regional Airport** (505-599-1395) in Farmington is provided by Mesa Airlines, Great Lake Airlines and Air Midwest.

BUS

Greyhound Bus Lines (800-231-2222; www.greyhound.com) provides service to Grants at Fins & Feathers, 907 West Santa Fe Avenue, 505-285-6268; and in Gallup, 255 East Historic 66, 505-863-3761.

TNM&O Coaches provides service from Albuquerque to Farmington. ~ 101 East Animas Street, Farmington; 505-325-1009.

TRAIN

Amtrak's "Southwest Chief" stops in Gallup. ~ 201 East Historic 66, Gallup; 800-872-7245; www.amtrak.com.

CAR RENTALS

A car is essential to touring this area. If you are flying in and out of Albuquerque, rent a car there (see Chapter Twelve for information). For rental cars in northwestern New Mexico, try **Enterprise Rent A Car**. Closed Sunday. ~ 2111 West Historic 66, Gallup; 505-722-7388, 800-736-8227.

For rentals at the Four Corners Regional Airport in Farmington, try **Avis Rent A Car** (800-331-1212), **Budget Rent A Car** (800-527-0700) or **Hertz Rent A Car** (800-654-3131).

FIVE

Albuquerque and Central New Mexico

Billy the Kid once roamed this area. Now you can, too. The vast ranchland plains east of the Rocky Mountains haven't changed much since the Kid rode into legend more than a century ago. But Albuquerque is another story. Just another small town on the banks of the Rio Grande downriver from Santa Fe in the heyday of the Wild West, it has been transformed into a bustling metropolis boasting a unique mosaic of lifestyles and cultures. This is the central New Mexico that intrigues the traveler: a mixture of the wild and the sublime, the cowboy and the Indian, the small town and the big city, the past and the present.

History is part of the enchantment of Albuquerque and its environs; geography is another. In fact, the setting is one thing the residents love most about their home. Sandia Peak towers a mile above the eastern city limit. Rural farmland follows the Rio Grande south. And to the west is a wide and beautiful emptiness. Visitors are often surprised by the abruptness with which the city gives way to wilderness at Albuquerque's edge. Route 40 plunges into a parched, overgrazed, alkaline high-desert wasteland that gradually reveals its stark beauty in twisting arroyos and jagged black-lava fields with fortresslike rock mesas and solitary mountains rising like islands from an arid sea.

Central New Mexico is a compelling combination of the high, cool forests of the Rocky Mountains to the north and the rocky, sunbaked Chihuahuan Desert stretching a thousand miles to the south. If you don't like the weather, you can just move on. In June, the hottest month of the year, when air conditioning becomes essential in Albuquerque, a short drive into the mountains offers shade, cool streams and occasional patches of unmelted snow. In January, skiers can enjoy nearby slopes and then return to lower elevations where snowfalls are infrequent and light.

The mix of mountain coolness, desert dryness and southern latitude produces evening temperatures that drop to about 50° even in mid-summer and daytime highs above freezing in the dead of winter. In autumn, people watch the month-long procession of bright-gold foliage gracefully descending from the mountain heights to the cottonwood bosquet along the rivers. In springtime, new greenery spreads slowly up the slopes toward the sky.

If you're headed toward Santa Fe from Albuquerque, consider taking the Turquoise Trail (Route 14), a more relaxed and less congested route that crosses the rugged San Pedro Mountains and offers a handful of interesting sights, including a restored old mission church and an old mining town.

Cultural contrasts are just as dramatic. This is a melting pot of Navajo and Pueblo Indians whose lifestyles were upset by the Spanish exploration that began in the 1500s. Also mixed in are Norteño descendants of Spanish and Mexican colonists (New Mexico was a province of Mexico from 1821 until the 1848 treaty that ended the Mexican War with the United States) and Anglos who began settling here in the early 1800s. All these cultures come together in modern-day Albuquerque, a polyglot of a city where ancient ceremonies and futuristic technological research, fiestas and hot-air balloon races, and cowboys and entrepreneurs exist side by side.

Equally fascinating sights await beyond Albuquerque's city limits. The eastern plains, where most travelers stop only to exit the interstate for gasoline and a bite to eat, offer beaches and water sports on several large, manmade lakes along the Pecos and Canadian rivers. You'll find the grave of Billy-boy himself in the town of Fort Sumner, along with sites long abandoned to wind, weather and wildflowers (but just aching to be discovered).

Near the small town of Mountainair at the foot of the Manzano Mountains, sightseers can explore Spanish and Indian ruins from centuries past, one-time American Indian trade centers and headquarters for missionary efforts during the colonial era. Outside Socorro, located just off the interstate, nature lovers visiting between November and March can witness the spectacular congregation of tens of thousands of snow geese, Canada geese and sandhill cranes.

Faint remnants of conquest can be found throughout the area, left by Spanish soldiers who explored central New Mexico in the first half of the 16th century. These reminders of the past include the site of Coronado's bridge near Santa Rosa and the ruins of the massacred pueblo of Kuaua at Coronado State Monument near Albuquerque.

This sounds like a lot to see and do, and it is. But the astonishing news is that every place described in this chapter is within three hours' drive of Albuquerque. What more incentive do you need?

▼▼▼▼▼▼▼▼▼▼
Albuquerque

If you plan to explore central New Mexico, make Albuquerque your starting point. You'll find that much of the sightseeing here is rooted in the past, but the city also offers a fine collection of art museums and nightspots. Many scenic wonders of nature are within the city limits or nearby. And when the day is done, there are plenty of places in which to eat and sleep.

SIGHTS

Perhaps the best place to begin is **Old Town,** the original center of Albuquerque during the Spanish colonial and Mexican eras. West of the modern downtown area, this lowrise district can be reached by taking Central Avenue west from Route 25 or Rio

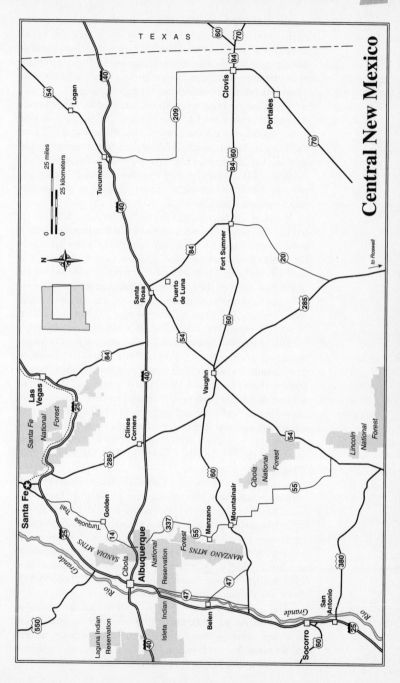

Central New Mexico

Grande Boulevard south from Route 40. Situated around an attractive central plaza with a bandstand, many buildings in Old Town date as early as 1780. After 1880, when the railroad reached Albuquerque and the station was constructed a distance from the plaza, businesses migrated to the present downtown and Old Town was practically abandoned for half a century.

Revitalization came when artists, attracted by bargain rents, established studios in Old Town. Galleries followed, as did gift shops, boutiques and restaurants. Today, it's easy to while away half a day exploring the restored adobe (and more recent "puebloized" stucco) structures, hidden patios, brick paths, gardens and balconies of Old Town, mulling over the handmade jewelry and pottery offered by American Indian vendors or just people-watching from a park bench.

Home of the largest public exhibition of rattlesnakes in the world, Old Town's **American International Rattlesnake Museum** could surprise you with some interesting facts about what may be the world's most misunderstood reptile. Bet you didn't know that our founding fathers almost elected the timber rattlesnake instead of the bald eagle as the national symbol. And while it may not have any hands-on exhibits, this museum overflows with rattlesnake artifacts and artwork. Admission. ~ 202 San Felipe Street Northwest; phone/fax 505-242-6569; www.rattlesnakes.com.

Two of the city's best museums lie on opposite sides of Mountain Road, about a block from Old Town Plaza. The **Albuquerque Museum** contains art and history exhibits, including the permanent "Four Centuries: A History of Albuquerque" display that features the largest collection of Spanish colonial artifacts in the United States. See armor and weapons that belonged to the conquistadors, medieval religious items brought by early missionaries and ordinary household items that evoke the lifestyle of early settlers along the Rio Grande. Closed Monday. Admission. ~ 2000 Mountain Road Northwest; 505-243-7255, fax 505-764-6546; www.cabq.gov/museum, e-mail info@albuquerquemuseum.com.

Nearby, the **New Mexico Museum of Natural History and Science** features unique and imaginative exhibits that let visitors walk through time, explore an Ice Age cave, stand inside an erupting volcano and sit on the back of a dinosaur. A planetarium and a five-story movie screen are also here. The museum is closed on non-holiday Mondays in January and September. Admission. ~ 1801 Mountain Road Northwest; 505-841-2800, fax 505-841-2844; www.nmmnh-abq.mus.nm.us.

Also in the area is Albuquerque's scariest tourist attraction, the **National Atomic Museum**. Exhibits here trace the development of nuclear weapons, from Albert Einstein's original letter (suggesting the possibility) to President Franklin D. Roosevelt to replicas of various atomic bombs from the 1940s and '50s and videos of

Exploring Albuquerque

The commercial hub of New Mexico, Albuquerque is not the tourist mecca that Santa Fe or Taos is, but it does have sights worth seeing. Since it's one of the few cities in this guidebook with a major airport, it's the first place that many visitors to the Southwest see. Here's how to see the best of the city in a day.

• Visit **Petroglyphs National Monument** (page 170) on the city's western edge for a look at the ancient Puebloan shamanic art. Allow one and a half hours, including driving time.

• Take your pick among the city's museums and nature parks. My suggestions: if you have kids along, go to either the **Rio Grande Zoo** (page 168) or the **New Mexico Museum of Natural History and Science** (page 166). Allow one and a half hours for either place. If not, your time might be better spent at the cool, calm **Albuquerque Aquarium** (page 168) and neighboring **Rio Grande Botanical Garden** (page 168), both included on the same ticket. Allow one and a half hours.

• Have lunch at the **Indian Pueblo Cultural Center** (page 168).

• Driving to the east side of the city, ride the **Sandia Peak Tramway** (page 171) to the summit of Sandia Crest. At the top there is a long, easy hiking trail with the best view in New Mexico, so plan to spend the afternoon.

• Late in the day, after descending from the mountaintop, head over to **Old Town** (page 164), a good place to stroll and dine.

ear tests. There are extensive exhibits on nuclear medicine,
ics and Madame Curie. Admission. ~ 1905 Mountain Road
vest; 505-284-3243, fax 505-284-3244; www.atomicmu
um.com, e-mail info@atomicmuseum.com.

Enclosures at the clean, imaginatively designed **Rio Grande Zoo** are designed to resemble the animals' natural habitats as much as possible. The most unusual residents are a pack of Mexican lobos, a small wolf subspecies that is extinct in the wild. Of the two dozen lobos that survive in a federal captive-breeding program, the majority has been bred at the Rio Grande Zoo. Closed Monday. Admission. ~ 903 10th Street Southwest; 505-764-6200, fax 505-764-6249; www.cabq.gov/biopark/zoo.

The **Rio Grande Botanical Garden** fills ten acres of the Rio Grande bosque west of Old Town with formal, walled theme gardens and a glass conservatory in which Mediterranean and desert environments are re-created. The 45,000-square-foot **Albuquerque Aquarium** traces the varied aquatic environments found along the Rio Grande as it makes its way from the Rocky Mountains to the Gulf of Mexico. There's a coral reef exhibit and an eel cave, but the aquarium's centerpiece is its 285,000-gallon shark tank. The zoo, the botanical garden and the aquarium, along with a planned water park, are collectively known as the **Albuquerque Biological Park**. Closed Monday. Admission. ~ Central Avenue Southwest and New York Street; 505-764-6200, fax 505-764-6249; www.cabq.gov/biopark.

North of downtown, the **Indian Pueblo Cultural Center**, jointly owned and operated by all 19 of New Mexico's pueblos, has one of the finest American Indian museums in the state. Through artifacts and dioramas, it traces the history of New Mexico's native population over a span of 20,000 years. Exhibits of traditional pottery and other arts and crafts show the stylistic differences between the various pueblos. The museum also features a collection of photographs from the Smithsonian Institution taken of Pueblo people in the late 19th century. The cultural center has retail galleries, a restaurant serving American Indian food, an indoor theater and an outdoor plaza where free dance performances and other special events are staged every weekend. Admission. ~ 2401 12th Street Northwest; 505-843-7270, fax 505-842-6959; www.indianpueblo.org.

East of downtown, the **University of New Mexico** offers a varied choice of on-campus museums and cultural events. ~ The campus is bordered by Central Avenue, Girard Boulevard, University Boulevard and Indian School Road; 505-277-0111, fax 505-277-2987; www.unm.edu.

The **Maxwell Museum of Anthropology** displays selections from the university's huge international collection of artifacts. Its "People of the Southwest" exhibit simulates an archaeological

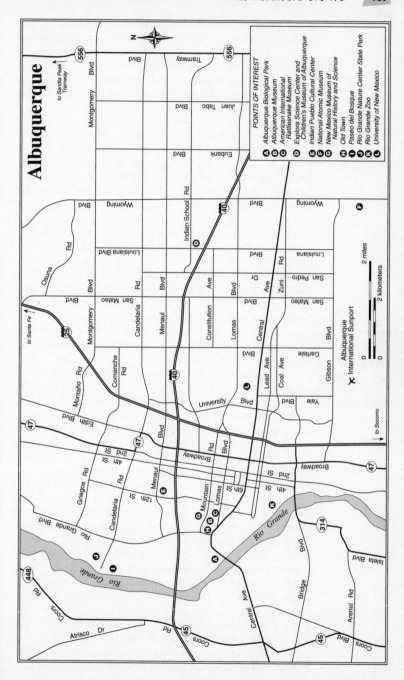

Albuquerque

to Sandia Peak Tramway

to Santa Fe

to Socorro

Albuquerque International Sunport

Rio Grande

POINTS OF INTEREST

- Albuquerque Biological Park
- Albuquerque Museum
- American International Rattlesnake Museum
- Explora Science Center and Children's Museum of Albuquerque
- Indian Pueblo Cultural Center
- National Atomic Museum
- New Mexico Museum of Natural History and Science
- Old Town
- Paseo del Bosque
- Rio Grande Nature Center State Park
- Rio Grande Zoo
- University of New Mexico

0   2 miles
0   2 kilometers

dig in progress. Closed Sunday and Monday. ~ University Boulevard, between Central Avenue and Lomas Boulevard on campus; 505-277-4404, fax 505-277-1547; www.unm.edu/~maxwell.

The **University Art Museum** has limited space but an outstanding collection of works by such well-known visual artists as Georgia O'Keeffe and Ansel Adams. Closed Monday. ~ Center for the Arts; 505-277-4001, fax 505-277-7315.

The university has a separate art museum, the **Jonson Gallery**, which displays selections from a 2000-piece collection of the works of early-20th-century New Mexico artist Raymond Jonson, as well as works from contemporary New Mexico artists. Closed Saturday through Monday. ~ 1909 Las Lomas Boulevard Northeast; 505-277-4967, fax 505-277-3188; www.unm.edu/~jonsong, e-mail jonsong@unm.edu.

Northrop Hall (505-277-4204), the geology building, has a **Geology Museum** and a **Meteorite Museum**, and next door in Castetter Hall is the university's **Museum of Southwestern Biology** (505-277-5340).

The **Explora Science Center and Children's Museum of Albuquerque** has hands-on exhibits designed to stimulate creative young imaginations. There are a giant loom, a bubble area, a capture-your-shadow wall, a puppet theater, the Creation Station for make-it, take-it art projects, and an interactive emergency room. The science section focuses on motion, light, fluids, air pressure and health. Admission. ~ Winrock Center, 2100 Louisiana Boulevard Northeast; 505-842-1537, fax 505-842-5915; www.esccma.org, e-mail media@esccma.org.

With 712,000 residents in the greater metropolitan area, Albuquerque accounts for more than a third of the state's entire population.

Along the dark volcanic escarpment on Albuquerque's western perimeter, visitors can find perhaps the largest assemblage of petroglyphs in the Southwest—more than 25,000 specimens in all. The drawings were chipped into the patina of rock surfaces 800 to 1000 years ago. Some are representational pictures of animal, human and supernatural figures, and others are abstract symbols, the meanings of which have provided generations of archaeologists with a fertile topic for speculation. A portion of the petroglyphs can be viewed in the **Petroglyphs National Monument**. In the Boca Negra Canyon there are several self-guided trails, including the Mesa Point Trail, that lead you past petroglyphs. To reach the visitors center, take the Unser exit from Route 40, then drive north for about three miles to the intersection of Unser Boulevard and Western Trail. Boca Negra Canyon is an additional two miles north of the visitors center, off Unser. ~ 4735 Unser Boulevard Northwest; 505-899-0205, fax 505-899-0207; www.nps.gov/petr, e-mail petr@nps.gov.

For many travelers, the ultimate experience is a trip up **Sandia Peak** (elevation 10,378 feet) east of Albuquerque. The mountain

rises so sharply on the city's eastern boundary that from eithe[
bottom or top it looks as if a rock falling from the cliffs along th[
ridgeline would land in someone's yard in the fashionable Nort[
east Heights neighborhood a mile below. On a typically clear day,
you can see almost half the state from the summit.

While the summit can be reached by car (see "Turquoise Trail"
Driving Tour on page 182) or on foot (see "Hiking" at the end
of the chapter), the most spectacular way to climb this mountain
is via the **Sandia Peak Tramway**. It takes just 15 minutes to as-
cend the 2.7-mile cable, and all the while you'll enjoy eagle's-eye
views of rugged canyons in the Sandia Wilderness Area; you may
even catch a glimpse of Rocky Mountain mule deer grazing on a
distant promontory. At the summit are an observation deck, a
deluxe-priced restaurant, a gift shop, a snack bar a short walk away
at the end of the auto road, the Four Seasons Visitors Center and
breathtaking views in every direction. The tram closes twice a year
(once in April, once in October) for regular maintenance. Admission. ~ 10 Tramway Loop Northeast; 505-856-7325, fax 505-
856-6335; www.sandiapeak.com, e-mail info@sandiapeak.com.

LODGING

As New Mexico's largest city, Albuquerque has lodgings for every
taste. One downtown grand hotel that predates World War II has
been restored to the height of luxury. The emerging bed-and-
breakfast scene features small, homey places that range from Victorian mansions to contemporary suburban guest houses. Rates
for Albuquerque accommodations are much lower than the cost
of comparable lodging in Santa Fe or Taos. *Note:* Reservations
are advised for all bed and breakfasts.

Conrad Hilton's second hostelry, built in 1939, has been lovingly restored as the city's showpiece downtown historic hotel,
La Posada de Albuquerque. The lobby, with its vaulted ceiling
and Indian murals, sets the tone—a blend of old-fashioned elegance and unique New Mexican style. Handmade traditional New
Mexico furniture graces the modern guest rooms. ~ 125 2nd Street
Northwest; 505-242-9090, 800-777-5732, fax 505-242-8664;
www.laposada-abq.com, e-mail info@laposada-abq.com. DELUXE.

Located within walking distance of Old Town, Route 66 and
downtown Albuquerque, the **Brittania & W. E. Mauger Estate
B&B** is a historic Queen Anne home with high ceilings and hardwood floors. The estate has eight bedrooms, each with a private
bath and refrigerator, and two townhouses. It offers full breakfast as well as wine and hors d'oeuvres in the afternoon. ~ 701
Roma Street Northwest; 505-242-8755, 800-719-9189, fax 505-
842-8835; www.maugerbb.com, e-mail maugerbb@aol.com. MOD-
ERATE TO DELUXE.

The **Old Town Bed and Breakfast** is actually east of Old Town
in a quiet residential neighborhood within easy walking distance

of restaurants, shops, the New Mexico Museum of Natural History and the Albuquerque Museum. It features pueblo-style adobe architecture, a patio and two guest quarters. The bottom two-room suite has a separate sitting area and a kiva fireplace. ~ 707 17th Street Northwest; 505-764-9144, 888-900-9144; www.inn-new-mexico.com, e-mail nancyhoffman@earthlink.net. MODERATE TO DELUXE.

Closer to the plaza, the **Böttger-Koch Mansion Bed and Breakfast Inn** is in a 1912 Victorian home listed on the National Register of Historic Landmarks. The eight guest rooms are individually decorated with Victorian furnishings; one includes a jacuzzi. ~ 110 San Felipe Street Northwest; 505-243-3639, 800-758-3639, fax 505-243-4378; www.bottger.com, e-mail bottgerk@aol.com. DELUXE.

Strolling among the Territorial-style lowrises of Old Town, it would be easy to imagine yourself in an earlier century were it not for the towering presence of the 11-story **Sheraton Old Town** a block away. The grounds preserve natural desert landscaping, while the large lobby bursts with Southwestern designs and colors. Views from the upper floors are arguably the most spectacular in town. ~ 800 Rio Grande Boulevard Northwest; 505-843-6300, 800-237-2133, fax 505-842-9863; www.flash.net/~sheraton, e-mail sheraton@buynm.com. DELUXE TO ULTRA-DELUXE.

Families traveling together who appreciate the extra space and amenities of a suite can find weekend bargain rates at several of Albuquerque's all-suite hotels. For example, the **Barcelona Suites Uptown** off Route 40 has suites with separate bedrooms and kitchen facilities that include refrigerators and microwaves. Rates include full breakfast. ~ 900 Louisiana Boulevard Northeast; 505-255-5566, 877-227-7848, fax 505-266-6644; www.barcelona suiteshotel.com, e-mail barcelonasuites@aol.com. MODERATE.

The **Crown Plaza Pyramid** is easy to spot; just look for its stepped pyramid shape along Route 25 in the commercial zone north of the city. Inside you'll find an atrium with a 50-foot waterfall, two glass elevators and Mayan and Aztec motifs. The 311 guest rooms feature such amenities as coffeemakers, hair dryers, full-size vanity mirrors and ironing boards. ~ 5151 San Francisco Road Northeast; 505-821-3333, 800-227-6963, fax 505-828-0230; www.crowneplazapyramid.com. DELUXE.

The **Amberley Suite Hotel** makes an excellent base for touring central New Mexico, plus it's a good bet for families. The 170 suites (one- and two-bedroom) and 24 rooms are decorated in soft tones, with floral spreads on the king-size beds. Garden-side units offer mini-kitchens with microwaves and refrigerators as well as dining areas. ~ 7620 Pan American Freeway Northeast; 505-823-1300, 800-333-9806, fax 505-823-2896; www.

amberleysuite.com, e-mail amberleysuitenm@aol.com. BUDGET
TO MODERATE.

Also on the city's north side off Route 25, and catering to a
business clientele, the **Wyndham Garden Hotel** offers some classy
touches, from the sunny atrium lobby to the bright, contemporary
Southwest-style guest rooms, not to mention the indoor-outdoor
swim-through pool. ~ 6000 Pan American Freeway Northeast; 505-
821-9451, 800-996-3426, fax 505-858-0239; www.wyndham.
com. MODERATE TO DELUXE.

Built in the 1930s by famed architect John Gaw Meem
(widely known as the father of Santa Fe style), **Los Poblanos Inn**
offers cozy indoor spaces that open onto beautiful courtyards,
spectacular mountain views and 25 acres of lush gardens. Hand-
carved doors and traditional tile fixtures are found in each of the
inn's lovingly furnished guest rooms. ~ 4803 Rio Grande Boulevard Northwest; 505-344-9297, fax 505-342-1302; www.los
poblanos.com, e-mail info@lospoblanos.com. DELUXE TO ULTRA-
DELUXE.

Near the eastern bank of the Rio Grande in Los Ranchos de
Albuquerque, **Sarabande Bed and Breakfast** is a six-room inn with
Southwestern–style accoutrements and *latilla* ceilings. Entered
through a lovely courtyard, this adobe-style home also offers fountains and private patios. The owners prepare extravagant breakfasts in their country kitchen and then serve them outside. Bicyclers
will find this a great location because of its proximity to a number
of scenic routes near the Rio Grande, and after a day of pedaling
visitors can look forward to soaking in the hot tub. There's also
a swimming pool. ~ 5637 Rio Grande Boulevard Northwest; 505-

AUTHOR FAVORITE

Bed and breakfasts abound in Albuquerque these days, and for my money the
most interesting is **Casas de Sueños**, three blocks from Old Town Plaza.
The 21 small houses and duplexes surrounding courtyard gardens began as
an artists' colony in the 1940s. Each living unit is individually designed and
furnished, and many have kitchen facilities, fireplaces or hot tubs. Over the
entrance to the main house is a large protuberance, which the innkeepers
refer to as "the snail." The sight of this architectural curiosity stops cars
on the street as drivers gawk. It was originally designed as a nonlinear
law office by young architect Bart Prince. A *Bon Vivant* breakfast, sure
to start your day on a delightful note, is included with your stay. ~
310 Rio Grande Boulevard Southwest; 505-247-4560, fax 505-842-
8493; www.casadesuenos.com. MODERATE TO DELUXE.

345-4923, 888-506-4923, fax 505-345-9130; www.sarabande bb.com, e-mail janie@sarabandebb.com. MODERATE TO DELUXE.

Step back into Southwest history by taking a room at the **Hacienda Antigua**. The 1790 adobe hacienda was built in the Spanish colonial era and still retains its 19th-century ambience. The five guest rooms are individually decorated with antiques including iron beds, kiva fireplaces and a century-old clawfoot bordello tub. There are plenty of opportunities to relax, whether you choose to take a dip in the pool, a soak in the outdoor hot tub or a turn in the orchard. The gourmet breakfast is a special treat. Discounted rates for extended stays in the winter. Gay-friendly. ~ 6708 Tierra Drive Northwest; 505-345-5399, 800-201-2986, fax 505-345-3855; www.haciendantigua.com, e-mail info@haci endantigua.com. DELUXE.

Visitors looking for budget accommodations should take Central Avenue east beyond the University of New Mexico campus. Central used to be Route 66, the main east–west highway through Albuquerque before the interstates were built. Although the old two-lane highway has become a wide commercial thoroughfare, several tourist courts dating back to that earlier era still survive along Central between Carlisle and San Mateo boulevards.

> Native New Mexican Conrad Hilton started his hotel chain in Albuquerque.

The affordably priced **De Anza Motor Lodge** is a prime example. Something about its pueblo styling and tepee-shaped sign recalls that small-town, halfway-from-home-to-California mystique that many people nostalgically associate with Old Route 66. This part of Central Avenue is just east of the hip Nob Hill District. ~ 4301 Central Avenue Northeast; 505-255-1654, fax 505-255-7459. BUDGET.

On the east edge of town, near the Central Avenue/Tramway Boulevard exit from Route 40, is another concentration of franchise lodgings. Although this area is a long way from central destinations like Old Town and the university, it is a convenient location from which to ride the tramway or drive up Sandia Peak.

One option is **Best Western American Motor Inn**. ~ 12999 Central Avenue Northeast; 505-298-7426, 800-366-3252, fax 505-298-0212; www.bestwestern.com/americanmotorinnalbu querque. Another hostelry is **Econo Lodge**. ~ 13211 Central Avenue Northeast; 505-292-7600, 800-553-2666, fax 505-298-4536. MODERATE.

Contemporary in style, the **Hilton Albuquerque** is the finest of several major hotels that cluster northeast of the Route 25 and Route 40 interchange. ~ 1901 University Boulevard Northeast; 505-884-2500, 800-274-6835, fax 505-889-9118. MODERATE TO DELUXE.

The first bed and breakfast to open in Albuquerque, **Casita Chamisa B&B** has two units with a private bath, entrance and fireplace in a 19th-century adobe home. The shady, forested acreage that is the Casita Chamisa's setting is also an archaeological site, and the innkeeper is happy to show a video that explains all about it. Children are welcome, and pets also, by prior arrangement. There's an indoor heated pool and hot tub. A hearty breakfast, complete with an informative narrative about the site by the innkeeper, is included with the room. You won't find a nicer host. ~ 850 Chamisal Road Northwest; 505-897-4644; www.casitachamisa.com, e-mail innkeeper@casitachamisa.com. MODERATE TO DELUXE.

Several first-rate, suburban bed and breakfasts are located in the Paseo del Norte area of Albuquerque and on the other side of the Rio Grande. **Adobe and Roses** rents a two-unit adobe guesthouse and a suite. The traditional New Mexico architecture features brick floors, Mexican tiles and *vigas*. All units have fireplaces as well as private entrances and kitchenettes. Full breakfast is included. ~ 1011 Ortega Road Northwest; 505-898-0654. BUDGET TO MODERATE.

Nearby, **Casa del Granjero B&B** sits on three and a half acres that are accentuated by a gazebo, lily pond, waterfall and hot tub that faces the Sandia Mountains, barn cats, chickens and horses. Three of the seven guest rooms are in the Main House, an adobe hacienda from the Territorial era that features a lovely enclosed courtyard. The Guest House is where the other accommodations are located. Kiva fireplaces, canopy beds, handmade willow furniture, French doors and Mexican-tiled bathrooms are highlights throughout all the rooms. There's also a sauna. ~ 414 C de Baca Lane Northwest; 505-897-4144, 800-701-4144, fax 505-897-9788; www.innewmexico.com, e-mail granjero@prodigy.net. DELUXE.

DINING

A photo exhibit by Jane Butel on Conrad Hilton's early years graces the walls of **Conrad's**, a Southwest-style restaurant featuring a green and white checkerboard floor and lacquered furniture. Drop by for a *cerveza* and appetizers at the bar or sit down for a full dinner of *paella valenciana*, saffron rice cooked in an iron skillet with lobster, green-lipped mussels, shrimp, chicken, pork and vegetables, or braised lamb *empanada* with a cucumber raita. ~ La Posada de Albuquerque, 125 2nd Street Northwest; 505-242-9090, fax 505-242-8664; www.laposadadealbuquerque.net. DELUXE.

La Placita Dining Rooms, in an adobe hacienda on the Old Town Plaza, features hand-carved wooden doorways and a garden patio. Replenish your strength after shopping in historic Albuquerque with *carne adovada* or an *enchilada ranchera*. The *sopapillas*, sprinkled with cinnamon and drenched in honey, are excellent for dessert. Salads, burgers and sandwiches will satisfy less adventurous eaters, and the youngsters can choose from special children's dishes. ~ 208 San Felipe Street Northwest; 505-247-2204, fax 505-842-9686. BUDGET TO MODERATE.

At **Zane Graze Cafe and News** you can pick up one of many local newspapers and settle down (on the patio if you please) to a light meal—perhaps homemade soup and a pita sandwich—and gourmet coffee drinks. No dinner. ~ 308 San Felipe Street Northwest; 505-243-4377. BUDGET.

A popular Mexican restaurant is **La Hacienda**. The Spanish colonial atmosphere, with *ristras* and lots of Southwestern art on the walls, fits right in with the Old Town experience. The menu includes steak and seafood dishes and local cuisine such as fajitas. ~ 302 San Felipe Street Northwest; 505-243-3131, fax 505-243-0090. MODERATE.

Arguably Albuquerque's most beautiful restaurant, **Maria Teresa** is located in the Salvador Armijo House, a National Historic Landmark dating back to the 1840s and elegantly furnished with Victorian-era antiques. Besides local specialties, the menu includes fine contemporary American and Continental dishes. Dinner only; brunch on weekends. ~ 618 Rio Grande Boulevard Northwest; 505-242-3900, fax 505-842-9733. MODERATE TO DELUXE.

In one of Old Town's oldest buildings, circa 1785, **High Noon** serves enchiladas and burritos as well as steaks and seafood to the strains of live flamenco guitar music. A house specialty is the pepper steak served with a pepper and cream cognac sauce. ~ 425 San Felipe Street Northwest; 505-765-1455, fax 505-255-4505. MODERATE TO ULTRA-DELUXE.

It's hard to top the New Mexican fare at **El Patio**, a charming brick bungalow renowned for its inexpensive *chiles rellenos* and beef fajitas. Dine out on the patio if it's nice out. ~ 142 Harvard Drive Southeast; 505-268-4245. BUDGET.

MADAME MCGRATH'S

McGrath's, the restaurant at the Hyatt Regency Albuquerque, is named after the madame of Vine Cottage, one of the most prosperous women in town at the turn of the 20th century. Always one step ahead of the authorities, Lizzie McGrath came up with a unique strategy for defeating the intent of an ordinance outlawing parlor houses in the vicinity of local churches. Rather than relocate her own house of ill repute, she bought the neighboring Lutheran Church and had it moved. (Her thriving business was allowed to stay put.)

Follow the crowds to **Carraro's Bar and Grill** for pizza pies as well as a variety of calzones and sandwiches. The decor won't win any awards, but the patrons couldn't care less; they're here for the homemade Italian bread. Take a table on the veranda if it's a balmy night. ~ 108 Vassar Drive Southeast; phone/fax 505-268-2300. BUDGET TO MODERATE.

While the decor of **The Original Garcia's Kitchen** raises a lot of questions (like what's that huge diamondback rattlesnake skin doing over the entry way to the dining room, and who decided to put all the family trophies in the window?), no one ever second-guesses the kitchen. Take a booth or counter seat and feast on the blue-corn enchilada plate, green-chili stew or *chicharrones* and beans. It's packed during the breakfast hour, when *huevos a la Mexicana* (scrambled eggs, jalapeños, tomatoes and onion) and *huevos locos* (eggs with shredded beef or ham) are among the entrées. Gringo breakfasts like french toast are also served. Breakfast and lunch. ~ 1113 4th Street Northwest; 505-247-9149, fax 505-765-1675. There are five other Garcia's Kitchen locations around Albuquerque. BUDGET.

The menu at **McGrath's**, the restaurant at the Hyatt Regency Albuquerque, features pork, beef, lamb and chicken prepared in a variety of ways. ~ 330 Tijeras Avenue Northwest; 505-766-6700, fax 505-766-6710. DELUXE TO ULTRA-DELUXE.

A different kind of local cuisine can be found at the restaurant in the **Indian Pueblo Cultural Center**. Open for breakfast and lunch, this restaurant serves traditional Pueblo Indian dishes such as fry bread, Indian tacos and *posole*. Hamburgers and other mainstream fare are also served. ~ 2401 12th Street Northwest; 505-843-7270, 800-766-4405; www.indianpueblo.org, e-mail info@indian pueblo.com. BUDGET.

For what many consider the best homemade green chile in Albuquerque, visit the 180-seat **Sanitary Tortilla Factory**. Lunch only. Closed Saturday and Sunday. ~ 403 2nd Street Southwest; 505-242-4890. BUDGET.

A favorite Albuquerque restaurant for unusual food is the **Artichoke Cafe**. Here the menu changes frequently to take advantage of fresh, seasonal ingredients. Choices are wide ranging, including all of your basic meats, pastas and salads. As one might expect, the first item on the menu is an artichoke—steamed and served with three dipping sauces. Paintings by local artists brighten the walls. No lunch on Saturday. Closed Sunday. ~ 424 Central Avenue Southeast; 505-243-0200; www.artichokecafe.com, e-mail articafe@aol.com. MODERATE.

Farther out on Central Avenue, you can get a green-chile cheese dog, a rich, thick chocolate shake and a big dose of nostalgia at the **66 Diner**, a 1950s-style roadside diner designed with

Historic Route 66 buffs in mind. Breakfast on weekends only. ~ 1405 Central Avenue Northeast; 505-247-1421, fax 505-247-0882. BUDGET.

A place where the green chile will knock (or maybe burn) your socks off is **Sadie's Dining Room**. This establishment is as local as it gets, with a view of a bowling alley. ~ 6230 4th Street Northwest; 505-345-5339, fax 505-345-9440. BUDGET.

New Southwestern cuisine is the specialty at **Casa Chaco**. Formerly the Hilton Albuquerque's coffee shop, Casa Chaco has become a full-scale restaurant featuring such delicacies as grilled Rocky Mountain lamb stuffed with spinach and pine nuts, roasted pork porterhouse grilled with prickly pear sauce and apples and mesquite-smoked prime rib. Breakfast, lunch and dinner. ~ 1901 University Boulevard Northeast; 505-884-2500, fax 505-889-9118. MODERATE TO DELUXE.

Firehouses seem to be a popular theme for Albuquerque restaurants. The **Monte Vista Firestation** is located in what was once a real fire station and today stands as one of the city's finest surviving examples of the "Pueblo Deco" architecture that sprang up along Old Route 66 in the 1930s. The fare at this restaurant is highly imaginative. The menu changes daily, but a typical dinner might include jalapeño fettuccine with roasted garlic cilantro cream topped with tequila-marinated shrimp or piñon-crusted pork loin and fried poblano chile rings. No lunch on weekends. ~ 3201 Central Avenue Northeast; 505-255-2424; www.nmbars.com/monte vistafirestation, e-mail montevistafirestation@nmrestaurants. com. MODERATE.

One of the most attractive restaurants on Nob Hill, **Scalo** is a contemporary split-level dining room with Tuscan-style banquette and table seating. The Northern Italian menu includes gourmet pizzas cooked in a wood-fired oven and pasta dishes like linguine with spicy tomato sauce, prosciutto, onions and herbs deglazed with vodka. The spinach salad served with house-smoked chicken, shaved red onion, roasted peppers and gorgonzola makes an excellent starter. ~ 3500 Central Avenue Southeast; 505-255-8782, fax 505-265-7850. MODERATE TO DELUXE.

Designed to look like the world's largest wine barrel, **The Cooperage** is graced with rock walls and etched glass. The surf-and-turf-oriented menu includes lean buffalo steaks, lamb chops rosemary and blackened salmon. ~ 7220 Lomas Boulevard Northeast; 505-255-1657, fax 505-266-0408. MODERATE TO ULTRA-DELUXE.

The Owl Café is one of those diners that offers a kind of "oh the hell with the fat content" menu (you know the type, with onion rings and chocolate cake). If you'd just as soon pass on the green-chili cheeseburger, healthy salads and nutritious drinks are available. Seat yourself at the formica counter (an interesting contrast to the faux marble pillars) or in one of the booths. Breakfast, lunch and dinner. ~ 800 Eubank Boulevard Northeast; 505-291-4900. BUDGET.

Neon cacti and painted *vigas* complement the Southwestern cuisine at **Papa Felipe's**. Booths and table seating are available, but the prices (and the food) are what satisfy customers at this adobe-style establishment, complete with whitewashed bricks and a saltillo tile floor. Specialties include *carne adovada* and chicken fajitas. ~ 9800 Menaul Boulevard Northeast; 505-292-8877. BUDGET TO MODERATE.

Located in the heart of the Nob Hill district, **Flying Star Cafe** is a popular hangout for anyone who wants to see and be seen. Grab a seat inside or at a table on the sidewalk anytime from 6 a.m. to midnight and anyone from university students to military personnel to neighborhood gay residents will be your neighbor. Famous for the goodies produced at their on-site bakery and for their coffee, which is roasted in-house daily, Flying Star also has a café menu with delicious homemade items. On the weekend there is an extended brunch menu. There are several locations. ~ 3416 Central Avenue Southeast, 4501 Juan Tabo Northeast, 8001 Menaul Northeast and 4026 Rio Grande Northwest; 505-255-6633, fax 505-232-8432. BUDGET.

Enjoy broiled orange roughy and grilled salmon at **Pelican's**, where captain's chairs and an outdoor deck done in a dock motif add to the fun. Prime rib, steaks and chicken Dijon round out the extensive menu, which, appropriately enough, focuses on fresh seafood. Dinners served before 6:30 p.m. are less expensive, and children can choose from special dishes. ~ 9800 Montgomery Boulevard Northeast; 505-298-7678, fax 505-293-5593. MODERATE.

Progressive for Albuquerque, **Woody's Cafe and Coffee Bar's** interior has lots of corrugated steel and bright colors. For breakfast there are pastries and four varieties of "espresso'ed eggs," and the lunch menu has an array of sandwiches, homemade soups and or-

AUTHOR FAVORITE

When in Albuquerque, I make a point of eating at the **Frontier Restaurant**, across the street from the main entrance to the University of New Mexico. It may not be fancy, but it's certainly cheap. I go there because they serve the best green chile stew anywhere, not to mention the biggest cinnamon rolls. The lively student environment blends intellectual conversation, video games and general rowdiness. Food choices include burgers and *huevos rancheros* (served all day). Open 24 hours. ~ 2400 Central Avenue Southeast; 505-266-0550, fax 505-266-4574. BUDGET.

ganic salads. The coffee bar features locally roasted coffee that can also be purchased by the pound. ~ 11200 Montgomery Boulevard Northeast, Eldorado Square; phone/fax 505-292-6800. BUDGET.

One of the city's better Asian eateries, ABC **Chinese Restaurant** is entered through a lacquered dragon and phoenix archway. Bas-relief Buddhas and colorful paper lanterns make this Chinese and Korean restaurant a delight. Specialties include boneless tenderloin pork marinated in a spicy Korean bean sauce and barbecued duck with lychee nuts, pineapple and a sweet orange sauce. ~ 8720 Menaul Boulevard Northeast; 505-292-8788. BUDGET TO MODERATE.

One of the finest restaurants in these parts is the **High Finance**. It's the setting that makes this restaurant so special. At the top of the Sandia Peak Tramway, the restaurant affords an incomparable view of Albuquerque glistening in a vast, empty landscape a mile below. Entrées include prime rib, steaks and lobster. Guests with dinner reservations here receive a discount on their tramway fares. ~ Sandia Crest; 505-243-9742; www.highfinancerestaurant.com, e-mail info@highfinancerestaurant.com. DELUXE TO ULTRA-DELUXE.

When the King of Spain granted a chunk of land to Domingo de Luna in 1692, he might have been pleased to know that 300 years later it would be the site of **Luna Mansion**, an elegant restaurant. After living here for many generations, the Luna family granted Santa Fe Railroad an easement across their historic property. In return, the railroad agreed to build the family a new mansion. Completed in 1881, this landmark was remodeled over the years into a handsome colonial-style adobe restaurant known for its eclectic menu. Specialties include a delicious red-chile linguine with chicken and portobello mushrooms. Closed Monday and Tuesday. ~ Los Lunas, east of Route 25 at the corner of Routes 6 and 314; 505-865-7333, fax 505-865-3496. MODERATE TO DELUXE.

SHOPPING   "We've got the hots for you," claims **Joan's Chili Pepper Emporium**, purveyor of hot sauces, pepper garlands and hundreds of other tongue-taunting products for the chili fanatic. This color-

AUTHOR FAVORITE

Inventive, sometimes whimsical modern Southwestern designs make **Tanner Chaney Gallery** a small gem with one of the most intriguing art collections in town. Drop by if you're in the market for Pueblo pottery, loomed rugs or Navajo pictorial weavings—and even if you're not. The gallery also carries folk art from Mexico. ~ 323 Romero Northwest; 505-247-2242.

ful store also stocks cookbooks, magazines and jellies. ~ 201 3rd Street Northwest; 505-766-9119.

An American Indian gallery, **Skip Maisel Indian Jewelry** carries Hopi and Zuni pieces, plus the requisite kachinas, rugs and pottery. Closed Sunday. ~ 510 Central Avenue Southwest; 505-242-6526.

Shoppers can buy directly from American Indian craftspersons along San Felipe Street across from the plaza in **Old Town**, which is also Albuquerque's art gallery and boutique district. Almost 100 shops can lure delighted visitors into making Old Town an all-day expedition.

Possibly the only candy store in America to be picketed by antipornography forces, **The Candy Lady** is an Old Town institution. This adobe-style candyland tempts sweet tooths with 21 brands of fudge, plus dipped strawberries, bonbons and other sugary yummies. But it's the X-rated section doubling as a human anatomy lesson that has caused all the ruckus. Candy molded into the shape of breasts and cakes with spicy frosting designs—even erotic sculptures—actually prompted the city of Albuquerque to attempt a crackdown. They also offer a huge selection of sugar-free treats. ~ 524 Romero Street Northwest; 505-243-6239, 800-214-7731; www.thecandylady.com, e-mail info@thecandylady.com.

The **Santo Domingo Indian Trading Post**, which specializes in jewelry, is owned and operated by a resident of Santo Domingo Pueblo. ~ 401 San Felipe Street Northwest; 505-764-0129.

The Good Stuff displays an array of American Indian and Western antiques. Closed occasional Sundays. ~ 2108 Charlevoix Street Northwest; 505-843-6416. At the **Christin Wolf Gallery** you'll see the artist's fine jewelry as well as Southwestern art. Metal and paper sculpture are also sold here. ~ 206½ San Felipe Street Northwest; 505-242-4222; www.christinwolf.com. **Perfumes of the Desert** carries unusual perfumes blended locally using desert-flower scents. ~ 208 San Felipe Street Northwest; 505-243-0859.

The **Indian Pueblo Cultural Center** has a series of gift shops surrounding the central dance plaza. All operated by the cultural center, the shops differ by price ranges from curio items to museum-quality collectors' objects. Because the cultural center is owned by a coalition of Indian pueblos, authenticity is assured, making this one of the best places to shop for American Indian pottery, sculpture, sandpaintings, rugs, kachinas and traditional and contemporary jewelry. ~ 2401 12th Street Northwest; 505-843-7270, fax 505-842-6959; www.indianpueblo.org.

For Southwestern furniture, kachinas and American Indian jewelry at discount prices, stop by **Albuquerque's Indoor Mercado**, across from the Indian Pueblo Cultural Center. With over 50 merchants hawking chile products, sandpaintings and dozens of other souvenirs, you're bound to find something to take home.

Open Friday through Sunday. ~ 2035 12th Street Northwest; 505-243-8111, fax 505-243-8419.

In Crowd sells folk art by Latin American artists plus New Mexico prison art. ~ 3106 Central Avenue Southeast; 505-268-3750.

Martha's Body Bueno Shop carries cards, gifts, lingerie and adult novelty items. Gay-friendly. ~ 3105 Central Avenue Northeast; 505-255-1122.

Spend some time browsing in **Page One**, the largest independently run bookstore in New Mexico. The friendly staff is always ready to help you find what you need. ~ 11018 Montgomery Boulevard Northeast; 505-294-2026; www.page1book.com.

Known for its broad line of quality boots, **Western Warehouse** offers a variety of popular styles at discount prices. They also carry concho belts, broomstick skirts, bolo ties and a wide array of shirts, Western-style, of course. ~ 6210 San Mateo Northeast; 505-883-7161.

For more practical shopping needs, Albuquerque's major shopping malls are **Winrock Center** (505-888-3038; www.shopwinrock.com), located at Louisiana Boulevard Northeast and Indian School Road Northeast, near the Louisiana Boulevard exit from Route 40, and **Coronado Center** (505-881-4600), located at Louisiana Boulevard Northeast and Menaul Boulevard Northeast.

If that's not enough, the **Chili Pepper Emporium** has the largest and most complete selection in New Mexico—and the world, probably—of chile items, ranging from spices, sauces and jellies to chile-motif T-shirts and chile-shaped Christmas tree lights. ~ 89 Winrock Center, Winrock Mall; 505-881-9225, 800-288-9648; www.chilipepperemporium.com, e-mail info@chilipepperemporium.com.

GAY SHOPPING It might not be a San Francisco or New York, but Albuquerque does have a growing gay and lesbian community. While there isn't a strictly gay area, the trendy Nob Hill neighborhood, home to several gay and lesbian bookstores and establishments, is probably where you'll find the closest thing to a "scene."

For a complete listing of gay and lesbian resources in Albuquerque and throughout New Mexico, pick up a copy of *Out! Magazine*, available at many newsstands and bookstores, or by contacting them at P.O. Box 27237, Albuquerque, NM 87125; 505-243-2540; www.outmagazine.com, e-mail mail@outmagazine.com. Or contact the **Albuquerque Lesbian and Gay Chamber of Commerce** for a copy of their free membership directory. ~ P.O. Box 27207, Albuquerque, NM 87125; 505-891-3647; www.algcc.org.

Sisters' and Brothers' Bookstore touts itself as one of New Mexico's only complete lesbian/bisexual/gay community bookstore. In addition to an endless selection of books, they also stock jewelry, flags, videos and anything with a rainbow on it. Closed Monday. ~ 4011 Silver Avenue Southeast; 505-266-7317, 800-687-3480; www.sistersandbrothers.com, e-mail ruth@sistersand brothers.com.

Alphaville rents films with gay and lesbian themes in a variety of genres including documentaries, experimental, feature films and erotica. Closed Sunday. ~ 3408 Central Avenue Southeast; 505-256-8243; www.alphavillagevideo.com.

NIGHTLIFE

A contemporary pianist tickles the ivories Wednesday through Friday evening at **La Posada de Albuquerque Lounge**. On weekends a variety of music can be heard, from *nuevo flamenco* to jazz to Western swing. ~ 125 2nd Street Northwest; 505-242-9090, 866-442-4224, fax 505-242-8664.

Wind down after a strenuous day of sightseeing at **Brewster's Pub,** where a balcony bandstand packs them in at happy hour. Dance on the hardwood floor to reggae, rhythm and blues, or jazz sounds or just sip a cocktail at the mirrored bar, the hub of a popular singles scene. Come early enough and you may even land a table. Occasional cover. ~ 312 Central Avenue Southwest; 505-247-2533.

The Sandia Peak Tramway is the world's longest aerial tramway.

Laffs Comedy Club features major national standup comedy acts five nights a week and has a full bar. Closed Monday and Tuesday. Cover. ~ 3100-D Juan Tabo Northeast; 505-296-5653.

The dancefloor is always busy at **Caravan East**. Hollywood-style lighting brightens this beam-ceilinged club, which features two country bands nightly. Native New Mexican musicians play on Wednesday. Weekend and Wednesday cover. ~ 7605 Central Avenue Northeast; 505-265-7877.

There's live music and dancing nightly except Sunday at **Club Rhythm & Blues**. The atmosphere is romantically dim and the music ranges from blues to Latin and world beat. ~ 3523 Central Avenue Northeast; 505-256-0849.

For country-and-western dancing, check out **Midnight Rodeo and Gotham Entertainment Complex**, where they offer line dancing. Besides country, they feature everything from hip-hop to '80s rock. Closed Sunday and Monday. Cover on Friday and Saturday. ~ 4901 McLeod Northeast; 505-888-0100; www.mid nightrodeonm.com.

Sometimes, there's nothing more exciting than seeing a big-name performer alongside hordes of rabid fans. With a seating capacity of 12,000, the **Journal Pavilion** fits the bill. The state-of-the-art concert venue hosts top musical performers, sports events and theater productions. ~ 5601 University Boulevard Southeast; 505-452-5100; www.journalpavilion.com.

OPERA, SYMPHONY AND DANCE There's a lively performing-arts scene in Albuquerque, most of which centers around the University of New Mexico. Productions at the university's **Popejoy Hall** (505-277-4569) include plays by touring Broadway shows, performances of the **Musical Theatre Southwest** (505-262-9301), the **New Mexico Ballet Company** (505-292-4245) and concerts by the **New Mexico Symphony Orchestra** (505-881-8999).

The Mexican name for the Rio Grande is "Rio Bravo."

Other theaters on campus include the Department of Theatre and Dance's **Theatre X** in the basement of the Center for the Arts and the **Rodey Theatre for the Arts** next to Popejoy Hall. ~ 505-277-4569.

The New Mexico Jazz Workshop hosts over 30 concerts a year at locations around the city including the Albuquerque Museum and the Hiland Theater. ~ 505-255-9798.

Another important performing-arts venue is the historic **KiMo Theatre**, which hosts performances by groups including the **Opera Southwest** (505-242-5837), the **Ballet Theatre of New Mexico** (505-888-1054) and the unique bilingual **La Compania de Teatro de Albuquerque** (505-242-7929). ~ 423 Central Avenue Northwest; 505-848-1370. The **South Broadway Cultural Center** offers theater, dance and film screenings. ~ 1025 Broadway Southeast; 505-848-1320. The **Albuquerque Children's Theatre** performs for the younger set. ~ 224 San Pasquale Southwest; 505-242-4750.

GAY SCENE If you're looking to dance, head for the high-tech gay hotspot, **Pulse**, located in the Nob Hill district. Designated danceclub nights feature a live deejay playing high-energy and retro music. Be forewarned: Thursday is "alternative gothic" night. Closed Sunday through Tuesday. Cover for special events. ~ 4100 Central Avenue Southeast; 505-255-3334, fax 505-244-9192; www.pulsenightclub.com.

The vast **Albuquerque Mining Co.** offers something for everyone with four bars under one roof, volleyball and barbecue on Sunday and special events. The dance bar is the most popular with its retro hip-hop and dance music. To take a break from dancing, kick back either on the patio or in the lounge. The clientele is both gay and lesbian. Cover Thursday through Saturday. ~ 7209 Central Avenue Northeast; 505-255-4022.

Another place to dance the night away is **Foxes Booze n Cruise**. The gay, lesbian, transgender and straight clientele boogie to deejayed disco music. There are drag shows on the weekend. ~ 8521 Central Avenue Northeast; 505-255-3060.

A leather bar is only one of the attractions that makes **The Ranch** a hit with the gay community. This Western-style club also features a wide-open dancefloor and a deejay operating out of a chuckwagon. If you're a little rusty on the Tennessee waltz, you can always work on your pool game. Weekend cover. ~ 8900 Central Avenue Southeast; 505-275-1616.

RIO GRANDE NATURE CENTER STATE PARK 🚶 This urban wildlife refuge is one of several access points to the bosque and riverbank. The visitors center has exhibits on the river's ecology; observation windows on one side of the building overlook a three-acre pond frequented by ducks, geese and herons, especially during migration seasons—November and April. The park is a favorite spot for birdwatching in all seasons. Two nature trails, each a mile-long loop, wind through the bosque, and one of them leads to several peaceful spots along the bank of the Rio Grande. Other facilities here are restrooms and a gift shop. Day-use fee, $1. ~ 2901 Candelaria Road Northwest, where Candelaria ends at the river a few blocks west of Rio Grande Boulevard; 505-344-7240, fax 505-344-4505; www.rgnc.org, e-mail rgnc@nmia.com.

PARKS

PASEO DEL BOSQUE 🚶🚲🐎 The bosque, or cottonwood forest, lining the banks of the Rio Grande is protected for future park development all the way through the city of Albuquerque. Most of this area remains wild, undeveloped and inaccessible to motor vehicles. A ten-mile paved trail for joggers, cyclists and horseback riders runs along the edge of the bosque, following the river north from the Rio Grande Zoo to Paseo del Norte Boulevard in the North Valley. ~ Trail access from Campbell Road, Mountain Road or Rio Grande Nature Center on Candelaria Road Northwest.

Exploring the area surrounding Albuquerque proper is well worth any visitor's time. Traveling north of Albuquerque on Route 25, motorists can explore a number of ancient and modern Indian pueblos, including the largest of the Rio Grande Indian pueblos.

Outside Albuquerque

Thirteen miles south of Albuquerque, **Isleta Pueblo** is a labyrinthine mixture of old and new houses comprising one of New Mexico's larger pueblos. Visitors who wander the narrow streets of the town will eventually find their way to the mission church, one of the oldest in the country. The pueblo operates a fishing lake and campground in the Isleta Casino and Resort. Several shops around the plaza sell the local white, red and black pottery. Photographing ceremonies is prohibited. ~ Route 25; 505-869-3111, fax 505-869-4236; www.isletapueblo.com.

SIGHTS

The two nearest pueblos to Albuquerque—Sandia Pueblo and Santa Ana Pueblo—are so small that they often go unnoticed.

Sandia Pueblo has an arts-and-crafts market and a Las Vegas–style casino. They also operate Sandia Lakes Recreation Area (505-897-3971), which is open to the public for fishing. Admission. The Sandia people number about 300 and speak Tiwa, a different language from that spoken at other pueblos in the vicinity. Kuaua was an ancestral home of the Sandia people. Photography and sketching are prohibited. ~ Route 313, about seven miles north of Albuquerque; 505-867-3317, fax 505-867-9235; www.sandiapueblo.nsn.us.

Just up the road, Santa Ana Pueblo has about 500 tribal members; nearly all live here, away from the old pueblo off Route 44. The tribe owns a golf course nearby and operates a nursery of native plants and a casino. The pueblo itself is only open to the public on July 25. ~ 2 Dove Road, off Route 313, two miles north of Bernalillo; 505-867-3301, fax 505-867-3395; www.santa ana.org, e-mail info@santaana.org.

Founded beside the Rio Grande around the year 1300, Kuaua was a thriving pueblo when a Spanish expedition led by Francisco Vasquez de Coronado arrived in 1540. The 1100 explorers spent the winter there and at first found the people of Kuaua hospitable, but as supplies ran short and demands on the pueblo increased, the Indians became uncooperative and Coronado destroyed the pueblo.

Today, the ruins of Kuaua are preserved at Coronado State Monument, 15 miles north of Albuquerque. The unique feature of this ruin is a ceremonial kiva (an underground chamber) that, when excavated, was found to have murals around its interior—the only pre-Columbian pueblo kiva paintings known to have survived the centuries. Archaeologists carefully removed and mounted the painted layers, and the original murals are now displayed in a room adjoining the visitors center along with diagrams that explain their meanings. The kiva itself has been fully restored and ornamented with replicas of the paintings, and visitors are welcome to climb down into it. The visitors center also contains exhibits about both the pueblo people and the Spanish conquistadors. Admission. ~ Route 550/44, one mile west of Route 25 from the town of Bernalillo; 505-867-5351, fax 505-867-1733.

Tradition is strong at San Felipe Pueblo, ten miles from Bernalillo north on Route 25. The pueblo is known for spectacular dances (the bowl-like central plaza has actually been worn down three feet below ground level by centuries of ceremonies) and beadwork. The pueblo's artisans specialize in *heishi* (disklike beads used for necklaces).The tribe's main source of income, though, is its flashy casino just off the interstate. Photographs and sketching are strictly prohibited. ~ One and a half miles west of Route 25 at Exit 252; 505-867-3381, fax 505-867-3383.

Santo Domingo is the largest of the Rio Grande Indian pueblos and one of the most conservative. After admiring the horses and other ornate designs painted on the church facade, visitors may wish to stroll through the narrow, old streets and hear the residents speaking in the native Keresan language. Pueblo artists sell fine silver jewelry and other crafts from their homes. ~ Five miles west of Route 25, Exit 259; 505-465-2214, fax 505-465-2688.

The mission church at **Cochiti Pueblo** dates back to 1628 and is among the oldest on the Rio Grande. Cochiti artisans originated the pottery storyteller figures that now are popular collectibles. At Cochiti Lake there is a campground and other lake services, and fishing is permitted in the Rio Grande at the bottom of the dam and also on the lake with a fishing license. Cochiti Pueblo is farther removed from the interstate than any of the other pueblos between Albuquerque and Santa Fe. ~ To get there, travel north on Route 25, then take Route 22 for about 15 miles; 505-465-2244, fax 505-465-1135.

◀ HIDDEN

American Indians have lived in **Zia Pueblo** since the middle of the 13th century, though diseases introduced by European set-

POINTS OF INTEREST
A Cochiti Pueblo
B Coronado State Monument
C Isleta Pueblo
D Jemez Pueblo
E San Felipe Pueblo
F Sandia Peak Tramway
G Sandia Pueblo
H Santa Ana Pueblo
I Santo Domingo Pueblo
J Zia Pueblo

Outside Albuquerque

tlers caused their population to dwindle from 15,000 to less than 100 by the end of the 19th century. But today this reservation, located 35 miles northwest of Albuquerque off Route 44, is thriving once more, with about 850 American Indians making their home here. Spread across 122,000 acres of piñon-juniper and ponderosa pine woodlands, the Zia reservation features a small cultural center that showcases arts and crafts. ~ Route 44, Zia Pueblo; 505-867-3304, fax 505-867-3308.

Zia Lake, on the north side of the Jemez River, is a popular fishing spot on the Zia Indian Reservation.

In the vicinity, **Jemez Pueblo** is also open to tourists. ~ On Route 4 just north of Route 44; 505-834-7359, fax 505-834-7331. And if you'd care to do some shopping for Jemez pottery and sculpture, you can visit the **Jemez Pueblo visitors center**, six miles north of San Ysidro on Route 4. Turquoise jewelry and drums are also sold here. ~ Off Route 4, three miles north of Jemez Pueblo; 505-834-7235, fax 505-834-2221.

LODGING

Corrales, a rural North Valley community located near Bernalillo and Coronado State Monument, is home to some of the Albuquerque area's best small bed and breakfasts. **Yours Truly Bed and Breakfast** offers four guest rooms with king-sized beds, cable TV and air conditioning in a modern adobe house with fireplaces, a spa and nearby hiking trails. A stay includes a full buffet breakfast and a complimentary coffee tray, with fresh-cut flowers, left on your doorstep. ~ 160 Paseo de Corrales, Corrales; 505-898-7027, 800-942-7890, fax 505-898-9022; www.yourstrulybb.com, e-mail yourstrulybb@aol.com. MODERATE TO DELUXE.

The Nora Dixon Place epitomizes New Mexico's unique Territorial-era architecture: the home is adobe brick with pine trim and has divided-light windows. Set on an acre and a half of wooded area by the Rio Grande, the property is filled with cottonwood, native plants, vegetable gardens and fruit and olive trees. Its three guest rooms come with a private bath, a fridge and a microwave. All open to an enclosed courtyard. A full breakfast is served. ~ 312 Dixon Road, Corrales; 505-893-3662, 888-667-2349, fax 505-898-6430; www.noradixon.com, e-mail noradixon@aol.com. MODERATE.

Upon passing through **Hacienda Manzanal**'s carved front door, guests will immediately feel as if they've reached their home away from home. This is in part due to the rocking chair in the courtyard and the relaxing room that overlooks the shaded veranda and sunny patio. The feeling is reinforced by its four guest rooms, which offer private baths and fireplaces; one has a whirlpool spa. A full breakfast is served (hosts Sue and Norm Gregory cater to special diets). ~ 300 West Meadowlark Lane, Corrales; 505-922-1662, 877-922-1662; www.haciendamanzanal. com, e-mail info@haciendamanzanal.com. MODERATE.

The **Chocolate Turtle Bed and Breakfast**, besides having a name that immediately evokes trust, is a lovely B&B on a one-and-a-half-acre spread in Corrales. The Territorial-style digs are cheerfully outfitted with Southwestern art, and each of the four rooms has a private bath. Full breakfast is included (if you're lucky, you'll get mangos and blue-corn pancakes). ~ 1098 West Meadowlark Lane, Corrales; 505-898-1800, 800-898-1842, fax 505-898-5328; e-mail turtlebb@aol.com. BUDGET TO DELUXE.

La Mimosa Bed & Breakfast is a private one-bedroom adobe house secluded in a large shady courtyard. There's a kitchen area with a refrigerator but no cooking facilities. Continental breakfast is served in the guesthouse or garden. ~ 1144 Andrews Lane, Corrales; 505-898-1354, fax 505-898-0635. MODERATE.

A quaint little diner with outdoor seating, the **Calico Café** offers substantial fare: burgers, sandwiches, salads and Mexican food. Breakfast and lunch served daily. ~ 4512 Corrales Road, Corrales; 505-890-9150. BUDGET TO MODERATE. **DINING**

Don't be alarmed if you find yourself sharing your meal with a flamboyant French ghost at **Rancho de Corrales**. The restaurant, well-known for its excellent Southwestern cuisine, housed a scandalous couple in the early 1800s; the adulterous wife was apparently shot to death by her jealous husband, and their spirits now wander the area. They may be motivated more by hunger than passion, however. The food here is delicious—try the Native Taco (frybread, meat and pinto beans, accented with your choice of chile and sprinkled with cheese). There's patio dining in the summer; cozy up to the fire in winter. No lunch during the week; Sunday brunch. Closed Monday. ~ 4895 Corrales Road, Corrales; 505-897-3131. BUDGET TO MODERATE.

The **Range Cafe** is a favorite spot among locals. Menu items include salads, Mexican-style entrées and gourmet vegetarian selections, including a grilled portobello mushroom "burger" with poblano chile aioli. If you're here for breakfast, try the oatmeal with cinnamon ice cream, walnuts and strawberries. Breakfast, lunch and dinner are served. ~ 925 Camino del Pueblo, Bernalillo; 505-867-1700; www.rangecafe.com, e-mail mail@rangecafe.com.

The elegant **Prairie Star** is 15 minutes north of the city off Route 25 in a sprawling, mission-style adobe house. Menu items include entrées such as seared house-smoked North Atlantic salmon served with gooseberry salsa and Chama Valley lamb chops accompanied by sun-dried-tomato polenta. Dinner only. Closed Monday. ~ 288 Prairie Star Road off Tamaya Boulevard, Santa Ana Pueblo; 505-867-3327; www.santaanagolf.com, e-mail pstar@santaanagolf.com. MODERATE TO ULTRA-DELUXE. ◄HIDDEN

COCHITI LAKE 🚲 🏊 ⛵ 🎣 🚣 🛶 🚤 ⤙ At the confluence of the Santa Fe and Rio Grande rivers lies Albuquerque's flood- **PARKS**

control reservoir and also its local water recreation area. Wind-surfing on the lake is popular, and some people paddle kayaks. Power boating is permitted but is restricted to no-wake speed. Fishing is good for largemouth and smallmouth bass, catfish and walleye. It's also a good place to swim. Facilities here include a picnic area, restrooms and showers. ~ Located 46 miles north of Albuquerque on Route 25 and then 15 miles northwest on Route 22; 505-465-0307, fax 505-465-0316.

▲ There are two campgrounds overlooking the lake, oper-ated by the Army Corps of Engineers. Cochiti has 60 sites (38 with RV hookups) and Tetilla Peak has 50 sites (39 with RV hook-ups); $5 to $8 per night for standard sites, $10 to $12 per night for hookups. Tetilla Peak is closed November through March.

Turquoise Trail

There are places worth visiting along Route 25 be-tween Albuquerque and Santa Fe—particularly San Felipe and Santo Domingo Indian pueblos. But if you want to take your time, avoid big truck traffic, and experience a taste of old-fashioned, undeveloped New Mexico, take the two-lane route known as the Turquoise Trail (see Driving Tour) around the back of Sandia Crest and over the Ortiz Mountains, and discover some hidden little towns that are short on water but long on personality.

SIGHTS

HIDDEN ►

About a mile from the Turquoise Trail on the Sandia Peak road is a small wonder for those traveling with children—the **Tinkertown Museum**, which exhibits a miniature Western town and a three-ring circus entirely hand-carved from wood with mechanical peo-ple and moving vehicles. The museum is easily recognized by its fence made of glass bottles. Closed November through March. Admission. ~ Route 536; 505-281-5233, fax 505-286-9335; www.tinkertown.com, e-mail tinker4u@tinkertown.com.

You won't have trouble discovering Madrid's roots if you go to the **Old Coal Mine Museum**. This block-long memorial pays tribute to an industry that peaked here in 1928. Your self-guided tour includes a visit to a coal mine shaft, a wide array of mining machinery, vintage railroad equipment and antique trucks—look in the parts storage building for a Model T pickup truck. Admis-sion. ~ Route 14, Madrid; 505-438-3780, fax 505-473-0248; e-mail coalminemuseum@earthlink.net.

Featuring a collection of gems, cattle skulls and pottery, the **Casa Grande Trading Post** is a good place to learn about the re-gion's geologic history. The offbeat, sometimes whimsical collec-tion of artifacts is highlighted by guides who are more than happy to fill you in on local lore. The collection in the **Turquoise Museum** ranges from prehistoric pieces to locally mined Cerrillos turquoise. Take your children next door to the **Petting Zoo**,

where they can feed the llamas, peacocks and goats. Admission.
~ 17 Waldo Street, Los Cerrillos; 505-438-3008.

The Turquoise Trail intersects Route 25 at the western edge of
Santa Fe, where it becomes Cerrillos Road, a busy main street.

LODGING

◄ *HIDDEN*

For those seeking a remote setting, still within easy commuting
distance of Albuquerque's attractions, **Elaine's** is the ideal choice.
This bed and breakfast, nestled among ponderosa pines, adjoins
Cibola National Forest near Cedar Crest. Outdoor enthusiasts
have ample opportunities for hiking, biking, skiing and horseback
riding. There's even a resident dog to accompany guests on walks
through the foliage. The three-story log house has five guest rooms,
big balconies, a grand country fireplace and European antiques
everywhere you look. Some rooms have jacuzzi tubs. A full breakfast is included. ~ 72 Snowline Estates, Cedar Crest; 505-281-
2467, 800-821-3092, fax 505-281-1384; www.elainesbnb.com,
e-mail elaine@elainesbnb.com. MODERATE TO DELUXE.

Located on the Turquoise Trail, **Madrid Lodging** is a quaint,
two-suite bed and breakfast that was once a 1930s boarding-
house. As one would expect, the atmosphere is casual and relaxed. The units are splashed with muted colors and accented
with Turkish *kalims* and other exotic touches. A large, outdoor
hot tub will soothe away any remnants of stress. Breakfast is included. ~ 14 Opera House Road, Madrid; 505-471-3450, fax
505-471-7916; www.madridlodging.com, e-mail info@madrid
lodging.com. MODERATE.

Hacienda Doña Andrea to Santa Fe is a charming blend of
New Mexico's past and contemporary comforts. Located in the
scenic Sangre de Cristo Mountains, the hotel is a peaceful de-
parture from the hustle and bustle of Santa Fe. The decor is classic Southwest: clean adobe walls with iron and tile accents. The
nine guest suites boast colorful hand-tiled showers, fireplaces,
custom linens; some have private patios. Breakfast is included. ~

LOOK WHAT'S COOKIN'

As every visitor discovers immediately, New Mexico boasts a distinctive culinary style. The two regional specialties that set it apart from Mexican food
familiar in other regions are blue corn, grown by the Pueblo Indians and
considered sacred in their traditions, and green chile. New Mexico produces virtually all the chile peppers grown in the United States, and while
most chiles are exported to the rest of the country in the form of red
chile powder, the local preference is to pick the chiles while green, then
roast, peel and eat them as a vegetable—chopped as a stew, breaded
and fried as *rellenos* or poured as a sauce over just about any entrée.

Turquoise Trail

A number of historical sights make the Turquoise Trail a rewarding route from Albuquerque to Santa Fe—and it takes just 30 minutes more driving time than the interstate. To find the Turquoise Trail (Route 14), take Route 40 eastbound from Albuquerque to the Tijeras/Cedar Crest exit, a distance of about ten miles from the city center, and turn north.

SANDIA PEAK   At Cedar Crest, a few miles from the interstate exit, a well-marked paved road, steep in places, forks off from the Turquoise Trail and leads up the eastern slope of the Sandias to Sandia Peak summit, with its spectacular views of central New Mexico.

GOLDEN   Midway between Albuquerque and Santa Fe, the Turquoise Trail crosses the San Pedro Mountains, a small but rugged range that was the site of major gold-mining operations from the 1880s to the 1920s. Once the area's residential hub, Golden is now practically a ghost town. Beside the highway, the ruins of an old stone schoolhouse and other collapsing buildings can still be seen. There is also a beautifully restored mission church dating back to 1830.

78 Vista Del Oro, Los Cerrillos; 505-424-8995; www.hdasanta fe.com, e-mail info@hdasantafe.com. ULTRA-DELUXE.

DINING   The oak floor and tables, New Mexican murals and a beam ceiling add to the charm of the historic **Mine Shaft Tavern,** home of the state's longest standup bar, 50 feet total. Mingle with the locals at the lodgepole pine slab or take a table and order a chef's salad, enchiladas or ribeye steak; wash it down with a local beer. For dessert, try the homemade ice cream or pie. Lunch is served daily; dinner served Wednesday, Friday, Saturday and Sunday. ~ Route 14, Madrid; 505-473-0743, fax 505-473-0248; e-mail dot mine@rt66.com. BUDGET TO MODERATE.

Located in the historic company store building, **Madrid Old Fashioned Soda Fountain** is known for its sundaes and phosphates. A loyal clientele packs the black formica counter. ~ In Maya Jones, Route 14, Madrid; 505-473-3641; e-mail random@maya jones.com. BUDGET.

At **Mamma Lisa's Ghost Town Kitchen,** everything from the soups and stews to the breads and desserts is homemade. The menu changes daily, and some of its most popular offerings are the New Mexican entrées and main-dish salads. Be sure to try

MADRID   Eleven miles away, on the other side of the pass, the town of Madrid (pronounced "MAD-rid") owes its existence to coal mining. The all-wood buildings, atypical of New Mexico architecture, give the community a look reminiscent of Appalachian coal towns. Abandoned after World War II, Madrid has since been partly repopulated by artists and historic-district entrepreneurs, but growth is limited due to a lack of water. (Water used to be brought in by a train that no longer runs.) Attractions in Madrid include a mining museum, a summertime melodrama and a baseball field where concerts are presented regularly.

LOS CERRILLOS   A third old mining town along the Turquoise Trail, Los Cerrillos (shortened to "Cerrillos" by locals) still retains the appearance of an old Spanish village. While silver, gold, copper, zinc and lead have all been mined in the hills north of town—and Thomas Edison once built a $2 million laboratory here in an unsuccessful attempt to develop a method for refining gold without water—Los Cerrillos is best known for turquoise. American Indians mined turquoise here as early as A.D. 500. Later, the people of Chaco and other Anasazi pueblos traveled from hundreds of miles away to dig pit mines for the stone, which was their most precious trade commodity. Others, from Spanish colonists to modern-day prospectors, have likewise wandered the maze of the Cerrillos hills in search of turquoise.

the red chili chocolate cake. Open daily during daylight hours only. ~ 2859 Route 14, Madrid; 505-471-5769. BUDGET.

Al Leedom Studio specializes in hand-blown glass and *really* expensive, high-quality jewelry. Call ahead for a schedule of glass-blowing demonstrations. ~ Route 14, Madrid; 505-473-2054.

SHOPPING

For Guatemalan clothing and crafts as well as new and used books, head to **Maya Jones**, a colorful shop with all sorts of inexpensive items. The handmade jackets and jewelry are particularly noteworthy. ~ Route 14, Madrid; 505-473-3641, fax 505-471-1090.

Gifted Hands Gallery features local and area artists. It's a hodgepodge of traditional American Indian jewelry, wall art, wearable art, Zuni fetishes, pottery and sculptures. ~ 2851 Route 14, Madrid; 505-471-5943; www.giftedhandgallery.com.

Madrid Melodrama offers memorable classic Victorian melodramas at the Engine House Theater in the Old Coal Mine Museum next to the Mine Shaft Tavern. Shows are on weekend afternoons and Saturday evenings from late May to mid-October. ~ Route 14, Madrid; 505-438-3780; www.madridmelodrama.com.

NIGHTLIFE

A solo guitarist or a duo or trio plays weekend afternoons at the **Mine Shaft Tavern**. There's live music on Friday or Saturday evenings. ~ Route 14, Madrid; 505-473-0743.

Santa Rosa Area

Drivers crossing eastern New Mexico on Route 40 may find the experience brain-numbing in its monotony—flat and featureless with an endless flow of speeding semi trucks. Those who venture a short detour from the main route, however, will discover a little bit of the special character of Santa Rosa, Fort Sumner and the other communities that dot the boundless prairie. This area is of particular interest to history buffs, for this is where the legend of Billy the Kid is rooted and, indeed, this is where the young outlaw is buried.

SIGHTS

Located along the Pecos River, the town of **Santa Rosa** (population 2700) lies 110 miles east of Albuquerque at the junction of Routes 40 and 54. It was settled by Spanish farmers during the 1860s, but its historic roots extend back to 1541, when Spanish explorer Vasquez de Coronado built a bridge across the Pecos River at **Puerto de Luna**, ten miles south of present-day Santa Rosa—or so the story goes. In the 1880s, Puerto de Luna was the largest community in the southeastern quarter of New Mexico Territory; today it is virtually a ghost town. But even though the bridge no longer exists and the stone county courthouse is beginning to crumble (along with a rock-faced church and a saloon where Billy the Kid hung out from time to time), Puerto de Luna still makes for an interesting short excursion off the interstate.

Santa Rosa's main vacation attractions are lakes, to the point that it calls itself "The City of Natural Lakes." Those who find the claim improbable for a town in the arid high plains of New Mexico will be even more surprised to learn that Santa Rosa is a mecca for scuba divers. (See the "Parks" section below.)

If you want to Kid around, drive 46 miles south to **Fort Sumner**, where Billy the Kid happened to be hiding out when the law caught up with him for the last time. You might expect that "Billymania" would be more prevalent in the outlaw's hometown of Lincoln, 100 miles to the south, where most of his escapades took place. But the fact is, Fort Sumner is the Billy the Kid capital of the Southwest. It was here (or at least at a ranch on the outskirts of town) that he was shot to death in 1881.

Two privately owned museums pay tribute to Billy the Kid's life and legend. Each is interesting enough to occupy the curious for an hour or two and spur speculations about whether Billy was a frontier Robin Hood, a psychopathic killer or a product of media hype. There is some duplication between the two museums, since a number of the documents on exhibit are photocopies of originals in the state archives.

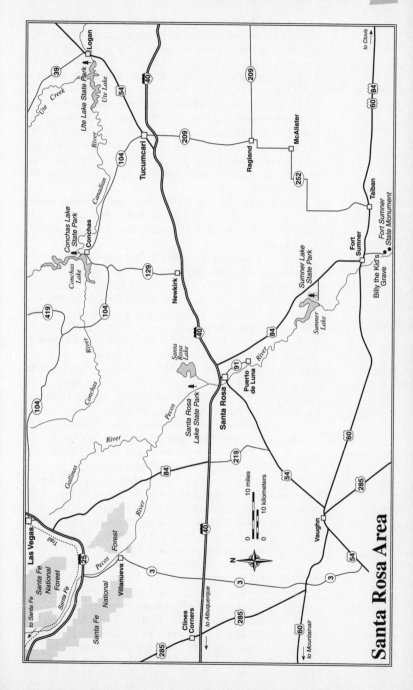

Santa Rosa Area

The **Billy the Kid Museum**, which showcases a large collection of Billy memorabilia and a jail cell, is near the eastern edge of town on the way to Fort Sumner State Monument. Closed the first two weeks of January. Admission. ~ 1601 East Sumner Avenue, Fort Sumner; 505-355-2380; www.billythekid.nv.switch board.com.

The **Old Fort Sumner Museum** displays letters written by Billy to the governor to negotiate a pardon, letters from Sheriff Pat Garrett to his wife describing his search for the outlaw, a history of impostors who have claimed to be the real Billy the Kid and a chronology of more than a dozen motion pictures about his brief, violent career. Admission. ~ Billy the Kid Road, Fort Sumner; 505-355-2942.

Billy the Kid's Grave, in the Maxwell family cemetery behind the Old Fort Sumner Museum, is locked securely behind iron bars because the headstone has been stolen twice. ~ Billy the Kid Road, Fort Sumner.

Just down the road from Billy the Kid's grave, **Fort Sumner State Monument** marks the site of the Army outpost for which the town was named. By the time Billy the Kid came to town, the fort had been converted to a ranch headquarters, and it was here that Sheriff Pat Garrett killed him. Just a few years earlier, the fort was the scene of larger and more infamous events. The leader of the U.S. Army in New Mexico ordered Colonel Kit Carson to force the entire Navajo tribe to walk 450 miles from their homeland to this place and help build Fort Sumner as a concentration camp. More than 8500 Navajo lived in captivity here for six years, and 3000 of them died of starvation and disease. Finally the government concluded that keeping the Navajo at Fort Sumner was too expensive and that their homeland was without value to the white man. Then the surviving Navajo people were allowed to walk back home. No trace remains of the original fort, but you can explore some of the subterranean ruins of the main fort buildings. The most moving part of the monument is a simple shrine of stones brought from all over the path of the Long Walk from the Navajo homeland and left here by American Indians in loving memory of those who lived and died here. Closed Tuesday. Admission. ~ Billy the Kid Road; 505-355-2573, fax 505-355-2573; e-mail hweeldi@plateaupel.net.

From Fort Sumner, it's about an hour-and-a-half drive to the border town of Tucumcari. Drive 11 miles east on Route 60/84 to Taiban. From here, Route 252 climbs the corner of Llano Estacado, a high mesa that covers much of eastern New Mexico, and heads northeast until the town of Ragland. At Ragland, the road drops off from the Llano Estacado into the Canadian River Basin and merges with Route 209. The view of the bluffs as you descend the mesa is quite dramatic and unusual for this character-istically flat area. Take Route 209 north until you reach Tucumcari.

Tucumcari, created by the Rock Island Railroad at the turn of the 20th century, is actually best visited during the day when the **Tucumcari Historical Museum** throws open its doors. What you'll see at this Richardsonian Romanesque complex is a compilation of American Indian artifacts, gems, a still from Prohibition days and other odd items donated by locals. Pioneer wagons and a pre-1900 windmill highlight the outdoor displays. Closed Monday from September to June. Admission. ~ 416 South Adams Street, Tucumcari; 505-461-4201; e-mail museum@cityoftucumcari.com.

Santa Rosa has more than a dozen budget-priced motels—most of them locally owned and operated. The exception is the **Best Western Adobe Inn**, which straddles the budget and moderate price ranges for its spacious, modern rooms. ~ Historic Route 66 (Will Rogers Drive) at Route 40 Exit 275, Santa Rosa; 505-472-3446, 800-528-1234, fax 505-472-5759; www.bestwestern.com. BUDGET TO MODERATE.

LODGING

The town of Tucumcari was named for a Comanche lookout.

A cruise down the main street, Will Rogers Drive, reveals that close to half the commercial buildings in Santa Rosa are motels. A good bet is the **Travelodge**, which has double-room units for families. ~ 1819 Historic Route 66 (Will Rogers Drive), Santa Rosa; 505-472-3494, 800-578-7878. BUDGET.

Billy the Kid fans might consider spending the night in Fort Sumner at one of the two motels, both budget-priced. The **Billy the Kid Country Inn** is a roadside motel with kitchenettes and cable TV; continental breakfast is included. ~ 1704 East Sumner Avenue, Fort Sumner; 505-355-7414, fax 505-355-7478. BUDGET. The **Coronado Motel** has all the basic amenities of motels everywhere. ~ 309 West Sumner Avenue, Fort Sumner; 505-355-2466. BUDGET.

Motels have been an important industry in Tucumcari since the 1940s, when the town was a natural stop along Old Route 66 because it was the only place for many miles. Today, billboards along Route 40 for hundreds of miles in each direction tout the fact that Tucumcari has 2000 beds for rent. A number of motels in town still offer the authentic flavor of roadside America half a century ago. Even their names—Buckaroo, Lasso, Palomino, Apache—evoke a notion of the West in an earlier era.

Lovely gardens, a big pool and generous patios make the **Best Western Pow Wow Inn** an ideal choice. Sixty-two modern rooms and suites appointed with American Indian prints and kachina-style lamps offer king- and queen-size beds as well as large vanity areas. ~ 801 West Tucumcari Boulevard, Tucumcari; 505-461-

Text continued on page 200.

Be a Road
Warrior

Albuquerque residents know it as the "Big I"—the congested freeway interchange in the middle of the city where two famous routes of bygone eras meet.

Interstate Route 25 follows the path of the oldest highway still in use in the United States. Originally known as El Camino Real de Tierra Adentro ("the Royal Road to the Inner Land"), it was established in 1598 to link Mexico City with New Mexico, the northernmost province of the Spanish empire in America. El Camino Real spanned a distance of 1700 miles, crossing brutal expanses of desert and venturing through lands guarded by hostile Apache warriors. Spanish soldiers in armor traveled its length, as did hooded monks on foot. Horses, cows and *vaqueros* (cowboys) first came to the American West via the old Royal Road.

Interstate Route 40 traces Old Route 66, the first paved highway connecting the eastern United States and the West Coast. Route 66 was the kind of highway dreams are made of. It ran across vast, sunbaked, brightly colored desert inhabited by cowboys and Indians all the way to Hollywood, capturing America's imagination as it went. John Steinbeck wrote about it. Glenn Miller immortalized it in song. The television series *Route 66* was one of the most popular programs of the 1960s. Old Route 66 became practically synonymous with the mystique of the open road.

Before the two-lane, blacktop road was replaced by today's high-speed, limited-access highway, travelers had no alternative to driving down the main street of each small town along the route—places like Tucumcari, Santa Rosa, Laguna and Gallup. Today, chambers of commerce in these towns enthusiastically promote Route 66 nostalgia, and what used to be cheap roadside diners and tourist traps are now preserved as historic sites.

While both El Camino Real and Old Route 66 have been paved and straightened into modern interstate highways, travelers willing to take the extra time can still experience much of what it must have felt like to travel either of these roads in times past.

Alternate highways, usually traffic-free and often out of sight of the busy interstate, parallel Route 25 almost all the way from the Indian pueblos north of Albuquerque to El Paso and the Mexican border. These secondary highways trace El Camino Real more exactly than the interstate does, and the New Mexico state government has put up historical markers along them to identify important landmarks from Spanish colonial days such as the stark landscape of the Jornada del Muerto ("Journey of Death").

Good Camino Real alternatives to the interstate include Route 313 from Albuquerque north to San Felipe Pueblo; Routes 47 and 304 south of Albuquerque on the opposite side of the Rio Grande from the interstate, serving old rural communities such as Bosque Farms, Valencia and Belen; Route 1 from San Antonio through Bosque del Apache Wildlife Refuge to Elephant Butte Reservoir; Route 187 from Truth or Consequences to Las Cruces; and Route 28 from La Mesilla, just west of Las Cruces, to El Paso and the border.

Most of Old Route 66 has been obscured by interstate Route 40. Only a few sections of frontage roads and old secondary highways—notably Route 124 from Mesita through the villages of the Laguna Indian Reservation to Acoma—give any hint of the road that used to carry travelers across the desert. The place to look for remnants of Old Route 66 is along the main streets of towns that the interstate has bypassed. Deco-style diners, quaint ma-and-pa motels and old-fashioned curio shops with concrete Indian tepees out front and signs like "Last Chance Before the Desert!" and "See the Baby Rattlers!" can still be found on Route 40 business loops all across New Mexico, from Tucumcari to Albuquerque's Central Avenue to Gallup, where the main street was recently renamed Historic Route 66.

Traveling any of these alternate routes takes twice as long as driving the interstate. The rewards are several—avoiding busy truck routes, discovering the offbeat charm of small-town New Mexico and sampling what cross-country travel used to be like in the American Southwest.

0500, 800-527-6996, fax 505-461-0135; www.powwowinn, e-mail jsullivan@powwowinn.com. MODERATE.

DINING

Settle into a booth at the **Comet II Restaurant**, one of the last original Route 66 restaurants in town. The Comet is a '50s classic, well-known for its Chimayo–style New Mexican specialties, particularly the blue-corn chicken and smothered *chiles rellenos*. Gringos may want to stick with burgers and the like, but everyone can enjoy the homemade pies. Closed Monday. ~ 217 Parker Avenue, Santa Rosa; 505-472-3663. BUDGET.

Santa Rosa also has a dozen other restaurants of more recent vintage, most of them either nationwide franchises or motel restaurants but all of them in the budget range. For Mexican food, we recommend **Mateo's Family Restaurant**. If you haven't had a Mexican breakfast, try it here. ~ Old Route 66, Santa Rosa; 505-472-5720. BUDGET TO MODERATE.

Steaks, seafood and New Mexican food are found at **Joseph's Bar and Grill**. Breakfast, lunch and dinner are served. ~ 865 Will Rogers Drive, Santa Rosa; 505-472-3361. BUDGET.

One of the most attractive dining rooms on this side of the state, the **Pow Wow Restaurant** features a Navajo storm design motif. Hand-painted lamps and American Indian blankets add a handsome touch to this cheery restaurant. Choose from New Mexican specialties like *carne adovada* or stick with the more standard rib-eye steak and rainbow trout. Breakfast, lunch and dinner are served. ~ Best Western Pow Wow Inn, 801 West Tucumcari Boulevard, Tucumcari; 505-461-0500, fax 505-461-0135. MODERATE.

If you've maxed out on New Mexican fare, why not head over to the **Golden Dragon** for a bowl of wonton soup and a generous serving of Mongolian beef. This Chinese restaurant overflows with shrines and Buddhas. ~ 1006 East Tucumcari Boulevard, Tucumcari; 505-461-2853. BUDGET TO MODERATE.

SHOPPING

We were so put off by the billboards advertising **Clines Corners** that we almost took a pass. Talk about a blight on the landscape! But like just about everyone else whistling along the interstate, we hit the brakes and drove on in to New Mexico's largest souvenir shop. The operating definition of kitsch, this tourist mecca warehouses thousands of moccasins, silkscreen lamps and baja jackets. It just might be the ultimate tourist trap. On the other hand, the prices aren't bad and there's plenty of selection. ~ Route 40 at Route 285, 1 Yacht Club Drive, Clines Corners; 505-472-5488.

The last of the original Route 66 curio shops in eastern New Mexico, **Tee Pee Curios**, a stucco tepee built in the '40s, offers a great photo opportunity for students of this region's recent past. Whether you're shopping for worrystones, twig baskets or authentic Navajo designs, this gift shop is a fun place to browse. If nothing else, buy a wooden postcard to send to your colleagues back at the office. ~ 924 East Tucumcari Boulevard, Tucumcari; 505-461-3773.

Joseph's Bar and Grill has a deejay, live bands or karaoke on Friday and Saturday nights. On weeknights, sports fans gather around the big-screen television to cheer on their favorite teams. ~ 865 Will Rogers Drive, Santa Rosa; 505-472-3361.

The kachina-style **Pow Wow** lounge offers a variety of live music on the weekends. ~ 801 West Tucumcari Boulevard, Tucumcari; 505-461-0500.

BLUE HOLE The amazingly clear water at this spot attracts dive-club caravans from Texas, Oklahoma and Colorado on most weekends. Formed by a collapsed cave and fed by a subterranean river, the lake is deeper (81 feet) than it is wide. Carp live in the dark reaches far below the surface. Swimming is popular, and on hot summer days teenagers can often be seen cannonballing into Blue Hole from the cliffs above even though the year-round water temperature is a very chilly 64°. Facilities include restrooms, a picnic area and a dive shop. ~ Blue Hole Road, at the southeast edge of Santa Rosa. Follow the signs from Will Rogers Drive (the business loop from Route 40). For information call the Santa Rosa Chamber of Commerce (505-472-3763, 505-472-3404, fax 505-472-3848). For diving permits, call Santa Rosa City Hall (505-472-3404).

SANTA ROSA LAKE STATE PARK A flood-control reservoir along the Pecos River, Santa Rosa Lake provides so much irrigation water to the surrounding farmlands that some years it can practically disappear in late summer. (Phone ahead to make sure the lake has water in it.) In wet years, the extensive shallows make for some of the best fishing in the state. Especially known for walleye, the lake is also stocked with crap-

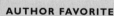

AUTHOR FAVORITE

Janes-Wallace Memorial Park is really no more than a local fishing hole. But don't be put off. It's a great place to drop a line and is stocked with what may just be your dinner. Expect to catch bass, catfish and rainbow trout. There are no facilities. ~ Follow 3rd Street, which becomes Route 91, south from Will Rogers Drive. For information about the park, call the Santa Rosa Chamber of Commerce; 505-472-3763, 505-472-3404, fax 505-472-3848.

pie, catfish and bass. Most fishing here is done from boats. Water-skiing is also popular. A short "scenic trail" starts from the state park's Rocky Point Campground. The park has picnic tables, rest-rooms, showers and a visitors center. Day-use fee, $4. ~ From Santa Rosa, take Exit 277 from Route 40. Turn left on 2nd Street; con-tinue to Eddy Avenue and turn right; continue north for seven miles; 505-472-3110, fax 505-472-5956.

▲ Rocky Point has 50 sites (23 with RV hookups), Juniper has 25 and Los Tanos has 15 (no hookups); $10 for standard sites, $14 per night for hookups. Reservations, from mid-May to mid-September: 877-664-7787; the rest of the year all sites are first-come, first-served.

SUMNER LAKE STATE PARK
On the Pecos River between Santa Rosa and Fort Sumner, this ir-rigation reservoir is one of New Mexico's most underused fishing lakes, with the added bonus of several quiet side canyons and a little village of summer cabins. The Y-shaped lake offers good spots for fishing from the shore in shallow, medium or deep water. Crappie, catfish, bluegill, northern pike and walleye are the common catches. State park areas below the dam provide access to both banks of the river. Swimming is permitted. There are picnic ta-bles, restrooms and showers. Day-use fee, $4. ~ Located six miles off Route 84. The marked turnoff is 35 miles south of Santa Rosa and ten miles north of Fort Sumner; 505-355-2541, fax 505-355-2542.

New Mexico was a province of Mexico from 1821 until the 1848 treaty that ended the Mexican War with the United States.

▲ There are 32 developed sites (18 with RV hookups); prim-itive camping is available. Fees per night are $8 for primitive sites, $10 for standard sites, $14 per night for hookups.

BOSQUE REDONDO   This Fort Sumner city park consists of a series of small lakes on 15 acres. The grassy shore, shaded by cottonwood trees, is a nice picnic spot. It's also a good place to fish. Ducks live on the lakes year-round. The park has outhouses. ~ Located two miles south of Fort Sumner on a marked road from the east edge of town.

CONCHAS LAKE STATE PARK
Conchas Lake, on the Canadian River north of Tucum-cari, is one of the most popular recreation lakes in New Mexico. Most of the 50-mile shoreline is privately owned, so the only easy public access to the lake is the state park, which includes developed areas on both sides of the dam. It's a good spot to fish and swim-ming and scuba diving are also permitted. There are picnic tables, restrooms, showers, marinas, bait and tackle, and groceries. Day-use fee, $4. ~ Located 25 miles north of Route 40 from the Newkirk/Route 129 exit, which is 27 miles east of Santa Rosa, or

31 miles northeast of Tucumcari on Route 104; 505-868-2270, fax 505-868-9641.

▲ There are 104 sites (40 are full RV hookups). Primitive camping available. Fees per night are $8 for primitive sites, $10 for standard sites and $14 for hookups.

GORDON WILDLIFE AREA 🏃 Tucumcari has a municipal wildlife refuge on the edge of town where a number of lucky birdwatchers have actually seen eagles. The 770 acres of wetlands provide a rest stop for migrating ducks and geese. There are hiking trails as well as an auto road. ~ Located just east of town, marked by a sign on Tucumcari Boulevard (Route 40 Business Loop).

UTE LAKE STATE PARK 🏃 ⛵ 🎣 ⛱ 🚤 ⛵ This reservoir was created in 1963 specifically for recreational purposes to bring tourism to the Tucumcari area. Records have been set here for the largest smallmouth bass ever caught in New Mexico. The park has picnic tables, restrooms, showers, a marina and hiking trails. Day-use fee, $4. ~ Located 25 miles northeast of Tucumcari on Route 54, or three miles west of Logan via Route 540; 505-487-2284, fax 505-487-2497.

▲ There are 110 standard campsites (77 with electric and water hookups) and three primitive camping areas. Fees per night are $8 for primitive sites, $10 for standard sites and $14 for hookups.

Clovis–Portales Area

The twin agricultural centers of Clovis and Portales, each just a few minutes' drive from the Texas state line, are located so far off the beaten track that few pleasure travelers ever find themselves there. Just in case you do—if you're passing through on your way from Fort Sumner to Muleshoe, Texas, for instance—here's what there is to tantalize you.

Clovis, the larger of the two towns, is the center of a grid of dirt roads that create identical plots of land, each exactly one mile square, as far as the eye can see. It's possible to get lost in the maze of farm roads for a whole day, but there's very little reason to wander into the countryside at all. The main crops, alfalfa and sugar beets, provide fodder for the town's huge cattle feedlots, which are said to be among the largest in the West.

SIGHTS

◄ *HIDDEN*

Clovis' greatest claim to fame is **Norman Petty Recording Studios,** where early rock-and-rollers Norman Petty, Buddy Holly, Waylon Jennings and Roy Orbison cut their first records. The studio, which is still in limited operation, is open for public tours by appointment only. ~ 1313 West 7th Street, Clovis; 505-356-6422.

Main Street in Clovis also has a collection of 1920s and Depression-era historic buildings that speak eloquently of the town's once-great expectations. The most impressive is the **Old Lyceum Theater**, where Shirley Temple, Tom Mix and John Philip Sousa performed during the age of vaudeville. It has been restored as a performing-arts center and is open to the public. Closed Sunday and Monday. ~ 411 North Main Street, Clovis; 505-763-6085.

Clovis is located alongside the Atchison, Topeka & Santa Fe Railway's Belen Cutoff, one of the busiest freight train routes in the Southwest; about 100 trains pass through town each day. Visitors can watch the railyard activity from the restored Clovis passenger station, which houses the **Clovis Depot Model Train Museum**. The museum contains elaborate electric train layouts depicting the history of the railroad in Great Britain and Australia, as well as a collection of American electric trains from the 1940s and 1950s, a working telegraph station and static exhibits on the history of the AT&SF Railway. Closed Monday and Tuesday, and in February and September. Admission. ~ 221 West 1st Street, Clovis; phone/fax 505-762-0066, 888-762-0064; www. clovisdepot.com.

HIDDEN ▶

The **Hillcrest Park Zoo**, located on the east edge of town, ranks as the second-largest zoo in New Mexico, even though it has only 500 animals and birds. Its inhabitants include bison, prairie dogs and other denizens of the region as well as the usual assortment of lions, elephants and bears. Closed Monday. Admission. ~ 10th and Sycamore streets, Clovis; 505-769-7873, fax 505-769-4800.

Seven miles north of town, the **H. A. "Pappy" Thornton Homestead and Museum** offers a look at life on the prairies of eastern New Mexico in the early years of the 20th century. There are an original dugout cabin and a farmhouse restored to its 1926 appearance, along with antique farming equipment. Open by appointment. ~ Ned Houk Park, Route 209, seven miles north of Clovis; 505-389-5146, fax 505-769-4800.

Clovis is best known, to anthropologists at least, as the namesake of one of the oldest known American Indian cultures, which flourished in the area about 11,000 years ago. Artifacts of the Clovis culture were first found in 1932 at Blackwater Draw, a large waterhole in prehistoric times, and the discovery of spear points and other small artifacts along with the bones of wooly mammoths, sabertooth tigers, dire wolves and Pleistocene camels provided the first evidence that humans had lived in North America much longer than had previously been believed. Many of the artifacts are now exhibited at Eastern New Mexico University's **Blackwater Draw Museum**, located midway between Clovis and Portales. Closed Monday from Labor Day to Memorial Day. Admission. ~ Route 70, Portales; 505-562-2202; www.enmu.edu.

HIDDEN ▶

The **Blackwater Draw Archaeological Site** is also open to the public. Following 13 major research digs by organizations includ-

HIDDEN ▶

ing the Smithsonian Institution and the National Geographic Society, the site is being actively excavated at present and is also protected for potential future excavations. Closed weekdays from October through February. Admission. ~ Route 467, between Portales and Clovis; 505-356-5235; www.enmu.edu.

A third the size of Clovis, **Portales** is the main peanut-farming area in New Mexico and the site of **Eastern New Mexico University**. On the university campus, Roosevelt Hall contains several museums. The **Natural History Museum** focuses on wildlife of New Mexico's eastern plains, with live exhibits of fish, amphibians, reptiles and insects including a living bee colony. There are also specimens of mammals and birds. Closed Saturday and Sunday. ~ Avenue K, off Route 70, Portales; 505-562-2723, fax 505-562-2192; www.enmu.edu.

Contrary to many visitors' misconceptions, green chile is *not* milder than red chile.

The **Roosevelt County Museum** presents exhibits on the area's early settlers and ranchers, with firearms, costumes, kitchen utensils, old photographs, a silent movie projector and other memorabilia. Hours may vary during the summer, so call ahead. ~ Avenue K, Route 70, Portales; 505-562-2592; e-mail mark.romero@enmu.edu.

The **Miles Mineral Museum** displays fossils, crystals, gems and other mineral samples from the local area and around the world. Closed Sunday. ~ Avenue K, off Route 70, Portales; 505-562-2651, fax 505-562-2192.

The most unique of the "museums" in Portales is **Dalley's Windmill Collection**. It contains more than 80 vintage windmills, all restored and erected in rank and file. Their purpose may not be entirely clear, but the photo possibilities are priceless. ~ 1506 South Kilgore Street, Portales; 505-356-6263.

◀ HIDDEN

The place to spend the night in Clovis is the **Clovis Inn**, the newest of several motels in town. The 97 guest rooms and suites feature contemporary decor in soft pink and gray hues, and there are a heated pool and a jacuzzi. A complimentary continental breakfast is included in the room rate. ~ 2912 Mabry Drive, Clovis; 505-762-5600, 800-535-3440, fax 505-762-6803; e-mail ci@yucca.net. BUDGET.

LODGING

In Portales, the charming little **Morning Star Bed and Breakfast** has three guest rooms and a two-bedroom suite with white wicker furniture and brass beds, original artwork and heirlooms, in a historic two-story adobe building that originally served as the home and clinic of Portales's only doctor in the early 20th century. The inn also has a common room with television and a cheerful dining room where a full complimentary breakfast is served. ~ 620 West 2nd Street, Portales; 505-356-2994; www.pdrpip.com/morningstarb&b, e-mail morningstarb&b@yucca.net. BUDGET.

◀ HIDDEN

DINING

Dining options in the Clovis–Portales area are about as routine as you'll find in any small Western town. In Clovis, the tantalizing aroma of Texas Panhandle–style barbecued beef and ribs wafts from **Ben's Barbecue**, an unpretentious place with long wooden tables. ~ 1421 Prince Street, Clovis; 505-763-4241. BUDGET.

Of the several good Mexican restaurants in Clovis, perhaps the most atmospheric is the **Guadalajara Restaurant**, serving standard Mexican fare along with a few house specialties such as *carne adovada*, pork strips marinated in a spicy red chile sauce. Closed Sunday. ~ 916-L Casillas Boulevard, Clovis; 505-769-9965. BUDGET.

In Clovis, a long-established favorite for south-of-the-border fare is **Juanito's Mexican Restaurant**, an unpretentious little place that has been serving enchiladas and combination plates at the same location since 1954. Its other location, in Portales, has been operating since 1994. No dinner on Sunday. Closed Monday. ~ 1608 Mabry Drive, Clovis, 505-762-7822; 813 South Avenue C Place, Portales, 505-359-1860. BUDGET.

If you want to go all-out for fine dining during a stay in Portales, the closest you're likely to find without leaving town is the **Cattle Baron Steak and Seafood Grill**, a family-style steakhouse that takes on an almost romantic ambiance after dark. The seafood may be pretty much limited to frozen breaded shrimp, but the thick slabs of steak sizzle and ooze juices guaranteed to appeal to the primal carnivore in almost anybody. ~ 1600 South Avenue D, Portales; 505-356-5587, fax 505-359-1937. MODERATE.

PARKS

OASIS STATE PARK 🧍🚴🐎🎣 This 194-acre park around a small lake in the barren badlands between Clovis and Portales may not have the waving palm trees of which its name conjures images, but 100-year-old locust and chinaberry trees planted by an early homesteader provide plenty of shade for picnicking, as do the relic native cottonwoods. In summer the lake is stocked with channel catfish; in winter, with rainbow trout. There is a wheelchair-accessible fishing dock. ~ Route 467, seven miles north of Portales; phone/fax 505-356-5331.

▲ There are 10 tent and RV sites (no hookups), $10 per night; and 13 RV sites with full hookups, $14 to $18 per night.

▼▼▼▼▼▼▼▼▼▼▼▼▼

Mountainair Area

For centuries, the Mountainair area was one of New Mexico's most populous regions. Three large Anasazi pueblos, dating back to the 1200s, flourished here. Salt from nearby dry lakebeds was gathered and traded to other pueblos and to the Plains Indians as well. The communities still flourished in 1598, when the first Spanish soldiers and priests arrived and began building their missions. The

Spanish colonial presence lasted less than 80 years before famine, drought, disease and Apache raids forced priests and Indians alike to abandon all the pueblos in the area, moving to Isleta and other Rio Grande pueblos. Today, the Mountainair area is sparsely populated but serves as the backdrop for exploring the ruins of these ancient peoples.

SIGHTS

East of Route 25, 39 miles from Belen via Routes 47 and 60, **Mountainair** serves the local ranching community and provides travelers a base for exploring the widely separated units of **Salinas Pueblo Missions National Monument**. The national monument preserves the ruins of three sizable ancient pueblos that date back to the 1200s. Massive, crumbling walls of Franciscan churches adjoin each pueblo site. The **park headquarters** in town is a good starting point for your exploration of the national monument's three units. ~ On the corner of Broadway (Route 60) and Ripley Street, Mountainair; 505-847-2585, fax 505-847-2441; www. nps.gov/sapu.

The **Abo unit** of the national monument is just off Route 60. Unexcavated pueblo ruins and the remains of the Mission of San

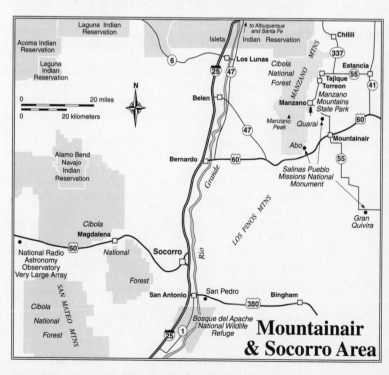

Mountainair & Socorro Area

Gregorio de Abo fill the small park area sandwiched between private farms. A ceremonial kiva built within the church *convento* at Abo puzzles archaeologists, since elsewhere in the Salinas pueblos priests destroyed kivas to halt native religious practices. ~ Off Route 60, nine miles west of Mountainair; 505-847-2400, fax 505-847-2441.

The red-walled Franciscan mission at **Quarai** was in operation from 1630 to the late 1670s. Today, in its tranquil setting alongside big cottonwoods at the foot of the Manzano Mountains, Quarai is perhaps the most photogenic of the three Salinas mission ruins. The adjoining pueblo remains are thoroughly buried and difficult to see. A small museum displays relics found at the site. ~ Route 55, eight miles north of Mountainair; 505-847-2290, fax 505-847-2441.

HIDDEN ►   **Gran Quivira** presents the national monument's most extensively excavated ruins. One of the largest pueblos in New Mexico, the limestone complex was home to about 2000 people at its height. Facilities include a visitors center with interpretive displays and a picnic area. There is no camping at any of the Salinas Pueblo Missions National Monument sites. ~ Route 55, 25 miles south of Mountainair; 505-847-2770, fax 505-847-2441.

LODGING   Because this area is sparsely populated and doesn't have much in the way of accommodations, people usually visit it as a daytrip from Santa Fe or Albuquerque.

However, if you need to rest your head while traveling through Mountainair, **El Rancho Motel** will do. It's sparse but adequate; its 17 units offer the bare basics (meaning no phone). ~ 901 Route 60 West, Mountainair; 505-847-2394. BUDGET.

DINING   Pickings are slim as far as dining options go in Mountainair. However, the **Kowboy Kafe** dishes up three meals a day. For breakfast you can count on standard fare such as egg dishes and pancakes; lunch brings sandwiches and burgers. Daily dinner specials may include an enchilada plate or chicken-fried steak. ~ 110 Broadway, Mountainair; 505-847-0950. BUDGET TO MODERATE.

Considered by some to be the jewel of Mountainair, the **Historic Shaffer Hotel & Dining Room** is a great place to eat. The food is good, but the surroundings are superb. Boasting a Tex-Mex menu, the Dining Room serves up ribeyes, nachos, burritos, combo plates and everybody's favorite: chicken-fried steak. Built in the 1930s by early resident "Pop" Schaffer, the establishment is a vision of American Indian–inspired handmade ceilings, chandeliers and furniture. ~ 102 West Main Street, Mountainair; 505-847-2888. MODERATE.

SHOPPING   For unique food and non-food gift items in Mountainair, visit the **Out of Tyme Shoppe**. Owner Joan Page's specialty is homemade chocolates. Call ahead to make an appointment to visit. ~ 505-847-2450.

Cibola Arts is a great place to pick up a gift and see what Mountainair's local artisans are up to. A co-op gallery, it sells a broad range of paintings, jewelry, tin works, handmade dolls, weavings, batik silks, greeting cards and hand-dipped wax candles. ~ 217 West Broadway, Mountainair; 505-847-0324.

MANZANO MOUNTAINS STATE PARK 🏃 Located in the foothills near the village of Manzano and the Quarai Unit of the monument, this small state park provides the most convenient camping for visitors to the Salinas Pueblo Missions National Monument. The forest road that continues past the state park turnoff leads to the Red Canyon trailhead at the Manzano Mountains Wilderness boundary. There are picnic tables, restrooms and nature trails. Closed November through April. Day-use fee, $4. ~ Off Route 55, 13 miles northwest of Mountainair, follow the highway signs; phone/fax 505-847-2820.

PARKS

> The quiet little town of Mountainair used to call itself the "Pinto Bean Capital of the World."

▲ There are 37 sites, one is handicapped reserved with a concrete ramp (8 with RV hookups); primitive camping is available. Fees for camping are $8 for primitive sites, $10 for standard sites, $14 per night for hookups.

CIBOLA NATIONAL FOREST 🏃🚴🐎🛶 The long, narrow range of the Manzano Mountains is one of seven separate units scattered across central New Mexico that comprise the 1,625,542-acre Cibola National Forest. Other units include the Sandia Mountains near Albuquerque and Mount Taylor near Grants, as well as several hard-to-reach areas such as the remote and rarely visited Apache Kid Wilderness southwest of Socorro. The Manzano Mountains unit is the only one with much to offer in the way of developed campgrounds. Like Sandia Peak, the Manzano Mountains are very steep on the west face, so most road and trail access is on the more gradual east slope. Osha Peak (10,008-feet) and Manzano Peak (10,098-feet), the highest points of the range, crown the Manzano Mountain Wilderness. ~ Accessible on numerous forest roads from Route 55 north of Mountainair; 505-346-3900, fax 505-346-3901.

▲ **Fourth of July Campground** near Tajique has 25 campsites, a picnic area and restrooms; day-use fee, $3; camping, $5 per night. **Red Canyon Campground**, up the road from Manzano Mountains State Park, has 52 campsites, no hookups; $5 per night. **New Canyon Campground** near Mountainair has 10 free campsites with no facilities except outhouses. Campgrounds are closed November through April.

Socorro Area

Seventy-five miles south of Albuquerque just off Route 25 is Socorro, a town so small that the strip of motels and gas stations along the interstate business loop overshadow its distinctive character. But take the time to look around; it will be worth it. This sleepy municipality of 8000 souls is actually one of the oldest towns in the state, dating back to 1615 when Franciscan priests began building a mission. A couple of detours off the interstate will pique the interest of birders and history buffs.

SIGHTS

Socorro's plaza is surrounded by a small, attractive historic district a short distance west of California Street on Manzaneras Avenue. Noteworthy are the restored **San Miguel Mission** (505-835-1620) at 403 El Camino Real, built in 1820 on the site of the church that was destroyed during the Pueblo Revolt of 1680; the old **Valverde Hotel** at 203 Manzaneras Avenue East, built in 1919 and now used as apartments; and the **Garcia Opera House,** one of two opera houses in town during the 1880s. The **Hilton Block,** near the opera house, is named for a relative of hotel tycoon Conrad Hilton, who operated a drugstore there in the 1930s. Hilton was born and raised in San Antonio, a town about nine miles south of Socorro that is so tiny it has no hotel or motel.

Northwest of Socorro's downtown area is the **Mineral Museum** at the New Mexico Institute of Mining and Technology. The museum's possessions have been combined with specimens donated by prominent mining speculator C. T. Brown to form one of the better rock collections in the Southwest. The more than 10,000 pieces include gems and mining artifacts. ~ Corner of Olive Lane and Canyon Road, Socorro; 505-835-5140, fax 505-835-6333; www.geoinfo.nmt.edu.

An 18-mile drive south of Socorro, **Bosque del Apache National Wildlife Refuge** is especially worth visiting between November and March when it presents one of the most spectacular birdwatching opportunities around. The refuge was established during the 1930s to protect the sandhill crane, which had nearly vanished along the Rio Grande. Local farmers grow corn for the birds on refuge land during the summer months. Today more than 12,000 cranes spend the winter at the refuge. Besides the four-foot-tall sandhill cranes and a couple of rare whooping cranes that were introduced into the flock in an unsuccessful breeding experiment, the refuge also provides a winter home for about 40,000 snow geese. The white geese often rise en masse from the manmade wetlands to fill the sky in a noisy, dazzling display. Admission. ~ Off Route 25 Exit 139; 505-835-1828, fax 505-835-0314.

Of several ghost towns in the Socorro area, perhaps the most interesting is old **San Pedro**, across the river from San Antonio where visitors exit the interstate to go to Bosque del Apache. An abandoned mission church and ruins of several adobe houses in Mexican and early Territorial styles are about all that remain of San Pedro, a town where people once grew grapes and produced champagne. Tamarisks have grown up through the floors of the houses to conceal much of the village. ~ To get to San Pedro, drive east from San Antonio for 1.4 miles on Route 380 and turn south on an unpaved road.

◄ HIDDEN

The Very Large Array is used in combination with other radio observatories around the world to explore the far limits of the universe.

Forty-six miles west of Socorro is the unusually named **National Radio Astronomy Observatory Very Large Array**. These 27 giant parabolic dish antennas, each weighing 235 tons, are used to search deep space for faint radio waves emitted by celestial objects. Together, the antennas can "see" as well as a telescope with a lens 20 miles in diameter. A visitors center at the site explains how it works, and a one-hour, self-guided walking tour lets visitors see the antennas up close. ~ Route 60; 505-835-7000; www.nrao.edu, e-mail info@nrao.edu.

Every motel in Socorro falls within the budget range. Accommodations are found in two clusters along California Street, the business loop from Route 25. The best in town is the **Best Inn**, about a block from San Miguel Mission. ~ 507 North California Street, Socorro; 505-835-0230, fax 505-835-1993. BUDGET.

LODGING

Representative of the good, clean independent motels found in Socorro is the **Payless Inn**. ~ 1009 North California Street, Socorro; 505-835-0276, fax 505-835-4142. BUDGET.

Don Juan's Cocina serves standard New Mexican fare. No lunch on Friday. Closed Sunday. ~ 118 Manzaneras Avenue, Socorro; 505-835-9967. BUDGET.

DINING

The **Valverde Steak House** serves steaks, seafood, enchiladas and other Southwestern dishes. There is also a salad bar. It's housed in an old hotel listed on the National Register of Historic Places. ~ 203 East Manzaneras Avenue, Socorro; 505-835-3380. MODERATE TO ULTRA-DELUXE.

Located in the center of the small town of San Antonio nine miles south of Socorro, the **Owl Bar & Cafe** offers everything from inexpensive sandwiches to moderately priced steak dinners. Their claim to serve the best green-chile cheeseburgers in the world may well be accurate. Breakfast, lunch and dinner are served. Closed Sunday. ~ Route 380, Main Street, San Antonio; 505-835-9946. BUDGET TO MODERATE.

▼▼▼▼▼▼▼▼▼▼▼▼▼▼

Outdoor Adventures

Although there aren't many options for skiing in the area, the easy access and reliable snowpack offered by the primary resort makes up for the lack of choices. You'll find both cross-country and downhill skiing right next to Albuquerque in the Sandia Mountains, and equipment rentals are readily available in town.

SKIING

ALBUQUERQUE   An average annual snowfall of 183 inches makes Sandia Peak one of the most popular ski slopes in New Mexico. Proximity to Albuquerque makes it the most crowded. **Sandia Peak Ski Area,** a short steep slope with an 1800-foot vertical drop, can be reached either by car or by the Sandia Peak Aerial Tramway. Snowboarding is allowed. The ski slope has six lifts serving trails rated 35 percent beginner, 55 percent intermediate and 10 percent expert. The ski season, which is unpredictable because there is little artificial snowmaking equipment, typically runs from mid-December to mid-March.

◆◆◆◆◆◆◆◆◆◆◆◆◆◆◆◆◆◆◆◆

Temperatures on the crest of Sandia Peak run about 20° cooler than on Albuquerque's downtown streets.

Sandia Peak also offers great cross-country skiing, especially on the Crest and 10-K trails, which begin near the Sandia Crest House at the top of the auto road. Alpine ski equipment and snowboards are available for rent. Adult and children's ski lessons are also offered. ~ 505-242-9133, fax 505-242-6549; www.sandiapeak.com.

Ski Rentals   In Albuquerque, cross-country skis are available for rent at **The Bike Coop Ltd.** ~ 3407 Central Avenue Northeast; 505-265-5170.

All manner of skis and equipment are also available for rent at **Sports Systems.** It also caters to the snowboarding crowd. ~ 1605 Juan Tabo Boulevard Northeast, Suite Z; 505-296-9111; www.nmsportsystems.com.

WIND-SURFING

New Mexico may not conjure up thoughts of windsurfing, but sailboards do shred the water at many of the state's lakes. Grab your board—or rent one—and hoist your sail. The sport is most popular at Cochiti Lake. Windsurfing is also permitted on Santa Rosa Lake, Conchas Lake and Ute Lake in the eastern part of the state.

BALLOON RIDES

Home of the annual balloon festival, Albuquerque has practically become synonymous with ballooning—at least, the sport is one of the city's major tourist attractions. If you rise early enough on a clear day (and most of them are), you'll see the multicolored creatures making their graceful ascent. Those who want to see what it's like to float above the city on the breeze can do so by contacting a local company like the **World Balloon.** They take to the air over Albuquerque with early-morning flights followed by champagne. ~ 4800 Eubank Boulevard Northeast; 505-293-

6800, 800-351-9588; www.worldballoon.com, e-mail info@world balloon.com.

Another outfitter that will allow you to touch the clouds is **Rainbow Ryders**, which offers one to one-and-a-half-hour expeditions over the Rio Grande River Valley. Riders are reputed to be able to see 70 miles in all directions. The day includes a continental breakfast with mimosas and a first-flight certificate upon completion. ~ 11520 San Bernardino Drive Northeast; 505-823-1111, 800-725-2477; www.rainbowryders.com.

GOLF

Central New Mexico is an excellent place to spend a day on the greens—whether you stay in Albuquerque or head to the outlying areas, you'll find a nice spot to swing your clubs. Most facilities have club and/or cart rentals, as well as golf pros who offer lessons. For information on golf courses statewide, contact the **Sun Country Amateur Golf Association**. ~ 10035 Country Club Lane Northwest, Suite 5, Albuquerque, NM 87114; 505-897-0864; www.newmexicogolf.org, e-mail scaga@prodigy.net.

ALBUQUERQUE Tee off in Albuquerque at the 18-hole **University of New Mexico South Course**. ~ 3601 University Boulevard Southeast; 505-277-4546. The public **Arroyo del Oso Golf Course** is also popular and has both a 9-hole course and an 18-hole course, plus a driving range and putting greens. ~ 7001 Osuna Road Northeast; 505-884-7505.

OUTSIDE ALBUQUERQUE Many Albuquerque golfers travel 40 miles north to play in a lovely setting below the rugged volcanic canyons of the Jemez Mountains at the Indian-owned **Pueblo de Cochiti Golf Course**, an 18-hole course in a beautiful lakeside setting surrounded by the multicolored foothills of the Jemez Mountains. ~ 505-465-2239.

SANTA ROSA AREA Work on your line drives at the **Santa Rosa Golf Course**, with nine holes. There are carts available to rent, but no clubs. ~ 535 Chuck-n-Dale Lane; 505-472-4653. The nine-hole **Tucumcari Municipal Golf Course** is also open for public golfing. Closed Monday. ~ 4465-C Route 66; 505-461-1849. You can also play the greens at the nine-hole **Conchas Dam Golf Course**. To get information about the course call the Conchas Dam Golf Association. There are a few carts available to rent, but no clubs. ~ 505-868-4563.

SOCORRO AREA Tee off at the 18-hole **New Mexico Institute of Mining and Technology Golf Course**. ~ 1 Canyon Road; 505-835-5335.

TENNIS

Tennis courts are very rare outside Albuquerque in central New Mexico. If you want to keep up your backstroke while on vacation, sign up for a court in Albuquerque at **Arroyo del Oso Park**. There are six unlit courts. ~ Wyoming Boulevard and Osuna Road Northeast. You can also serve and volley at the six lit courts at **Los Altos Park**. ~ 10300 Lomas Boulevard Northeast. **Jerry Cline Tennis Courts** has twelve public courts in Albuquerque, seven of them lit. ~ Constitution Boulevard at Louisiana Boulevard Northeast; 505-256-2032. You can also play a couple of matches on one of the 16 hardtop, unlit public courts at the **Albuquerque Tennis Complex**. Fee. ~ 1903 Avenida Cesar Chavez Southeast; 505-848-1381. **Sierra Vista West** has full facilities and ten courts: eight hard and two omni. ~ 5001 Montano Road Northwest; 505-897-8819.

RIDING STABLES

Whether you rent a horse or go on a guided tour, the mountains, rivers and canyons around Albuquerque are ideal for riding.

ALBUQUERQUE   Albuquerque has two popular areas for horseback riding—the Rio Grande bosque and the foothills of Sandia Peak. Individual rentals and group tours in the Manzano foothills are available at **Turkey Track Stables**, east of the city near Route 40. ~ 1306 Route 66, Tijeras; 505-281-1772.

Another lesser-known area that offers good horseback riding trails is the foothills of the Manzano Mountains. **Town and Country Feed Stables** leads one-hour guided tours along its hilly and circuitous paths. A party of eight to ten people will allow for a night ride. ~ 15600 Central Avenue South; 505-296-6711.

BIKING

Central New Mexico is a popular place to pedal, with both on-road and off-road riders. Hit the trails to explore petroglyphs on an extinct volcano, or simply use your wheels to explore the urban outback of Albuquerque.

ALBUQUERQUE   A well-developed system of bike trails runs throughout Albuquerque. **Paseo del Bosque** is a paved bike and horse trail running for over 20 miles along the Rio Grande from south of Rio Bravo Boulevard to the northern edge of town, passing through the Rio Grande Nature Center. The **Paseo del Norte/ North Channel Trail** (7 miles) connects the Paseo del Bosque with the **Paseo del Noreste**, a six-mile trail, allowing residents of the fashionable Northeast Heights area to commute downtown by bicycle. **Paseo de las Montañas**, a 4.2-mile biking and jogging trail between Tramway Boulevard Northeast and the Winrock Shopping Center on the northeast side of the city, offers grand views of Albuquerque. For more information about bike trails and bike routes, contact the **Outdoor Recreation Division of Parks and Recreation**. ~ P.O. Box 1293, Albuquerque, NM 87103; 505-768-2453, fax 505-857-8220.

OUTSIDE ALBUQUERQUE   In a little-known area on the edge of the Cochiti Pueblo Grant, **Cochiti Canyon**'s rough unpaved road

In the Land
of Hot Air

On any weekend morning you can see as many as 50 hot-air balloons soaring gracefully across the sky above Albuquerque—or sometimes, when the air temperature is wrong, bouncing off suburban rooftops—with their gas burners roaring like dragons. Indeed, hot-air balloons are so much a symbol of Albuquerque that they appear as a motif decorating everything from fast-food restaurants to New Mexico's license plates.

Balloon fever, of course, is the result of the **Albuquerque International Balloon Fiesta**, the world's largest balloon event, which now lasts for nine days in early October. The fiesta's most spectacular events are dawn mass ascensions, in which more than 700 hot-air balloons, tethered to the ground, are illuminated from the inside in a colorful display. In between are many other events, from "splash-and-dashes," in which contestants try to touch the bottoms of their baskets in the Rio Grande without crashing, to a gas balloon distance race in which contestants start from Albuquerque and see who can fly farthest, sometimes landing as far away as the East Coast.

A victim of its own popularity, the Balloon Fiesta now requires advance planning and more than a little endurance of its audience. Part of the problem is that balloons fly best just after dawn, when the air temperature is cool and rising. To be at the Albuquerque Balloon Park before dawn means getting on the road by 3 a.m. so that you can get in line for the parking lots in time. Worse yet, in recent years the number of vehicles attending the Balloon Fiesta has exceeded the capacity of the parking lots, causing traffic jams that paralyzed Route 25 for hours. Then, too, there are not nearly enough hotel and motel rooms in Albuquerque to accommodate all the Balloon Fiesta spectators. Santa Fe's hotels are also packed, and many visitors end up searching for vacancies as far afield as Grants and Socorro.

While the city of Albuquerque experiments with solutions such as shuttles from other parts of the city, the best strategy—one that few people try—may be to spend the night in a campground on the back side of Sandia Crest, drive to the top ridge of the mountain before dawn, and view the mass ascension from above. ~ 4401 Alameda Northeast, Albuquerque, NM 87113; 505-821-1000, 888-422-7277, fax 505-828-2887; www.balloonfiesta.com, e-mail balloons@balloonfiesta.com.

splashes through creeks as it climbs to Tent Rocks, the site of an old ghost town that takes its name from huge tepee-shaped rock formations created millennia ago when steam vents hardened volcanic ash like concrete so that the massive cones remained in place while the ash around it eroded away. The canyon is so remote that bears are commonly spotted there. To find it, follow the tribal road past Cochiti Lake and through Dixons apple orchards, where the pavement ends; then keep right where the road forks.

MOUNTAINAIR AREA   The roads in the vicinity of **Fourth of July Campground** in the Manzano Mountains are popular with mountain bikers.

SOCORRO AREA   Outside Albuquerque, popular cycling trips include the level, unpaved 15-mile tour loop at **Bosque del Apache National Wildlife Refuge** near Socorro. ~ 505-835-1828.

Bike Rentals & Tours   **Rio Mountain Sports** rents mountain bikes (as well as inline skates) and does repairs. Closed Sunday. ~ 1210 Rio Grande Boulevard Northwest, Albuquerque; 505-766-9970. For information on bike routes, call or pass by **Two Wheel Drive**, a good shop although they don t rent bikes. Closed Sunday. ~ 1706 Central Avenue Southeast, Albuquerque; 505-243-8443. **Old Town Bicycles** rents mountain and road bikes as well as the ever-popular comfort bikes. Lock, helmet, tools and maps included in the rental fee. ~ 2412 Central Avenue Southwest, Albuquerque; 505-247-4926. Another shop that supplies mountain and road bikes is **Northeast Cyclery**. Its 24-hour rentals include a helmet. ~ 8305 Menaul Boulevard Northeast, Albuquerque; 505-299-1210. Knowledgeable guides at **New Mexico Mountain Bike Adventures** lead bike tours of the Turquoise Trail and Jemez Mountains. Reservations required. ~ 49 Main Street, Los Cerrillos; 505-474-0074; www.bikefun.com.

HIKING   The trails of Central New Mexico, with their varied elevations, let you explore a variety of terrain and your hike can be as convenient to Albuquerque or as remote as you wish. Hike in a lush north-facing valley or on a barren western slope, in a forest of Douglas fir, maple or quaking aspen or in no forest at all. Climb 10,000-

AUTHOR FAVORITE

My favorite mountain-biking area in Albuquerque is the series of five extinct volcanoes that make up a city-owned open space on **West Mesa**, the western skyline of the city. Dirt roads ramble all around the volcanoes and lead to petroglyphs at the edge of the West Mesa Escarpment.

foot peaks or do a bit of spelunking underground, the choice is yours. Just be prepared for changeable weather . . . and breathtaking views. All distances are one way unless otherwise noted.

ALBUQUERQUE Sandia Peak, the 10,378-foot mountain that fills Albuquerque's eastern skyline, offers hiking trails for every preference, from gentle strolls to ambitious ascents.

The easiest way to hike Sandia is to either drive or take the aerial tramway to the crest of the mountain and walk the well-worn trail between the restaurant at the top of the tramway and the gift shop at the end of the auto road, a distance of about a mile with continuous views of the city below. The **Crest Trail** continues along the top ridge through the Sandia Wilderness Area all the way down to Canyon Estates, 10.5 miles to the south near Route 40, and Placitas, almost 16 miles to the north.

The **10-K Trail** (4.8 miles) starts at a trailhead two miles down the road from the crest and reaches the top ridge at the broadcast towers north of the gift shop. The hike to the summit leads through shady forests of Douglas fir, aspen and spruce with a 1000-foot elevation gain. A continuation of the trail follows the road back down to the trailhead to close the loop.

A trailhead midway up the Sandia Peak road marks the **Tree Spring Trail** (2 miles), which climbs to the top ridge, joining the Crest Trail a mile and a half south of the tram station. It is a 1400-foot climb from the trailhead to the crest.

One of the most challenging trails on Sandia Peak is **La Luz Trail** (5.8 miles), which takes expert hikers up the seemingly sheer west face of the mountain from Juan Tabo Picnic Ground to the tram station on the crest. It's a climb from 7060 feet elevation at the foot of the mountain to 10,378 at the summit. You can ride the tram to the top and hike back down the trail. The **Pino Canyon Trail** (4.7 miles) is newer—and even more difficult, some hikers say—rising 2800 feet from Elena Gallegos Picnic Ground to the summit. The hike is quite scenic and shadier than La Luz Trail.

On the north side of Sandia Peak, lush **Las Huertas Canyon** is accessible by the road that leads from Route 25 through the village of Placitas or by a steep, narrow road that descends from the Sandia Crest auto road. Near the upper end of the canyon, an easy .75-mile trail takes hikers along the canyon wall to **Sandia Man Cave**, where University of New Mexico archaeologists found artifacts left by Indians during the last Ice Age. A flashlight is needed to reach the inner recesses of the cave—plan on getting dirty. For more information on trails in the Sandia area, call 505-281-3304, fax 505-281-1176.

OUTSIDE ALBUQUERQUE To experience solitude amid a unique landscape of yellow, red, chocolate brown and black banded cliffs, mushroom-shaped rock formations and natural bridges that arch over miniature canyons, search out the virtually undiscovered **Ojitos Wilderness Study Area**. This 10,000-acre expanse of badlands under Bureau of Land Management jurisdiction has been reserved as a potential wilderness area since 1982, though no congressional action has been taken to extend permanent protection. There are no established hiking trails, but walking is easy in the open juniper woodland. The area is on an unpaved road that heads west from Route 44 approximately three miles southeast of the village of San Ysidro, or 23 miles from Route 25.

MOUNTAINAIR AREA   A profusion of bigtooth maple trees makes Fourth of July Campground near Tajique, located about 30 miles south of the Tijeras exit from Route 40, a favorite for fall hiking. The moderate **Fourth of July Trail** (1.3 miles) leaves from the campground and climbs northwest to the **Manzano Crest Trail** (22 miles), which affords great views of the Rio Grande and Estancia valleys. The moderate **Albuquerque Trail** (3.4 miles roundtrip) begins at the end of Forest Road 55C, a half mile northeast of the Fourth of July Campground, and runs north to the Isleta Indian Reservation boundary.

The southern Manzano Mountains offer excellent hiking opportunities. Two of the best trails here start from the unpaved road past Manzano Mountains State Park near the town of Manzano, just north of the Quarai unit of Salinas Pueblo Missions National Monument.

The difficult **Red Canyon Trail** (2.4 miles) follows a creek with small waterfalls into the Manzano Mountain Wilderness until it's within scrambling distance of the summit of Gallo Peak, elevation 10,003 feet. It is a strenuous climb with a 2000-foot altitude gain.

The **Kayser Mill Trail** (3.3 miles) climbs 2000 feet to intersect the **Manzano Crest Trail**, which runs along the top ridge of the Manzanos. To reach the summit of Manzano Peak, elevation 10,098 feet, follow the Crest Trail for about a mile south of the intersection. Those who plan to hike only the lower portion of one of these trails should choose the Red Canyon Trail, since the first part of the Kayser Mill Trail, outside the wilderness boundary, has been heavily logged. For more information, contact the Mountainair Ranger District of Cibola National Forest. ~ 505-847-2990, fax 505-847-2238.

SOCORRO AREA   From the upper ridges of the Magdalena Mountains, you can see Sandia Peak in the distance. Notice the difference. While hiking any of the Sandia trails on a summer day can be a very social experience, few people visit the Magdalenas. **North Baldy Trail** (6 miles), the best hiking access, is a challenge to reach. Beyond Water Canyon Campground, off Route 60 about 16 miles west of Socorro, eight miles of unpaved, narrow, rocky road lead to the trailhead. The trail starts near the summit, where the state operates a laboratory to study thunderstorms. After a short, steep climb, the main trail runs along a ridgeline of high mountain meadows to the North Baldy summit (elevation 9858 feet).

Transportation

CAR

Two major interstate highways, **Route 25** and **Route 40**, cross near the center of Albuquerque, an intersection known locally as the "Big I." Santa Rosa is on Route 40, two hours east of Albuquerque, and Tucumcari is another hour east of Santa Rosa.

The most direct way to reach Mountainair from Albuquerque is by exiting Route 25 at Belen and taking **Route 47**, which merges into **Route 60** and runs through Mountainair. Route 60 parallels Route 40 across eastern New Mexico and runs through Fort Sumner. A straight and very empty two-lane highway through pronghorn antelope country, **Route 41** is the most direct route between Santa Fe and the Mountainair area. Driving south of Albuquerque on Route 25 will bring you to Socorro. For New Mexico road conditions, call 800-432-4269.

AIR

Albuquerque International Sunport is the only major commercial passenger terminal in the state. Carriers include America West, American Airlines, Continental Airlines, Delta Air Lines, Frontier Airlines, Mesa Airlines, Northwest Airlines, Rio Grande Air, Southwest Airlines and United Airlines. ~ 505-842-4366.

Taxis and hotel courtesy vans wait for passengers in front of the airport terminal. **Herrera/Santa Fe Shuttle** (505-243-2300, 888-833-2300) and **Sandia Shuttle** (505-243-3244, 888-775-5696; www.sandiashuttle.com) provide transportation to and from Albuquerque and Santa Fe. **Twin Hearts Express** (505-751-1201, 800-654-9456) and **Faust's Transportation** (505-758-7359, 888-830-3410) provide transportation between Albuquerque and Taos. **Sun Tran**, Albuquerque's public bus system, also serves the airport. ~ 505-843-9200.

BUS

Greyhound Bus Lines (800-231-2222; www.greyhound.com) and **TNM&O Coaches** provide service to Albuquerque, Tucumcari, Fort Sumner, Clovis, Portales, Santa Rosa and Socorro. ~ Albuquerque Bus Transportation Center: 300 2nd Street Southwest; 505-243-4435. Tucumcari: 2618 South 1st Street; 505-461-1350. Socorro: 1007 South California Street; 505-835-1767. Portales: 215 East 2nd Street; 505-356-6914.

TRAIN

Amtrak's "Southwest Chief," which chugs between Chicago and Los Angeles, stops daily at the Albuquerque passenger station. ~

214 1st Street Southwest; 505-842-9650, 800-872-7245; www. amtrak.com.

CAR RENTALS

Agencies at Albuquerque International Sunport include **Advantage Rent A Car** (800-777-5500), **Avis Rent A Car** (800-331-1212), **Budget Rent A Car** (800-527-0700), **Dollar Rent A Car** (800-800-4000) and **Hertz Rent A Car** (800-654-3131). Located just outside the airport, **Alamo Rent A Car** (800-327-9633) offers free shuttle service to and from the terminal. ~ 2601 Yale Street Southeast.

Any of the more than 60 agencies listed in the Albuquerque Yellow Pages can arrange car pickups and drop-offs at the airport or a hotel.

PUBLIC TRANSIT

Sun Tran, Albuquerque's metropolitan bus system, has routes covering most parts of the city, including the airport, the bus depot, Old Town, the University of New Mexico and all major shopping malls. ~ 100 1st Street Southwest; 505-843-9200.

TAXIS

Taxi services in Albuquerque include **Albuquerque Cab Co.** (505-883-4888), **Yellow Checker Cab Co.** (505-243-7777) and **Yellow Cab Co.** (505-247-8888).

SIX

Southern New Mexico

Southern New Mexico has little in common with the northern part of the state. In pre-Columbian times, when the Anasazi Indians were building cities in the Four Corners area, Mimbres people occupied the southern region, living in small cliff-dwelling communities. Their pottery has long been famed for the imaginative artistry of its animal motifs, but scientists are only now realizing what a sophisticated knowledge of astronomy the Mimbres possessed. They vanished without explanation centuries before nomadic Apaches moved into the region and the first European settlers arrived in New Mexico.

The Spanish colonists who settled Santa Fe avoided the south, where the land was parched and arid, and Apache Indians terrorized any outsider who set foot in their territory. Most of the development in southern New Mexico has come in the 20th century, from air force bases to ski resorts and huge boating reservoirs. Today descendants of the Apaches operate exclusive recreation facilities at the edge of the Mescalero Apache Indian Reservation near Ruidoso.

With the exception of Carlsbad Caverns National Park, southern New Mexico is less visited by vacationers than other parts of the state. That's surprising, and somewhat disappointing, for this region boasts enough outdoor sports and road-side sightseeing to fill a two-week vacation easily. Cool islands of high mountain forest offer relief from the scorching summers of the Chihuahuan Desert. On top of this, they're great for winter skiing. The lowlands enjoy a much longer warm season for spring and fall outdoor activities than Albuquerque, Santa Fe or Taos, making the entire region an attractive year-round destination.

Southern New Mexico is divided into several geographic regions. The area east of the mountains is, for all practical purposes, indistinguishable from west Texas. Carlsbad Caverns is closer to the Texas state line than to any New Mexico town. Ruidoso, the horse racing and skiing town in the mountains west of Roswell, caters almost exclusively to visitors from Texas. South of Ruidoso, memories of the Wild West live on in Lincoln, once among the most lawless towns on the frontier, now a low-key historic district.

Driving on Route 25 or the older highway that parallels it, motorists find an empty landscape flanking a series of large recreational lakes. Taking Route 54 through the Tularosa Basin, the sights are more unusual—a giant lava field, many ancient Indian petroglyphs, and miles of pure white sand dunes. In the mountains just west of Alamogordo, charming little Cloudcroft is a bustling ski town in the winter and a cool, quiet haven the rest of the year.

The southwestern part of the state is filled with national forest. Driving to the boundary of the roadless Gila Wilderness, the largest wilderness area in the lower 48 states, you won't find any gas stations or grocery stores along the route, but you will discover many scenic lookouts, mountain lakes and hiking trails. Travel within the Gila Wilderness is restricted to horseback riders and hikers. A driving trip from Gila Cliff Dwellings National Monument in the canyonlands at the heart of the wilderness to the Catwalk on the western perimeter and then north through the ghost town of Mogollon to Snow Lake on the high mountain slopes can take several scenic, pleasurable and adventurous days.

Southeastern New Mexico

Travelers to Southeastern New Mexico won't be disappointed. Carlsbad Caverns National Park, one of New Mexico's top vacation destinations, offers a vast, silent world of gemlike crystals and massive stalactites deep below the earth's surface. Those who venture to this region can also discover Carlsbad's peaceful river park and desert museum and Roswell's unique "bottomless" lakes. The Lincoln historic district recalls the bloody days when six-guns ruled the land, while the Mescalero Apache operate a five-star ski resort in Ruidoso. Technicolor sunsets, secluded mountain lakes and great mountain biking are just the extra attractions.

SIGHTS

Carlsbad Caverns National Park takes you 750 feet underground inside a limestone reef in the foothills of the Guadalupe Mountains, where ancient standing groundwater dissolved and hollowed out a spectacular honeycomb of caves. Eons of dripping dampness decorated the cave with an amazing display of natural mineral spires, curtains, crystals and lace. Bottomless pits, fairy temples and alien landscapes challenge your imagination. There are more than a hundred known limestone caves in the park, nine of which are open to cavers with permits; only three are open to the public. Admission. ~ The entrance to Carlsbad Caverns is either off Route 285 or off Route 62/180. It is 23 miles northeast of the town of Carlsbad and only 17 miles from the Texas state line; 505-785-2232, 800-967-2283, fax 505-785-2302; www.nps.gov/cave, e-mail cave_interpretation@nps.gov.

Carlsbad Cavern is the cave most people visit, the big one with the visitors center on the surface and an elevator that runs to the cave's Big Room 750 feet below. Visitors can choose from two self-guided tours or a ranger-led tour. On the easy Big Room Tour,

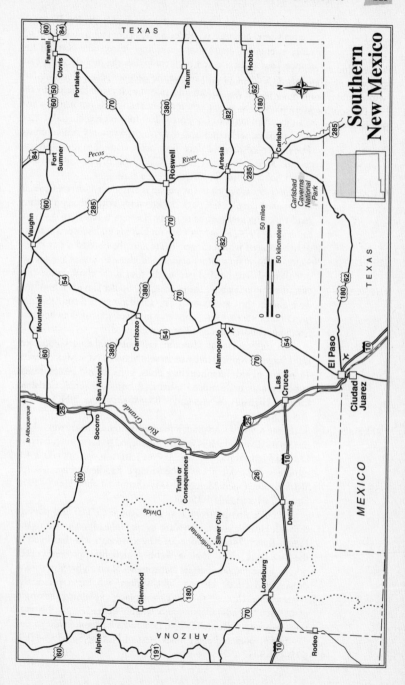

Southern New Mexico

TEXAS

Farwell
Clovis
Portales
Tatum
Hobbs
Fort Sumner
Pecos River
Roswell
Artesia
Carlsbad
Vaughn
Mountainair
Carrizozo
Alamogordo
Las Cruces
El Paso
Ciudad Juarez
San Antonio
Socorro
Rio Grande
Truth or Consequences
Silver City
Deming
Continental Divide
Glenwood
Lordsburg
Alpine
Rodeo

Carlsbad Caverns National Park

to Albuquerque

TEXAS

MEXICO

ARIZONA

N

50 miles

50 kilometers

0

0

they ride both ways on the elevator to see only the Big Room on a mostly level one-mile paved loop trail. Those who pick the much more strenuous—and more rewarding—three-mile Natural Entrance Tour walk a switchback trail from the mouth of the cave down to a depth of 750 feet at the deepest point, climb 80 feet back up to the Big Room and ride the elevator back up to the ground level. However you reach it, the Big Room inspires awe with its seven acres of floor area, 200-foot-high ceiling and massive, looming stalactites and towering stalagmites and columns. The ranger-led King's Palace Tour takes visitors to four different rooms: King's Palace, Queen's Chamber, Papoose Room and Green Lake Room. Be sure to bring a flashlight.

HIDDEN ▶   Another cave open to the public is **Slaughter Canyon Cave**, in an isolated part of the park backcountry reached via a county road that is gravel part of the way. Though it has been open for tours since 1974, Slaughter Canyon Cave is undeveloped and can only be toured with a ranger. Tours must be booked a day in advance at the main visitors center, and children under age six are not allowed. The hardest part of the tour is the climb to the cave

HIDDEN ▶   entrance 500 feet above the parking lot. **Spider Cave** is a primitive cave also in the backcountry. The small ranger-led tour (Sunday only) takes about four hours and involves lots of crawling and climbing; children under 12 are not allowed.

The **Million Dollar Museum**, just outside the park entrance, is the largest historical museum in southeastern New Mexico, with 11 rooms of exhibits including dolls, guns, music boxes, ranch antiques and mummified Indians. Admission. ~ 25 Carlsbad Caverns Highway, Whites City; 505-785-2291 ext. 204, fax 505-785-2283.

In the town of **Carlsbad,** a marked auto tour route runs along the Pecos River, which is partially dammed to form long, narrow Carlsbad Lake through town. At **Port Jefferson** you can take a 40-minute scenic tour aboard the vintage paddlewheeler, *George Washington*. Open Memorial Day through Labor Day. ~ Park Drive, Carlsbad; 505-885-1600.

If you're driving from Texas via Route 62/180 and passing through Hobbs, you might want to plan ahead for a visit to the **Linam Ranch Museum**, operated by a woman who has lived in the area since 1906. Thelma Webber's delightful pioneer collection includes pie safes, quilts featuring local ranch brands, squaw dresses and butter churns. Mrs.Webber will often personally guide visitors through this little showplace, explaining the origin of the arrowheads, wagons and wagon-wheel lamps. Reservations required. ~ Route 62/180, two and a half miles west of Lea County Airport and eight miles west of Hobbs; 505-393-4784, 505-393-9032.

Living Desert Zoo and Gardens State Park offers a close-up look at the animal and plant life of the Chihuahuan Desert. Inhabitants include a mountain lion, a bear, Mexican wolves, bison and javelinas. There is a mineral exhibit in the visitors center and an indoor exhibit that contains giant tropical cactus species from around the world. Admission. ~ Just off Route 285; 505-887-5516, fax 505-885-4478.

The largest town in southeastern New Mexico, with a population of nearly 50,000, **Roswell** is the shipping and commercial center for thousands of square miles of ranchlands in the region. At first glance, Roswell does not look like the kind of place that would have much to offer vacationers. But explore a bit and you'll discover some little-known sightseeing treasures. Bottomless Lakes State Park and Bitter Lake National Wildlife Refuge are described in the "Parks" section below.

The **Roswell Museum and Art Center** is one of the best in the state, with collections ranging from Western art and Indian artifacts to early rockets. The museum's highlight is a collection of

Southeastern
New Mexico

paintings by famed landscape painter and portraitist Peter Hurd, who was born in Roswell and spent most of his life on his ranch nearby. Other artists represented here include Georgia O'Keeffe and Marsden Hartley. The museum's other claim to fame is the **Robert H. Goddard Planetarium** (admission), the largest planetarium in New Mexico, which presents educational programs and laser lightshows daily during the summer and one week a month the rest of the year. ~ 100 West 11th Street, Roswell; 505-624-6744, fax 505-624-6765; www.roswellmuseum.org, e-mail rmac@roswellmuseum.org.

Satellites use south central New Mexico as a landmark to calibrate their cameras—the jet black lava flows of the Valley of Fires and the dazzling dunes of White Sands form the highest-contrast terrain feature on the entire surface of the earth.

Roswell is perhaps most famous as the site where UFO buffs believe an extraterrestrial spacecraft crashed in 1947. At the time, the "flying saucer" was officially dismissed as a stray weather balloon. In the decades since, with the general fading of the federal government's credibility, the Roswell myth has been enhanced through movies and television.

At the **International UFO Museum and Research Center**, docents include retired military personnel on duty at the time of the 1947 retrieval of alleged space aliens. There's a flying saucer exhibit, a gift shop and a research library where you can learn about mysterious abduction reports and unusual personal experiences. ~ 114 North Main Street, Roswell; 505-625-9495, fax 505-625-1907; www.iufomrc.com, e-mail iufomrc@iufomrc.com.

What do football great Roger Staubach and New Mexico artist Peter Hurd have in common, other than that they're good with their hands? Both were students at New Mexico Military Institute, an institution that has sent more than 2800 graduates into combat duty since the Spanish American War. The proud heritage of NMMI is captured at the **General Douglas L. McBride Museum**. Grouped by war, the exhibit areas showcase many little-known treasures, including a machine-gun-toting Harley Davidson used by one of General Pershing's squadrons in the assault on Pancho Villa in 1916. Closed Saturday through Monday and when school is not in session. ~ 101 West College Boulevard, Roswell; 505-624-8220, fax 505-624-8258; www.nmmi.cc.nm.us, e-mail hardman@email.nmmi.edu.

Experience turn-of-the-20th-century New Mexican life at the **Historical Center for Southeast New Mexico, Inc.**, a museum that spans the period from 1865 to 1940. It's located in a grand 1910 prairie-style structure and is decorated with pioneer antiques and Victorian furniture. The collection of artifacts is drawn from local Chaves County residents. Children will be fascinated by the display of vintage toys. ~ 200 North Lea Avenue,

Roswell; 505-622-8333, fax 505-623-8746; www.dfn.com/hssnm, e-mail hssnm@dfn.com.

About 70 miles west of Roswell, and a world apart, is **Ruidoso**. Set among soaring pines and secluded valleys, Ruidoso is a year-round resort offering skiing, sledding, hiking, fishing and, its biggest summer draw, horse racing.

The race track, **Ruidoso Downs Racetrack and Casino**, is located five miles east of town. Quarter horses and thoroughbreds run here Thursday through Sunday afternoons during the summer season, climaxing with the All-American Futurity, the world's richest quarter horse race with a $2 million purse. At the end of the racing season, high-priced horse auctions are a last burst of excitement. The Ruidoso Downs Casino offers pari-mutuel betting on simulcast races year-round. The racetrack is closed Saturday and Sunday from September to late May, but the casino is open daily. Parking fee. ~ Route 70 East, Ruidoso; 505-378-4431, fax 505-378-4631; www.rdracing.com.

Adjacent to the racetrack is a noteworthy collection of horse memorabilia at the **Hubbard Museum of the American West**. An upstairs gallery traces 30,000 years of equine history and offers some surprising insights on the development of the West. Exhibits explain horse breeding, biomechanics and racing. Downstairs, there is a collection of other horse-drawn vehicles. Admission. ~ 841 Route 70 West, Ruidoso; 505-378-4142, fax 505-378-4166; www.zianet.com/museum, e-mail moth@zianet.com.

A 45-minute drive from Ruidoso is the historic town of **Lincoln**. The village of Lincoln would have faded from the map generations ago had it not been the scene of an infamous "war" between two competing groups of storekeepers and ranchers in 1878. After the leader of one faction was assassinated, one of his employees, a professional gunman known as Billy the Kid, avenged him by killing all the participants in the ambush and their bosses. The Lincoln County War ultimately brought down the territorial government of New Mexico and made Billy the Kid a legend.

The whole village and its surrounding area is now a historic district, giving Lincoln the authentic feel of a late-19th-century town. The focal points of a walking tour of Lincoln are several units of **Lincoln State Monument** as well as other structures. The Old Courthouse contains exhibits explaining the Lincoln County War and an actual bullethole made by Billy the Kid during a jailbreak. The restored Montaño Store Museum represents the Hispanic culture of the area with exhibits about the Montaños, who lived here during the Lincoln County War. Admission. ~ Off Route 380, Lincoln; phone/fax 505-653-4372; e-mail rangers@pvtnetworks.net.

The **Historical Center Museum**, a branch of the Hubbard Museum, displays Victorian-era frontier artifacts and has exhibits

Text continued on page 230.

In the Land
of Outlaws

No other character in New Mexico's history captures the imagination like Billy the Kid. He was the west's enigmatic "live fast, die young" character, a sort of 19th-century James Dean who has lived on in novels and movies. More than a century after his violent death at the age of 21, Billy the Kid's legend seems stronger than ever. Travelers can explore throughout southern New Mexico, from Lincoln to Mesilla to Silver City and beyond, following historical markers that recall the outlaw's exploits.

Lincoln is where the foundation was laid for Billy the Kid's immortality. There, visitors learn about the 1878 Lincoln County War, a violent conflict between a naive newcomer and a ruthless cattle baron that spread to involve the whole county in gunfights and arson for months and finally toppled the government of territorial New Mexico. Billy the Kid was on the side of the "good guys," legally deputized to capture the gunmen who had murdered his employer. Instead of arresting them, however, he shot them to death, causing modern scholars to believe that he was a violent sociopath.

After ridding Lincoln County of its nest of cattle rustlers, robber barons and corrupt politicians, Billy was granted amnesty by the new governor of New Mexico, Lew Wallace. Many people throughout the county reputedly saw him as a Robin Hood character. Yet he became the region's leading cattle rustler himself before he was hunted down for the murders of two sheriffs and a deputy and shot to death by the newly appointed Lincoln County sheriff, his old friend Pat Garrett.

One of the things Billy the Kid did best was escape. Two of his most daring escapes—one from a burning house under siege by a local posse and federal troops, the other from a makeshift jail cell in the old courthouse that houses the Lincoln State Monument head-quarters today—took place in Lincoln.

South of Lincoln, in Ruidoso, visitors can see the water wheel of Dowlin's Mill, where gunmen cornered Billy the Kid seeking revenge for a friend he had shot. Billy escaped by hiding in a flour barrel. Located south of Ruidoso, Blazer's Mill near Mescalero was the site of a furious shootout during which the leader of the band of gunmen known as the Regulators was killed, after which Billy, the youngest and wildest member of the gang, took command.

Billy the Kid enthusiasts—and southern New Mexico sees its fair share of them—can find traces of the outlaw and his legend all across the state. On the outskirts of Fort Sumner (see Chapter Five for more information) is the site of Billy the Kid's grave near the ranch where Pat Garrett caught up with him. Fort Sumner also has the two biggest Billy the Kid museums in the state.

On Route 70 east of Las Cruces, a state sign marks the spot where Garrett himself was later killed in a dispute over goat grazing. In old Mesilla, just outside of Las Cruces, visitors can see the courthouse where Billy was convicted and sentenced to hang for murdering a lawman. (He escaped.)

North of Carrizozo on the way to Corona, a marker tells of yet another siege in which Billy and his gang were trapped by a posse inside a burning stagecoach station but escaped in the confusion after a deputy sheriff was killed in the crossfire while trying to negotiate a surrender.

Before the Lincoln County War began, Billy the Kid worked in a general store at Seven Rivers. The townsite is lost beneath the waters of Brantley Dam, but details can be found in the small historical museum in Artesia. Earlier, Billy spent part of his boyhood and attended school briefly in Silver City. His childhood cabin and his mother's grave are there, along with the first jail he ever escaped from—at the age of 15 while in custody for robbing a Chinese laundry.

Populist hero or psychopathic killer? Historians and Hollywood scriptwriters are still guessing. But one thing's for sure: Billy the Kid wandered far and wide across some of the prettiest country anywhere.

about buffalo soldiers (black troops stationed in the West after the Civil War) and the Apaches they fought. Some of the most popular exhibits feature Billy the Kid. Admission. ~ Off Route 380, Lincoln; 505-653-4025, fax 505-653-4627.

A few miles west of Lincoln, the sightseeing highlight in the small town of Capitan is **Smokey Bear Historical State Park**. A must for kids and anyone interested in the history of advertising, this small museum traces the career of America's best-known bear from early artist's sketches through more than 40 years of forest service propaganda, children's comics and commercial kitsch. A film tells the story of the "real" Smokey the Bear (1950–1976), who was rescued by rangers from a fire in Lincoln National Forest and sent to live in a Washington, D.C., zoo. The live bear was named after the imaginary character, not vice versa as legend suggests. Admission. ~ 118 Smokey Bear Boulevard, Capitan; 505-354-2748, fax 505-354-6012; www.smokeybearpark. com, e-mail smokeybear@state.nm.us.

LODGING   Visitors to Carlsbad Caverns may choose to stay at Whites City by the national park entrance or in the town of Carlsbad, a 20-minute drive away.

In Whites City, the **Whites City Resort** includes the **Best Western Cavern Inn** and the **Best Western Guadalupe Inn**, both of which offer fairly standard motel accommodations. ~ 17 Carlsbad Canyon Highway, Whites City; 505-785-2291, 800-228-3767, fax 505-785-2283; www.whitescity.com, e-mail whites city@whitescity.com for both inns. MODERATE.

In the town of Carlsbad, the **Quality Inn** offers spacious rooms surrounding a courtyard patio and pool. A buffet breakfast is included. ~ 3706 National Parks Highway, Carlsbad; 505-887-2861, 800-321-2861, fax 505-887-2861 ext. 310; www.carlsbadnm. com/qualityinn, e-mail qualityinn@carlsbadnm.com. BUDGET TO MODERATE.

AUTHOR FAVORITE

Whenever I need to pamper myself, I check into the **Apple Tree Inn & Retreat Center**, which has five full-kitchen suites and five suites with bedrooms and living rooms, as well as a two-bedroom stone house. Most rooms have fireplaces and in-room jacuzzis; all have private baths and entrances. All open onto the spa pavilion with its hot tubs, steam room, and massage and exercise area. ~ 100 Lower Terrace, Ruidoso; 505-257-1717, 877-277-5322, fax 505-257-1718; www.appletreebb-spa. com, e-mail appletreebb@zianet.com. MODERATE TO DELUXE.

Roswell's lodging scene is unexceptional. The top of the line is the **Best Western Sally Port Inn**, with its tropical atrium, spa facilities and guest rooms with tall picture windows and some with refrigerators and microwaves. ~ 2000 North Main Street, Roswell; 505-622-6430, 800-528-1234, fax 505-623-7631; www. bestwestern.com, e-mail swijmf@pvtnetworks.net. MODERATE.

One of the better low-priced motels is the **Frontier Motel**. ~ 3010 North Main Street, Roswell; 505-622-1400, 800-678-1401, fax 505-622-1405; www.frontiermotelroswell.com. BUDGET.

The **Inn of the Mountain Gods** on the Mescalero Apache Indian Reservation near Ruidoso is one of New Mexico's most exclusive resorts. It is owned by the Mescalero Apaches, whose mountainous reservation extends from Ruidoso south to Cloudcroft. All of the rooms have balconies and most overlook Lake Mescalero. Facilities include a golf course (closed in winter), a horseback riding stable, fishing, an outdoor heated swimming pool and a spa, along with a casino and card rooms. Many activities are open to nonguests for a fee. Some of the facilities are closed in winter. ~ Carrizo Canyon Road, Mescalero; 505-464-5141, 800-545-9011, fax 505-464-6173; www.innofthemountain gods.com. MODERATE TO DELUXE.

Cuckoo clocks, massive stone fireplaces and panoramic views await guests at **Swiss Chalet Inn**. Decorated Pennsylvania Dutch style, the 82-room inn features knotty pine paneling, mahogany furniture and Western antiques. Newlyweds should ask for the honeymoon suite with canopied bed. There's an indoor pool and spa here along with easy access to the Lincoln National Forest and Ski Apache. ~ 1451 Mechem Drive (Route 48), Ruidoso; 505-258-3333, 800-477-9477, fax 505-258-5325; www.ruidoso. net/swisschalet, e-mail swisschalet@zianet.com. MODERATE.

A romantic establishment with a covered veranda and a garden frequented by hummingbirds, **Shadow Mountain Lodge** is a tranquil retreat in the pines. In addition to fieldstone fireplaces (a warm treat after a day on the nearby slopes), all 19 rooms come with kitchenettes, king-size beds and air conditioning. Shadow Mountain offers direct access to Rio Ruidoso. Adults only. ~ 107 Main Road, Ruidoso; 505-257-4886, 800-441-4331, fax 505-257-2000; www.smlruidoso.com, e-mail lodge@looking glass.net. MODERATE TO DELUXE.

For more than half a century **Dan Dee Cabins** has been the ◄ HIDDEN quintessential cottage resort, a tradition among families who know this mountain region well. Thirteen pine-paneled cabins—with one to three bedrooms each—spread across five nicely landscaped acres with picnic and barbecue areas. Equipped with kitchenettes, fireplaces, wicker and pine furniture, these units are just steps away from a fishing stream and convenient to year-round resort activities. Dan Dee Cabins is one of the friendliest places we found in New Mexico. ~ 310 Main Road, Ruidoso; 505-257-2165, 800-345-4848; www.storybookcabins.com, e-mail cabins@ruidoso.net. MODERATE.

Several complexes near the Ruidoso River rent cabins in the pines with kitchens and fireplaces, including **Story Book Cabins**. ~ 410 Main Road, Ruidoso; 505-257-2115, 888-257-2115, fax 505-257-7512; www.storybookcabins.com, e-mail cabins@ruidoso.net. **Whispering Pines Cabins** is another such establishment, renting 17 cabins, all with fireplaces and many with kitchens. ~ 422 Main Road, Ruidoso; 505-257-4311. MODERATE.

Lower-priced motels in the Ruidoso area cluster east of town on Route 70 near the Ruidoso Downs racetrack. For low-cost lodging, try the comfortable, 17-room **Economy Inn**. It's clean and simple and has color televisions. ~ 2019 Route 70, Ruidoso; 505-378-4706, fax 505-378-4398. BUDGET.

Monjeau Shadows Bed & Breakfast Establishment is an attractive B&B in the mountains. A completely restored four-story Victorian farmhouse located on eight wooded acres with walking paths, this seven-room inn is furnished with antiques and heirlooms. There's a big gameroom on the premises and the owners can arrange historic tours of Billy the Kid country, as well as skiing, horseback riding and golf. ~ Take Route 48 north from Ruidoso for nine miles until it intersects with Route 37; the B&B is two miles past the intersection, Alto; 505-336-4191; www.ruidoso.net/shadows, e-mail shadows@zianet.com. MODERATE TO DELUXE.

Lincoln has a small selection of memorable places to stay, and advance reservations are essential at all of them.

There are several bed and breakfasts located in town. Located in the oldest building in Lincoln County, **Ellis Store Country Inn**, a Territorial-period adobe, offers eight rooms and two suites in a separate house with private and shared baths. A full breakfast is included; a six-course gourmet dinner is available by reservation. ~ Mile Marker 98, Route 380, Lincoln; 505-653-4609, 800-653-6460, fax 505-653-4610; www.ellisstore.com, e-mail ellistore@pvtnetworks.net. MODERATE TO DELUXE.

Casa de Patron Bed & Breakfast is nestled between two hillsides in the Bonita River Valley. There are three moderate-priced rooms in the main house, and two deluxe-priced *casitas*. Located in the Trailhouse behind the main house are the Vaquero room, decorated in a Spanish cowboy theme, and the Eastburn room, which has a country garden flavor. Complimentary breakfast is included. Closed January and February. ~ Route 380, Lincoln; 505-653-4676, 800-524-5202, fax 505-653-4671; www.casapatron.com, e-mail patron@pvtnetworks.net. MODERATE TO DELUXE.

Art lovers should seek out the **Hurd Ranch Guest Homes**, where artist Michael Hurd designed the four adobe *casitas* (two with one bedroom each, one with two bedrooms, and one with three bedrooms) with a blend of traditional Southwestern and contemporary furniture. Part of the 2300-acre Sentinel Ranch, all units—with saltillo tile, antique cabinetry and wood-burning fireplaces—come complete with kitchens and patios. The main house (the Henrietta Wyeth House) has two bedrooms. Also available is the more expensive contemporary suite in the Hurd–La Rinconada Gallery. This two-story unit, which features a private balcony, is decorated with original paintings by members of the famous Hurd family. ~ Mile Marker 281, Route 70, San Patricio; 505-653-4331, 800-658-6912, fax 505-653-4218; www.wyethartists. com. DELUXE TO ULTRA-DELUXE.

DINING

Cavern Coffee Shop serves inexpensive fare in the national park visitors center. It is often crowded enough to make hungry sightseers wish they'd brought a picnic lunch. Inside the cave, near the elevators that carry visitors back to the surface at the end of the tour, the restaurant serves box lunches containing fried chicken or ham sandwiches. ~ Carlsbad Caverns National Park; 505-785-2281, fax 505-785-2302; www.nps.gov/cave. BUDGET.

Cortez has been a popular place with locals for more than 50 years with its affordably priced Mexican dishes. Closed Tuesday during the summer, and Monday and Tuesday from Labor Day to Memorial Day. ~ 506 South Canal Street, Carlsbad; 505-885-4747. BUDGET.

The best budget bargain in town is catfish and homemade pie at **Hazel's Cajun Kitchen**. Breakfast, lunch and dinner are served. Closed Saturday and Sunday. ~ 5800 South Main Street, Roswell; 505-623-7441. BUDGET TO MODERATE.

The Ruidoso area has an abundance of fine dining establishments. Of the two restaurants at the exclusive Inn of the Moun-

AUTHOR FAVORITE

Follow the locals at lunchtime and you're likely to wind up at **The Deck House Restaurant**, one of the best affordably priced restaurants in southeastern New Mexico. Dine out on the deck or indoors among the Southwestern antiques and adobe-style painted walls. The New Mexican menu features corn bread made with whole corn, green chiles and cheese and "squawbread" (the house specialty), a sweet and chewy concoction served with homemade strawberry preserves. I'm also partial to the chicken *compuestas* with green chile and sour-cream sauces. Sandwiches and burgers are all served on fresh-baked bread. Closed Labor Day to mid-May. ~ 202 Mechem Drive, Ruidoso; 505-257-3496, fax 505-630-1106. BUDGET.

tain Gods, the finest is **Dan Li Ka**, the main dining room, with a wide-ranging menu that offers everything from wild game to shrimp diablo. The lake and mountain view is incomparable. Guests are served on burgundy or teal linen and seated in metal captain's chairs painted maroon. Dan Li Ka's decor features American Indian weavings, baskets and modern paintings. Breakfast, lunch and dinner are served. ~ Carrizo Canyon Road, Mescalero; 505-464-7555, fax 505-464-6173; www.innofthemountain gods.com. DELUXE TO ULTRA-DELUXE.

An even more elegant possibility is the **La Lorraine**. Located in an adobe building with green canopies, the chandeliered dining room has upholstered chairs, fine silver, white linen and a good collection of regional art. Entrées include rack of lamb, châteaubriand and roast duck. Lunch is served Wednesday through Saturday. Dinner is served Monday through Saturday. Closed Monday from November through May; closed Sunday. ~ 2523 Sudderth Drive, Ruidoso; 505-257-2954, fax 505-258-9060; e-mail lalorraine@zianet.com. DELUXE TO ULTRA-DELUXE.

Ruidoso has the **Flying J Ranch** featuring the summer evening combination of an authentic chuckwagon dinner of chicken or beef served on a tin plate, and singing cowboys. Reservations recommended. Closed Sunday from Memorial Day to Labor Day; open Saturday only from September to mid-October. Closed mid-October to Memorial Day. ~ Route 48, Ruidoso; 505-336-4330, 888-458-3595; www.flyingjranch.com, e-mail info@flyingjranch.com. MODERATE.

SHOPPING In Carlsbad, the **Horticultural Gift Shop** at Living Desert Zoo and Gardens State Park sells an assortment of cacti that make good souvenirs. ~ 505-885-9988.

Ruidoso has a number of art galleries that seem to keep a lot of racetrack winnings from leaving town. More than a dozen of them can be found along Mechem and Sudderth drives.

The Ruidoso Store, a reincarnation of one of the oldest general stores in the area, carries a hodgepodge of merchandise from vintage photographs to saddles and spurs. The store has a large

BEAUTY'S IN THE EYE OF THE BEHOLDER

One painting you won't see on display at the Hurd–La Rinconda Gallery is Peter Hurd's famous "official" portrait of President Lyndon Baines Johnson, completed in 1967. Hurd's fellow Southwesterner was less than taken with the likeness, describing it as "the ugliest thing I ever saw." (This portrait can now be seen at the National Portrait Gallery in Washington, D.C.)

collection of "cowboy and Indian" jewelry and the walls are lined with framed paintings and prints by famous Western artists, past and present. Closed Wednesday from January through April. ~ 2615 Sudderth Drive, Ruidoso; 505-258-2552.

Ceremonial weapons of war along with peace pipes share the shelves at **White Dove**. However, the shop's real specialty is authentic American Indian art and jewelry, especially Hopi, Navajo and sterling silver designs. ~ 2501 Sudderth Drive, Ruidoso; 505-257-6609.

"We Cheat You Right" is the whimsical slogan at **Rio Trading Company**. It's a barnlike store, well stocked with everything from donkey carts to miniature windmills and American Indian dreamcatchers. ~ 2200 Sudderth Drive, Ruidoso; 505-257-9274.

The museum shop located at **Historic Lincoln**, a division of the Hubbard Museum of the American West, sells a remarkable array of Billy the Kid books, comics, posters and motion picture videos. How the outlaw's legend has endured! ~ East Route 380, Lincoln; 505-653-4025.

Peter Hurd, his wife Henrietta Wyeth and their son, Michael Hurd—three of the best-known painters in the Southwest—show originals of their work at the **Hurd–La Rinconada Gallery**, one of the most important art collections in New Mexico. Also on display in this adobe gallery are the works of Henrietta's distinguished father, N. C. Wyeth and her brother, Andrew Wyeth. Paintings, lithographs and signed reproductions are all available. Closed Sunday. ~ Mile Marker 281, Route 70, San Patricio; 505-653-4331, fax 505-653-4218; www.wyethartists.com.

Ranked among the best galleries in southern New Mexico, **Benson Fine Art** exhibits an outstanding array of works by period and contemporary Southwestern artists along with museum-quality American Indian and ethnographic art and artifacts. It is located in a late 1800s adobe hacienda in the San Patricio historic district south of Ruidoso. ~ On the east end of Route 013 off Route 70, San Patricio; 505-653-4081, fax 505-653-4065.

For evening entertainment, nothing can compete with the sunset flight of almost half a million Mexican freetail bats from the entrance of **Carlsbad Caverns**. The bats put on their show nightly from May to mid-September. They migrate to the tropics for the winter. Call ahead for information. ~ 505-785-2232, fax 505-785-2302; www.nps.gov/cave.

NIGHTLIFE

Ruidoso's **Spencer Theater for the Performing Arts** is as spectacular as the performances it presents. The 514-seat hall's futuristic architecture features 450 tons of mica-flecked Spanish limestone facing, a gleaming lobby faceted with 300 panes of glass—none of them the same size—and an artificial waterfall. The year-round calendar of events includes everything from dance and classical music to Broadway shows and children's theater. ~ Airport Road, Ruidoso; 505-336-4800, 888-818-7872, fax 505-336-0055; www.spencertheater.com.

The **Flying J Ranch** near Ruidoso represents a traditional Western genre of tourist entertainment. After a barbecue-beef dinner served "chuckwagon style" (that is, in a chow line), singing cowboys take the stage to perform classics like "Red River Valley" and "Git Along, Little Dogie." It's corny, but lots of fun. Closed Sunday from Memorial Day to Labor Day; open Saturday only from September to mid-October. Closed mid-October to Memorial Day. Reservations highly recommended. ~ Route 48, Ruidoso; 505-336-4330, 888-458-3595; www.flyingjranch.com.

Ruidoso is the liveliest town after dark in this part of the state. Blues bands play on Sunday while classic rock outfits entertain Wednesday through Saturday night at **The Quarters**. There is karaoke on Monday and Tuesday. There's a dancefloor, a big bar and comfortable table seating at this lounge. ~ 2535 Sudderth Drive, Ruidoso; 505-257-9535.

You'll find live country-and-western music every night at **Win Place & Show Lounge**. ~ 2516 Sudderth Drive, Ruidoso; 505-257-9982.

PARKS

CARLSBAD MUNICIPAL PARK This large park runs through town for more than a mile along the west bank of Lake Carlsbad, a portion of the Pecos River that has been dammed to make it wider and deeper. It is used for waterskiing, swimming, fishing and sailing. A playground, a golf course and tennis and handball courts are also located in the park. On the shore, the park has broad lawns and shade trees. There are restrooms and picnic areas. Paddlewheel boats are available to rent. ~ Take Greene Street east several blocks from Route 285 to the river; 505-887-6516.

SITTING BULL FALLS Although it is a long drive through uninhabited backcountry, Sitting Bull Falls is a locally popular spot, likely to be crowded on summer weekends. It's one of the largest falls in New Mexico—130 feet high—and practically the only running water in the arid foothills northwest of Carlsbad. Swimming is permitted in the pool at the bottom of the falls. There are hiking trails, including a wheelchair-accessible trail to the falls, a picnic area and restrooms. Day-use fee, $5. ~ From Route 285 about 12 miles north of Carlsbad, take Route 137 southwest for 25 miles and watch for a sign to Sitting Bull Falls. The falls are at the end of an eight-mile paved road off Route 137; 505-885-4181, fax 505-887-3690.

BRANTLEY LAKE STATE PARK This irrigation reservoir on the Pecos River north of Carlsbad offers several opportunities for water recreation from boating and

fishing to scuba diving and waterskiing. The park features a picnic area, restrooms, showers, volleyball, horseshoe pits, a nature
trail and a children's playground. There is also a fishing dock. Day-
use fee, $4. ~ County Road 30, just off Route 285, 12 miles north
of Carlsbad; 505-457-2384, fax 505-457-2385; e-mail brant-
leylkstpk@pvtnetworks.net.

▲ There are 51 sites with RV hookups; $14 to $18 per night.
Primitive camping is allowed; $8 per night.

BOTTOMLESS LAKES STATE PARK
New Mexico's oldest state park consists of seven natural lakes,
small in surface area but as much as 90 feet deep, formed by collapsed underground salt caves. The largest, Lea Lake, is the only
one where swimming is allowed. It also has a public beach and
pedalboat and paddleboard rentals (Memorial Day to Labor Day
only) and is a popular site for scuba diving. There's a visitors center near Cottonwood Lake. Trails lead to beautiful Mirror Lake,
surrounded by red cliffs. Ducks, geese and other waterfowl abound
on the lakes during spring and fall migration seasons. The park
has a picnic area, restrooms and showers. Day-use fee, $4. ~ From
Roswell, take Route 380 for 12 miles east, then turn south on
Route 409 for two miles to the park entrance; 505-624-6058, fax
505-624-6029.

▲ There are 32 sites, some with RV hookups; $10 to $18
per night.

BITTER LAKE NATIONAL WILDLIFE REFUGE   Small wetlands
along the Pecos River attracts a lot of migrating waterfowl as
they cross this arid region. As many as 30,000 snow geese, 15,000
sandhill cranes and 12,000 ducks stop at Bitter Lake each year.
The wilderness area is open for hiking. There's also an auto-tour
route. ~ From Route 285 go east on Pine Lodge Road and follow the signs to the refuge headquarters; 505-622-6755, fax 505-
623-9039.

LINCOLN NATIONAL FOREST   Outdoor
recreation in the part of this 1,103,000-acre forest that lies north
of the Mescalero Apache Reservation centers around the White

BOMBS AWAY

Even as recently as 1945, southern New Mexico was considered so godfor-
saken that the U.S. Army picked it as the perfect place to test the first
atomic bomb. There was hardly anyone to evacuate from the area. Today
the population of this region lives along two main north–south routes
separated from each other by the huge White Sands Missile Range,
which is off-limits to all nonmilitary persons.

Mountain Wilderness, a cluster of peaks northwest of Ruidoso that reach elevations of over 10,500 feet. Forest access from Ruidoso is by several forest roads branching off Routes 532 and 37. Another White Mountain Wilderness trailhead is on the other side of the mountains at the end of the road past Three Rivers Petroglyph Site north of Alamogordo. The Guadalupe district contains a number of limestone caves ideal for exploring (permit required). A rarely explored part of this national forest unit is the low mountain range east of White Oaks, an old mining town reached by Route 349 from Carrizozo, where a maze of rough roads provides access to dozens of hidden springs and old mining tunnels. ~ 505-434-7200, fax 505-434-7218.

▲ *South Fork Campground* northwest of Ruidoso has 42 tent and RV sites and 18 tent-only sites without hookups; $10 per night. A smaller campground north of Ruidoso, *Skyline* has 17 campsites. There is no fee; drinking water is not available.

▼▼▼▼▼▼▼▼▼▼▼▼▼▼▼▼▼▼

South Central New Mexico

Birthplace of the atomic age, a favorite resting place of Apache revolutionary Geronimo and a bonanza for petroglyph buffs, south central New Mexico is famous for its gypsum dunes and lava fields. Juxtaposing desert and mountains, this Rio Grande region offers a number of popular dammed lakes ideal for outdoor enthusiasts. It is also a must for ghost-town buffs.

SIGHTS

The northern part of the Tularosa Basin, which begins north of Carrizozo and extends 80 miles to the south, is a jagged wasteland of black lava. At **Valley of Fires Recreation Area**, a self-guided nature trail, the first half of which is fully wheelchair-accessible, leads across a portion of the 2000-year-old lava field for a closeup look at this strange and forbidding landscape. There is also a visitors center and a bookstore. Admission. ~ Off Route 380 just west of Carrizozo; phone/fax 505-648-2241.

From Carrizozo to Alamogordo, Route 54 runs along the eastern edge of **White Sands Missile Range**, a vast area used by the military to test weapons; turn west on Route 70 at Alamogordo to enter the site. It's been off-limits to the public since World War II, when it was the site of the first atomic bomb test. Open year-round, however, are the museum and missile park, where you can see examples of tested missiles. A tour of the Trinity Site where the original bomb was exploded is given twice a year, on the first Saturday in October and April. ~ Route 70; 505-678-1134, fax 505-678-7174; www.wsmr.army.mil.

HIDDEN ▶

Halfway between Carrizozo and Alamogordo, the **Three Rivers Petroglyph Site** contains thousands of pictures chipped into the dark patina of boulders by artists of the Mimbres people, an

American Indian culture centuries older than the Anasazi of the Four Corners area. An often-steep three-quarter-mile trail follows the crest of a high hill to let you see the mysterious pictures of animals, humans and magical beings as well as abstract symbols whose meanings can only be guessed at. A pleasant picnic area lies at the foot of the trail. Admission. ~ Five miles off Route 54; 505-525-4300, fax 505-525-4412.

In Alamogordo, the **New Mexico Museum of Space History** houses one of the world's largest collections of space exploration artifacts. The gleaming five-story gold cube on the hillside contains antique rockets, space suits, Apollo and Gemini capsules, moon rocks, satellites and lots more. An outdoor park displays larger rockets and the Sonic Wind Rocket Sled, which was used to test the effects of rocket acceleration on humans. Adjoining the museum is the **Clyde W. Tombaugh IMAX Dome Theater**, a planetarium that presents IMAX movies as well as educational astronomy programs. It is named after the man who discovered the planet Pluto. Admission. ~ At the top of Route 2001, Alamo-

South Central
New Mexico

El Camino Real

Route 25 follows the path of the oldest highway still in use in the United States. Originally known as El Camino Real de Tierra Adentro ("the Royal Road to the Inner Land"), it was established in 1598 to link Mexico City with New Mexico, the northernmost province of the Spanish empire in America. Today, Route 25 has taken the place of the old Camino Real, but it keeps its distance from the Rio Grande. For most of the distance from Albuquerque to Las Cruces, slower, traffic-free, two-lane highways follow the original Camino Real, usually out of sight of the interstate. The New Mexico state government has put up historical markers along them to identify important landmarks from colonial times such as the stark landscape of the Jornada del Muerto ("Journey of Death"). There are three separate segments of this parallel highway; taking them all requires about twice the time the interstate would.

gordo; 505-437-2840, 877-333-6589, fax 505-437-7722; www.spacefame.org, e-mail spacepr@zianet.com.

To learn more about the exploration of space, drive up to the National Solar Observatory–Sacramento Peak on the crest of the mountains to the east. First, take the 16-mile drive on Route 82 from Alamogordo to the village of **Cloudcroft**. Nestled in the pines near the crest of the Sacramento Mountains, Cloudcroft has seen little of the rampant resort development evident at Ruidoso on the other side of the Mescalero Apache Indian Reservation, and it retains the weathered charm of a little Rocky Mountain logging town.

Explore a pioneer barn, granary and hand-hewn log house chinked with mud at the **Sacramento Mountains Historical Museum**. Of special interest is an exhibit about the Cloudcroft Baby Sanatorium, a high-country facility that saved the lives of hundreds of children suffering from summer heat sickness in the nearby lowlands between 1912 and 1932. There is also a pioneer village and a farm and ranch exhibit. The collection of artifacts includes an Edison cylinder talking machine and a rifle once owned by explorer Zebulon Pike. Closed Wednesday and Thursday. Admission. ~ Route 82, across from the chamber of commerce, Cloudcroft; 505-682-2932, fax 505-682-3638.

From the museum, take Scenic Byway 6563 for 16 miles, following the signs to "Sunspot." Maintained by the National Science Foundation for the use of various universities, the **National**

ISLETA PUEBLO   Route 47 leaves Route 25 at Exit 215 to Isleta Pueblo (page 185) just south of Albuquerque. It passes through 40 miles of farmlands and small towns like Bosque Farms and Los Lunas before rejoining the interstate north of Socorro, where the old highway reaches the boundary of Sevilleta National Wildlife Refuge, which is closed to the public.

BOSQUE DEL APACHE NATIONAL WILDLIFE REFUGE   Twenty-eight miles farther south, at Exit 147 in Socorro, the old highway resumes as Route 1. It skirts the edge of Bosque del Apache National Wildlife Refuge (page 210), continuing for 58 miles before merging with the interstate again near **Elephant Butte Lake** (page 249).

CHILE COUNTRY   Another 25 miles south on Route 25, the old highway splits away again at the lower end of **Caballo Lake** (page 248) to become Route 187. From here, it takes you another 56 miles through the green chile farmlands around **Hatch** (page 247) before arriving in historic **Mesilla** (page 242) on the west side of Las Cruces.

Solar Observatory–Sacramento Peak has several solar telescopes. The main one extends from 20 stories below ground level to 13 stories above. Visitors on self-guided tours of the facility can view solar flares on a video screen and other displays in the visitors center and often watch scientists studying the sun on similar screens. Open daily from April through October; call for hours from November through March. Admission. ~ Scenic Byway 6563; 505-434-7000, fax 505-434-7079; www.sunspot. noao.edu, e-mail sunspot@nso.edu.

A trip to this area would not be complete without a stop at the world's largest gypsum dunefield, **White Sands National Monument.** The monument, encompassing 275 square miles of sand, protects the southernmost part of White Sands for public use. A 16-mile roundtrip scenic drive takes you into the heart of the white-as-snow gypsum dunes, where you can park and step out into this strange landscape. The juxtaposition of pristine white sand and bright blue sky can make you feel like you're walking on clouds. Several readers recommend the sunset ranger stroll. Admission. ~ Off Route 70 between Alamogordo and Las Cruces; 505-479-6124, fax 505-479-4333; www.nps.gov/whsa.

As beautiful as it is unusual, the landscape is ever-changing: Desert winds constantly reshape the dunes, creating pure white sculptures that disappear with each fresh gust. Surrounded by a spectacular wasteland, with an occasional yucca plant the only sign of life, it's difficult to decide whether this is heaven, hell or simply the end of the earth. Hiking is allowed without limitation, but camping is only permitted at a backcountry campground (for backpackers only) with ten sites, available first come, first served. Camping fee is $3 per person. Rangers conduct evening nature walks.

Most of the population of southern New Mexico is centered in and around **Las Cruces** (population 74,000). The name Las Cruces, Spanish for "The Crosses," pays tribute to the gravemarkers of settlers killed here in the 1800s by Apache Indians. A busy, spirited college town, home to New Mexico State University, Las Cruces is situated in an otherwise quiet landscape—an agricultural zone along the Rio Grande where farmers specialize in chili peppers and pecans. This county seat—one of the fastest growing cities in the nation—recently surpassed Santa Fe to become the second-largest city in New Mexico. Las Cruces is noteworthy for the Organ Mountains that loom east of the city. Vaulting 5000 feet above the valley, these peaks derive their name from the spires and minarets that resemble the pipes of a church organ cast in stone.

The Gadsden Purchase, signed in Mesilla in 1854, fixed the current international boundaries of New Mexico and Arizona.

At the handsome adobe-walled **Cultural Complex** are two museums. The **Branigan Cultural Center/Historical Museum** (500 North Water Street) tells of local and regional history. The **Las Cruces Museum of Fine Art & Culture** (490 North Water Street) exhibits a variety of contemporary paintings, sculpture and arts and crafts. Closed Sunday. ~ Las Cruces; 505-541-2155, fax 505-525-3645; www.lascruces-culture.org, e-mail bcc1@zianet.com.

A short distance southwest of Las Cruces on Route 10, the village of **Mesilla** is one of the state's prettiest and best-preserved historic districts, dating back to 1598. Mesilla achieved further historical significance by serving as the Confederate capital of the Arizona Territory for a short period during the Civil War. The downtown plaza and several of its surrounding Territorial-style buildings have been designated as **La Mesilla State Monument**. Points of interest around the plaza include the **San Albino Church**, the oldest in the area, built in 1853. Also here is the **Gadsden Museum**, with folk art and artifact collections representing the Anglo, Spanish and Indian cultures of the region. Admission. ~ 1875 Boutz Road, Mesilla; 505-526-6293.

Fifteen miles north of Las Cruces, **Fort Selden State Monument** includes the ruins of an adobe fort used by the Army from 1865 to 1891. It was a base for troops guarding the Mesilla Valley and providing protection for wagon trains and later the railroad. A small museum recalls what life was like at the fort during the Territorial era. Closed Tuesday. Admission. ~ Off Route 25 Exit 19; 505-526-8911; www.nmoca.com.

Farther north along Route 25 is **Truth or Consequences**—that's "T or C" to most New Mexicans. The sprawling retirement community of Truth or Consequences merits a look-see, and maybe even a soak in its bubbling hot springs. Long before it was founded, the site was an American Indian place of healing and a hideout for Geronimo, the renegade Apache leader. Truth or Consequences now serves as the food and lodging center for visitors to nearby Elephant Butte Reservoir, the largest lake in New Mexico at 38,000 acres.

The main point of interest in town is the geothermally heated **Geronimo Springs Museum**. It is a fairly large museum with 12 exhibit rooms full of Mimbres pottery, ranch antiques, fossils and petrified wood, works by local artists, awards for wool production and other curiosities from all over Sierra County. A highlight of the museum is the Ralph Edwards Room, commemorating the television show that inspired Hot Springs, New Mexico, to change its name to Truth or Consequences in 1950. Closed Sunday. Admission. ~ 211 Main Street, Truth or Consequences; 505-894-6600, fax 505-894-1244.

Truth or Consequences' popularity as a spa resort has long since faded, but the hot springs themselves remain intact. Next to the Geronimo Springs Museum is a 105° natural spring where Apache leader Geronimo himself is said to have relaxed. One spring open to the public for bathing is **Sierra Grande Lodge and Health Spa**. Admission. ~ 501 McAdoo Street, Truth or Consequences; 505-894-6976; www.sierragrandelodge.com, e-mail sglodge@riolink.com.

The most interesting of the several ghost towns in the Truth or Consequences vicinity is **Chloride**, 29 miles off the interstate on Route 52 and then just over two miles on a marked, unpaved forest road. This is one of the few New Mexico ghost towns that looks the way you expect a Western ghost town to look, with about a dozen falsefront buildings still standing along a deserted main street. In its heyday during the late 19th century, Chloride was a center for silver mining and had a population of about 500.

◄ *HIDDEN*

Virtually all Alamogordo accommodations are standard highway motels and with few exceptions their rates are in the budget range. Representative of the type is the **Satellite Inn**, which has phones, cable TV and an outdoor pool. A continental breakfast is included. ~ 2224 North White Sands Boulevard, Alamogordo; 505-437-8454, 800-221-7690, fax 505-434-6015; www.satellite inn.com, e-mail satellite@totacc.com. BUDGET.

LODGING

A more interesting option is to spend the night in Cloudcroft, high in the mountains and just 16 miles from Alamogordo. The most elegant hotel in town is the **Lodge at Cloudcroft**, with both rooms and suites. The three-story lodge has been in operation since the turn of the century and has been completely refurbished and modernized. Rooms have high ceilings and some antique furnishings. ~ 1 Corona Place, Cloudcroft; 505-682-2566, 800-395-6343, fax 505-682-2715; www.thelodgeresort.com, e-mail info@thelodge-nm.com. MODERATE TO DELUXE.

The lodge also operates the **Lodge Pavilion Bed & Breakfast**, offering accommodations in the town's oldest building. Both the Lodge and the Pavilion are listed on the National Register of Historic Places. ~ 199 Curlew Street at Chipmunk Avenue, Cloudcroft; 505-682-2566, 800-395-6343, fax 505-682-2715; www.thelodge resort.com, e-mail info@thelodge-nm.com. MODERATE.

For more modest, quiet and cozy lodgings, Cloudcroft has numerous cabins for rent. For example, **Buckhorn Cabins**, located in the center of town, has rustic-style cabins ranging from single rooms with kitchenettes to two-bedroom cabins with living rooms and fireplaces. ~ Route 82, Cloudcroft; 505-682-2421; e-mail gloryb@zianet.com. BUDGET TO MODERATE.

Equipped with fireplaces and tucked amid the pines, **Tall Timber Cabins** is a prime choice for a family holiday. All nine cottage and duplex units offer picnic tables and grills that allow guests to take advantage of the setting—a quiet residential area—as well as full kitchens. After a day behind the wheel, you'll be happy to fall into the comfy king- or queen-size beds. ~ 1102 Chatauqua Canyon Boulevard, Cloudcroft; phone/fax 505-682-2301, 888-682-2301; e-mail ttimbercabins@zianet.com. MODERATE.

In Las Cruces, the most luxurious hotel is the **Hilton Las Cruces**, situated in the foothills on the east edge of town off Route 25 and across the street from Mesilla Valley Mall. The modern seven-story hotel features bright, attractive guest rooms, and the swimming pool is surrounded by palm trees. ~ 705 South Telshor Boulevard, Las Cruces; 505-522-4300, 800-445-8667, fax 505-522-7657; e-mail hiltonlascruces@buynm.com. MODERATE.

Budget motels cluster along West Picacho Avenue. Try the **Economy Inn**, which offers all standard amenities including an outdoor pool, phones and cable television. ~ 2160 West Picacho Avenue, Las Cruces; 505-524-8627, fax 505-523-2606. BUDGET.

More unusual lodging can be found at the **Lundeen Inn of the Arts**, where each of the 16 units, including two second-floor two-bedroom suites with kitchenettes, are named after well-known New Mexican and American Indian artists. A kiva fireplace and clawfoot tub are featured in the Frederick Remington Room, while the Henrietta Wyeth Room has a kitchenette and a breathtaking view of the mountains. ~ 618 South Alameda Boulevard, Las Cruces; 505-526-3327, 888-526-3326, fax 505-647-1334; www.innofthearts.com, e-mail lundeen@innofthearts.com. MODERATE.

Nearby in historic Mesilla is the **Meson de Mesilla**, an elegant boutique hotel. All 15 rooms in this modern adobe inn have private baths and are appointed in Southwestern decor. Guests may stroll the flagstone pathway through a courtyard filled with yuccas, cacti and desert blooms or enjoy the sweeping views of the Organ Mountains from the inn's lawn. There is a swimming pool. Full complimentary breakfast served in the dining room atrium. ~ 1803 Avenida de Mesilla, Mesilla; 505-525-9212, 800-732-6025, fax 505-527-4196. MODERATE TO DELUXE.

Accommodations in Truth or Consequences range from a scattering of very low-priced older independent motels to quality contemporary motor inns.

With a hot-springs mineral bath setting it apart from other hostels (guests soak for free), **Riverbend Hot Springs** provides clean, air-conditioned dorm-style accommodations; private rooms and kitchenettes are available, as are outdoor accommodations (tents, tepees). There's a common kitchen and a barbecue, and if you're game, you can join in the organized activities. Reservations recommended. ~ 100 Austin Street, Truth or Consequences; 505-894-6183; www.nmhotsprings.com, e-mail hostel@riolink.com. BUDGET.

The **Quality Inn**, which has lovely lake views, belongs in the latter group. ~ Route 195, off of Route 25 Exit 83, Elephant Butte; 505-744-5431, 800-228-5151, fax 505-744-5044. MODERATE.

In Alamogordo, fast-food places are the norm, with the exception of a few family-style restaurants such as **Angelina's Italian Restaurant**, serving pizzas and pastas. Dinner only. Closed Sunday. ~ 415 South White Sands Boulevard, Alamogordo; 505-434-1166. BUDGET TO MODERATE.

DINING

Cloudcroft has a number of good restaurants, many featuring Texas-style cuisine. In the middle of town is the cafeteria-style **Texas Pit Barbecue**, a real find for hickory-and-pecan-smoked beef and *chile con carne*. Closed Tuesday and Wednesday from mid-September to late February. ~ Route 82, Cloudcroft; 505-682-2307, fax 505-682-3335. BUDGET.

For fine dining, consider **Rebecca's**, the dining room at the Lodge at Cloudcroft, where steaks, seafood and Continental selections are served in an atmosphere of Victorian elegance with

AUTHOR FAVORITE

In Las Cruces, I like to check out the scene at **Nellie's Cafe**. This long-time local favorite serves New Mexican and Old Mexican dishes like *carne adovada, chiles rellenos* and *sopapilla compuesta* (which is like a Mexican pizza). Breakfast and lunch served all day; dinner also served on Thursday and Friday. Closed Sunday and Monday. ~ 1226 West Hadley Avenue, Las Cruces; 505-524-9982. BUDGET.

a view of the pine forest. White linen, wicker furniture, historic portraits and a pianist make this a romantic spot. Breakfast, lunch and dinner are served. ~ 1 Corona Place, Cloudcroft; 505-682-2566, fax 505-682-2715; www.thelodge-nm.com. DELUXE TO ULTRA-DELUXE.

Fine restaurants surround the plaza in Mesilla. The most elegant of them is the **Double Eagle**, with a Continental menu and museum-quality period decor in a restored Territorial adobe listed on the National Register of Historic Places. ~ 2355 Calle de Guadalupe, Mesilla; 505-523-6700, fax 505-523-0051; www.doubleeagledining.com. DELUXE TO ULTRA-DELUXE.

South Central New Mexico is home to the only city in America renamed for a game show—Truth or Consequences.

La Posta de Mesilla, a favorite with locals, is another restaurant on the plaza that serves New Mexican food in a historic building. Closed Monday. ~ 2410 Calle de San Albino, South Plaza, Mesilla; 505-524-3524, fax 505-541-0317. BUDGET TO MODERATE.

Break for caffeine at **Kokopelli Café**, where lattes and mochas are the order of the day. Smoothies, lemonade and ice cream treats will satisfy the non-caffeine addicts. Gourmet sandwiches and salads are also available. No dinner. Closed Tuesday. ~ Calle de Parian west of the Plaza, Mesilla; 505-524-1929. BUDGET.

Most Truth or Consequences restaurants present standard interstate highway exit fare. One exception is the **Damsite Restaurant**, located five miles east of town on the dam road. In an old adobe overlooking Elephant Butte Lake, the restaurant serves steaks and other American fare. Call for winter hours. ~ Englestar Route, Truth or Consequences; 505-894-2073. MODERATE TO ULTRA-DELUXE.

SHOPPING   **Moore's Trading Post** is one of the few places we know that has live rattlesnakes. But if you'd just as soon not drive home with a fanged pet, Moore's carries plenty of reptilian "accessories," everything from skins and heads to snake-bite kits. If slinky critters give you nothing but the jitters, choose instead from the thousands of secondhand items: combat boots, military fatigues—you name it. ~ 215 Route 82 East, Alamogordo; phone/fax 505-437-7116.

Local artists and craftspeople display their works at galleries around the small plaza in the old Spanish village of **La Luz**. ~ Located eight miles northeast of Alamogordo via Route 70 and Route 545.

If you need souvenirs, try **Bear in the Woods**, an eclectic shop that carries one-of-a-kind quilted jackets, country crafts and antiques. ~ 94 James Canyon Highway, Cloudcroft; 505-682-2094.

Well stocked with contemporary works by local artists, folk art and children's toys, **Branigan Cultural Center Gift Shop** offers a variety of gift items. You could as easily walk out with an original watercolor as with a Southwestern desk set. ~ 500 North Water Street, Las Cruces; 505-541-2155, fax 505-525-3645.

Pick up a thriller for the trip home at **Coas: My Bookstore**. This is one of the largest bookstores in southern New Mexico, with more than 100,000 titles—new, used and rare. (Coas also carries games as well as used CDs, videos and DVDs.) ~ 317 North Main Street, Las Cruces; 505-524-8471.

A five-block collection of shops dubbed "Nostalgia City" can be found in Las Cruces lining West Picacho Avenue from Valley Drive to Alameda Street. If poking through antique stores searching for that perfect treasure is your activity of choice, this is where to go. Shops range from the **Elegant Junque Shoppe** to the **High Class Junk Joint** to the ever-honest **Things for Sale**. Keep poking, you'll find it.

Every Wednesday and Saturday morning 50 to 120 exhibitors head for the **Las Cruces Farmers and Crafts Market** on the downtown mall. These vendors generally offer the top pick in local produce, nuts and flowers, though they plug everything from honey and salsa to Southwestern furniture. The toys and dolls make first-class gifts. ~ North of Las Cruces Avenue on the downtown mall, Las Cruces; 505-541-2554.

It's hard to beat a generous scoop of the pecan-praline ice cream at **J. Eric Chocolatier**, but the homemade candy and cashew clusters come close. This sweets shop also sells toffee, almond bark and other delectables. Definitely a class act. ~ The Plaza, Mesilla; 505-526-2744.

Hatch, located midway between Las Cruces and Truth or Consequences off Route 25, has a reputation for producing the best-tasting chile in New Mexico, and most of the stores in the little town are **chile shops**. In September, they sell fresh-roasted green chiles. The rest of the year, they stock it dried, canned, powdered, shaped as Christmas tree lights and as a T-shirt motif.

Up in the mountains, the **Lodge at Cloudcroft** has a piano player most evenings in the dining room. ~ 1 Corona Place, Cloudcroft; 505-682-2566; www.thelodge-nm.com.

NIGHTLIFE

Las Cruces, a lively college town, has nightspots such as **O'Ryan's Tavern & Brewery**, which has beers brewed on-site, as well as cocktails and a full menu. Occasional live and deejayed music rounds out the bill. Occasional cover. ~ Mesilla Valley Mall, 700 South Telshor Boulevard, Las Cruces; 505-522-8191.

New Mexico State University provides a steady flow of cultural activities. Stop by the Corbett Center Student Union during the school year or check out their website. ~ Locust Street, Las Cruces; 505-646-3235; www.nmsu.edu/~upc.

After a day of shopping on the Mesilla Plaza, why not take in a good foreign film at the Mesilla Valley Film Society's **Fountain**

Theater? Enjoy evening performances and Sunday matinees in the beautifully restored mission-style theater. ~ 2469 Calle de Guadalupe, Mesilla; 505-524-8287.

PARKS
Several dams on the lower Rio Grande form lakes used for recreation, ranging from little Leasburg Lake (hardly more than a wide spot in the river) to huge Elephant Butte Lake (one of New Mexico's largest bodies of water). From south to north, these lakes are:

LEASBURG DAM STATE PARK This park is located near a small dam on the Rio Grande, set in a desert of creosote bushes and cholla cacti near Fort Selden State Monument. It is a popular area for swimming and boating (canoes and rafts). Fishing is also permitted. The park also features a nature trail, picnic areas, restrooms, showers and a playground. Gates close at sunset. Day-use fee, $4. ~ Off Route 25 at Radium Springs, 15 miles north of Las Cruces; 505-524-4068, fax 505-526-5420.

▲ There are 50 sites (18 with RV hookups); primitive camping is allowed. Fees are $8 for primitive sites, $10 for standard sites and $14 for hookups.

PERCHA DAM STATE PARK Another small dam widens the river at this park, which is primarily a campground and riverbank fishing area with sandy beaches. Unlike Leasburg Lake, Percha Dam has tall old cottonwoods to provide shade on hot summer afternoons. Fishing is permitted. Facilities at the park include a picnic area, restrooms, showers and a playground. Day-use fee, $4. ~ Off Route 25 near the village of Arrey, 53 miles north of Las Cruces (21 miles south of Truth or Consequences); 505-743-3942, fax 505-743-0031.

▲ There are 31 sites (6 with RV hookups); $10 per night for standard sites, $14 for hookups. The camping area features green lawns—a rarity in southern New Mexico. Reservations: 877-664-7787.

CABALLO LAKE STATE PARK The name, Spanish for "horse," comes from the days when wild horses used to live in Caballo Canyon before it was dammed in the 1930s to form Caballo Lake. The lake is more than a mile wide and 12 miles long, with more than 70 miles of shoreline. It is popular, especially in the spring, with anglers fishing for channel catfish, bass and walleye pike. The visitors center, main campground and picnic area are on the west side of the lake (one mile north from Exit 59 off Route 25). From there, Route 187 follows the shore all the way to the upper end of the lake. Below the dam is a river fishing area with drinking water and campsites shaded by cottonwood trees. The park has restrooms and showers. Day-use fee, $4. ~ Off Route 25, 60 miles north of Las Cruces (20 miles south of Truth or Consequences); 505-743-3942, fax 505-743-0031.

▲ There are 135 sites (63 with RV hookups) and primitive camping along the shoreline. Fees are $8 for primitive sites (located on the east side of the lake), $10 for standard sites and $14 to $18 for hookups. Reservations: 877-664-7787.

ELEPHANT BUTTE LAKE STATE PARK The dam creating this 40-mile-long reservoir, the second-largest lake in New Mexico, was originally built in 1916 to impound irrigation water for the whole Rio Grande Valley downriver. Today, it is New Mexico's most popular state park. Recreational activities include fishing, boating (there are marinas and boat rentals), waterskiing, windsurfing, sailing and even houseboating. The lake also has miles of sand beaches and several protected swimming areas. On display at the visitors center are dinosaur and early mammal fossils found in the area, including a tyrannosaurus rex jawbone. A network of unpaved roads provides access to a series of remote points along the lake's west shore, but all of the east shore can only be reached by boat. In addition to nature trails and a playground, there are picnic areas, restrooms and showers. Day-use fee, $4. ~ The main entrance to the park can be reached from Route 25 by taking either Exit 79 or Exit 83 and following the signs; 505-744-5421, fax 505-744-9144.

> New Mexico was a province of Mexico from 1821 until the 1848 treaty that ended the Mexican War with the United States.

▲ There are 127 sites (104 with RV hookups) and an area for primitive camping. Fees are $8 for primitive sites, $10 for developed sites and $14 for hookups.

Southwestern New Mexico

Geronimo's base, southwestern New Mexico is home to Mogollon, one of the state's finest ghost towns, as well as the Gila (pronounced "hee-lah") Wilderness, cliff dwellings and the frontier boomtown of Silver City. If you like to pack in to high-country lakes, cycle through national forests or explore cliff dwellings, this remote area is your kind of place. While here you can learn about the legend of Pancho Villa, who made the mistake of invading this area in 1916.

SIGHTS

Gila Cliff Dwellings National Monument, 44 slow miles north of Silver City, preserves five natural caves that were inhabited by peoples of the Mogollon culture about 700 years ago. Visitors who have seen the Southwest's great Indian ruins, such as those at Chaco Canyon, Mesa Verde or the Jemez Mountains, sometimes find Gila Cliff Dwellings a disappointment because they consist of only 40 rooms, which housed a total of 10 to 15 families. But the small scale of these ruins and nearby pit houses, representative of the many communities scattered throughout the Gila country, is marvelous in the context of the vast surrounding canyonlands. Admission to the dwellings. ~ Route 15; 505-536-9461, fax 505-536-9461; www.nps.gov/gicl.

The real reason a national monument exists at Gila Cliff Dwellings is to administer the central trailheads for one of the nation's most important wilderness areas. Encompassing much of the 3.3 million-acre Gila National Forest, the rugged mountain and canyon country of the **Gila Wilderness** and adjoining **Aldo Leopold Wilderness** comprise the largest roadless area in the United States outside of Alaska. The Gila was the nation's first designated wilderness area, established by an act of Congress in 1924. Aldo Leopold, a New Mexico forest ranger, originated the idea of wilderness protection.

An **overlook** on Route 15 just before the descent to Gila Cliff Dwellings gives a good idea of the Gila's extent and complexity. Three forks of the Gila River join near the cliff dwellings. One of the three main hiking and horse trails into the Gila Wilderness follows each fork through a river and high mesa canyon that meanders between mountains for many miles. A treacherous tangle of side canyons off the main ones defied all pioneer efforts at settlement and provided a stronghold for renegade Apache leaders, including Geronimo.

Today mounted rangers take a full week to cross the wilderness as they patrol, and hiking from boundary to boundary is practically impossible without a horse, mule or llama to carry your food supply. The rugged mountains visible from the overlook— the Black, Diablo, Mogollon, San Francisco and Tularoso—are also part of the wilderness area. Of the many natural hot springs in the vicinity of the Gila Wilderness, the most popular is a series located a short hike up the Middle Fork from the Forest Service visitors center.

While the main roads are paved, visitors should not underestimate the trip to Gila Cliff Dwellings. The 44-mile drive from Silver City on Route 15 will take at least two hours; for the 99-mile trip via Routes 152 and 35 from Exit 63 on Route 25 south of Truth or Consequences, allow about three hours. There are no gas stations or other travelers' services along the way, with the exception of a small store with a gasoline pump less than four miles from the cliff dwellings on Route 15. Even if you're not planning to hike into the wilderness, it is wise to allow a full day for any trip to the Gila.

Also rewarding is a drive around the western perimeter of the Gila Wilderness, taking Route 180 west from Silver City, 63 miles to the little town of **Glenwood**. Just outside of Glenwood, to divert water for a small hydroelectric generator in the 1890s, a mining company suspended a water pipeline from the sheer rock walls of **Whitewater Canyon**. To maintain the pipeline, workers had to balance on it 20 feet above the river. Today the mining company and its pipeline are gone, but the forest service has installed a steel mesh walkway, known as **The Catwalk**, along the old pipeline route, affording visitors a unique look at this wild canyon. The upper end of Whitewater Canyon is a wilderness trailhead.

Seven miles north of Glenwood, Route 159 turns off to the east and takes you four miles to **Mogollon** (pronounced "moh-gi-YONE"), one of New Mexico's most intriguing and beautifully located ghost towns. A silver and gold mining boomtown in the 1890s, Mogollon had a population of more than 2000—larger than in any town in the area today. It boasted a theater, several stores and saloons, two churches and two separate red light districts (one Anglo, the other Spanish). Many of Mogollon's historic wood and stone buildings still stand in various states of disrepair. One portion of the street was spruced up for use as a motion pic-

◄ *HIDDEN*

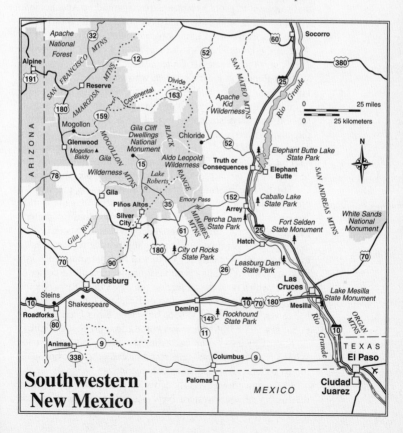

Southwestern New Mexico

ture location in the 1970s, and since then a few people have taken up residence here during the summer months to restore old buildings, create artwork and engage in low-key tourist enterprises. However, fewer than a dozen people live here year-round.

Past Mogollon, the road turns to dirt, passable by regular automobiles but not by long motor homes or vehicles with trailers. It winds along the northern wilderness boundary through the **Mogollon Mountains,** the highest in the Gila with four peaks more than 10,000 feet high, giving access to several hiking trails, forest service campgrounds and fishing streams and lakes.

Seven miles north of Silver City on the way to Gila Cliff Dwellings via Route 15, the historic town of **Piños Altos** also offers a look at life in southwestern New Mexico a century ago. While this "ghost town" has never been completely abandoned, it is a mere shadow of its glory days.

Among the points of interest in Piños Altos are a replica of **Santa Rita del Cobre** (also referred to as Fort Webster)—the original was built to protect residents from marauding Apaches who lived in the Gila Wilderness—and a turn-of-the-20th-century opera house. Also here are a gift shop built where Judge Roy "Law West of the Pecos" Bean's store was located before he moved to Texas, and the Hearst Art Gallery, dedicated to the memory of William Randolph Hearst's father, who struck it rich mining in Piños Altos. Admission. ~ Main Street, Piños Altos.

Silver City is a pretty hillside town of 10,500 people, a quarter of them college students. Located in the Piños Altos foothills, the city's Victorian commercial district turns back the clock to frontier days. Bisected by a steep canyon, this town could easily be a set for a Hollywood Western. It's also the jump-off point for one of the state's most picturesque mountain ranges, the Mogollon.

The best sightseeing highlight in Silver City is the **Western New Mexico University Museum.** The museum has the world's largest collection of 700- to 1000-year-old Mimbres pottery, painted with the distinctive animal designs that have been revived as a popular decorative motif throughout southern New Mexico in recent years. Not easy for visitors to find, the museum is in a four-story white building with light-brown trim in the center of campus, which is on the hillside on the west side of town. Closed during university holidays. ~ Top of 10th Street, near the library bell tower, Western New Mexico University, Silver City; 505-538-6386, fax 505-538-6178; www.wnmu.edu/univ/museum.htm.

Silver City also has an interesting downtown historic district. While a few of the old buildings stand vacant, others provide space for art galleries and student-oriented stores.

In the downtown area, the **Silver City Museum** is devoted to the history of southwestern New Mexico. Collections include ranch and business relics as well as pottery and artifacts from the Mimbres and Mogollon peoples. There is also an extensive photo archive, a research library and a gift shop. Closed Monday. ~ 312 West Broadway, Silver City; 505-538-5921, fax 505-388-1096; www.silvercitymuseum.org, e-mail silvercitymuseum@zianet.com.

Silver City was home for a time to young **Billy the Kid**, as several minor historical sites attest. His mother's grave is located on the east side of town on Memory Lane. For information and tour maps contact the **Silver City/Grant County Chamber of Commerce** (closed Saturday and Sunday), which also operates the visitors center (closed Sunday from late October to mid-April). ~ 201 North Hudson Street, Silver City; 505-538-3785, 800-548-9378; www.silvercity.org, e-mail scgcchamber@cybermesa.com.

One of the West's premier ghost towns, **Shakespeare** flourished in an 1870s silver boom, when some 3000 miners came here seeking their fortunes. After a second boom played out in 1935, the town was purchased by the Hill family, which has done its best to preserve local history, going so far as to stage dramatic re-enactments (given on the second weekend of the month) of 19th-century Shakespeare murders and hangings. Guided tours (held the second Sunday and preceding Saturday of each month) take you to the old Butterfield stagecoach stop, a saloon, the Stratford Hotel, the mail station, a blacksmith shop, an assay office and a gunpowder magazine. (Call ahead for a schedule of the re-enactments, staged on the fourth weekend of the month in April, June, August and October.) Admission. ~ Take Exit 22 off Route 10 at Lordsburg and follow the signs south two and a half miles; 505-542-9034; www.shakespeareghostown.com, e-mail visit@shakespeareghostown.com.

> Of the many natural hot springs in the vicinity of the Gila Wilderness, the most popular is a series located a short hike up the Middle Fork from the Forest Service visitors center.

Another well-preserved ghost town with a different character, **Steins** began as a way station on the short-lived Birch Stage Line in 1857. It was later taken over by the Butterfield Overland Stage Company and then, when the railroad came through in the early 1880s, became the major work station for the railroad on this desolate part of the route, growing to a population of 1300 and boasting a general store, a boarding house, two bordellos and three saloons (though no church). Modern-day visitors to this open-air museum will find 11 intact wood and adobe buildings filled with antique furniture, books, clothing and tools, as well as the crumbling walls of the original stagecoach station and other ruins. Admission. ~ Route 10, Exit 3, Roadforks; 505-542-9791.

New Mexico's southwesternmost corner, known as the **Bootheel**, is so remote and uninhabited that the most isolated parts of the Gila Wilderness seem almost busy by comparison.

Most of the Bootheel is taken up by a single vast ranch, the Gray Ranch, one of the few grasslands in New Mexico that can be called "undergrazed." Ownership of the ranch was the object of a bidding war between The Nature Conservancy and a Japanese investment group in the 1980s, but was finally acquired by cable-TV tycoon Ted Turner, who has directed that it be operated with environmental protection as a priority. No part of the ranch is open to the public.

Adventurous souls who want to experience the awesome solitude of the Bootheel firsthand can follow Route 338 south from Animas, the last town on the road, for about 50 miles to the place where the dirt road to Douglas, Arizona (Geronimo Trail) forks off into the small fragment of Coronado National Forest that spills over the Arizona state line into New Mexico. The road climbs through scrub forest and makes its way over the rocky Peloncillo Mountains, where several trails lead into canyons and springs.

HIDDEN ▶

Hiking options range from **Blackwater Canyon**, a two-mile hike along an intermittent stream to a waterhole that attracts many species of birds including some not seen elsewhere in the

HIDDEN ▶

United States, to **Skeleton Canyon**, a 19-mile loop trail on which a two-day trek brings you to the spot where Apache war chief Geronimo surrendered in 1886.

About 60 miles east of Lordsburg on Route 10 and 52 miles southeast of Silver City via Route 180 is **Deming**, where troops once defended the United States border against the raids of Pancho Villa. Now primarily a ranching center, Deming is home to the red-brick **Deming Luna Mimbres Museum**. The museum is located in a former National Guard armory that housed these same troops. Among the treasures here are 2500 bells gathered from near and far, quilts dating back to 1847 and a 900-year-old Mimbres kiva. Kids will enjoy the collection of more than 600 dolls from around the world. ~ 301 South Silver Street, Deming; 505-546-2382.

The sleepy little town of **Columbus** lies 32 miles south of Deming on Route 11. Its main claim to fame is that in 1916, Mexican revolutionary leader Pancho Villa invaded the United States with

A STREET NO MORE

Big Ditch Park, a tree-lined 50-foot-deep arroyo with a small promenade, runs right through the center of Silver City. In fact, it was originally Silver City's main street, but floods washed it away to its present depth, which explains why some of the original storefronts face the ditch instead of the street.

1000 soldiers, intent on robbing a train carrying a gold shipment. His information was bad, and the train turned out to be carrying coal. After a battle in which 18 Americans and more than 100 Mexicans died, Villa and his men retreated into Mexico with General Pershing and 6000 United States soldiers with motor cars and airplanes in hot pursuit.

The story is recalled at the **Columbus Historical Society Museum** in the restored train station at the crossroads in the center of town and in the smaller state park museum in the old customs house building across the street. Closed late May to September. ~ Corner of Routes 9 and 11, Columbus; 505-531-2620.

Cooperation between the United States and Mexico is commemorated by a monument at **Pancho Villa State Park,** a desert botanical garden where cholla, *ocatillo*, large prickly pears, century plants, tall yuccas and other plants of the Chihuahuan Desert grow in profusion on the slopes of the only hill around. Visitors may wish to drive the three miles to the border and walk across to the Mexican village of Palomas. Admission. ~ Corner of Routes 9 and 11, Columbus; 505-531-2711, fax 505-531-2115; e-mail ahmartinez@state.nm.us.

LODGING

The sign for the 70-acre **Casitas de Gila Guesthouses** warns wanderers: "Entering a stress-free zone." The signage is not hyperbole: You can wander the semi-isolated grounds, doze in a hammock, watch the sunset while you barbecue buffalo meat, peer through the telescope or just sit in the hot tub gazing at the evening constellations and congratulating yourself on your luck. There are five individually decorated *casitas*, each with its own bath, kiva and fully stocked kitchen. ~ 310 Hooker Loop, Gila; 505-535-4455, 877-923-4827, fax 505-535-4455; www.casitas degila.com, e-mail info@casitasdegila.com. DELUXE.

Besides conventional motels, Silver City has a couple of special, surprisingly affordable places to stay. The **Palace Hotel** is a bed and breakfast in a former bank building (circa 1882) located on the main street of the downtown historic district. The guest accommodations, which range from five small rooms with showers only to spacious three-room suites (with full bath), feature quaint Territorial-period furnishings and open onto a central sitting room where a continental breakfast is served. ~ 106 West Broadway Street, Silver City; phone/fax 505-388-1811; www.zianet.com/palacehotel. BUDGET.

Deming, an agricultural and mining community on an interstate highway, holds no surprises where lodging is concerned. Every motel in town is budget-priced. The town's top-of-the-line hotel is **Grand Motor Inn.** ~ 1721 East Spruce Street, Deming; 505-546-2631, fax 505-546-4446. BUDGET. An older independent motel with rock-bottom rates is the **Mirador Motel**. ~ 501 East Pine Street, Deming; phone/fax 505-546-2795; e-mail verna@zia net.com. BUDGET.

Columbus, a little town about as far off in the middle of nowhere as any place that can be reached by highway, has a few unexpected touches of sophistication. One is **Martha's Place**, a bed and breakfast. The five elegant second-floor guest rooms have balconies overlooking the rooftops of this one-story town. Full breakfast included. ~ Main and Lima streets, Columbus; 505-531-2467, fax 505-531-2376. MODERATE.

HIDDEN ►

DINING

The fanciest dining in the area is at the **Buckhorn Saloon** in the historic town of Piños Altos, seven miles north of Silver City on Route 15. The restaurant and saloon are in a beautifully restored adobe building from the 1860s with big stone fireplaces and elegant place settings. Steaks are the specialty. Dinner only. Closed Sunday. ~ 32 Main Street, Piños Altos; 505-538-9911. MODERATE TO ULTRA-DELUXE.

In between the chain fast-food places, Deming has a number of local restaurants that feature Mexican and American food. **La Fonda Restaurant** serves fajitas and has a good salad bar. Breakfast, lunch and dinner are served. ~ 601 East Pine Street, Deming; 505-546-0465. BUDGET TO MODERATE.

Sí Señor has stuffed *sopapillas* and red or green *huevos rancheros*. No dinner on Sunday. ~ 200 East Pine Street, Deming; 505-546-3938. BUDGET TO MODERATE.

The **Grand Restaurant** features a comprehensive menu of steak, seafood and Mexican food. Breakfast, lunch and dinner are served. ~ 1721 East Spruce Street, Deming; 505-546-2632, fax 505-546-4446. BUDGET TO MODERATE.

Even more authentic is the Mexican food at any of the hole-in-the-wall *taquerías* across the border in **Palomas, Mexico**—nothing fancy, but certainly foreign.

SHOPPING

The gift shop at the **Western New Mexico University Museum** has a good selection of T-shirts, jewelry, local artworks, Mimbres ceramic reproductions, coffee cups, tote bags, stationery and anything else they determined could brandish the unique Mimbres animal motifs from ancient pottery. ~ Top of 10th Street, near the library bell tower, Western New Mexico University, Silver City; 505-538-6386.

A number of local artists have studios in Silver City's downtown historic district. Many of them are well-hidden in the residential blocks north of Broadway. You can pick up a gallery guide at the Chamber of Commerce or the Yankee Creek Gallery. The latter is home to the **San Vicente Artists of Silver City**. ~ 300 North Bullard Street, Silver City; 505-538-5232.

A visit to **What's a Pot Shop** is like taking a trip through Silver City native Harry Benjamin's imagination. Pottery, painting, photography, sculpture and American Indian–inspired "corn angels" are among the offerings in this wonderful shop, which also serves as the artist's home and studio. ~ 300 North Arizona Street, Silver City; 505-388-2007; www.harrybenjamin.com.

NIGHTLIFE

Near Silver City, the historic **Buckhorn Saloon** in Piños Altos is as authentic as Old West saloons come, complete with a collection of paintings of nude women, a buffalo head on the wall and a pot-belly stove to warm the saloon in winter. Live bands perform Wednesday through Saturday. Closed Sunday. ~ 32 Main Street, Piños Altos; 505-538-9911.

Down in the town of Columbus, the favorite nighttime entertainment is to cross the border to Palomas, where **mariachi bands** perform on the plaza on weekend evenings.

PARKS

LAKE ROBERTS 🚶 🚵 🐴 🚗 🚤 🛥️ 🎣 Gila National Forest has a number of pretty little mountain lakes, of which Lake Roberts is the best known and most accessible. Boating and rainbow trout and catfish fishing (seasonally good) are popular on the 69-acre lake. The southeast shoreline is only accessible by foot trail or by boat (electric motors only). One of the two campgrounds is on a mesa overlooking the lake and the other is at the upper end of the lake. About a quarter-mile from the shoreline are summer cabins. The park has a picnic area and restrooms. ~ Just off Route 35, about three miles east of the intersection with Route 15 (a narrow mountain road), which is 25 miles north of Silver City on the way to Gila Cliff Dwellings; phone/fax 505-536-2250.

▲ Mesa Campground has 24 sites; $7 per night. There are 12 additional sites at the upper end of the lake; $7 per night. Closed mid-October to mid-May.

SNOW LAKE 🚶 🚣 🚗 🚤 🎣 This beautiful 100-acre mountain lake is at the north boundary of the Gila Wilderness at the foot of the Mogollon Mountains. Anglers consider it a great trout lake, especially in the springtime. Some people also catch, boil and eat the abundant crawfish. Use is limited to canoes, row-

JORNADA DEL MUERTO

Jornada del Muerto ("Journey of Death") is the name Spanish colonists gave to the bone-dry, barren sands of the Chihuahuan Desert, which extends up from Texas and Northern Mexico into the Carlsbad and Alamogordo regions of Southern New Mexico. These pioneers dreaded crossing that sun-cracked expanse on their way from El Paso to Santa Fe and Taos.

boats and other small boats without gas motors. There is a picnic area and restrooms. ~ Follow unpaved Route 159 from Mogollon for about 30 miles. This is a slow, sometimes narrow, winding and quite scenic unpaved mountain road. The road is passable by passenger cars when dry, but tight curves pose serious problems for long motor homes and towed vehicles. An alternate route is the 50-mile Forest Road 141 from Reserve, the last half of which is gravel; 505-533-6231, 505-533-6232, fax 505-533-6605; e-mail ambaca@fs.fed.us.

General John Pershing and his troops—who thwarted Pancho Villa's 1916 invasion of the U.S.—were the first to use cars and airplanes in combat.

▲ Dipping Vat Campground has 40 tent/RV sites (no hookups) overlooking the lake; $5 per night. Primitive camping is allowed at the north end of the lake outside the recreational boundaries; no fee.

CITY OF ROCKS STATE PARK 🚶 🚲 South of Silver City on the way to Deming, this park makes an extraordinary spot for a picnic stop. At first sight, it appears to be a no-big-deal rockpile in an otherwise featureless desert marred by open-pit copper mines. As you approach, the strangeness of this little geological park becomes apparent. Picnic sites surround a rock dome that has been fractured and eroded into a fantastic maze of oddly shaped stone monoliths and passages that form a natural playground that children and the young at heart can explore for hours. It is impossible to get lost in the maze, since the park road surrounds it on all sides. The park has a visitors center, restrooms and showers. Day-use fee, $4. ~ Route 61, three miles off of Route 180, 28 miles east of Silver City, or 23 miles west of Deming on Route 180; 505-536-2800, fax 505-536-2801.

▲ There are 52 sites, 10 with hookups; $10 per night for tent sites; $14 per night with hookups.

ROCKHOUND STATE PARK 🚶 Mainly of interest to rock collectors in search of the garnets and other semiprecious stones found here, the park has the best public campground in the Deming-Columbus area and offers a close-up look at the arid, rocky slopes of the Florida Mountains. The park features trails, a visitors center, a picnic area, a playground, restrooms and showers. Day-use fee, $4. ~ Off Route 143, 14 miles southeast of Deming; 505-546-6182.

▲ There are 29 sites, 24 with hookups; $10 per night for tent sites, $14 per night for hookups.

Outdoor Adventures

SKIING

Even though you're pretty far south, the high elevations here translate into good skiing. You can swoosh down a 12,000-foot mountain at an Indian-owned resort, or explore the backcountry on skinny skis. So strap the boards on your feet and take to the hills!

SOUTHEASTERN NEW MEXICO Ski Apache, 16 miles north-west of Ruidoso on the slopes of 12,003-foot Sierra Blanca, is one of New Mexico's most popular downhill ski areas. Owned and operated by the Mescalero Apache Indians, Ski Apache has 11 lifts and 55 groomed runs and trails, evenly divided between beginner, intermediate and expert, with vertical drops of up to 1900 feet. There are no restrictions on snowboarding. Ski lessons are available for adults and children. Ski rentals are available. ~ 505-336-4356, fax 505-336-8327; www.skiapache.com.

Some trails and primitive roads in **Lincoln National Forest** outside Ruidoso are used for cross-country skiing in the winter. For current trail information and snow conditions, contact the **Smokey Bear Ranger Station**. ~ Ruidoso; 505-257-4095, fax 505-257-6174.

Although this region is full of horse-breeding ranches, southern New Mexico offers surprisingly little in the way of public horse rentals or tours.

RIDING STABLES

SOUTHEASTERN NEW MEXICO Near Ruidoso, the **Inn of the Mountain Gods** offers guided one-hour trail rides, as well as half-day and full-day trips in the mountains west of the hotel complex; reservations are required for the half-day and full-day rides. ~ 505-464-5141; www.innofthemountaingods.com. Also in the Ruidoso area, **Buddy's Riding Stable** leads gentle half-hour to one-hour trail rides in the pine and oak forest. ~ Gavilan Canyon Road; 505-258-4027. **Cowboy Stables** leads rides of one hour or longer for up to 20 people to mountain overlooks above town. ~ 1027 North Lane, Ruidoso Downs; 505-378-8217.

Despite the arid climate, golf enthusiasts manage to keep Southern New Mexico green. Grab your caddy and head to one of several private or municipal courses. Most courses offer cart and equipment rentals.

GOLF

SOUTHEASTERN NEW MEXICO The **Lake Carlsbad Municipal Golf Course** has both a 9-hole and an 18-hole course open to the public. ~ 901 Muscatel Avenue, Carlsbad; 505-885-5444. In Roswell, check out the 18-hole **Spring River Golf Course**. ~ 1612 West 8th Street; 505-622-9506. Closed during winter but open the rest of the year is the course at the tribally owned 18-hole **Inn of the Mountain Gods** near Ruidoso. ~ Carrizo Canyon Road, Mescalero; 505-257-5141; www.innofthemountaingods.com. **The Links at Sierra Blanca** is another winning 18-hole semipublic Scottish-style links course in Ruidoso. ~ 105 Sierra Blanca Drive, Ruidoso; 505-258-5330.

SOUTH CENTRAL NEW MEXICO Visitors to the Alamogordo area can work on their swing at the driving range of the 18-hole

Desert Lakes Golf Course. ~ 2351 Hamilton Road, Alamogordo; 505-437-0290. Play a nine-hole round at **The Lodge Golf Course**. ~ 1 Corona Place, Cloudcroft; 505-682-2098. Nearby is the public, nine-hole **Ponderosa Pines Golf Course**. Located in the middle of Lincoln National Forest, it has an elevation of 8000 feet. Closed in winter. ~ 878 Cox Canyon, Cloudcroft; 505-682-2995.

SOUTHWESTERN NEW MEXICO The public, 18-hole **New Mexico State University Golf Course** is near the intersection of University Avenue and Route 25. ~ Las Cruces; 505-646-3219. In Silver City is the **Silver Fairways Golf Course**, an 18-hole public green. ~ South of Silver City off of Ridge Road; 505-538-5041. Hopefully your concentration won't put your game in jeopardy at the public, nine-hole **Truth or Consequences Golf Course**. ~ 685 Marie Street, Truth or Consequences; 505-894-2603.

TENNIS

Tennis is pretty scarce in this neck of the woods, but there are some courts to be found.

SOUTHEASTERN NEW MEXICO Nine lighted courts are available at **Carlsbad Municipal Park**. A tennis pro is available for lessons. ~ 700 Park Drive, Carlsbad; 505-887-1980. There are six lighted courts at **Cahoon Park**. ~ 1101 West 4th Street, Roswell; 505-624-6720. For a fee, nonguests can use the six lighted courts at **Inn of the Mountain Gods** near Ruidoso. Pros are available for lessons. ~ 505-257-5141; www.innofthemountaingods.com.

SOUTH CENTRAL NEW MEXICO In Las Cruces, public courts are at **Apodaca Park** (two courts; Madrid Road at Solano Drive), **Lions Park** (twelve courts; Picacho and Melendres streets), **Young Park** (two courts; Nevada and Walnut streets) and **Frenger Park** (two courts; Parkview Drive). All the courts are hard-surfaced, lighted for night play and open to the public except during scheduled group lessons. Call the Las Cruces Recreation Department for a current lesson schedule. ~ 505-541-2554.

BIKING

Low-elevation summers can be sweltering, and high-elevation winters can be frigid, but aside from climactical concerns, cyclists will find good places to pedal in Southern New Mexico. You'll even find a few shops offering rentals, cycling equipment and ride recommendations.

SOUTHEASTERN NEW MEXICO The nine-and-a-half-mile unpaved scenic drive that begins near the visitors center in **Carlsbad Caverns National Park** makes for a good mountain-bike ride during the spring or autumn. (In summer months, the drive is too hot and often has too much car traffic for enjoyable biking.)

In the Roswell area, cyclists ride the back roads in the ranchlands east of town, particularly the paved roads through **Bitter Lake National Wildlife Refuge** and **Bottomless Lakes State Park**.

Mountain bikers around Ruidoso use the six-mile unpaved forest road from the Ski Apache Road up to Monjeau Campground or any of several jeep roads going into the national forest around Bonito Lake.

SOUTHWESTERN NEW MEXICO   Mountain bikes are prohibited within the Gila Wilderness, but several jeep roads in the **Piños Altos** area lead into other parts of the national forest. Ambitious cyclists may wish to tackle unpaved Route 159, which skirts the northern boundary of the wilderness beyond Mogollon.

Bike Rentals   Rent mountain bikes in Ruidoso at **High Altitude**, a full-service bike shop. Closed Tuesday from September to late May. ~ 2316½ Sudderth Drive; 505-257-0120.

In Silver City, the place for mountain-bike rentals and repairs is **Gila Hike & Bike**, which offers free information sheets on day hikes, road rides and mountain-bike rides in Gila National Forest. ~ 103 East College Street; 505-388-3222.

Whether your interests lean toward history, geology, panoramic views or just plain exercise, you'll find the hiking options in this area tempting. Explore a quarter-mile-long cave on your own; scale the steep sides of Sierra Blanca; seek out the grave of the notorious Apache Kid; or examine ancient petroglyphs and cliff dwellings. All distances are one way unless otherwise noted. Happy trails!

HIKING

SOUTHEASTERN NEW MEXICO   About three-fourths of **Carlsbad Caverns National Park** is a wilderness area restricted to horse and foot travel, with a system of seven trails ranging in difficulty from easy to strenuous. Backcountry trails are primitive and not well marked; take water, a compass and a topographical map. Overnight camping is allowed with a free backcountry permit. Some of the trails are accessed from the scenic drive that starts near the visitors center, while others start from inconspicuous dirt roads off of Route 62/180.

AUTHOR FAVORITE

My favorite hiking trail in south central New Mexico is the difficult **Three Rivers Trail** (6.5 miles) in the White Mountain Wilderness. It starts at the Three Rivers Campground at the end of the unpaved road beyond Three Rivers Petroglyph Site, midway between Carrizozo and Alamogordo. Eventually the trail climbs up to Elk Point on the north side of Sierra Blanca, where it intersects several other major trails leading to all parts of the wilderness area. Many more hikers enter the wilderness from the other side, near Ruidoso, than from Three Rivers.

One of the more interesting hikes is **Yucca Canyon** (2 miles), which leads through piñon and oak forest and past old cabins to cool Longview Spring, with a magnificent view of the Carlsbad Caverns Wilderness. This is part of the longer **Yucca Ridge Trail** (11-mile loop), which climbs 1520 feet from the canyon floor to the top of the ridge.

The **Slaughter Canyon Trail** (6 miles) leads past **Goat Cave** on its 1850-foot climb to Guadalupe Ridge. Goat Cave is only about a quarter of a mile long, but the size of its single room is impressive. Persons wishing to enter the cave must first obtain a special permit (a process that can take a month) from the **Cave Resource Office** (505-785-2232 ext. 363 or 368, fax 505-785-2133) at the Carlsbad Caverns visitors center, which is also the place to ask for up-to-date information on these and numerous other hikes in the national park.

Several side trails off the Apache Kid Trail lead to hidden canyons and midway along the trail is the Apache Kid's gravesite, where he was shot down by local ranchers.

Lincoln National Forest has a network of more than 50 miles of trails throughout the **White Mountain Wilderness** northwest of Ruidoso.

From the Ski Apache ski area, a three-mile trail leads to the summit of **Lookout Mountain**. This is a strenuous hike with an elevation gain of 2100 feet. In summer and fall, people hike to the summit to enjoy the spectacular view.

Another great hike is up **Argentina Canyon** (2.5 miles) with its lush ancient forest and streams fed by mountain springs. To get there, take Route 48 north out of Ruidoso to County Road 37. Follow the signs west to Bonito Lake and Argentina/Bonita trailhead.

SOUTH CENTRAL NEW MEXICO The main feature of **Oliver Lee Memorial State Park** (505-437-8284, fax 505-439-1290), 12 miles south of Alamogordo, is Dog Canyon, a hidden oasis in the barren-looking foothills of the Sacramento Mountains. The easy **Dog Canyon Interpretive Trail** (.6-mile loop) runs from the visitors center up along a small creek between steep slopes covered with ocatillo and giant prickly pear cacti to a lovely little spring seeping out of the canyon wall.

The steeper, longer **Dog Canyon National Recreation Trail** (5.5 miles) follows a different route and reaches a higher spring. The trail continues, climbing out of the canyon to a high ridgeline. Note that this trail rises more than 3000 feet in elevation, making it a very challenging hike.

In the Organ Mountains just east of Las Cruces, the easy **Dripping Springs Trail** (1.5 miles) leads up a steep-walled canyon to Dripping Springs, the former site of a stage stop, a major turn-of-the-20th-century resort and a tuberculosis sanitarium.

The **San Mateo Mountains** west of Truth or Consequences are probably the least-visited mountains in New Mexico. This is a beautiful area characterized by rugged, narrow canyons. It is hot for summer hiking but far enough south to be relatively snow-free in the early spring.

The heart of the San Mateos is the 45,000-acre Apache Kid Wilderness, named for a renegade who hid out here in the late 19th century. The main route through the wilderness is the **Apache Kid Trail** (a total of 21.1 miles, 12.9 of which are located within the Apache Kid Wilderness), an ambitious hike that follows Nogal Canyon for about a mile from the trailhead at Cibola National Forest's Springtime Campground and then climbs steeply to the upper ridge of the mountains. Hiking the whole trail takes three days and two nights.

SOUTHWESTERN NEW MEXICO The **Gila Wilderness** is restricted to just foot and horse travel, and more than 400 miles of trails extend to all areas of the wilderness. Several guidebooks devoted to hiking trails in the Gila Wilderness are locally available in Silver City. A few of the top hiking options in the Gila include:

The **West Fork Trail** (15.5 miles) is, for the first five miles, the most used trail in the Gila Wilderness. For an adventurous day hike, follow the moderate trail upriver about three miles to a narrow, deep section of canyon where caves containing ancient cliff dwellings can be seen high on the sheer rock faces. The trail fords the cold river 32 times in the six-mile roundtrip. The trail begins at the Gila Wilderness National Monument parking lot.

Those planning longer backpacking trips should note that the trails following the river forks from the Gila Cliff Dwellings area all eventually climb several thousand feet from canyon floors to mountain slopes. A less strenuous approach to the Gila high country is to hike one of the numerous trails that cross the unpaved forest route from Mogollon to Snow Lake on the north boundary of the wilderness. The trails there start at higher altitudes, so less climbing is involved.

Nine major side trails branch off the moderate **Crest Trail** (11 miles), which starts at the marked Sandy Point trailhead, 14 miles up the road from the ghost town of Mogollon. Through lush ancient forest, the main trail climbs to the crest of the mountain range and follows it to the 10,770-foot summit of Mogollon Baldy, where an old fire-lookout station affords a panoramic view of boundless wilderness. It is a moderate two- to three-day backpacking expedition. For a one-day hike, take the first four miles of the trail to Hummingbird Spring.

Another major Gila hiking area, the **Aldo Leopold Wilderness**, is accessible from the top of 8100-foot Emory Pass on Route 152, the most direct way from interstate Route 25 to the Gila Cliff Dwellings. The main trail runs north from the pass through stately ponderosa and Douglas fir forest up 10,011-foot **Hillsboro Peak** (5 miles). On the way up the mountain, it intersects six other major trails that go to all corners of the wilderness.

Transportation

CAR

Carlsbad and Roswell are on **Route 285**, a two-lane highway that crosses unpopulated plains from Santa Fe all the way to Del Rio, Texas. The distance from either Santa Fe or Albuquerque is about 200 miles to Roswell and another 100 miles to Carlsbad Caverns National Park. From El Paso, it is a 150-mile drive to Carlsbad Caverns via **Route 62/180**.

Ruidoso and Lincoln are both about 65 miles west of Roswell via **Route 70/380**. The highway forks 47 miles west of Roswell at Hondo, with Route 70 going to Ruidoso and Route 380 going to Lincoln.

Two highway corridors run north and south through south central New Mexico: interstate **Route 25** along the Rio Grande through Truth or Consequences and Las Cruces, and the more interesting and isolated **Route 54** down the Tularosa Valley through Carrizozo and Alamogordo. Both highways lead to El Paso, Texas. Four-lane **Route 70/82** links Alamogordo with Las Cruces, making a loop tour of the south central area an enjoyable possibility.

Southwestern New Mexico is the most remote, undeveloped part of the state. The most convenient hub for exploring this area is Silver City, 52 miles north of **Route 10**. An apparent shortcut, **Route 152** from Route 25 south of Truth or Consequences over the Mimbres Mountains to Silver City, saves mileage but not much time compared to driving south to Deming and then north again.

AIR

Mesa Airlines (800-637-2247) provides passenger service to Carlsbad's **Cavern City Air Terminal, Alamogordo Municipal Airport** and the **Silver City–Grant County Airport** from Albuquerque. Mesa also flies to the **Roswell Industrial Air Center** from both Albuquerque and Fort Worth, Texas.

Many visitors to Carlsbad Caverns fly into the airport at El Paso, Texas, and rent cars for the trip to the caverns. America West, American Airlines, Continental Airlines, Delta Air Lines, Frontier and Southwest Airlines service **El Paso International Airport**. ~ 915-780-4749.

Silver Stage Lines shuttles passengers from Deming to the international airport in El Paso. ~ 800-522-0162. In Alamogordo, airport transportation is available from **Alamo–El Paso Shuttle Service**. ~ 505-437-1472. In Las Cruces, call **Las Cruces Shuttle Service**. ~ 505-525-1784.

BUS

In the southeastern part of the state, **TNM&O Coaches** has daily bus service to the terminals in Carlsbad at 1000 South Canyon Street, 505-887-1108; in Roswell at 1100 North Virginia Street, 505-622-2510; in Ruidoso at 138 Service Road, 505-257-2660; in Alamogordo at 601 North White Sands Boulevard, 505-437-3050; in Las Cruces at 490 Valley Drive between Picacho and

Amador streets, 505-524-8518; and in Truth or Consequences at 718 North Route 51, 505-894-3649.

Greyhound Bus Lines (800-231-2222; www.greyhound.com) stops in Las Cruces at 490 North Valley Drive, 505-524-8518; in Truth or Consequences at 8 Date Street, 505-894-3649; in Deming at 300 East Spruce Street, 505-546-3881; and in Lordsburg at 112 Wabash Street, 505-542-3412.

In Carlsbad, **Hertz Rent A Car** has its agency at the Cavern City Air Terminal. ~ 800-654-3131.

CAR RENTALS

Avis Rent A Car (800-331-1212) and **Hertz Rent A Car** (800-654-3131) are your options at the Roswell airport.

Grimes Aviation offers rentals at the Silver City–Grant County Airport. ~ 505-538-2142, 800-725-2142. **Taylor Car Rental**, for a fee, offers pickup and delivery from the airport, which is 30 miles outside of Silver City. You may also rent cars from their location in Silver City. Closed Sunday. ~ 808 North Hudson Street; 505-388-1800.

At the El Paso airport try **Advantage Rent A Car** (800-777-5500), **Avis Rent A Car** (800-331-1212), **Budget Rent A Car** (800-527-0700), **Dollar Rent A Car** (800-800-4000), **Enterprise Rent A Car** (800-736-8222), **Hertz Rent A Car** (800-654-3131) or **National Car Rental** (800-227-7368).

Pecos Trails operates a fixed route through Roswell. ~ 515 North Main Street; 505-624-6766. **Roadrunner Transit** offers bus service in Las Cruces. No service on Sunday. ~ 1501-A East Hadley Street; 505-541-2544.

PUBLIC TRANSIT

In Alamogordo, taxi service is provided by **TNT Cab**. ~ 505-437-2292. In Las Cruces, **Yellow Cab of Las Cruces** supplies citywide service. ~ 505-524-1711.

TAXIS

Index

Lodging Index

Dining Index

HIDDEN GUIDES

Adventure travel or a relaxing vacation?—"Hidden" guidebooks are the only travel books in the business to provide detailed information on both. Aimed at environmentally aware travelers, our motto is "Where Vacations Meet Adventures." These books combine details on unique hotels, restaurants and sightseeing with information on camping, sports and hiking for the outdoor enthusiast.

THE NEW KEY GUIDES

Based on the concept of ecotourism, The New Key Guides are dedicated to the preservation of Central America's rare and endangered species, architecture and archaeology. Filled with helpful tips, they give travelers everything they need to know about these exotic destinations.

Ulysses Press books are available at bookstores everywhere. If any of the following titles are unavailable at your local bookstore, ask the bookseller to order them.

You can also order books directly from Ulysses Press
P.O. Box 3440, Berkeley, CA 94703
800-377-2542 or 510-601-8301
fax: 510-601-8307
www.ulyssespress.com
e-mail: ulysses@ulyssespress.com

Order Form

HIDDEN GUIDEBOOKS

___ Hidden Arizona, $16.95
___ Hidden Bahamas, $14.95
___ Hidden Baja, $14.95
___ Hidden Belize, $15.95
___ Hidden Big Island of Hawaii, $13.95
___ Hidden Boston & Cape Cod, $14.95
___ Hidden British Columbia, $18.95
___ Hidden Cancún & the Yucatán, $16.95
___ Hidden Carolinas, $17.95
___ Hidden Coast of California, $18.95
___ Hidden Colorado, $15.95
___ Hidden Disneyland, $13.95
___ Hidden Florida, $18.95
___ Hidden Florida Keys & Everglades, $12.95
___ Hidden Georgia, $16.95
___ Hidden Guatemala, $16.95
___ Hidden Hawaii, $18.95
___ Hidden Idaho, $14.95

___ Hidden Kauai, $13.95
___ Hidden Maui, $13.95
___ Hidden Montana, $15.95
___ Hidden New England, $18.95
___ Hidden New Mexico, $15.95
___ Hidden Oahu, $13.95
___ Hidden Oregon, $15.95
___ Hidden Pacific Northwest, $18.95
___ Hidden Salt Lake City, $14.95
___ Hidden San Francisco & Northern California, $18.95
___ Hidden Southern California, $18.95
___ Hidden Southwest, $19.95
___ Hidden Tahiti, $17.95
___ Hidden Tennessee, $16.95
___ Hidden Utah, $16.95
___ Hidden Walt Disney World, $13.95
___ Hidden Washington, $15.95
___ Hidden Wine Country, $13.95
___ Hidden Wyoming, $15.95

THE NEW KEY GUIDEBOOKS

___ The New Key to Costa Rica, $18.95

___ The New Key to Ecuador and the Galápagos, $17.95

Mark the book(s) you're ordering and enter the total cost here ⇨ [   ]

California residents add 8.25% sales tax here ⇨ [   ]

Shipping, check box for your preferred method and enter cost here ⇨ [   ]

☐ BOOK RATE   **FREE! FREE! FREE!**

☐ PRIORITY MAIL/UPS GROUND cost of postage

☐ UPS OVERNIGHT OR 2-DAY AIR cost of postage

Billing, enter total amount due here and check method of payment ⇨ [   ]

☐ CHECK   ☐ MONEY ORDER

☐ VISA/MASTERCARD _____EXP. DATE_____

NAME _____PHONE_____

ADDRESS _____

_____

CITY_____ STATE _____ ZIP _____

MONEY-BACK GUARANTEE ON DIRECT ORDERS PLACED THROUGH ULYSSES PRESS.

ABOUT THE AUTHOR

RICHARD HARRIS has written or co-written 20 other guide-books including Ulysses' *Hidden Bahamas*, *Hidden Cancún and the Yucatán*, *Hidden Arizona* and the bestselling *Hidden Southwest*. He has also served as contributing editor on guides to Mexico, New Mexico and other ports of call for John Muir Publications, Fodor's, Birnbaum and Access guides. He is a director and past president of PEN New Mexico and president of the New Mexico Book Association. When not traveling, Richard writes and lives in Santa Fe, New Mexico.

ABOUT THE ILLUSTRATOR

GLENN KIM is a freelance illustrator residing in the San Francisco Bay area. His work appears in numerous Ulysses Press titles including *Hidden Southwest*, *Hidden Arizona* and *Hidden Belize*. He has also illustrated for the National Forest Service, several Bay Area magazines, book covers and greeting cards, as well as for advertising agencies that include Foote Cone and Belding, Hal Riney and Jacobs Fulton Design Group. He is now working with computer graphics and having lots of fun.